Paolo Segneri, William Humphrey

The panegyrics of Father Segneri, of the Society of Jesus

Paolo Segneri, William Humphrey

The panegyrics of Father Segneri, of the Society of Jesus

ISBN/EAN: 9783742835918

Manufactured in Europe, USA, Canada, Australia, Japa

Cover: Foto ©Lupo / pixelio.de

Manufactured and distributed by brebook publishing software
(www.brebook.com)

Paolo Segneri, William Humphrey

The panegyrics of Father Segneri, of the Society of Jesus

THE PANEGYRICS

OF

FATHER SEGNERI,

OF THE SOCIETY OF JESUS.

TRANSLATED FROM THE ORIGINAL ITALIAN,
WITH A PREFACE,
BY THE REV. WILLIAM HUMPHREY,
PRIEST OF THE SAME SOCIETY.

LONDON:
R. WASHBOURNE, 18 PATERNOSTER ROW.
1877.

CONTENTS.

PAGE

PANEGYRIC IN HONOUR OF THE IMMACULATE CONCEPTION OF THE BLESSED VIRGIN.—AN ORIGIN ILLUSTRIOUS IN PROPORTION TO ITS OBSCURITY 1

PANEGYRIC IN HONOUR OF THE BLESSED VIRGIN MARY.—THE HIGHEST IN THE EYES OF GOD; THE LOWEST IN HER OWN EYES 28

PANEGYRIC IN HONOUR OF SAINT JOSEPH, AS SPOUSE OF THE BLESSED VIRGIN 54

PANEGYRIC IN HONOUR OF SAINT JOHN THE EVANGELIST.—THE HIGHEST IN EVERY GIFT 81

PANEGYRIC IN HONOUR OF SAINT JOHN BAPTIST.—THE ABSENCE OF MIRACLES A PROOF OF SANCTITY . . 110

PANEGYRIC IN HONOUR OF SAINT STEPHEN, THE PROTOMARTYR: THE FIRST WHO FOR CHRIST'S SAKE LAID DOWN HIS LIFE 135

PANEGYRIC IN HONOUR OF SAINT IGNATIUS OF LOYOLA, FOUNDER OF THE SOCIETY OF JESUS: WHO CONTINUALLY SOUGHT THE GREATER GLORY OF GOD, AND WHOM GOD, THEREFORE, GREATLY GLORIFIED . 162

PANEGYRIC IN HONOUR OF SAINT FRANCIS XAVIER: IN WHOSE CASE MIRACLES WERE THE RULE INSTEAD OF THE EXCEPTION 192

CONTENTS.

PAGE

PANEGYRIC IN HONOUR OF SAINT ALOYSIUS GONZAGA.—
THE INNOCENT RANKING HIMSELF WITH PENITENTS. 221

PANEGYRIC IN HONOUR OF SAINT THOMAS OF AQUIN . 247

PANEGYRIC IN HONOUR OF SAINT PHILIP NERI: WHO
PRACTISED THE VIRTUES OF THE CLOISTER WHILST
LIVING IN THE WORLD 273

PANEGYRIC IN HONOUR OF SAINT ANTONY OF PADUA.—
SANCTITY RECEIVES A WORLD-WIDE HOMAGE IN THE
PERSON OF SAINT ANTONY OF PADUA . . . 297

DISCOURSE IN HONOUR OF THE BLESSED SACRAMENT.—
TO PROVE THAT GOD CONFERS ON US GREATER BENE-
FITS BY REMAINING HIDDEN BENEATH THE SPECIES
OF BREAD, THAN HE WOULD HAVE DONE HAD HE
OPENLY SHOWN HIMSELF 323

DISCOURSE IN HONOUR OF THE HOLY WINDING-SHEET.—
IN WHICH IT IS SHOWN THAT WE OUGHT TO LOVE
CHRIST ON ACCOUNT OF THE DISFIGUREMENT PRO-
DUCED IN HIS BODY BY CONTINUAL SUFFERINGS . 342

DISCOURSE UPON THE ANGEL GUARDIAN: IN WHICH HE
IS PROVED TO BE THE TRUEST FRIEND OF MAN . 358

PREFACE.

BOTH the intellectual and the moral lives of individual men depend, for their direction and character, for their type and tone, not only on what such men are by nature and within themselves, but on their surroundings, and on influences which affect them from without. Antecedent circumstances, such as early training and associations, present circumstances of society, occupation, and the like, leave their impress upon the soul, and have their share in making the intellectual and the moral life of a man to be what it is.

This must be so, necessarily, and from the very nature and constitution of man's spiritual being. The ideas which he conceives are suggested to him in great measure from without, and therefore depend for their character upon the external circumstances of time and place, of persons and things. He is in contact with them, and he cannot escape their influence. They affect him insensibly, and, not seldom, all the more because he is unconscious of the power of their presence.

The ideas which he conceives are stored in his memory, and become the food of his mind. His mind feeds upon them and digests them. It assimilates some, it rejects others, it modifies the rest. What he retains, he retains not merely in his memory; it has passed, as it were, into the texture of his spiritual being; it is woven into the web of his mental and moral life; it has come to form part and parcel of his mental and moral self.

The result is expressed in his words and actions. His words, if true and adequate, are the verbal expression of his mental life. His actions, if otherwise unrestrained, are the term of his purposes and resolves, of his desires and aims.

These have their mainspring and motive in the ideas presented by his understanding to his will; while the ideas are themselves the fruit and offspring —of his inner self indeed, but—of his inner self as affected, as moulded and fashioned from without.

Now, among the circumstances which so affect a man, few are more important than his reading. As he takes his tone, in a measure, from those with whom he associates, so does ho also in a measure receive it from the minds with which his is brought in contact by means of books.

His soul cannot fail to be affected for good or for evil by his intellectual food, any more than his body by the food which is its sustenance, which it assimilates, and which comes to form part of itself.

And what is true of man in the natural order— mentally and morally, as well as physically, is true of him also in the supernatural order. Besides his physical life, the result of the union of his soul and body, besides the moral and intellectual life, which belongs to him as he is a free intelligent and spiritual being, with a natural light illuminating his understanding, and a natural law engraven on his conscience, he possesses, if he is in the estate of grace, a *supernatural* life. Habitual and sanctifying grace is *anima animæ*—the soul of his soul. By the presence within it of this grace, his soul is quickened and lives; in the absence of that grace, his soul is dead.

This life-giving grace is the free gift of his Creator and Lord. Man can, of himself, do nothing to merit its bestowal. He can no more acquire it for himself, or bestow it upon others, than a dead body can restore its own life, or than a living man can bestow life on a dead body. If man is impotent to give life in the natural order, *a fortiori* is he so in the supernatural order. God alone is the Lord and Giver of life in the natural order; and so certainly is this also His prerogative in the supernatural order.

But, life once given, it depends for its character not only on the being who possesses it, but also on the circumstances amid which he lives, and on the external influences brought to bear upon him. This is true of all lives. The life of the body is affected by the atmosphere which the body breathes; and there are intellectual and moral atmospheres which in like manner affect the soul. As there is a supernatural life of the soul, so is there also a supernatural atmosphere, the action of which produces its influence upon that supernatural life. The principle of that life is from within, but the type and character of that life are, in their measure, determined from without.

The intrinsic principle of supernatural life is sanctifying grace; but that grace is determined and directed in its operations by extrinsic agencies and influences. These are called *external graces*. Pious parents, careful education, wise direction, edifying companionships, are external graces. They are given by God, as means of sanctification, in His supernatural providence.

To their number we may add preaching and spiritual reading; and, as an important branch of spiritual reading, we may include the Lives of Saints.

In the natural order, the biographies of the great and good do much to mould the characters of men. The greatest and the best pass away, as do the meanest and the least worthy; but, in the records of their lives, the memory of their virtues and of their deeds remains. They leave their mark not only on their own generation, but on all generations, so long as their names are held in benediction. In their day they may have formed the public opinion, and given the tone to their society; and the effect of their influence survives themselves. It passes into a tradition, and it creates a moral atmosphere.

Next in value to direct contact and living association with the great and good, is that familiarity with them which comes to us from a knowledge of their lives. We know their principles of action, their aims and their methods, the ends they set before themselves, and the means which they used in order to secure them. If we admire, we are led to imitate. If they commend themselves to us, they become our models. We assimilate their principles; and our lives are moulded, more or less consciously, on the lines of theirs. It is clear, then, that whatsoever serves to preserve a tradition, or to create an atmosphere, in the moral order, is a great gain; and those deserve well of their fellow-men who lend themselves to the task of chronicling the sayings and doings of the great and good of other days.

But, what the great and good are in the natural order, that the Saints of God are in the supernatural order.

If the lives of the former are invaluable in order to the development of the moral life, in like manner are the Lives of the Saints efficacious in order to the development of that supernaturally moral life, resting upon and springing from a supernaturally mental life, which we commonly call *the spiritual life.* They preserve the true supernatural tradition; and they diffuse a pure supernatural atmosphere. The soul that lives in this atmosphere, derives from it health and vigour. The soul that adopts this tradition, is strengthened in its principles, has higher aims, and a clearer knowledge of the means by which those aims are to be attained to and secured.

The Lives of Saints have contributed to the formation of other Saints; and even those who are not Saints have, by means of these, become more saint-like. Even where this has not been the result, such

Lives have yet served to keep alive the true idea of what sanctity is. In both ways, they have their special value for those who live in a Protestant country, with an obscured tradition, and surrounded by a tainted atmosphere.

The spirit of the world is in direct antagonism to the spirit of sanctity. The maxims of the world are in direct contradiction to the maxims of the Saints. The life of the world is but a living death in the eyes of those who are dead to the world, and whose lives are "hid with Christ in God." We who live in the world, are commanded to be not of the world. To be in the world and yet not of the world is, therefore, possible to us; for it is repugnant that our Creator and Lord should lay on us, His creatures and servants, a command which it is impossible for us to obey. It *is* possible to us; but possible only through our use of those means which He has ordained and provided in order to this end. And among those means, external graces, as well as internal graces, have their place. If we neglect the former, it must be to the prejudice of the latter. In daily contact with the world, if we are careless to counteract its influences, to which we are daily subject, we shall sooner or later become penetrated with its spirit; its views will colour ours, its maxims will enter into our language, and our lives will be practically indistinct from those of the wise and prudent of this world.

Among the men of the world, some deny the existence of sanctity, as Catholics understand it; others doubt its possibility; while to not a few it is folly. That it is possible, and that it does exist, the Lives of the Saints bear witness; its wisdom those only can appreciate who have learned the *Verbum Crucis*.

The doctrine of the Communion of Saints and of their intercession before the Throne of God, in union with their Human King and Head, is a bulwark of the doctrine of the Incarnation of the Word, of His sacrifice of Himself on the Cross, and of the extension and continuation of that sacrifice in the sacrifice of the Mass.

It was a natural consequence that, when in Protestant England the intercession of the Saints ceased to be believed in, and their invocation to be practised, the daily sacrifice should be taken away, the sacrifice of the Cross should be misconceived, and the Incarnation itself should be, to say the least, inadequately understood.

The Lives of the Saints are in like manner a bulwark of the Life of Jesus Christ Himself; nay! more, or, still more truly, they are themselves His own life under another aspect.

There was His hidden life, and His public life, both here on earth. There is His present life, alike in Heaven and on earth—His life of glory and exaltation at the right hand of the Father, and His life of obscurity and humiliation in our midst behind the sacramental veils. There is, besides these, His life in His mystical Body; and that life is in a special manner manifested in those whose lives are hid with Him in God, who continue with Him in His tribulations, who with Him are nailed to His Cross, who can say with His Apostle the vessel of His election, chosen to bear His name—"I live, yet not I, Christ liveth in me," who have put on Christ, and in His strength can do all things, and who, in their sufferings of soul and body in Christ and for Christ, make up those things which were wanting to His sufferings, for His Body's sake, which is the Church.

Christ, says St. Peter, suffered, leaving us an example that we should follow in His footsteps. Twice in one Epistle to the Corinthians, and again, to the Philippians, does St. Paul write, "Be ye followers of me, even as I also am of Christ." "Be followers of me, brethren, and observe them who walk so, as you have our model."

"Be ye holy even as I am holy," was the Divine command under the Old Law, reiterated in the New by Him who said, "Be ye perfect as your Heavenly Father is perfect." Setting before our eyes His Saints, God closes our mouths, and opens alike our minds and our hearts. He teaches us that what has been may be, that what others have done we may do; as by an interior voice He said to Saint Augustine, "*Et tu non poteris quod isti et istæ?*"

God might command us, but He could not persuade us by the force of His own example. He could not, not only because He is Himself invisible, inaccessible, incomprehensible, but also because the manner of His sanctity is not the manner of ours. Ours is inseparable from penance, submission, obedience, and self-contempt. He has supplied in His Saints what was lacking in Himself, as He is our model.

No, man, says St. John, hath seen God at any time, the Only Begotten Son Who is in the bosom of the Father, He hath declared Him. He the "First-born of every creature" is the "Image of the Invisible God." Through Him is God made manifest to men, in Whom dwelleth all the fulness of the Godhead corporeally.

Through every work of His hands is its Creator known, but most of all is He known through His greatest work, that Sacred Humanity, which in a special manner has he coveted, appropriated, and made His own through its subsistence in the unity of a Divine Person.

Next in exemplary value to that human life, wedded through the Hypostatic union to the Divine life, is the life of Her whom we invoke as *Speculum Justitiæ*. But besides these,—the greater and the lesser light,—we have a firmament of stars, each differing from the other in its special glory, and yet shining one and all with the same brightness—derived to them from their central sun. Even in the natural order, the invisible things of God, from the creation of the world, are clearly seen, being understood by the things that are made, His eternal power also and divinity, *Cœli enarrant gloriam Dei,* but *Mirabilis Deus in sanctis tuis, in quibus,* as St. Leo adds *et præsidium nobis constituit et exemplum.*

Next, then, in value to the Life of our Lord, as we have it recorded to us in the Holy Gospels, come the Lives of His Saints; and they have, moreover, as we have seen, a special value of their own, relatively to us, and in order to our imitation. Tertullian's words are true: "*Solutio totius difficultatis Christus.*" It is true also that He was in all things made like unto us His brethren, that He was tried in all things even as we are, that He was a Man of sufferings and acquainted with grief; that He allowed a real, human fear to take possession of His human soul; that that Soul really bent beneath the weight of a sadness, which, had He not been sustained, would have slain Him before His time: "*Tristis est anima mea usque ad mortem ;*" that He knew the strength alike of human friendship and of filial love; that He knew, in consequence, what bereavement and separation cost; that in His mortal Body He suffered hunger and thirst, and weariness and pain ; and yet, with all this, the "*Ecce Homo!*" sounds in the ears of some with a sense of almost unreality; for, blinded by the brightness of His Divinity, their eyes fail to see His oneness, as our example, with ourselves.

And our Mother too, even she, so dazzling in her glory, seems almost beyond our reach, and outside our sphere. Our faith tells us that, with all her glory, she is yet a creature, and a human creature, with her created human personality as well as with her created, human nature; that she, in her whole being and subsistence, is one of ourselves; but, as the eyes of that same faith carry us away to the land that is far off, and we gaze on the Queen in her beauty, the Woman clothed with the Sun, and set high above the Seraphim, the Immaculate Mother of our God,—her peerless position, her unparalleled prerogatives, the singleness of her unequalled glory, her nearness and closeness to her Divine Son, while they quicken and deepen our worship and our love, yet tend, and that almost in the same proportion, to obscure in our eyes her value as our example, as a pattern shown on the Mount, and set before us for our imitation.

This, it may be, ought not so to be. And yet, such is our frailty and such our little faith, that, with most of us sometimes, and with many not seldom, so it is. And so He Who knoweth whereof we are made, and Who hath compassion on our infirmities, has, besides Himself and Her—our King and Queen, our Father and our Mother—given us as our models, our brethren and our fellow-citizens, our fellow-soldiers and our fellow-servants.

These, at least, have laboured in the same vineyard with ourselves, and borne the same burden. They have fought in the same warfare, and against the same enemies. Men of like passions with ourselves, they have experienced the same difficulties, doing battle with the forces of evil from without, and with the frailty of the flesh within.

To all His subjects, to the whole race, to each individual human being, is the same appeal made, is the same invitation given by the King Eternal, Christ our Lord:—"My Will is to subdue the whole world, and all Mine enemies, and so to enter into the glory of My Father. Whoso wills to come with Me must be content with the same food, with the same clothing, with the same lodging, as I Myself. He must labour with

Me by day, he must watch with Me by night, and so, sharing with Me My toils and sufferings, shall he be made partaker of My victory, and follow Me into My glory."

It requires but judgment and prudence, but right-mindedness and sound reason, to prompt the answer to an appeal so generous.

But there are those who, not content with enrolling themselves beneath the standard of their Lord and Leader, and fighting in the ranks against His enemies, whom they have declared their own, desire to distinguish themselves in His presence, and burn to do great deeds in order to His greater glory. Not content with resisting the onset of the foe, they will attack him, and that in his citadel, within their own borders, *agendo contra;* doing violence to their own sensuality, to their own carnal love, and to their own love of the world.

To their own sensuality—not only refraining from licentious gratification of the senses, but denying themselves even such satisfactions as are not unlawful.

To their own carnal love—not only resisting the attacks of concupiscence, but mortifying even such desires of the flesh, the indulgence of which is not forbidden, and such affections as in themselves are pure.

To their love of the world—not only by a holy indifference as to their possession or as to their lack of those things which the world esteems and longs for, strives after, and rests satisfied with; but by a disesteem and even contempt of riches and of honours, of pleasure and of power, and by a holy covetousness of those very things which the world abhors and shrinks from—of poverty and obscurity, of a life of labour unrequited, and suffering unsympathised with, of contempt and the hatred of their fellow-men.

The Saints did not, do not, more than do other men, have any *natural* liking for these things, one and all repugnant to our human nature; but, fixing their eyes on Him Who led the way, and seeing Him deliberately *choose* to be a poor man, to lead a life of labour, to be despised and hated, to suffer all that human nature is capable of suffering, and to die in agony and by a death of shame,—they saw this life of poverty and obscurity, of mortification and toil, of subjection and obedience, in that it was chosen, undertaken, and undergone by Him,—elevated, ennobled, yes! and divinised by its being made the mode of the human life on earth of a Divine Person. Looking at it from this point of view, they saw its supernatural excellence and value, they conceived for it a supernatural esteem, and this esteem begot in them a supernatural desire, wherewith they burned to make it their own. In the satisfying of this desire they grew into the likeness of Jesus Christ; and thus they became Saints. They distinguished themselves beneath His standard on the field of battle, following closely where He Himself led the way. Thus it was that through labour and conflict they won their position as the flower of His army, as the chivalry of His Church.

It is most true that a man may lead a holy life, and

b

that, thank God, many a holy life has been led in the midst of riches and surrounded by all that honour, and by all those pleasures which riches procure for their possessor,—that opportunities of pleasure may be made opportunities for the exercise not only of temperance but of mortification,—that rank and riches may be valued and used solely for the greater glory of His Divine Majesty; but it is no less true, that a life with such surroundings of material comfort, of social and domestic joys, and of earthly honour is, with all its holiness, a life in its circumstances singularly unlike the life on earth of Jesus of Nazareth.

This is all that can be said against it; and yet this has sufficed for motive to make men turn their backs upon all that the world covets, and seek that which the world abhors. It was their clear view of this truth that gave the Saints their strange attraction for that cheerless, unwedded life of childlessness and poverty and toil and suffering, which so many deliberately chose, and which so many more would most gladly have embraced, had God in His adorable Providence not ordered otherwise their lot on earth. Had they been free to follow their own attraction, they would have followed in His footsteps even to the death, rejoicing with His Apostles *contumeliam pati pro nomine Christi*, so that in living and in dying they might not only be His, but be also in all things made like unto Him.

To the men of the world, who live for what the world can give them, what is this but folly?

And folly indeed it would be, were this life the only one, and were there no Crucified, Risen, and Ascended Jesus. The Saints would then be of all men most miserable, and those would be words of wisdom, "Let us eat and drink, for to-morrow we die."

Here do we see that Word of the Cross which in past times as in the present, was to the Jews a stumbling-block, and to the Gentiles foolishness; but which, to the Apostle and to us, to all who believe, is the power of God and the wisdom of God. St. Paul calls it a hidden Gospel, hidden to those who perish, whose minds the god of this world hath blinded, that the light of the Gospel of the glory of Christ, Who is the image of God, should not shine unto them. "But," says he, "God, Who commanded the light to shine out of darkness, hath shined in our hearts, to give the light of the knowledge of the glory of God in the face of Christ Jesus. In all things we suffer tribulation, but are not distressed; we are straitened, but are not destitute; we suffer persecution, but are not forsaken; we are cast down but we perish not; always bearing about in our body the dying of Jesus, *that the life also of Jesus*, may be *made manifest* in our bodies; for we who live are always delivered unto death for Jesus' sake, that the life also of Jesus may be *made manifest* in our mortal flesh. For this cause we faint not, for, though our outward man is corrupted, yet the inward man is renewed day by day. For our present tribulation, which is momentary and light, worketh for us above measure exceedingly an eternal weight of glory;

while we look, not at the things which are seen, but at the things which are not seen; for the things which are seen are temporal, but the things which are not seen are eternal."

Such is the Gospel of the Cross; a hidden treasure, lying not on the surface, but beneath the soil. To many it may seem an hard saying, and yet who can deny but that this is *Christianity?* It is Christianity pure and simple, and in its quintessence. It is Christianity as Christ taught it, as Paul preached it, as the Saints have in all ages understood it. They, more truly than Paul's written words, are his "epistles read and known of all men."

It comes to this,—that those are not the men most to be congratulated, and to be envied, who have health and wealth, family and home, prosperity and pleasure. All these are gifts of God, and to be received with thanksgiving, but they are not His choicest gifts and the tokens of His tenderest love. Those are the men to be congratulated, the men to be envied, on whom He has bestowed His other gifts of poverty, and suffering, and subjection, who recognize these as from the treasury of His bounty, and receive them with joy and thanksgiving, from their Father's hand. The former may be of the number of His faithful servants, whom He calls His friends, whom He has made His children; but the latter are the dearest to His Father's heart; for they remind Him, as it were, the most of His Only begotten and His Well-beloved Son.

This folly of the Cross is the wisdom of the Saints;

and it is a wisdom with which the wisdom of this world is in unceasing conflict. These two wisdoms are striving for the victory ever around us, and sometimes also within us. We Catholics possess this hidden wisdom, but it is a treasure which we have in earthen vessels. Living in the world, surrounded by its atmosphere, with its maxims ever sounding in our ears, it is impossible, in the order of things, that we should not be in some measure affected by its spirit. Hence the necessity, on our part, not only of ceaseless vigilance, but also of continual effort. The Spirit of God drives us into the Desert, or leads us along the way of the Cross, or lifts us Heavenward to where Christ sitteth at the Right Hand of God. The spirit of this world leads us into the bustle of life, shows us the kingdoms of this world, and the glory of them, and drags us earthwards to seek our satisfaction, and to find our peace in those things which the world can both understand and bestow. It would tempt us to ascend from Thabor, instead of taking the way to Olivet, which leads through Gethsemani. It suggests to us the prize without the race, the wage without the labour, the victory without the conflict, the Crown without the Cross.

Hence we must be upon our guard, and upon our guard especially as to this, that we do not lower our standard to the level of our practice; that we do not, in order to excuse our shortcomings, if not to others, to ourselves, darken our understandings, or shut our eyes to the light, afraid of facing the fact as to what Christianity really is. For the children of light to live like the children of this world is bad indeed; but for them to adopt the maxims, to speak the language, and to breathe the spirit of the world is hopeless.

One great protection against this danger is the conviction and remembrance that Christianity, in its breadth and fulness, is not that which we ourselves practise, is not that which we see in the majority of men around us, but is that which we see incarnated in the Saints of God. A definition of a Saint is,—a perfect Christian.

Thus, whether we lead Christian lives or not, we shall at least have in our minds a clear and true idea of what our lives ought to be, of that to which our Baptism binds us, and of that of which by our name of Christians we make profession. And to see this clearly and to hold this firmly is of itself a great grace. It is a triumph of the grace of Divine faith within our souls. It then needs but our co-operation with the twin-grace of inspiration, inflaming and strengthening our wills, as the grace of illumination enlightened our understandings, to make us stretch forward to the race set before us, and endure hardness as good soldiers of Jesus Christ.

Such being the value of the Lives of the Saints as a means of promoting the growth and development of sanctity within our souls, by preserving the true idea of Christianity in our minds, the same value attaches to their Panegyrics. For what is a Panegyric save the Life of a Saint in an especially convenient and attractive form? It gives a condensed, a bird's-eye view of his life, dwelling either upon the great deeds he did for God, or upon the Christian virtues of which such deeds were but the fruit. In a word, it sets before us that aspect under which he more especially imitated Jesus Christ.

God will have His Saints honoured, not in heaven only and in the future, but on earth and now; and God Himself is honoured in His Saints; a ray of the eternity of their glory and recompense penetrates even into the darkness of this present time, in the worship given to them by the Church on earth, a worship which shall endure from generation to generation throughout the ages, till time shall be no more. "*Justi autem in perpetuum vivent; in memoriâ æternâ erit justus,*" says the Psalmist, and in view of this prodigality of their recompense he cries again: "*Nimis honorificati sunt amici Tui Deus!*" To perpetuate their memory, and to extend their glory is the end of a panegyric; and, were it the only one, it would suffice. By this means, as in other ways, those who despised all earthly honours while on earth, receive greater honour even from the earth than they could ever have obtained had they striven for it, than they could ever have hoped for from any triumph of statecraft, or from any feats of arms.

But, then are the Saints most honoured, and with that honour which they themselves desire, when men through them "learn Christ." And so, just as God has wedded together His own greater glory with man's salvation and sanctification, so has He also bound in one the honour of His Saints and our imitation of them. To procure both is the twofold end of a Panegyric; or, the one end under its twofold aspect.

With this view Segneri preached. With the same view the translator places his Panegyrics within reach of English readers. The name of Segneri is too well known and too justly celebrated for his works to need words of commendation. May they accomplish their end in the souls of those who read them; and let those who read remember what St. Augustine says: "*Summa religionis est imitari quem colimus.*"

WILLIAM HUMPHREY, S.J.

[NOTE OF THE TRANSLATOR.]

The reader is reminded that the Panegyric on the Immaculate Conception (page 1) was written some 150 years before the Immaculate Conception of our Lady was defined by the Church, at a time when it was denied by a certain school of theologians and considered doubtful by others. The Panegyric bears witness to a good deal more than the individual opinion of its author; he could not have used the language we find in it unless his words had been in harmony with the general instinct of the faithful, and the traditions of the Christian Church.

PANEGYRICS OF FATHER SEGNERI.

PANEGYRIC

IN HONOUR OF THE IMMACULATE CONCEPTION OF THE BLESSED VIRGIN.

An origin illustrious in proportion to its obscurity.
"Jacob begot Joseph, the husband of Mary, of whom was born Jesus, who is called Christ."—MATT. i. 16.

It cannot be denied that the light of the moon is a gift bestowed on her by the sun. And, nevertheless, at the same time we are compelled to admit that the sun shows himself as jealous of the moon as he is beneficent towards her; for it appears that he only enriches her with his gifts under the express condition that she shall never adorn herself with them in his presence hence the more brilliantly he enlightens her at a distance, the more completely is her light obscured when she is nigh to him.

Very differently do we to-day behold Christ acting with regard to Mary. For, although Mary derives all her glory from Christ in exactly the same manner as the moon derives hers from the sun, she is not on this account obliged to remain far from him in order to shine. On the contrary, she never appears so resplendent as when in His immediate presence; and this is perhaps the principal reason why the gospel of to-day sets them both before us in such close proximity.

It appears to me that in this same gospel St. Matthew has simply depicted a most glorious firmament —a firmament in which the illustrious personages whom he enumerates at so much length, take their place as stars of lesser magnitude, some being distinguished on account of their sanctity, others on account of their high birth or exalted position. Amongst all these Christ shines forth as the sun, and Mary as the moon. But in order that Mary might shine with greater splendour on this her first appearance, it was not necessary that the Evangelist should separate her from her sun; therefore no sooner has he mentioned the husband of *Mary* than he hastens to add that of her was born Jesus. Hence, if we would prove her to be perfect in every respect, the fact of her nearness to Christ is the argument of widest application and greatest force. Why was she holy at her very birth? Because this was meet for the Mother of Christ. Why did she contract no stain in childbirth? Because such purity was required in the Mother of Christ. Why was her life blameless? Because the Mother of Christ must needs lead such a life. Why was she so favoured in the hour of her death? Because in her character of the Mother of Christ she deserved these privileges. Thus the more plainly we see her very nearness to Christ conferring on her a greater lustre in every respect, the stranger does it appear that the festival of to-day should not dispel any existing doubt as to the stainless nature, not only of her life, but also of her conception. It it said of Mary that she it is of whom was born Jesus; can it then for a single instant be doubted whether her conception was impure or whether it was immaculate? Still less can I believe that the world contains any one foolish enough to persuade himself that Christ permitted her to be conceived in sin from a feeling of jealousy; that is to say, because he was unwilling that beside himself the moon should shine with perfect purity and unclouded splendour; for the divine sun loses nothing of his light, because from his fulness he enriches all the lesser planets. And it is well known that ever amongst these latter there exists this difference: that whilst the light possessed by some is natural to them, in others it is but a gift bestowed upon them; so that in the case of the former it may be considered as inherent, in the case of the latter as borrowed.

Let us, therefore, endeavour this morning to investigate, with a holy curiosity, the reasons why the Church in her prudence has hitherto abstained from defining the dogma of the Immaculate Conception, seeing that in support of it there exists abundant evidence deduced from the authority of Scripture, the force of argument, and popular belief. In fact, so convincing are the proofs, that we feel a moral certainty that God could never permit falsehood so completely to assume an appearance of truth and effect so widespread a deception. I say the Church has abstained from defining this dogma, although it is true that our Chief Pastor Alexander VII. has, in a famous Bull, renewed all those decrees which were in favour of it; has explained, confirmed, and amplified them in some respects; but yet we must fain confess that he adds a special clause to the effect that this proceeding is not intended to have the weight of a decision. Nay, he even allows any one to lawfully entertain an opposite opinion in his own mind, without scruple of conscience, and without incurring the guilt of heresy or impiety.

And inasmuch as the objection, which I myself have heard from the lips of more than one person, is one worthy of consideration and elucidation, I propose this morning to enter on the subject, and satisfy at once all objections, by showing wherefore the wise Providence of God has permitted that to remain so long a matter of uncertainty in the Church, which He could in a single moment have made evident to all. This might, perhaps, be productive of much good; it may bring great glory to Mary, and to ourselves no small profit. I ask, then, for your attention while I proceed to open the subject.

Some may perhaps be of opinion that this uncertainty has been permitted, because it is a matter of but slight importance to the Blessed Virgin that she should be pronounced exempt from all sin, not only actual, but original. This idea can, however, hardly be entertained, if we consider how universal is the value set upon noble birth, and the contempt in which a low origin is held. And this is the very point which remains doubtful in regard to the Blessed Virgin: whether her birth was noble. Not, indeed, in the order of nature, but what is of far greater consequence, in the order of grace. The question now at issue is whether she is a member of the guilty race of Adam; whether she too, in her conception, is not free, but a slave; not a friend, but a foe; not a saint, but a sinner. And yet some affirm this to be a matter of no moment to her!

It has often occurred to me to wonder how it is that men set such great value on noble extraction. For tell me in truth, how are we responsible in the matter of our birth? It is no merit of our own if we are well-born; it is no fault of ours if our origin is base. It is a mere gift of nature, determined by fate, and not by choice. And yet how averse is every one of us to hear that he comes of ignoble parentage! We can better bear to be accused of poverty, ignorance, or cowardice, than of low birth. For my part I think this state of things must have come about because the fault of low birth is a stain which is almost indelible. If a man be poor, he may by means of industry acquire wealth. If he be ignorant he may by means of study, make himself an accomplished scholar. If he be a coward he may, by long effort, become a valiant man. But if he be a plebeian, efforts of his own can scarcely avail to procure him a place among the nobles of the land. Certainly it is possible that by dint of exertion he may achieve great distinction for himself, but one blot remains which can never be wiped out; he comes of ignoble race, his blood is tainted, his forefathers were slaves. The rich man who has won for himself wealth does not require us to ignore the fact that he was once poor; but let no one presume to remind the self-made noble that his rank is acquired. Baldus, an oracle for those amongst you who are lawyers, used to compare such persons to patients recovering from a wound: "they are like a sick man recovering from a wound, some mark of which always remains." In the case of other sufferers, as soon as the malady itself is removed, the traces of it speedily disappear; but with wounds it is otherwise, however perfectly they may be healed the scar will always remain.

Now consider that this would be equally applicable to the Blessed Virgin, if she had been conceived in sin. From its very nature original sin is of all others the very last for which we deserve to be blamed, because, properly speaking, it is not committed, but inherited; and as only by a special interposition of Divine Goodness could we be exempted from it, so in all justice it cannot be our own fault if we are contaminated by it. From this point of view then, it appears of little consequence that Mary should be declared free from original sin. But again, on the other hand, it appears evident that, had she not been free from original sin, this taint, born with us at our birth, would have been enough to blight all her subsequent glories. For in that case even after she had attained to the most exalted position a pure creature can ever occupy in the order of grace, her mean origin might have been called to mind, and she might have been reproached with her unfortunate race. Would not such a blot as this cause her greatness to lose much of its lustre? Imagine for a moment that she was conceived in sin, and then tell me: What do we know about her? That she is the Queen of Heaven? Yes, but previously she was a subject of hell. That she is the Mother of grace? Yes, but previously she was the daughter of wrath. That she is the Advocate of sinners? Yes, but first of all she was their fellow-sinner. If she was the Mother of the Divine Word, can it be denied that she had formerly been His enemy? The Holy Ghost took her for His Spouse; but before that had not the hellish tyrant held her captive ? The Eternal Father adopted her as His Daughter; but the archrobber had been beforehand in possessing her. When all has been told of the Blessed Virgin, if we cannot add that her origin was immaculate, that primeval blot will suffice to darken all her subsequent splendour. Shall we, then, delude ourselves into the belief that the Blessed Virgin does not care that we should recognise her origin to be immaculate? Moreover, if in the order of nature she so highly valued noble birth that, notwithstanding her lowliness, she thought it a glory to belong to David's royal race, would she have prized it so little in the order of grace as to be willing that, notwithstanding her sanctity, she should appear to be of impure origin ?

We see, then, that this is a question of great consequence to the Blessed Virgin; it is most momentous, it is all-important. But if so, it will be asked, why has not God interposed with His absolute authority? Why has He not defined it more clearly? Why has not He uttered a final verdict ? Why has not His voice been heard ? I should not venture of myself to examine into so weighty a question, did not the same Holy Virgin, who inspires my mind now also, put words into my lips. St. Bridget was the recipient of her confidences; to her she discovered this secret; to Bridget, I say, with whom Christ Himself used to converse so frequently, so affectionately; and whose revelations it is as just to revere as it would be presumptuous to despise, since, although belief in them is not binding on the faithful, they have received the unanimous sanction of four supreme Pontiffs, after a protracted investigation. In one of these revelations, our Lady thus speaks to St.

Bridget: "It is a certain truth that I was conceived without original sin." "But if this be true, O my Lady, why has there been no definition?" Let us hear the answer she makes to this our objection. "God so willed it, that His friends should feel a holy doubt concerning my conception, to give opportunity for the display of zeal, until in due time the truth should shine forth brightly." These few words are seeds, fruitful in strength, which give me courage to enter upon this subject with a view to promoting the honour of Mary.

It cannot be doubted that God, in the first instance, permitted this uncertainty in order to bring greater glory to His Mother, whose honour He, as a loving Son, has always been as anxious to promote as if it were His own. He delights to see us applying our intellect to the task of delineating her perfections, and tracing out her peculiar characteristics; and therefore He has left a wide field open to our research. And this I believe to be the reason why we find so little information given us respecting the Blessed Virgin in Holy Writ. Of her Son Himself we do not read that He ever conversed about her with others, much less did He hold her up for praise. Do we generally find Him so sparing of His encomiums of persons far inferior to her? What did He not say of His Precursor Saint John, alone? Did He not of His own accord assume the part of an orator to proclaim his worth to the assembled crowd? of an advocate to plead his cause with the Pharisees? He commended a poor widow for offering two mites in the temple; He praised a wretched publican for performing a single act of humiliation; no sooner did He behold the converted Magdalen at His feet, than He broke forth into eulogiums of her charity. He lauded the perseverance of the Canaanitish woman, the faith of the centurion, the guilelessness of Nathanael; and yet we never read that He spoke a word in commendation of the Blessed Virgin. On the contrary, when a certain woman in the crowd gave utterance to those well-known words of praise : " Blessed is the womb that bore thee," He immediately silenced and rebuked her, giving another direction to the eulogium, undeniably just though it was, by pronouncing him to be far more blessed who listens to the Word, the Son of her womb, and obeys that Word. " Blessed are they who hear the word of God, and keep it." And why did Christ thus act ? Was He perhaps ignorant of His Mother's surpassing virtues, did He not love her, did He not appreciate her ? Such a supposition would be madness. And wherefore did He enjoin on others the same silence concerning her which He Himself observes in the Gospel ? Wherefore if not because the less we find decided and determined about her, the more eagerly shall we prosecute our researches and carry out our speculations. Thus, if you proceed to consider the subject, you will observe that almost everything which we now clearly and certainly know about the Blessed Virgin, was, for a long time, wrapped in far greater obscurity than the question of her Immaculate Conception is at the present day.

Each dogma was disputed in the schools, discussed in books, examined by several councils, ere the Holy Ghost saw fit finally to reveal it to us. Now tell me, what more glorious title has Mary than that of Mother of God ? Such a title was certainly worthy to be published for the first time by the mouth of the Holy

Ghost Himself, speaking in the Divine Scriptures; and yet it was His Will that the tongues of the Ephesian Fathers should first give utterance to it, that their pens should first subscribe it. In our own day we all agree in proclaiming Mary to be a virgin before childbirth, a virgin in childbirth, a virgin after childbirth. But where do we find this so expressly stated in the Scriptures as to be beyond dispute? It was needful that many lofty intellects should weary themselves in bringing forward arguments to prove the orthodoxy of this belief, and in discussing and expounding them, in order to silence the arrogance of the Heloidians, Valentinians, and various other sects, which have contested her right to this glorious prerogative. At how much length did the Fathers deliberate upon her birth into the world, and her assumption into heaven, before they considered themselves warranted in authoritatively pronouncing as to whether the former should be regarded as holy, and the latter be believed to be corporal. Thus, as the stream of time flows on, her glorious prerogatives gradually unveil themselves in their full splendour; and she, from on high, notes down how many great minds are employed in her service, how many vigils are consecrated to her, how many pages are written and how many hours of toil are dedicated to her honour. In our day, little yet remains with regard to the Mother of God in which we are left in doubt, awaiting a final definition from the voice of the Church, except her Immaculate Conception: on this subject how many researches have been made and are still being made! How many willing hands are engaged in turning over the pages of Holy Writ! How many learned pens are employed in compiling books! How many loving tongues are indefatigable in recapitulating arguments! What wonder, then, that God permits this question to remain doubtful, ánd delays to interpose His indisputable and infallible authority, since this uncertainty which has so long prevailed in the Church, has redounded so much to the glory of Mary.

And in truth, as often as I apply my mind fixedly to the subject, it strikes me that God has acted towards the Blessed Virgin as nature towards the Nile. Follow me carefully in what I am about to say, for I am aware that perhaps the comparison will seem to you weak, rather than unbecoming. It is undeniable that nature has endowed the Nile with unusual virtues and properties peculiarly its own. What is the next thing we hear? That nature has also ordained, that the source of that river should be hidden, and thus no man can know whether it is clear or muddy, whether it is grand or insignificant. And incredible as it may appear, this obscurity, which seemed its only drawback, has turned out to be its choicest prerogative. Nature could have invented no better means of rendering the Nile illustrious. The discovery of this unknown source has been the object of incessant competition amongst men. Long hours of study have been directed to this end, wearisome journeys undertaken, abundant treasures expended. What can be said more than this? we find Nero himself, the ruler of the world, organising a vast expedition. By his command beasts of burden are brought from all parts, individuals are assembled together, money is collected, carriages are constructed, stores of provisions are prepared, suitable for journeys by sea and land. Several noble Roman Senators are appointed leaders of the band: prayers are offered on its departure, vows recorded for its safe return, when at last this famous expedition starts from Rome, the capital of the world. Every nation through whose territory it passes, inquires with curiosity whither it is bound? and to all the same answer is returned. "We are going to discover the sources of the Nile." There is no province, no city, no habitation where the fame of it does not spread. The news are passed from hand to hand, they fly from mouth to mouth; each man asks his neighbour: "Have you not heard that Rome is sending to discover the sources of the Nile?" Rome is sending to discover the sources of the Nile! What is the reason of this? Has the Nile no other marvellous properties for which it deserves to be famous? It is not universally acknowledged that this, of all rivers, is the one most favoured by nature? When the waters of other streams are dried up through the summer heats, she renders those of the Nile more plentiful, as if she would compel all men to owe their subsistence to it alone, since, as Lucan says, "In that torrid clime, the Nile is present lest the heat should consume the earth;" its ample stores being thus provided as a supply in the time of universal drought. The Egyptian husbandman does not need to turn his eyes heavenwards; he has the Nile; to it he makes his vows, to it he addresses his supplications. And the friendly river, copiously overflowing its banks, spreads over the face of the land, filling the valleys, and turning the villages into so many happy isles, whose inhabitants, besieged by the water, gladly betake themselves to their agile boats, there with trumpets, with viols, with pipes and drums, to give expression to their joy, rejoicing the more in proportion as they see their lands disappear under the waters. We need not marvel at this, for the turbid river flowing over the freshly-sown fields, does not carry along with it devastation as other rivers are wont to do, but on the contrary renders them fertile. On this account Isaias bestows on it these words of praise: "The seed of the Nile in many waters; the harvest of the river is her revenue" (Is. xxiii. 3), for those fields which most richly receive the deposit of the waters, afford the best promise of an abundant harvest. And were not the wonders we have enumerated worthy of being publicly honoured by such an expedition as this? Most undoubtedly; they were well worthy of it. But the nature of man leads him to pay slight attention to the marvels which lie open to his view, and eagerly to hunt after those that are hidden. Whatever rare properties the Nile might have possessed, it would never have obtained such world-wide fame, if its source had not remained a secret. The mystery of its birth was the inducement which led the Romans, under Nero, to send out their memorable expedition; and even long before their time the Assyrians under Cambyses, the Persians under Sesostris, the Macedonians under Alexander, impelled by a like motive, had embarked on a similar enterprise. And in spite of the stubborn manner in which this river has refused to yield up its secret, it preferred that nations should admire the mystery of its origin rather than discover it. So that after so many efforts and so many speculations in the past its tendency to concealment still prevails: yet nothing has been able to quench the sanguine hopes of posterity, for men still strive to search out that which preceding ages have left in uncertainty. Wherever it appears it is sought, and the glory of discovering it falls to the lot of no people, as we read in Lucan.

Now who shall forbid us, O my hearers, after contemplating the remarkable manner in which God acts in the order of nature, to rise higher, and acquaint ourselves with His proceedings in the order of grace? I once more repeat what I have already said, that if I am not mistaken, God has dealt with the Blessed Virgin as nature has dealt with the Nile. For a long time He has permitted her origin to be wrapped in mystery; and this fact, more, perhaps, than anything else, has contributed to promote her glory. Nor is this the only point of similitude between her and the Nile; for when the Sun of Divine Justice, hotly kindled, arms himself with his fiercest rays and sharpest arrows, to burn up the earth in his wrath, it is the prerogative of Mary to interfere to appease his wrath. *Et ne terras dissipit ignis,* she alone, *adest mundo,* to extinguish by the compassionate tears falling from her eyes the fire which the sins of men have called down from heaven. Even when the royal streams of other saints are impotent to quench the burning, Mary is never found wanting; on the contrary, her waters flow in greater force and abundance, for God often withholds graces asked through the intercession of His other servants in order that mortals may have recourse all the more to the intercession of His Mother. Many, having her for their advocate, feel no need to turn their eyes elsewhere; confiding in her patronage, to her they offer their supplications, to her they make their vows. And the happy effects of their confidence are made manifest when they readily obtain from her which they vainly looked for from another. She pours forth her graces in no sparing measure, enriching all, repulsing none; differing, however, from the Nile in this one point, that, whereas the benefits conferred by that river are restricted to a single province, the graces of Mary are the portion of the whole earth. But what do I say? these prerogatives of Mary have often been enumerated; many lips have recounted them; on this account the busy world no longer takes interest in investigating them. This is plain to an ordinary observer; any man of sense can comprehend it; for the more hidden anything is, the more efforts will the human intellect expend on searching it out.

And because we are left in greater ignorance about the origin of the Blessed Virgin than about anything else concerning her, and however much we study, however much we speculate, the tendency to concealment still remains, for this very reason it forms the object of our most indefatigable researches. But who shall say how greatly her glory has hereby been advanced? From almost every realm of Europe solemn deputations have gone forth to the Holy See; they have passed mountains, they have crossed the Ocean, and with what object? In order to ascertain what was the origin of the Blessed Virgin, in order to learn whether her conception was noble or base, stainless or impure. For this end how many potentates are constantly sending one representative after another! how much gold is lavished, how many instructions are issued, how many petitions presented, how great exertions are made! Nor does the failure of past efforts destroy present hope; as long as the origin of the Blessed Virgin remains involved in mystery, so long will men strive to penetrate that mystery. They will increasingly continue to make her the topic of their discourses, the object of their speculations, the subject of their writings, like miners working a rich vein of ore which yields the more the farther it is pursued.

And now, my hearers, what do you say in answer to all this?

Is it not apparent that God, by this plan of action chosen by Him, has singularly promoted the glory of His Mother? If the immaculate nature of her conception had from the first been plainly revealed, what greater, what more universal honours could she have received than those which all nations have paid to her whilst it was yet a matter of obscurity?

But, if I am not mistaken, God has had a further object in thus acting, namely, that of providing for the faithful a means of advancing themselves in the favour of the Blessed Virgin. For, indeed, those truths respecting the Blessed Virgin which the incontrovertible authority of Holy Church obliges us to believe and confess, may be compared to a compulsory tribute, which if we refuse to pay constitutes us rebels, and, if paid, cannot gain for us the title of generosity.

Nothing remains for us but humbly to bow our heads, and thus modestly address Our Lady. We have done that which we ought to do. If it would be an act of disloyalty, O my Queen, to refuse you this homage, it cannot be a meritorious work to perform it. But it seems that I can make you my debtor, if I freely offer you that which I am at liberty to withhold. It is perfectly legitimate for me to entertain the belief that you were conceived in sin, provided that I refrain from giving utterance to my opinions in print, from preaching or arguing on the subject, from teaching or defending them even in private. The Church in her wisdom has tied my hands and closed my lips; the famous Bulls, published by several Sovereign Pontiffs, and especially the last, issuing from Alexander VII., leave me no choice but to conceal such opinions in the inmost recesses of my mind. However, in this hiding-place, at least, I may safely cherish them, without laying myself open to the charge of audacity or presumption.

But I do not wish to avail myself of this liberty; unless the Church expressly enjoins on me a contrary belief, it will ever remain my firm persuasion that you are free from all sin, whether original or actual. To maintain this I am ready to exhaust my strength, to spend my breath, and even to shed my blood. Now tell me, my hearers, do you not think such an act of homage must be singularly pleasing to Our Lady, as being an act which cannot be commanded even by those who have a right to rule our inward beliefs, and which is therefore all the greater proof of love?

Most certainly it is, and must be so, otherwise Saint Jerome, in answering Jovinian, would have been incorrect when he asserted a free gift to be more worthy of thanks than a compulsory one. Furthermore, do we not see that God Himself desires that similar voluntary acts of service should be rendered to His Majesty? With a view to this, He has ordained that a part only of those things which conduce to His glory should be enjoined on us as a precept; it is His Will that many should be in the form of counsels, as, for instance, perpetual obedience, voluntary poverty, virginal chastity; so that if we embrace them we are worthy of praise, but if we do not embrace them we incur no blame. Must not every one perceive that such a proceeding as this cannot fail to redound to the greater glory of God? For, notwithstanding the liberty left to us, many undertake of their own free will to carry out not only that which He enjoins, but that also which He counsels, and these form a select band of followers whose service, because voluntary, is all the more acceptable in His sight. In this way He can test the love we bear Him; for Love, as Saint Augustine says, does not wait for a command, it is ready to obey the slightest sign. For a soul that loves, it is sufficient to know the wish of him whom she loves; she embraces it, and seeks to forward it in every way.

To me it appears that what we have just said holds good in regard to the Blessed Virgin; we all owe her a manifold tribute of praise, the nature of which the Church expressly determines for us; in one matter nevertheless, room is left for the exercise of our free will, namely whether we do or do not hold her conception to have been immaculate. In this one matter, I say, the Church has hitherto left us liberty to form our own opinions; we may in our heart of hearts believe what we choose: yet he who seeks to know her mind on the subject will have no difficulty in perceiving to which side she inclines. She allows the immaculate nature of the conception of the Virgin to be openly maintained, to be proved by argument, to be taught publicly and privately, with the proviso that under the term conception should be understood the first instant in which her body was animated by a living soul. The Festival of the Conception is solemnised with double rites, a special Mass and a special Office are appointed for the day, and in both of these the conception of Mary is spoken of in exactly the same terms which are applied to her nativity. It is not said to have been sanctified, but to be of its nature holy, which may be taken to mean more than being immaculate; and more it certainly is, because if the meaning of the word be weighed, we shall see that "immaculate" only expresses the absence of impurity, whilst "holy" expresses the presence of many additional perfections, a solid and stable purity, a purity which brings its possessor into the closest union with God. For, as Saint Thomas says, "Two things belong to the name of sanctity—purity and strength." Not that the Church hereby intends to forbid any one from entertaining a contrary opinion in his secret heart; she reckons it to him as no sin, she utters no word of censure. Her real object is plain. Love does not wait for a command, it is ready to obey the slightest sign. What is the result of the small amount of liberty which the Church has wisely seen fit to leave us upon this head? The result is, that a countless multitude of faithful souls are brought to light, zealous servants of Mary, who when the honour of their mistress is concerned, delay not to obey until a command is laid on them, but are quick to follow a sign. And do they not succeed in honouring her? If this proves nothing else, at least it proves to her how anxious we are for her exaltation, since we spontaneously attribute to her a perfection which it were no sin to deny her; we do not care to wait for the presence of a command, the absence of a prohibition is enough for us.

This being so, can the Blessed Virgin doubt that we

shall willingly receive all that is enjoined on us respecting her, since we believe that which it is not obligatory on us to accept ? "He who resolves to do more than has been commanded, shows that less has been enjoined on him than he is able to perform," says Saint Augustine, speaking of those who, not content with obeying the Evangelical precepts, show themselves ready to follow the counsels. And it appears to me that the same thing on a lesser scale will apply to my present subject. If we, in order to honour the Blessed Virgin, show ourselves prompt to affirm more than that which is required of us, it follows that less is required of us than we are prepared to affirm. Let the Church then only state what she would have us believe about Mary, and however great her requirements, she need not fear, we shall not hold back. Does she perchance desire us to credit Our Lady with the possession of that rare prerogative of pre-natal sanctity, a prerogative conceded to others inferior to herself, as to Saint John Baptist, and to Jeremias ? This seems to us but a small thing. Does she desire us to believe that in virtue of this sanctity the Blessed Virgin was endowed with a measure of grace so abundant as to preserve her from committing any actual sin, however venial, and consequently that in the very outset of her earthly career, she stood on a higher summit of perfection than that reached by any other traveller at the close of his journey ? We are prepared to go further than this. Does she desire us to believe that in Mary were united two prerogatives as mutually incompatible as those of Virgin and of Mother ; so that neither did her Virginity render her barren, nor her Maternity interfere with her purity ? This is not sufficient to satisfy our devotion.

Let the Church speak again, and not hesitate on account of the sublimity of the verities she would propose to us. What will she tell us of Mary? That she is to be universally acknowledged as the Mother of God? We reply, so let it be; and should any follower of the vile heresy of Nestorius venture to contest her claim to this glorious title, let him be accursed, let him perish, let him be cast into the depths of hell. Are we required to believe anything else? Yes, we are required to believe that she was exalted above all the choirs of Angels, above all the company of the Blessed; that in heaven, she is present not only in spirit, as we are bound to believe, but also in body, as we have every reason to think; and that she stands before the Throne of God, as the Advocate of sinners, the Refuge of the miserable, the Dispenser of graces, the Patroness of the Church, the Queen of the universe. And is this all? or does there perchance yet remain something more for our acceptance, if we are desirous of honouring as far as possible the Blessed Virgin? What, something more! and who amongst us but will gladly concede to Our Lady this further prerogative? As far as we go the Church shall have no need to take from her armoury the weapons of justice, the excommunications and penalties which she is wont to hurl against those contumacious persons who resist her decrees; for is it likely we shall rebel against her commands after having shown ourselves so docile to her suggestions? He who resolves to do more than has been commanded, shows that less has been enjoined upon him than he is able to perform.

May we not venture, then, to hope that Mary will look down from heaven and accept this homage at our hand? Surely it is no inconsiderable homage, no small tribute that we pay her; she cannot fail to rejoice at the sight of so many faithful who lay at her feet a freewill offering of praise, one which the Church merely invites them to present, and does not extort by an indisputable command. And indeed it seems to me that an offering of such magnitude warrants us in expecting from the Blessed Virgin great things in return. Therefore I do not wonder that God, in order to give us the means of obtaining so rich a reward, has left this mystery as yet undecided, though he shows to us how reasonable it is to believe in it, still he does not reveal it to us as a subject for faith. But on this account we should not cease to hope for the publication, and that on no distant day, of the decision already promised to Saint Bridget, since it appears that now opportunity has been afforded for the display on all sides of holy zeal and earnest endeavours to discover the truth: and that thus the preordained time is near at hand in which the dogma revealed to us by Mary, full three centuries ago, shall be formally promulgated from the Vatican. "It is an undoubted truth that I was conceived without original sin."

SECOND PART.

Now if we hold the Blessed Virgin to be immaculate in her conception, although we are at liberty, under the restrictions above mentioned, to believe the contrary, what may we expect that she will do for us in return? She will do great things for us in return, as I learnt in my youth from the lips of one equally distinguished for his great learning, and for the high position he filled. And what she will do will be this:—

She will defend us in the hour of our death, as we defend her in the instant of her conception. Listen to me attentively. The thing of present importance to us is to ensure for ourselves a holy death, since the subject of our conception no longer concerns us. And that which is of present importance to Mary is to establish the belief in her immaculate conception, since the question of her death has been already set at rest. Now if we do our utmost to promote that which the Blessed Virgin has most at heart, may we not hope that she will interest herself in that which is of chief moment to us? Does not perfect gratitude require that the return made should be equivalent in degree if not in kind? But tell me, what can we do to spread the belief in her Immaculate Conception? The supreme authority of the Vatican does not rest in our hands; we are not empowered to speak from that chair, or to constitute ourselves the mouthpiece of that Oracle. This, my hearers, is no reason why you can do nothing in favour of the Immaculate Conception; I tell you rather, there is a great deal which is in your power to do, if you have the good will. For it is evident that so long as an article is not decreed to be of faith, it can always receive more or less probability, at least extrinsic, according as to whether it is upheld by a large or small number of authors, and whether those who believe in it are few or many.

With regard to all such dogmas as have been pronounced *de fide*, it does not lie within our power either to diminish or augment their certainty. If we receive them we do not render them any the more true; nor if we refuse to believe them are they any the less so. Were the doctrines taught by the Church rejected by every human intelligence, they would on this account be none the less infallible; and it matters little whether we speak in their defence or whether we keep silence. But in the case of truths which are not yet decided there is much which we can do; the number of votes in their favour being an argument for their truth, and *vice versâ*; and everything which adds to the weight of their probability tends in equal measure to prepare the way for the final and indubitable definition. Thus much being certain, we know further that the Immaculate Conception, of which we are now speaking, is amongst the number of those truths as yet not positively defined. The Church has, until now, not seen fit to declare *ex-cathedrâ* whether the Blessed Virgin was or was not conceived in sin. Let us take our stand with those who frankly, boldly, and unhesitatingly pronounce her conception to be immaculate; and there is no doubt but that, by so doing, we shall help to spread a belief already well-nigh universal, just as even the tiniest grain may add to the weight of a scale already quivering in the balance.

And is it not apparent to all that this opinion is daily acquiring new strength, for do we not see all classes of persons unanimously concurring to approve it—men and women, nobles and plebeians, learned and unlearned, religious and seculars, ecclesiastics and laymen, princes and subjects, royalists and republicans? Do we not listen gladly to him who speaks in its favour, whilst we cannot tolerate one who takes the opposite side? Do we not give outward expression to the inward conviction of our hearts in books, in the schools, in our writings, in our teachings in academies, in pictures, by festivals and by solemnities? Do we not erect splendid churches and dedicate magnificent altars to the honour of the Immaculate Conception? Do we not visit them frequently, celebrating there the appointed Mass and reciting the prescribed Office? Do we not follow the custom prevalent in many great Universities—as those of Paris, Cologne, Mayence, Vienna, Valentia, Salamanca, Alcala, Louvain, Barcelona, Evora, Coimbra, and others which I will not name here, to the number of thirty-eight, all of which refuse to confer a doctor's degree upon any one who will not previously pledge himself to further the cause of the Immaculate Conception, as long as the question may remain open to discussion? Do we not unite our entreaties to those of the many illustrious cities and famous capitals, which, in the name of the people, have petitioned the Holy Father to hasten on the final decision? Do we not construct Oratories, found Congregations, establish Confraternities under the title of the Immaculate Conception, as so many other people have already done, that from the Confraternity established in Rome alone, seven hundred different offshoots may be reckoned? Do we not strive to introduce our friends into these Oratories, and multiply the number of those who frequent them? And even in time of war, do not our troops bear the name of the Immaculate Conception? Is not this name given to the gates of our cities, to the bulwarks of our fortresses, to the quarters of our guards, to the vessels of our navy, to the ports of our coast, as is the custom prevalent in many kingdoms of the Indies; not to speak of Austria, Poland, Naples, Sardinia, Sicily, Portugal, and Spain, who have all publicly taken the Blessed Virgin for their Patroness, under the title of Our Lady of the Immaculate Conception? In a word, do we not manifest as plainly as we can, by hearty demonstrations of approval and applause, how much we have this matter at heart?

Now tell me, can any fail to see that a cause upheld by so vast a number of advocates must have far more probabilities in its favour than could belong to one destitute of them? Shall we not strive, then, at least, to do something where there is so much that may be done, from the performance of which no one can interfere to prevent us? If you are academicians, let this mystery often be represented in your works; choose for the subject of your compositions the Immaculate Virgin, crushing the Serpent under her foot and inflicting on him a mortal wound, rather than a Pagan Venus treading on the thorns in order to turn them into roses. Strive, all of you, to elucidate this mystery; if you are preachers, you may do it with your eloquence; if men of learning, with your arguments; if writers, with your pens; if painters, with your pencils; if sculptors, with your chisels. At least, let there be no one amongst you who has not some image of Mary Immaculate in his house, so that all who enter there may see at once which side of this question is adhered to by him who lives there. If you possess influence, if you possess authority over others, consider diligently how you can best employ these gifts to the honour of this same mystery. And can you believe that, if you do all this, the Blessed Virgin will not espouse your cause with the same ardour with which you have taken up hers? I can only repeat to you the definite promise she gives us by the mouth of the Ecclesiasticus: "They that explain me shall have life everlasting." (Eccles. xxiv. 31.) Now what are we, my brethren, to take as the meaning of the word explain? To explain is to throw light on that which is dark, to discover that which is hidden, to make certain that which is doubtful. There is but one alone of all the mysteries respecting Our Lady which still affords us an occasion of rendering her this homage. We need no longer explain her nativity, since it is *de fide* that it is holy; nor her childbearing, since it is *de fide* that it was virginal; we need no longer discuss the purity of her life or the glory of her death, for these also are enjoined on our belief. What is there, then, with regard to Mary, which yet remains for the unerring torch of the Church to enlighten, except her Immaculate Conception? It is right therefore that to him who labours in this cause, everlasting life should be promised in an especial manner; a life on which he shall enter through the portal of a good, a tranquil, a happy death; a death such as we all hope for, and which I entreat our Blessed Lady to grant in the most abundant measure to all those who have a devotion to her Immaculate Conception.

THE BLESSED VIRGIN MARY.

THE HIGHEST IN THE EYES OF GOD: THE LOWEST IN HER OWN EYES.

" And Mary said, Behold the handmaid of the Lord."
LUKE i. 38.

IT is related of the famous sculptor Phidias that he had on one occasion carved a statue equally remarkable for its great beauty and for its vast size, the proportions of which were so colossal that although the figure was not erect but in a sitting posture, its head reached to the ceiling of the studio in which it had been made. On this work being for the first time exposed to view, many persons, as is usual under such circumstances, came together to inspect it. Expressions of admiration were not wanting; one beholder praised the majesty of the countenance, one the life-like ease of the attitude, one the anatomy of the muscles, one the elegance of the drapery, another the proportion of the limbs, a thing all the more worthy of praise when on so large a scale. At length a certain person who thought himself more knowing than the rest, remarked that Phidias had made a great mistake in his art, because if it should occur to the statue to rise and stand upright, it must either break its head or shatter the ceiling. Phidias overheard the objection of this presumptuous individual and replied with good-humoured irony: "You need not fear that catastrophe, my friend, for I have provided against it; the statue, let me inform you, is made of so weighty a material that however it might wish to arise it would never be able to do so." This answer provoked a smile from the bystanders, and obtained for the artist an easy triumph over the objector, who was silenced and put to shame. It appears to me that these words, uttered in joke about a statue, may be applied in all gravity to the Blessed Virgin. Among the bold mortals who have presumed to pass censure upon the infinite works of God, there have not been wanting those who assert that He has gone too far in raising a woman to such pre-eminent dignity, in conferring upon her such privileges, such rare gifts, such titles, such dominion as we believe to be the portion of Mary. And for this reason, viz, that had Mary chosen to magnify herself, she could with the greatest facility have passed herself off as a goddess, for Dionysius himself almost fell into the error of worshipping her. But those who speak so foolishly prove they know nothing respecting the structure of so rare a piece of workmanship; for the great Artificer Himself, who gave to the Virgin a dignity so sublime, so surpassingly great, made her also to be firmly rooted and established in humility, so that whatever lofty and unwonted honours might be paid her, she could never leave the position in which she had been placed. And what day could possibly present an occasion more calculated to inspire her with pride than that on which she saw herself unanimously chosen to be the Daughter of the Eternal Father, the Mother of the Only Begotten Son, the beloved Spouse of the Holy Ghost? On that day the whole universe was made subject to her; on that day the Angels paid homage to her as one who was to be the means of filling the vacant places in their ranks; on that day the demons trembled before her as one who was to snatch many victims from their abyss. And yet on that very day she ventures to appropriate to herself no other title than that of a servant. *Ecce Ancilla Domini.* With what lowliness she conducts herself, with what prudence, with what modesty, just as if not one of these rare gifts had been hers. "Behold what humility!" exclaims Saint Ambrose in astonishment; "she terms herself a handmaiden, who is chosen to be the Mother; nor is she suddenly elated by the promise." What shall we say then? Was not God, in creating the Holy Virgin, justified in departing from the rules He was accustomed to follow, since at the same time He constituted her exempt from instability and changefulness? But it appears to me that I should be doing what is very pleasing to her and profitable to ourselves, if, conformably to the spirit of her whose festival we celebrate this morning, I set before you, not the eminent glory she received, but the profound humility by which she merited that glory; taking as the theme of my discourse these most admirable words, that as among all the pure creatures of God none was more exalted in His sight than Mary, so none was lower than Mary in her own eyes.

And now, my hearers, I am not about to affirm that Mary had not the most acute perception of all the gifts both of nature and grace with which she had been endowed above other created beings. No, my brethren; true humility does not rest upon blind ignorance, that will not permit us to recognise clearly our own gifts; it is not deficiency of understanding, but modesty of will. Wherefore, since the intellectual powers of the Blessed Virgin were of the highest order, one can readily believe that no finite intelligence has ever appreciated more fully than she did the beauty of her soul, the plenitude of her graces, the magnitude of her glory, the excellence of her dignity. She knew well under what innumerable forms and figures the Prophets of old spoke of her in their profoundest utterances. She possessed indeed the knowledge of the law, and had made herself acquainted, says Origen, by daily meditation, with the predictions of the Prophets. Whence we see that she understood herself to be prefigured in that flowering rod of Jesse, foretold by Isaias; in that precious Ark of the Testament, adored by the Hebrews; in that fleece heavy with dew, which Gedeon found; in that lofty and celestial ladder shown to Jacob; in that enclosed garden of delights of which the Canticle sings; in that lofty Cedar of Libanus, whose praise is found in Ecclesiasticus; finally, in that Eastern Gate of the Temple described by Ezekiel. Nor were these all; for everything that the holy Doctors of the Church have since written of the glories of Mary was most clearly manifest to her, far more clearly than to them. Thus she knew full well, long before Saint Thomas taught it in the schools, that by reason of her divine Maternity she shone with a splendour infinitely superior to that of any other creature; nor from the voice of Saint Bonaventure did she first learn that God could indeed have fashioned a brighter sun, a more glorious firmament, an ocean more abundant in treasures, a world more vast; but, in respect to the Mother of God, Omnipotence Itself could do no more when Mary had been created. She was conscious of being herself that miracle—"the rarest of all miracles," as she has been termed by Saint John Chrysostom; that miracle—"the newest of all miracles," as Saint John Damascene calls her: nor did the writings penned by her beloved Suarez first enable her to apprehend the marvellous accumulation of new and ever new degrees of grace, which increased in her every moment, nay, every instant, multiplying with a rapidity inconceivable by us, until their united amount is sufficient to submerge, as it were in a sea of wonder, every human intelligence. These and all her other glories she beheld in herself with perfect clearness, with absolute fulness of vision. Wherefore, if Saint Paul could say of himself: "Now we have received, not the spirit of this world, but the Spirit which is of God; that we may know the things that are given us from God" (1 Cor. ii. 12), shall we not believe that Mary could say the same of herself? Nevertheless, so profound was her humility that the Abbot Guerricus could with justice affirm respecting her that, "as no created being equalled the Blessed Virgin in the greatness of her merit, in like manner, none was ever found to equal her in the greatness of her humility."

And, in very truth, what else could have been the reason why she led a life so obscure, so simple, during the time of her sojourn upon earth? You know well that all those supernatural graces by one or more of which we find the other saints severally distinguished, all meet in her, and are collectively possessed by her in a higher degree than they are severally by any other. "For the plenitude of grace, given to others in part, was infused in its entirety into Mary," as says Saint Jerome. And not only was she adorned with the aforesaid graces, called *gratum faciens*, but also by those which are designated *gratis datæ*, namely, the gift of prophecy, the discernment of spirits, authority over devils, power over diseases, dominion over death. Yet tell me, where do you read that Mary ever, during her whole life, exercised any such powers? Unless, indeed, that most sublime canticle may be looked upon as in some measure prophetical—I mean the Magnificat; the first canticle sung under the New Testament dispensation to celebrate the astounding wonder God had wrought in clothing Himself with mortal flesh; the canticle, as some opine, referred to by the Psalmist when he speaks of the new canticle which, his own lips being unable to sing it, he greatly desired to hear. "Sing ye to the Lord a new canticle, because He hath done wonderful things" (Ps. xcvii. 1). Moreover, when have you heard that she ever removed a mountain, as did Thaumaturgus? that she raised the dead or healed the sick? that she calmed the tempest, called rain from heaven, or worked any of those miracles, which, though in reality they added naught to the eminence of the Saints, at least made their sanctity more venerated? I certainly have not read that she did any such things; but I am not ignorant that she possessed the power to do far more than any other Saint, according to the dictum of the great Saint Bernard. For was not hers a faith far stronger than that of James, of John, or of those other disciples of our Lord, who returned to Him with joy, telling him how they had trodden upon scorpions, trampled under foot serpents, and seen all the power of the enemy tremble before them. "Lord, the devils also are subject to us" (Luke x. 17). Yes, verily: therefore does not the fact that Mary worked no such miracles give proof of a consummate discretion on her part, which, conforming itself to circumstances, led her to ask all miraculous favours from her Son, as we know her to have done at the marriage feast in Cana, rather than to work them herself?

Are you surprised at this? I have somewhat yet more wonderful to repeat to you; it is a remark of the Abbot Rupert, who gives it as his opinion that the Blessed Virgin, at least during the thirty-three years of Christ's life on earth, never revealed a single one of the rare prerogatives with which she was endowed to any person, however intimate or beloved. Never did she speak of the perfect use of reason which had been hers even before she left her mother's womb; nor of the total suppression of concupiscence within her breast, of the complete subjugation of her passions; she did not speak of the sanctifying grace conceded to her from the very first instant of her Immaculate Conception; nor of the encomiums addressed to her by the Archangel Gabriel at the Annunciation, of the Incarnation of the Eternal Word effected within her; nor finally of that marvellous union by virtue of which she joined the fruitfulness of a Mother to the chastity of a Virgin. And does not so modest a silence strike you as worthy of all admiration? See to what danger she was exposed when her espoused husband, Joseph, unacquainted with all these profound mysteries, was on the point of abandoning her. "He was minded to put her away privately" (Matt. i. 19). She need merely have taken him aside and said to him: My husband, I am well aware of the suspicious thoughts which agitate your mind: you cannot hide them from me, despite your smiling countenance and gentle manner. Yet be assured that my present condition is the work of that God Who, as He renders the shells of the sea fertile by means of celestial dew, can also by the operation of His Holy Spirit, cause a Virgin to be at the same time a Mother. Listen, and I will relate how, one day, when I was alone in my chamber, the Archangel Gabriel appeared before me, and revealed to me such and such hidden things of God. And then she might have gone on to tell the objections she had made, and the rejoinders of the angel; and by quoting the authority of the prophets and the testimony of Scripture, she might so fully have convinced Joseph of the truth of her words as to dispel every shade of jealousy from his mind. Nevertheless, she would not upon any consideration avail herself of these legitimate means of clearing her character; putting her cause into the hands of God, she was ready, had not a celestial messenger been promptly sent to prove her innocence, to submit to the accusation of adultery rather than declare herself to be the Mother of the Divine Word. O noble conduct, worthy of the highest admiration! I am well aware that instances are not uncommon in which people have displayed reticence or timidity in divulging their own merits, even when conversing with friends in whom on other points they reposed the utmost confidence. But, on the other hand, when an unjust aspersion on their good name gave them the indisputable right to speak in their own justification, these very persons have not scrupled to proclaim their virtue, not indeed to make themselves esteemed, but to repulse calumny and blunt its point.

Who does not know that the Prophet Samuel was a most humble man? Nevertheless, to stop the mouth of murmurers he had no hesitation in boldly protesting how upright he had always been in his judicial capacity; how far from either interfering with the course of justice through interested motives, or abusing his power to oppress the innocent. For the same reason the patient Job passed in review, in the hearing of his friends, a long list of praiseworthy actions; did he not tell them how he had been an eye to the blind and a foot to the lame, a guide to the wanderer, a father to the fatherless, a protector of widows? Did he not commend the continency which had led him to abstain from casting an amorous glance at the beauty of any woman? "I made a covenant with mine eyes, that I would not so much as think upon a virgin" (Job xxxi. 1). Did he not recall to mind his readiness in listening to requests, his liberality in relieving mendicants, his hospitality in receiving strangers; with these and similar boasts wearying the ears of his listeners? In like manner the Apostle Paul, in his Second Epistle to the Corinthians, enumerates his apostolic labours and the divine revelations vouchsafed to him. Ignatius the Martyr also does the same in his Sixth Epistle to the Philadelphians, whom he reminds of the purity of his life and the justice of his rule. And to take an example more analogous to our present subject, how anxious was the beautiful Judith on her return from the pavilion of Holofernes, whom she had decapitated, to dispel every sinister suspicion which might have attached to her. For this purpose she did not deem it in any way inconsistent with modesty and humility to proclaim that an angel had come in person to protect her amidst the lascivious glances and licentious soldiery amongst whom she had so courageously adventured herself. "As the same Lord liveth," such were her words, "His angel hath been my keeper both going hence, and abiding there, and returning from thence hither: and the Lord hath not suffered me His handmaid to be defiled; but hath brought me back to you without pollution of sin, rejoicing for His victory, for my escape, and for your deliverance" (Jud. xiii. 20). Wherefore it appears that we have every right to publish either our own virtues or the divine favours we have received, provided this is the only means left to us whereby we can support a tottering reputation. What then can be said of the unfathomable depth of Mary's humility, since, under circumstances of such urgent necessity, she refused in her own justification to utter a single word of self-praise? Shall we not feel ourselves constrained to repeat: "None was ever found like to her in the greatness of her humility!"

If even from her beloved spouse Mary concealed the rare privileges bestowed on her, you may imagine that she was far from divulging them to any persons less closely connected with her. Yet how great honour would have been hers had she announced to her friends, announced at least to some chosen few, the divine nature of her offspring! My womb has given birth to one who is both God and man. Nor do I think that her statement would have been doubted, especially at the time when her Son wrought wonders so numerous, so glorious, so awful, that the people wished to take Him by force and make Him a king. Nevertheless, so far was she at all times from any such ostentation that when the fame of His miracles had raised the renown of our Lord to its highest point, she never mingled with the multitude in the hope of being recognised as His Mother, and pointed out as such. And when on one occasion she desired to speak with Him, she waited apart, on the threshold or in the street, like any ordinary woman, refusing to exercise the right her maternal relation to Him gave her, of penetrating into the room where He was preaching. "She stood without, desiring to speak with her Son; nor, in virtue of her maternal authority, did she either interrupt His discourse or enter the house where He was speaking," exclaims St. Bernard in astonishment.

But need we wonder at this, since we know that no sounds were more unwelcome or more discordant in her ear, than words spoken in her praise. Never, except at the time when she heard the salutation of the angelic messenger, is it recorded that any stormy gust or breath of tempest disturbed the calm surface of that soul, incomparably greater than all the fabled deities of Olympus. I know some have before now asserted that her chastity took alarm at the unexpected apparition of so young and so beautiful a man; nor is it a new thing to see in this circumstance an example from which virgins should learn that it becomes them to be on their guard in the presence of any man, even though he seem as an angel.

But Eusebius Emissenus, with greater penetration, bids us observe that the exact words of the sacred text are not, "she was troubled at his *sight*," but "she was troubled at his *saying*." This was not the first time that an angel had appeared to Mary; the sight of these celestial visitors was probably familiar to her, and she must have known them individually. It was, therefore, those magnificent and royal titles so unexpectedly applied to her that from the first caused her uneasiness. For, as Origen points out, nowhere else in the pages of Holy Writ do we find an instance of any one having been distinguished by so great an honour as that of being styled full of grace. *Gratia plena.* Hence it follows that the Blessed Virgin, well versed as she was in the Sacred Scriptures, could not fail to feel her humility wounded on hearing herself saluted with a title before unknown to the world—one which had not been given to a Sara, a Rebecca, a Rachel, an Anna, a Judith. For had Mary known that to any one else similar words had been spoken, they would not have alarmed her as an unknown salutation.

It was, therefore, the sound of her own praise which at first agitated her, and constrained her even to ask herself what manner of spirit that could be which had addressed her thus. She thought within herself what manner of salutation this should be (Luke i. 29). It is at all events certain that when, with prophetic light, her cousin or kinswoman Elizabeth recognised in her the Mother of her Lord, "Whence is this to me, that the Mother of my Lord should come to me?" (Luke i. 43). and assigned to her as such, a position above all illustrious women, "Blessed art thou among women," she was so far from feeling gratified that she cut short the words in the mouth of the speaker. She interrupted the speech and turned it aside. And Mary said, "My soul doth magnify the Lord." Thus she refused to appropriate to herself the honours paid her, but ascribed all the glory to God; and mentally retreating into the abyss of her primeval nothingness, said, in deep self-abasement, that God had mercifully looked upon her lowliness. "He hath regarded the humility of His handmaid." A famous Spanish theologian, lately deceased (P. Antonio Perez, equally eminent for his acute intelligence and vast erudition), lost in admiration of such humility, draws from the circumstance a conclusion, unexpected indeed, but in my opinion both legitimate and conclusive, in proof of the Immaculate Conception of the Blessed Virgin. I ask your kind attention while I explain how this pious inference may be deduced from such premises; it will not, if I judge aright, be any digression from the theme we are pursuing, but rather help us in our course to the desired end.

It is evident that the Blessed Virgin sought to bring together in that canticle of the Magnificat, wherein her humility found expression, all possible arguments which could serve to represent her most clearly in the light of a woman unworthy of the rare favours with which God had graciously vouchsafed to distinguish her. On this account she said that He had not despised her low condition, her poverty, her insignificance, her nothingness; for what else but this do the words quoted above signify—"He hath regarded the humility of His handmaid"—according to the meaning attached to them by nearly all of the commentators? Can it be doubted then that, had the Blessed Virgin deserved, even for one single brief moment, the name of sinner, she would have let pass so suitable an opportunity of declaring herself to be one, in order to make the divine bounty stand out more brightly in contrast to her own demerits? And is it not plain that it would have been a cause of far greater abasement to her had she been able to say, "He hath regarded the iniquity of His enemy," rather than, "He hath regarded the humility of His handmaiden?" Certainly if she had spoken thus she would have adduced a much stronger proof of her unworthiness; therefore that she did not do so shows that she could not have done so without falsehood. And, indeed, I cannot imagine that Mary would have omitted making so noble, so meritorious an act of humility as that of publishing her own sin, had truth permitted such an act. We see Saints far inferior in virtue practising this humility in a very high degree. With what ingenious eloquence does Saint Jerome confess in his letters the follies of his youth! With no less frankness does Saint Anselm accuse himself in his lamentations; and, what is still more apposite, did not Saint Augustine compose a whole book, in order to immortalise, for all future ages, the memory of his misdeeds? And, on looking more closely, you will perceive that not one of all his voluminous writings has been composed with more elegance of style, charm of expression, or brilliancy of ideas, that it might offer greater attractions to the reader, and lead him to study it intimately. Saint Matthew tells us in his Gospel that his original calling was that of a publican. And Saint Paul has recorded in his Epistles that in past times he had persecuted the Church. Saint Peter caused Saint Mark, whom he employed as his amanuensis, to relate the sad story of his three-fold denial with more minute details and in more forcible language than did either of the other Evangelists. Moses also, in the book of Numbers, records his sins of unbelief. Solomon, in Ecclesiastes, bears witness to his former dissolute life; and so many holy men have done the same that it has come to be considered one and the same thing to be a just man and one's own accuser. The just is first accuser of himself (Prov. xviii. 17). Now is it possible to conceive that if the Blessed Virgin had ever been defiled by any single fault, she would studiously have concealed it, and that on an occasion when an avowal of it would have been extremely well-timed? To allege this would be equivalent to asserting that Mary was surpassed in candour and in humility by the Saints who acted as we have described. And who would be found bold enough to venture on such a statement, since we know it to be indisputable that no one was ever found equal to this Virgin in the grace of humility?

I know that if you who are theologians were now to break silence, you would answer me that actual sin and original sin are two very different things; that the former affords matter for confession, but not the latter. And since the Saints, whilst they accuse themselves of transgressions of thought, of word, and of deed, which were actual sins, nowhere bring forward original sin as a cause of humiliation, we need not wonder that it is not mentioned by the Blessed Virgin. But do you not see that this is no real answer to the point in question? It is undeniably true that original sin does not supply matter for sacramental confession, as Saint Thomas teaches in the third part of his Summa; but this is no reason why it should not supply matter for confession, for self-abasement, for humiliation. It is at any rate certain that of itself it would have sufficed for the end the Blessed Virgin had in view, because by the simple fact that she had once been the enemy of God, she might have abundantly proved how unsuitable, how unworthy, she was to be selected as His chosen Mother. Therefore, if the Saints, in seeking a subject for humiliation, passed over their original sin in silence, they only did so because the mention of it would seem superfluous in those who were guilty of so many actual offences against God. But what will you say when I prove to you that it was not passed over by them in silence? Listen to David: "Behold I was conceived in iniquity, and in sin did my mother conceive me." What is your opinion of that? Is David proclaiming his actual transgressions, or his original guilt? What does he mean? To which does he refer? Of which is he speaking? Does he not state the fact that he, like the rest of mankind, was conceived in sin, merely for the purpose of increasing his confusion? Forgive me, therefore, O Mary, my Lady, my Queen, if I call upon you this morning to justify your conduct; if I ask you, did you not often read this confession of the royal Prophet? Did you not approve of the example he sets? did you not commend it to others, as Holy Church has since not hesitated to do? Why then did you blush to imitate it, when so suitable an occasion presented itself? Something was wanting to your complete humiliation when you called yourself a servant of God, a most lowly one; you omitted to state that you once deserved to be called a sinner. "Humble thy spirit very much," says the wise man (Eccl. vii. 19), very much, very much. Therefore, when you thought fit to say you were the handmaid of the Lord, you ought to have added that you had originally been the slave of Satan. It appears to me that the only answer to be made is that it was impossible for you to speak thus without a sacrifice of truth; to entertain any other belief would be to wrong you. Thus, notwithstanding all you alleged in your generous self-abasement before God, you could not go so far as to declare, "Behold, I was conceived in iniquity," but were compelled to content yourself with saying, "He hath regarded the humility of His handmaiden," unable to say, "He hath regarded the iniquity of His enemy."

Such, my hearers, is the ingenious chain of reasoning pursued by the theologian I mentioned above, a master whom I ever reverenced, and whose loss I shall never cease to lament; and it seems to me that his argument is possessed of no small force as well as beauty, if we examine the foundation on which it rests. And what indeed gives it this force, if not the extraordinary humility of the Blessed Virgin, which we this morning are wondering at? A humility extraordinary indeed, for (to return to the path whence we deviated, in order the better to honour her), we find it almost impossible to comprehend the solicitude with which she not only closed her ears against her own praises, but ever made the most of her imperfection, if indeed that can be termed imperfection which only falls short of the infinite perfection of God.

If we deem it a still greater act of humility to bear with patience the contempt of others, especially of vulgar and low persons, how much must not the Blessed Virgin have had to suffer in this respect. When the Jews in their malice wished to lessen the opinion in which Christ was held by the multitude, and bring Him into discredit and derision, they used to say: "Who is this man? is He not the son of Mary?" "Is not this the carpenter, the son of Mary?" (Mark vi.

iii). Words which, as Saint Bonaventure points out, offer a greater insult to Mary than to Christ, for they show that she must indeed have been looked upon as a poor and common woman, since, in order to stamp our Lord as mean and despicable, nothing more was needed than to proclaim Him to be the offspring of such a mother. And although it must often have been her lot to listen to bitter sneers of this sort, yet she was so far from evincing the slightest sign of resentment, that she used to choose the very occasions on which she was likely to hear such taunts, to leave for a time her accustomed seclusion and appear in public. For Mary, who was nowhere seen in Jerusalem when her Son made His triumphal entry there, was beheld by all men when He was led forth thence to be put to death; faithfully following every step of His way until He reached the summit of the shameful Mount of Calvary. I leave you to imagine, if you can, what insults, what reproaches, what disgrace she must have had to bear as the mother of a condemned criminal! For as at an earlier stage the scorn of a blasphemous multitude was excited against Christ by the words: "Is not this the son of Mary?" would not now the sneering taunt be employed against Mary: Is not this the Mother of Jesus? and thus, though it may seem incredible, that which formed her proudest boast was converted into a term of derision.

But when, on His resurrection from the dead and ascension into heaven, the divinity of Christ was made manifest, then perhaps the Blessed Virgin might think fit to relax somewhat of the severity of her profound abasement, seeing she could no longer conceal, at least from the eyes of the faithful, her supreme dignity and surpassing merit. Was such, think you, the case? Pliny, in his celebrated panegyric, relates of Trajan as an act of consummate virtue, that after the divinity of his adopted father Nerva had been proclaimed, according to the foolish custom of the heathen, he never thought of arrogating any glory to himself on that account. "Nothing of arrogance was added to thee on account of the immortality of thy father," he exclaims in astonishment; and goes on to tell us with admiring wonder that he dressed as usual, went about as usual, conversed as usual, and was just as familiar with his friends, bearing himself on all occasions, both in public and in private, as had ever been his wont. But let us borrow these words uttered by the mouth of adulation, and ask, as we can do in all truth and justice respecting the Blessed Virgin : *Num illi ex immortalitate filii aliquid arrogantiæ accessit?* Was she any the less humble when she had seen her Eternal Son ascend into heaven; when she beheld Him adored by so many nations; when she heard Him extolled by so many tongues; when she saw so many ready for His sake, not only to despise riches, contemn honours, and abandon their country, but even to go forward to meet death with a joyful step? On the contrary, as Saint Bernard assures us, she was even more unassuming than ever; her dress was as poor, her manner of life as frugal, and, what is still more admirable, she showed such respect to even the least of our Lord's disciples, that when they were gathered together in the Cenacle awaiting the glorious descent of the Paraclete, Mary occupied the lowest place amongst them all.

And now, my hearers, I ask you, are not these marvellous instances of humility? Let us contrast them with the conduct of Lucifer, that unhappy spirit, who, because conscious of possessing preëminent gifts of virtue and beauty, was so puffed up with pride that he aspired to take his seat on the very throne of God. "I will exalt my throne above the stars of God; I will sit in the mountain of the covenant, in the sides of the north; I will ascend above the height of the clouds" (Isa. xiv. 13). What would he have done had he beheld his soul adorned with the far higher gifts and greater graces which were the portion of Mary? I verily believe he would have considered himself entitled to wrest from God the sceptre of the starry spheres, and not merely share His throne on terms of equality, but rule in heaven as sole and absolute monarch. And yet Mary, a being more exalted far than Lucifer, stooped to place herself beneath the feet, not of Christ alone, but of His apostles, of His disciples and followers; never behaving towards them as their queen, but always as their servant. "Behold, let thy servant be a handmaid;" thus spoke the true and far more humble Abigail—" a handmaid to wash the feet of the servants of my Lord " (1 Reg. xxv. 41).

Who will not therefore see it to be right that Mary should now be raised to so sublime a height of glory that she, who was willing to place herself below the servants, should be chosen by their Master as His own beloved Mother? Open then wide, O ye] heavens, for the time has come; distil from above that dew which shall fertilise her virgin womb, and cause it to bring forth the wondrous Child, the desire of all ages. Drop down dew, ye heavens, from above, and let the clouds rain the just (Isa. xlv. 8). She is fit to be the shell which shall contain the goodly pearl; the mine which shall beget the precious treasure. And if those mountains which conceal within their bowels veins of gold, possess no outward show and external attractions, and bare of every plant or shrub, are content that others should adorn themselves with loftiest trees and clothe their sides with thickest foliage, is it not right that the purest gold, destined to form the priceless treasure of a ransomed race, should derive its being from one so modest, so humble, so free from the faintest shade of ostentation as her whose portrait I have to-day feebly endeavoured to trace? Solomon long since told us that where humility is, there is also wisdom; and if he is right, can it be denied that in the breast of the most lowly Mary, Eternal Wisdom will find His most fitting abode on earth?

SECOND PART.

It may seem a strange thing to you, my hearers, that I should discourse upon humility before people in the world, the object of whose schemes is none other than to make themselves known, to advance their own interest, to promote their own advantage. They are like the crocodile, which alone among all animals never attains maturity, but whose growth only ceases with its life. Unenviable truly is the condition of such persons, who thus lack that very gift which of all others is most dear and beloved to the heart of Mary. For it was on account of her rare humility, according to the unanimous opinion of the Fathers, that she deserved to be chosen from amongst all other women for the signal honour of being the Mother of God. "Doubtless the humility of Mary drew the King of Heaven down to earth," as Richard of Saint Laurence, among many others, expressly states. Therefore whenever she perceives in any soul the presence of this virtue which was productive of so much glory to herself, she feels impatient, so to speak, to pour out upon that soul an abundant and overflowing measure of grace. "Thou sendest forth springs in the vales" (Ps. ciii. 10). And now, in reference to this, let me make one more observation, namely, that although as a general rule, even in the case of pious persons, Mary waits to be invoked before coming to their aid, on behalf of the humble she makes an exception to this rule. She shows herself, so to speak, anxious to anticipate their requests; she does not require them to seek her out, but goes to meet them, offering them her gracious protection and making them the recipients of gifts equally abundant and unexpected. I could take illustrations of this among others from the lives of Saint Bonito, the Bishop; of Saint Hermann, a priest, who, by virtue of their humility, were found worthy to receive from the Blessed Virgin honours such as it never entered into their minds to conceive. But I prefer to select an instance from the history of a man who lived in the world; listen, therefore, while I relate to you an adventure which befell a captain named Leo, a native of Thrace.

One day when he was passing through a wood, I know not whether in the course of a journey or whilst following the chase, or when merely walking out for his own pleasure, he heard, apparently at some distance, a plaintive voice as of a man entreating help. On standing still in order the better to ascertain whence the sound came, he discovered that it proceeded from the very thickest part of the wood; nevertheless, with

4

the courage that characterised him, he dauntlessly plunged into the thicket, and finally found a poor blind man, who had lost the right path, and whose efforts to extricate himself from the bushes only resulted in his further entanglement. As soon as he came in sight of him, Leo bade him take heart and be comforted, and not content with merely conducting the wanderer back to the safe road, he did not disdain to offer his arm to lean on for a considerable distance, manifesting great charity as well as humility; for with his disengaged hand he put aside the branches which encumbered the path, and even removed from the ground the brambles, underwood, and stones which might have hurt the feet of his blind companion. Thus after great labour he at length brought him out into the highway, and deposited him on a seat by the roadside. He was about to leave him when the poor man, not satisfied with the services already rendered to him, began in piteous accents to beg for a draught of water to refresh his parched lips and cool his fevered frame. What was Leo to do? The country was barren, the soil sandy, it was long since rain had fallen. Yet, to appease the thirsty wanderer, he returned once more to search diligently in the wood if he could not perchance discover the trace of at least some stagnant pool, if of no crystal spring. But all was in vain. At last when he had for some time, with indefatigable patience, been wearying himself in the hope of finding some water for the poor man, he suddenly heard a voice from on high calling him by name: "Leo, Leo!" He looked up in astonishment, but saw nothing. However, on the call being repeated, he stopped again to listen, and heard distinctly these words: "Proceed a little farther, and thou wilt find both water and clay; with the former thou canst relieve the blind man's thirst, with the latter thou shalt restore him to sight. Know, furthermore, with regard to thyself, that in recompense of what thou hast done the imperial Sceptre shall be thine; and I enjoin on thee that, when seated on the throne, mindful of the favour shown thee by Mary, thou erect a solemn temple in My honour on the spot whence thou dost take the water and the clay." I leave you to imagine the effect produced on Leo by these unwonted communications; and I know not whether the feeling predominant in his mind was amazement at so novel a miracle, astonishment at so splendid a promise, or emotion at the munificence of Mary. Penetrating farther into the bushes, he soon came upon a marshy pool from which he filled his helmet with water, taking some of the mud away in his hand. With these he returned to the blind man, to whose lips he held the water that he might quench his thirst; then he spread the clay upon his eyes, thus restoring his sight. Afterwards he returned home, singing the praises of Mary; and long time did not elapse before, on the Emperor Mercianus dying without a lawful heir, he was invested with the imperial purple by common consent of the Senate, the people, and the soldiery. The hero of my tale was Leo the Great, the first of that name, who, by his salutary laws and pious example, did much to further the cause of the Catholic religion. Amid the splendours of royalty he persevered in the humility of his private life, nor did he deem it derogatory to his princely grandeur frequently to ascend the column of Daniel the Stylite, and kneeling before him, embrace with profound respect those saintly feet on which worms had already begun to feed. You will doubtless have been beforehand with me and discovered for yourselves the truth which the anecdote I have just related was intended to teach you. Leo had not once invoked the Great Mother of God, he had not asked her assistance, he was not even thinking of her; yet she could not refrain from hastening to the spot where might be seen so pleasing a sight as that of a noble knight stooping to render service to a ragged beggar. And although she might have sent down from heaven some Saint or Angel in her place to give the needed aid, yet she preferred to be the personal spectator of so fair a deed, one which afforded her so much delight and satisfaction, and of which she did not deem the Empire of a world to be an unfitting recompense.

How unhappy then, my hearers, is the condition of those worldlings who imagine the practice of that virtue which is so pleasing to Mary to be at variance with the duties of their rank and office! But why should it be at variance with them? Would they banish humility to dwell in the hovels of the poor, or hide her head in the cloister, as if ashamed to be seen in the halls of the wealthy? It might perhaps have been so in earlier times before the Blessed Virgin taught us by her example the way to practise this virtue. But now, after all we have seen, how shall the subjects of so humble a Queen dare to be so proud? *Quomodo opponet ultra magnificare se homo super terram?* Shall those servants strive after notoriety whose mistress led so hidden a life; shall they aspire to rule whose mistress loved to obey? Let it not be said of you, my hearers, that your actions do not come up to your profession. Why are you so punctilious, why so proud? why such lovers of ostentation, such seekers after pomp and show? Why should you blush to be seen listening with kindly attention to the plaints of the poor? Why do you even in the performance of your charitable actions crave for the vain plaudits of the crowd, and sigh for the trumpet-blast of a short-lived fame? Can you not free yourself from these trammels in order to follow in the footsteps of our great Queen? O, happy we, if we do but succeed in learning from her such salutary lessons! But in any case let none hope to share her glory who have not first imitated her humility. Humility goeth before glory. (Prov. xv. 33.)

PANEGYRIC IN HONOUR OF SAINT JOSEPH

AS SPOUSE OF THE BLESSED VIRGIN.

"Joseph her husband being a just man."—MATT. i. 19.
"Happy is the husband of a good wife."—ECCL. xxvi. 1.

THERE is no one whose services the great ones of the earth would be willing to purchase at a higher price than they would those of an able panegyrist, did it lie in their power to meet with such a person, and engage his talents in their own behalf. The celebrated Macedonian thought himself unhappy, even when he had attained the climax of power and prosperity, because he had no Homer to praise him. Nor was he ashamed to weep over the tomb of Achilles, his tears being prompted by no appreciation of the worth of the departed, but by envy of his good fortune in having had such an eulogist. Nor was Alexander singular in this respect; the Spartans, who, before they went out to battle, would not condescend to commend themselves to Mars, the God of War, yet did not think it beneath them to sacrifice to the peaceful Muses, showing by this that the more confident they felt in their own powers of conquest, the more eager were they to secure the meed of praise which their heroic deeds would deserve. Thus Marius Rusticanus flattered Plotius; thus Pompey the Great employed Theophanus; thus Decius Brutus lavished favours on Accius, in the hope of being immortalised in their writings. And I remember having read something stranger still, related by Philostratus of a certain Varus, a wealthy youth, who used to lend money to his poorer fellow-students, on the condition that when his turn came to declaim publicly in the Academy, they should, as if unable to restrain their admiration, burst out into open applause, and rising from their seats with astonished looks, cry out, "Well done!" these acclamations were to stand in lieu of pecuniary interest on the loans. Thus we see how high is the value men are accustomed to set upon praise, even when they know it to be not spontaneous, but obtained through their own solicitations.

And if all this be true of human praise, what would not one give to have God Himself for one's Panegyrist? He alone cannot be led to exaggerate through affection, to err through ignorance, or to garble the truth through unworthy motives. But how few have enjoyed so happy a lot!

It cannot be denied that one of the foremost amongst that favoured few is Joseph, whose praises you have this morning come together to hear, with more eagerness and joy than if I had invited you to listen to your own. Not from my lips, however, but from those of the Eternal Truth Himself, will Joseph receive a high eulogium, comprised in one brief word. For as we speak of the faithful Abraham, the God-fearing David, the wise Daniel, the meek Moses, so Joseph will ever be remembered as the just: "Joseph being a just man" (Matt. i. 19). But what does this name of Just signify? What does it tell us? What are we to understand by it? Let him speak who, as an exponent of Scripture, has merited the title of the Great Doctor. Let, I say, Saint Jerome speak; for his words are worthy of being listened to with the fullest confidence: " Notice that Joseph is called a just man." And why? Listen to the answer. "Because of the perfect possession of every virtue." Not because he excelled in one particular virtue, nor in several virtues, no, nor even in many, but in all. And enough is not yet said; for he not only possessed all virtues, but possessed them in the very highest degree. Because of the perfect possession of every virtue. And what more can be said of any man than that he possessed every virtue in the highest degree? Is not this a sublime eulogium? Is not this the greatest praise?

And now let us go on to consider more at length the height of perfection to which Saint Joseph was raised, or to which he may have raised himself; not indeed as if we doubted what is certain, namely, that he merited the name of Just, but rather to see if this name warrants us in regarding him as that great Saint, that exalted, that super-excellent personage which he must of necessity be, if the explanation given above be a correct one. But since we know little about his life, and still less about his death, what is to be done? We must draw our conclusions from those scanty records which are within reach of all. All are aware that he was the spouse of the Blessed Virgin—" her husband," as such every one knows him, every one reveres him. With what perfection, then, may we not credit him, since such was the position he filled—a position which proclaims him to be that most fortunate spouse, whose lot of all others the Wise Man declared to be enviable when he wrote: "Happy is the husband of a good wife."

Joseph was then the husband of Mary, of a good wife, or, to speak more correctly, of the best of wives. But here we have need of caution, for he was not a consort given to her by chance, or blindly drawn by lot, as was the foolish custom of the Lacedemonians, but specially designed for her by Providence, and given to her in accordance with the rules of reason. Hence we may gather that Joseph, beyond all other men, resembled the Blessed Virgin in his character, his habits, and his disposition, as well as in his lineage, which was royal; for, as is known to all, the first requisite for a suitable marriage is similarity and agreement of tastes between husband and wife. From this I infer that those learned Doctors were not, perhaps, mistaken who affirm that Saint Joseph was sanctified from his mother's womb; for, although, this cannot be affirmed with absolute certainty, yet it may reasonably be looked for in him who was the destined consort of the Blessed Virgin, and who, by this very destiny, was proclaimed to be the man of all others most similar to, and suitable for her. Otherwise it is apparent that a greater resemblance to the Blessed Virgin might be claimed for Jeremias and for John the Baptist, both of whom were sanctified before their birth. And can it be thought that to these so great a privilege would be conceded on the ground of their being heralds of the Saviour, the one afar off, the other His immediate forerunner, whilst it was denied to one who was to be neither His herald nor His precursor, but His guardian, His nurse, His protector, His very father, by adoption if not by nature? Saint

Thomas has beautifully said, that the more nearly anything approximates to its source, the more perfectly it partakes of the special properties of that source. Thus the light which is nearest to the sun is the most dazzling, the heat which is nearest to the fire is the most ardent, and he of you who may chance to draw water will find that the clearest, the purest, the most crystal water is that which comes from the fountain-head itself. The purest water is to be sought from the spring; and if this be true, how could it possibly be imagined that Joseph, who by blood-relationship and by duty was so near to the source of all sanctity, should have participated in it less fully and less perfectly than those who were further removed from it. Who, except the Blessed Virgin, enjoyed more familiar intercourse with Christ? Who more often held Him in his arms? Who pressed Him more closely to his bosom? Who more frequently carried Him upon his shoulders? Who so often embraced and caressed Him? Who, finally, so repeatedly disposed of Him at his pleasure? What man could say to Him with greater truth: "You are mine." I said with "greater truth," for, although Joseph neither by co-operation nor by participation took part in the generation of the Divine Word, yet it seems to follow that since he was verily and indeed the husband of her who conceived that Word, he could with perfect truth call Him his own. Listen, all you who are acquainted with the law. Who is there amongst you so little versed in civil institutions as not to know that in order to call any produce one's own, it is not necessary to have sown, or planted, or grafted it, or in any way contributed to its growth? nothing more is needed than that it should have sprung up on one's own land, or, as the text has it, "on one's own soil." Whatever the manner of its production, whether it be generated by the natural fertility of the soil, or whether it be produced by a manifest miracle of Heaven, one may with equal justice claim this fruit as one's own. Is it not so? This being granted, I once more repeat that Joseph took no part in producing that fruit which was conceived by an undoubted miracle in the virgin soil of Mary's womb. But tell me, was he not the proprietor of that soil? Most assuredly, for in this, as the Apostle says, lies the essence of the matrimonial union. "The wife hath not power of her own body, but the husband; and in like manner the husband also hath not power of his own body, but the wife" (1 Cor. vii. 4), although by mutual consent they may refrain from the exercise of that power. Therefore, since he was incontestably the rightful owner of the soil which gave birth to so rare a fruit, it follows of necessity that the fruit also belonged to him. Wherefore if Joseph enjoyed such close proximity to the Source of all sanctity, if he was able to recognise it as belonging to him, and as such could call it his own, can it be supposed that he would participate in it less copiously than others who had no such rights? Where could the man be found who, whilst owning a mine, should yet lack gold? or, having a spring on his land, should want water? or, being master of a warehouse, should yet be short of the merchandise it contains? If you will find me such an one, I will acknowledge it possible for Joseph to hold in his hands the Giver of all sanctity, and yet fail to be eminent in holiness.

From the principle we have established, it appears

highly probable that not only was Joseph sanctified in his mother's womb, which is all we have hitherto attempted to prove, but that he was afterwards confirmed in grace, and was so free from all sin that we may boldly state that no greater saint ever existed upon earth. No greater saint? Perhaps some timid, cautious, or scrupulous persons may be shocked at this, and think it temerity to make such bold comparisons, which outdo those of the astronomers, who endeavour to ascertain the relative magnitude of the stars. And yet what would you have me do? Retract my words? I will retract my words, for I was wrong in saying that there was not ever a saint who excelled Saint Joseph; I ought to have said, Saint Joseph was superior even to the greatest saints that ever existed, excepting always his holy Spouse. If you condemn my boldness, you at the same time condemn the boldness of Gerson, the famous Chancellor of Paris; of Bernardine of Busto; of John of Carthage; of Isidore, surnamed Isolanus; and finally of Suarez, a man whose opinion is equivalent to the unanimous voice of an university. And does Suarez employ ambiguous or obscure words? Hear them and judge for yourselves. " I do not consider it overbold or improbable, but rather a pious and probable belief, to hold Saint Joseph to have surpassed all in sanctity and grace; for Scripture contains nothing contrary to this." You cannot suppose that so great a man would allow himself to write these words heedlessly, or when carried away by feeling, and without a due consideration of those other words—which have undoubtedly already occurred to your mind as apparently contradicting those uttered by him: " There hath not arisen a greater than John the Baptist." No, my brethren, nothing escaped his comprehensive glance: with regard to that which bears so closely on the subject before us, amongst other wise answers he gives it as his opinion that, " in interpreting sweeping statements such as this, 'There hath not arisen a greater,' we must remember that there exists exceptions to the rule; that those are not included in the general law whose lofty position raises them above it, unless the contrary be definitely expressed." And who will deny that Saint Joseph may be numbered amongst these latter, as being the faithful Servant whom his Lord has appointed over His family? Over what family? Over the first, the chief family, that appertained immediately to the service of the sacred Hypostatic Union. " He constituted him," as Saint Bernard writes, "the solace of His Mother, He constituted him the guardian of the Sacred Humanity; finally, He constituted him alone of all the world the faithful coadjutor in His lofty counsels." Relying then on the countenance and support of these great writers, I again repeat that probably no one ever surpassed Joseph in sanctity, but, on the contrary, that his sanctity surpassed that of every other man; and this not only for the reasons given above but also for others, more brilliant and more convincing still, which I shall now proceed to unfold if you will lend me your kind attention.

It is indisputably true that a wife ought to love no one more tenderly than her husband. To him should belong the first place in her thoughts, and in her prayers; and if she is a really good wife, she will not desire her own welfare and interests more than she does those of her husband. This being granted, is there one among you who could imagine for a single moment that Mary could fail to perform her duty perfectly in this respect? Does not the conduct of Joseph show the immense esteem he felt for her? Did he not toil for her, did he not labour, did he not undergo a thousand hardships for her sake? Truly nothing was wanting in their reciprocal discharge of conjugal obligations, except that by mutual consent they preserved their virginity intact, living together in chastity, as bees do in their hive. This would serve to increase rather than to diminish the love of the Holy Virgin for her Spouse; because it proved to her the pure and celestial nature of the affection he bore her, he being content to stand towards her in the relation of the elm when it is wedded to the vine, since he espoused her for no selfish ends or lower pleasures, but only in order to acquire the right to bear her burdens. Thus it remains my firm conviction that towards no other man did Mary cherish a love so tender, so devoted, so heartfelt, as she did towards Joseph; how constantly, then, must she have prayed for him, how many graces must she have obtained for him, how much glory must she have won for him! This is the good which above all else we ought to seek for those we love. Artemisia showed the love she felt for her husband Mausolus, by erecting to his memory a tomb which was one of the wonders of the world. Sulpicia showed her love for Lenturlus by submitting for his sake to the hardships of exile. Chilonides showed her love for Theopompus by enduring for love of him the hardships of imprisonment. Portia showed her love for Brutus by swallowing live coals for his sake. And Ipsicratia, to show how dearly she loved Mithridates, was willing to deny, so to speak, her very sex; for with masculine courage she clipped her flowing locks, she accustomed herself to manage horses and learnt to wield the spear, and followed him bravely to the battle-field (in this way proving herself to be the reverse of that woman spoken of in Ecclesiasticus, who "with feeble hands and disjointed knees doth not make her husband happy"). If therefore these women, whose affection for their husbands fell far short of that entertained by the Blessed Virgin for hers, were yet willing to do and suffer so much for them; is it probable that she, animated by stronger feeling and purer love, would neglect the performance of an evident duty, and omit to intercede for Joseph, and thus earn for him an abundant measure of grace? Truly the feeble and faint-hearted wife who fails in her duty in this respect is sufficiently blamed in Ecclesiasticus: "a woman who doth not make her husband happy" (Eccles. xxv. 32).

There was, however, no necessity for the Blessed Virgin to make great exertions to attain this end. The power of holiness in a wife is capable of exercising a mysterious influence over the husband; even should he be an evil-doer, it is possible that through her he may be changed into a martyr; for, as Saint Paul says, the unbelieving husband is sanctified by the believing wife (1 Cor. vii. 14). And since it may not be superfluous to bring forward in this place some sublime examples of the truth of my assertion, let me point to the conduct of Theolinda in regard to Agilulf, king of the Lombards; of Ingonda, with regard to Hermengild, king of the Goths; of Clothilde, in regard to Clovis, king of the Franks; or to turn to some of less exalted birth, let me remind you of Cecilia, who incited her husband Valerianus to suffer martyrdom; of Bridget, whose persuasions induced her consort Wolfarus to become a monk. How then can we doubt that Mary, whose sanctity was so great, so eminent, so abundant, would impart of her fulness to the heart of Joseph—a heart already by its own nature as disposed to receive these treasures as ever was dewy cloud to reflect the splendours of the sun. It is acknowledged that the mere sight of anyone whom we highly esteem on account of his virtue, may suffice to awaken in us a vehement desire to imitate him; many astonishing examples of this power being recorded in the Lives of the Saints. For instance, we read of Saint Lucian, that his appearance alone did as much to convert unbelievers to the faith of Christ as did the miracles worked by other men; so that the Emperor Maximinus, when he gave him audience before condemning him to death, caused him to be screened from his sight by a curtain, as was the custom in Athens when criminals were brought before the Senate; dreading lest if he looked upon the Saint's countenance he should feel himself irresistibly compelled to become a Christian. And not only the persons of the Saints, but the sight of their portraits or their statues has been known to possess the like potency, so that it is not surprising that the powers of hell caused a furious attack to be made on all sacred pictures and images exposed for public veneration in the churches. For these pictures, representing the triumphs of holiness, produced a marvellous effect on multitudes of those who gazed on them, leading to the conversion of sinners and the edification of the faithful; exciting some to the practice of penance, arousing in others the desire of martyrdom, or animating them to bear suffering with patience. Saint John Chrysostom was wont to be filled with zeal and fervour at the mere sight of the statue of Saint Paul; Saint Gregory Nyssensus felt his heart melt in the sweetness of devotion whilst gazing on the effigy of the Patriarch Abraham. And we know that the pictures of the Blessed Virgin are especially remarkable for the wonderful nature of the effects they have been known to operate; recalling wanderers, inflaming the tepid, strengthening the tempted, and awakening in many pious breasts fresh fervour of charity, of faith, of purity, of mortification, of humility. To this abundant testimony is borne by Saint Bernardine, that glorious ornament of the Seraphic Order. What effect then must her constant society have produced on Joseph, what flames of charity must have consumed the heart of him who had continually before his eyes not the sculptured image, but the living presence of Mary, who could converse with her, listen to her, accompany her whithersoever she went; who dwelt in the same room, and eat at the same table with her; who, with the familiarity of a husband, might observe her ways, acquaint himself with all her actions, and even penetrate into the secret recesses of her heart! Can we think it possible that he failed to profit by the opportunities afforded to him beyond any other mortal man of becoming a saint; and can we imagine that any can boast of having surpassed the spouse of Mary in his faithful reflection of her virtues, his exact imitation of her example, his close following in her footsteps?

But there is still more to be said. It follows that he who has espoused a Queen should become a King. And this law is of so widespread an application that down to our own days, I can discover no exception to it in any age or nation. Yet, in general, it would be a foolish thing for a man to imagine that he could ennoble himself by the mere fact of marrying a wife in a station superior to his own, since by common consent the wife takes the rank of her husband, not the husband that of his wife. In this way a lady of rank loses rank by marrying a commoner, the husband in such case merely remaining what he was; but, nevertheless, this rule ceases to hold good when applied to women enjoying titles of the highest rank, and still less when the woman is ruler over large dominions, and invested with sovereign dignity. "Then," as Baldus asserts (all jurisconsults agreeing with him), "the reverse takes place, the husband being raised to the rank of the wife, not the wife stooping to that of her husband; so that whoever married a queen, were he but a simple shepherd, would by this act be constituted a king, and entitled to share in all the wealth and honours of royalty. What right had Marcianus to the imperial purple except on account of the marriage bond which united him to Pulcheria, (although by mutual agreement they preserved their virginity inviolate); or Anastasius, except on the score of being the husband of Arianna; or Páphlagonius, except in respect of his union with Zoe: all these three women being Empresses regnant? Now, I ask you, my brethren, is there one amongst you who would venture to call in question, or for one moment to doubt the fact that Mary is Queen of Saints? If such a heretic were here present, he would stand corrected—I will not say by an Epiphanus, a Basil, a Bernard—but by any old woman who day by day has heard chanted that glorious invocation: "*Regina Sanctorum omnium, ora pro nobis.*" And if Mary is Queen of all Saints, is it not right, conformably to the above-mentioned law, that Joseph her Spouse should be their King? And if he is King, how can he be inferior to those Saints over whom he reigns supreme? Amongst strong men, who is king but he who excels all in feats of strength? amongst wise men, who merits the title of their king but he who in wisdom surpasses all the rest? and who can be called king of beauty, but he who is fairest among the sons of men? And shall not the King of Saints exceed all others in sanctity? Thus, my hearers, it suffices to say that Joseph was the husband of Mary to prove beyond a doubt that in him dwelt every perfection and every virtue; the happy husband of a good wife. But this will be seen yet more plainly if we consider attentively the other stupendous ends which this mysterious union was intended to serve.

The principal reason wherefore Joseph was wedded to Mary, was not in order that he might use his rights as husband, but that he might be the faithful guardian of her virginity; and with what continency, what sincerity, what purity, must not he have been gifted to fit him for this task! It is affirmed by some authors that concupiscence of the flesh was in him either entirely extinguished or completely deadened. It is, nevertheless, a matter of small moment, since his virtue produced the self-same results. Thus, I say, the Blessed Virgin in her intercourse with Saint Joseph, could feel the most perfect security, and without the slightest shadow of distrust dwell with him, show herself in his company abroad and abide with him at home, reposing in his care by night and by day, in public and in private, in solitary places or amid the throng of men. On what a solid foundation must not Joseph's virtue have rested, since in their closest, most intimate intercourse, Mary never felt the least apprehension in respect to the virginity she so jealously guarded, a virginity so supremely delicate and sensitive as to cause her to take alarm at finding herself alone even with an Angel, when that Angel appeared to her under the form of a man. But on the other hand it is impossible to over-estimate the tact required on Joseph's part whilst acting as the guardian of this spotless virginity, to prevent the real state of affairs from being suspected, lest the holy offspring of Mary should be thought illegitimate, and thus the loss of reputation and life be entailed on the Mother, and on the Child that of His good name and the respect due to Him. Since Joseph proved equal to conduct a matter of so much difficulty, what prudence must he not have possessed, what circumspection, what talent, what address, for he continued in his relations with Mary to unite the loving familiarity of a husband with the respectful reticence of a stranger. Let it suffice to say that in this way he deceived the very devil himself. For it is the declared opinion of Saints Leo, Ambrose, Basil, Bernard, Jerome, Damascene, and many others, following in this the opinion of the great martyr, Saint Ignatius, that the enemy of mankind for a long time held Jesus to be in deed and in truth the son of Joseph, as did all the Jews. And if it is but seemly that we should accept the authority of such eminent doctors, I leave you to decide what wisdom that must have been which could succeed in deceiving the Arch-deceiver himself. Now I will pass on to a further consideration, for to-day I am like the pearl-fisher who, when he finds one pearl, sees in it an earnest of the rich harvest his nets will bring in to him. If Joseph made it his continual study to appear the real Father of Christ, Christ must also have done His part in order to appear to be the son of Joseph. What follows from this? We may at least conclude therefrom that Christ resembled him strikingly in outward appearance, that He had the same features, the same complexion, the same colouring, the same air, carriage, and manners, it being in the due course of nature that a man's children should resemble him. Hence it is that they are called images of him: "A man is known by his children" (Eccl. xi. 30). And if Polybius is to be believed, when the Libyans, whose custom it was to have their wives in common, wished to discover the rightful person on whom devolved the duty of supporting and bringing up a child, they contented themselves by selecting as his father the man to whom he bore the closest resemblance. How great was the honour God bestowed on Joseph, His beloved servant, in that when He willed to become incarnate, He chose to be made like to him, in preference to any other man, and took upon Himself his exact likeness and image in order to appear more truly his son! It is evident that, to say the least, Joseph's exterior bore the impress of the most exalted sanctity, that in him there shone forth a dignity more than human, an angelic grace, a majesty not unworthy of a God-man!

But what do I say? These are ordinary gifts, these are slight favours in comparison with those of which I am now going to speak. Be silent, O heavens! be silent; stay your course, O winds; listen in amazement, O ye Angels, whatever your rank or degree, and hearken to a thing which could not be believed were it not matter of faith. The God from Whom all nature, animate or inanimate, takes her law; Who governs the spheres, Who presides over the course of events, the Monarch before Whom all rulers bow, under Whom they stoop that bear up the world (Job ix. 13), that God Himself was willing, in order to be considered the son of Joseph, to obey him, to submit to his domestic discipline, to his paternal direction, and as if incapable of governing Himself, chose to be subject to him. Now judge for yourselves what must have been the skill and ability possessed by one who was selected to rule a God-man. Philo most truly says that as the brute creation will only obey a being of a superior order to themselves, so he who governs men ought in reason to be more than man. If it is so, tell me, O my hearers, what must he then be to whom not a man but a God is subject? The Infant Jesus was committed by Heaven into the charge of Joseph that he might guard Him from the snares of royal persecutors, preserve Him amid the dangers of foreign lands, carry Him over difficult paths, through unknown solitudes, amid thick darkness; provide Him with food, with clothes, with shelter, and supply Him with all other necessaries of life. He it was whose lot it was to watch over Him with loving care throughout those sufferings which He, oblivious of what was due to Himself and His Majesty, willingly took upon Himself when He became man and shared the lot of our common humanity. The fact that Joseph was chosen by Heaven out of all mankind, and that to him was confided this sacred trust, sufficiently proves that he was of all men most fitted to accomplish the task committed to him;

a task for which the love of Seraphs would seem too cold.

And, doubtless, this great Saint acquitted himself admirably of the duties laid on him, not only in directing the divine Infant, but in taking care of Him, so that he might in truth have said to Jesus: To me do you owe your life. For although Joseph had not given Him being in the same sense in which His Mother had, he had yet preserved His life from the attacks of those who had drawn the sword to deprive Him of it; and every one knows that to preserve a life is as great a thing as to give it, if not even greater, since the former is an act of nature, the latter a work of skill. But, be this as it may, must not the man to whom a God owes His life be peculiarly favoured by Him, be very near to Him, and specially beloved by Him? "He that is keeper of his master shall be glorified," says Solomon (Prov. xxvii. 18). And if, as is well known, for this reason alone regal honours were decreed to Mardochai throughout the realm of King Assuerus, may we not justly believe that Joseph would, in like manner, be highly exalted in the kingdom of Christ? Most assuredly we may. For, after all, if we look closely we shall see that the most Mardochai did was to perform a deed of loyalty, by disclosing the plot directed against his master's life, whereas Joseph did far more; he not only revealed the plot as soon as it was made known to him, but defeated it, rendering the scheme abortive and bringing it to nought. In this, I think, we may see an additional reason for believing that Joseph occupies the chief place in the kingdom of heaven, a place to which he is moreover entitled on various other grounds; so that, although he can never take the precedence of his Virgin Spouse, yet he also possesses his throne, wields a special sceptre, and wears a peerless crown; King over all, subject only to the King of kings!

But we need not any longer wonder at finding Joseph thus raised above his fellow-men, so that we have to employ different terms in speaking of him, and are obliged openly to make him an exception, to exempt him even from those rules which are most universal in their application. Other men, when they have done for God all that lies within their knowledge and their power, when they shall have done all these things, are forced at last frankly to acknowledge: We are unprofitable servants; because there is nothing which can be of any advantage to God. "What doth it profit God if thou be just?" (Job xxii. 3) asks one of Job's friends. For if we slay victims, God does not feed on our flocks and herds; if we burn incense, the fragrance of our perfumes adds nothing to His sweetness; if we offer of our goods, our adornments in no wise increase His beauty. God has need of nothing, and therefore we can be of no profit to Him. But, O wonder inconceivable! these rules cannot be applied to Joseph; he alone needs not to acknowledge before God his uselessness; for he was important, he was even necessary to Him; his labours prevented the spectacle of a God publicly soliciting alms from His creatures. It was he who prevented his God from dying of hunger, from perishing with cold, from blushing in nakedness; he it was who succoured his God in all the necessities to which the Sacred Humanity was liable. And now methinks I hear the blast of the final trumpet; I see approach the day of universal judgment; the tribunal is set, the just willingly present themselves, the reprobate also draw near, the Judge appears. After glancing with wrath at the reprobate, He turns upon the elect a look of complacency, addressing to them these consoling words: "I was hungry, and you sustained me with food; I was thirsty, and you brought me refreshment; I was a wanderer, and you gave me shelter; I was naked, and you provided me with clothing." At these unexpected words, the just will lift up their eyes in astonishment and be compelled to answer: "O dear Lord, do not speak thus to us! Though it has been our happiness to have loved and esteemed Thee much, yet how canst Thou attribute to us miserable creatures such loving deeds as those? When did we ever see Thee hungry, so as to be able to supply Thee with food? or thirsty, so that we might bring Thee refreshment? when a wanderer, that we might give Thee shelter? when naked, that we might provide Thee with clothing?" And then, in very truth, if Christ would make good His words, He must reply that He had taken everything given to the poor as bestowed upon Himself. "As long as you did it to one of these my least brethren, you did it to me" (Matt. xxv. 40). But when He speaks to Joseph, will any such explanation be necessary? In addressing him, Christ can literally say of Himself: "I was hungry, and you gave me to eat; I was thirsty, and you gave me to drink; I was a stranger, and you took me in; naked, and you covered me." And will Joseph be astonished to hear this? will the words sound strange to his ears? will modesty prompt him to answer in terms of gentle self-depreciation? On the contrary: "Thou hast not then forgotten," he will be able to reply to his former foster-son and present Judge, "Thou hast not forgotten how when Thou wast a child of five years and more, I led Thee back with Thy Mother from Egypt to Palestine. Oh, how many times during that journey I saw Thee languishing from hunger, and, not having any bread to offer Thee, I went to seek amongst the trees of the wood for some wild fruit wherewith to sustain Thee! How often beneath the glowing sky I saw Thee parched with thirst, and, no river being nigh, I hastened over the mountains to find among the rocks some spring with whose cool waters I might revive Thee! Worn out with fatigue, Thou wast often unable to proceed farther, then I remember taking Thee in my arms and carrying Thee over a long portion of the road; and never did I walk with greater speed or greater ease than when charged with this sacred burden! How often did we pass the night under the open heaven, and I remember how, absorbed in the thought of Thee, I formed with my garments a sort of tent to shelter Thee! When thieves overtook us on dangerous paths, I remember that, only solicitous for Thy safety, I concealed Thee with my own hands under a thicket, lest I should lose Thee! And oh! on how many other and subsequent occasions was it true that I saw Thee hungry and gave Thee to eat; I saw Thee thirsty, and gave Thee to drink; I saw Thee a stranger, and took Thee in; and, although thou wast He Who clothes the birds in their varied plumage, and the flocks in their soft fleeces, in spite of this, I saw Thee naked; I saw Thee naked, and, taking off my own cloak, I covered Thee!" In this manner will Joseph in all truth be able to make answer to Christ; and if those who have succoured our Lord in the person of His poor will receive a great recompense, how much greater will be the recompense of one who succoured Him in His own person? He that receiveth a prophet in the name of a prophet, we are told, shall receive the reward of a prophet; and he that receiveth a just man in the name of a just man, we are also told, shall receive the reward of a just man; how therefore should he who receives a God in the name of a God fail to receive the reward of a God; that is to say, a reward proportionate, as far at least as this is possible, to the greatness of the guest he entertains? But although all that has been said admits of no doubt, Joseph would be the last to deny that all his glory is attributable to the fact that he was the Spouse of the Blessed Virgin; the happy husband of a good wife. It was this that afforded him the opportunity of exercising paternal affection towards Christ, and receiving from Him filial affection in return; it was this that promoted him to the enjoyment of such great happiness, that acquired for him such eminent virtue, such exalted honour; so that he might truly say in speaking of Mary: "All good things came to me together with her" (Wisd. vii. 11).

And I think we shall in nowise detract from the glory due to the Saints, if we hold Joseph not to have been inferior, or, as many believe, to have been far superior to them all. On the contrary, it appears to me that to affirm the reverse, would be to cast a slight on the dignity of the Blessed Virgin. For what would be thought of a queen who allowed her subjects to enjoy higher dignity than her husband, and did not rather raise him above them all? Moreover, Christ Himself did not disdain to yield the preference to His foster-father, by submitting to him for thirty years as his subject, his servant, his apprentice in the workshop; obeying him in every sense of the word, "the Lord obeying the voice of a man" (Jos. x. 14). Wherefore let him who would rashly give to Joseph a second place, pause and consider well before he thus acts.

SECOND PART.

It appears to me that one objection on this subject may yet remain in your minds, which it is my duty to remove as briefly as possible. If Joseph was, as we have seen, a Saint so distinguished, so eminent, so sublime, greater perhaps than any other, how comes it that the Church has not paid to his memory that tribute of solemn acclamation and applause, which from all that has gone before, appears to be his due? Many Saints inferior to him have received more honour at her hands; for a long time there was neither Office nor Mass appointed for his day, and it is only within the last few years that the observance of his Feast has been enjoined upon the faithful. My brethren, do you wish to hear the reason of this in one word? I will tell it you. It is to be accounted for by the very fact that Joseph was the Saint we have shown him to be, distinguished, eminent, sublime, greater perhaps than any other. This may seem strange, but lend me your kind attention and I will make it plain. There were in the Early Church some heretics, and at their head the heresiarch Cerinthus, who, in order maliciously to detract from the glory of our Incarnate God, asserted that He had been conceived in the ordinary course of nature, and in consequence was in very deed the son of Joseph, as He was the true son of Mary. A monstrous blasphemy this, as you perceive, which the Church was compelled to use every effort to confute. Yet perceiving that to decree to Joseph an exalted place in public homage would only tend to increase the number of those who were led astray by this error, and give it an appearance of truth in the eyes of the simple, by, as it were, granting to it her sanction, she in her wisdom took a contrary course; she showed for Joseph but slight esteem and ordinary consideration, and apparently placed before him many who doubtless had no claim to stand on a par with him. Such is the rare discretion which the Church has seen fit to employ in order to preserve intact the prerogatives of Christ.

But I will not follow the example of one in our own day, one otherwise illustrious, who, addressing Joseph in the name of the whole world, has asked pardon of him for the slight esteem in which for so many centuries he was held. No, no, my hearers. I am well aware that it is a distinguishing mark of greatness to take time to make itself known and appreciated, at least by the greater part of mankind; in fact, the magnitude of the sun itself, which is, so to speak, a giant amongst the planets, was for a long time so greatly underrated that it was actually estimated by Empedocles to be but a foot in diameter. Thus, again, the treasures of the vast eastern oceans were only discovered gradually; the same is likewise true of the properties of the most precious stones, and of the virtues of the choicest herbs. It is not necessary, however, that I should have recourse to such explanations; in all her operations the Church of God is guided by a special light. Therefore, it remains my glad belief that if Saint Joseph has not always been held in universal honour, as at present, this was not the result of any negligence for which his pardon ought to be publicly asked, but was in conformity with the designs of Providence, and the wise foresight of the Church.

In our own day it would indeed be most inexcusable were we not to honour Joseph, since the truth respecting him has been fully unfolded, and made clear as the noonday; nor is there any cause to fear lest the homage paid to him should in the least degree diminish the glory due to Christ, or even obscure its brightness. And if this is so, which of you, my hearers, will fail to give the first place amongst his favourite patron Saints to Saint Joseph? The other Saints have truly great power with Christ, but at the most they can only ask, they cannot demand; whereas he who is supreme among them needs not to ask; he has the right to command; he commends not, but commands, as Gerson forcibly remarks. Is there not every ground for supposing that even in heaven Christ is willing to sustain the relations which existed on earth between Him and His foster-father, and that He still, if we may so speak, exhibits towards Joseph a like filial love, a like filial submission? Nor can there be any doubt that every request coming from Joseph will have the force of a paternal command, and as such, will be more favourably received and more speedily responded to by Christ than those proffered by any other Saint; the Lord obeying, as formerly on earth, so now in heaven, "the Lord obeying the voice of a man." Take him, then, take him all of you for your protector; he is worthy of your confidence, and all may find a plea for claiming him as their special patron; take him, priests, that of him you may learn the reverence due to the God you hold daily in your hands; take him, you who are married, that of him you may learn to put an end to discord among yourselves; take him, virgins, that of him you may learn how to preserve your chastity intact; take him, travellers, for he will prove a faithful guide in your journeyings; take him, artisans; take him, ye poor; take him more especially you who, formerly of noble rank, have by the reverses of fortune been reduced to a state of poverty; take him, fathers, for he will teach you how to bring up your children aright; take him, masters, for he will teach you how to rule your dependents well; take him, princes, for he will teach you the art of governing wisely all your subjects, be they high or low; above all, let those take him for their patron who desire peace at their latter end, and who for this purpose have specially enrolled themselves in that solemn and salutary confraternity of the Bona Mors, which I rejoice to see flourishing amongst you. Jesus and Mary stood by Joseph at the hour of his death; Jesus and Mary sped his parting soul; Jesus and Mary with their own hands closed his eyes; and if, as may well be imagined, his last words breathed nothing but divine love, what were the final accents of his expiring lips save the sweet names of Jesus and Mary! O happy we, if he wins for us a like blessed privilege! Yes, my brethren, let us ask it of him earnestly, let us ask it confidently, for if he will vouchsafe to exert his prerogatives on our behalf, he can at the moment of death lead to our bedside Jesus and Mary; so that, beholding them, and ardently longing to be with them, we may breathe forth our souls in a transport of love, we may expire amidst their greetings, we may expire in their embraces, we may expire, as God grant may be the case with each and all of us, we may expire, I say, amid the consolations of celestial sweetness, in the embrace of the Lord!

PANEGYRIC IN HONOUR OF SAINT JOHN THE EVANGELIST.

THE HIGHEST IN EVERY GIFT.

"He shall exalt him among his neighbours."—Eccl. xv. 4.

That is but a natural feeling which makes the noble heart unwilling to see itself surpassed on every side, and causes it to aspire after the attainment of eminence on some one point at least. But to crave for universal pre-eminence betokens a proud and haughty spirit, impatient of all superiority which is not its own. Let Aristotle make it his ambition to soar above his fellows by aid of his pen, but he must not grudge to Alexander the prominent position he won for himself with his sword. Let Tully find his pleasure in returning from the rostrum accompanied by the blast of trumpets, but he should not aspire to make the theatre re-echo with the harmonies of his lute, lest perchance mocking Fame should open her hundred mouths to deride him. Let him hand over the lyre to Virgil and to Homer, and they, in their turn, will not dispute with him that glory which is his due. Let Cato be content that his wise counsels prevail in the Senate, nor let him marvel that Cæsar should surpass him in his exploits upon the battle-field. It would be too much for a single individual to excel all in everything. Nor has God ordained that in His Church any single Saint should shine with the lustre of every perfection. For instance, he whose mantle is dyed with the Martyr's purple cannot encircle his brow with the aureole of a Doctor; he who is distinguished for the gift of prophecy does not likewise possess the authority of an Evangelist; he who carries in one hand the staff of the Apostle is not permitted to bear in the other the lily of the Virgin. Such, my brethren, is at least the ordinary rule, laid down by Saint Paul in the well-known words: "God hath indeed set some in the Church, first Apostles, secondly Prophets, thirdly Doctors, after that workers of miracles, then those who serve" (1 Cor. xii. 28). Hence, Saint Gregory Nazianzen used to say that in his opinion the man of greatest worth was either he who possessed many virtues in a comparative degree, or he who possessed one in a superlative degree. But is this rule so absolute, so unalterable, as to admit of no exception? This is not for me to say. Still I think that if you pass in mental review all bygone ages, if you search in all climes and amongst all peoples, unless I am mistaken, your eyes will light upon one person only who forms an exception to this rule, and that is the great Saint John, whom the Church commemorates to-day with due solemnity and glad rejoicings. He was a Virgin, an Apostle, a Doctor, an Evangelist, a Prophet, and a Martyr. What other wreaths can seem wanting to this one brow? Can one say more than that we know Christ loved to exalt him amongst the disciples, as His own chosen favourite, that on him He conferred every dignity, on him He bestowed every gift? He exalted him among his neighbours. This is not all, it seems indeed but little, when we proceed to consider his greatest glory, namely, that each of these rare gifts was possessed by Saint John in a high degree, in a degree so superlative, that either of them alone would have sufficed to constitute him not only a Saint, but a Saint of the rarest perfection. And now listen to what I am about to say, if you would have me explain this further and prove it more clearly.

Putting out of sight for a moment all the other wondrous gifts we find in Saint John, let us at present consider him solely in his character of Virgin. Who will be found bold enough to dream of surpassing him in this respect, who will dare even to place himself on an equality with him? He was, as we have said, a Virgin, and not only in the time when virginity had been inculcated by Our Lord in so many discourses and pointed out as a virtue specially dear to Himself, but even at a period when virginity was known to few, hated by many, practised by almost no one. Even from his earliest years, if Eutimius is to be believed, John regarded purity both of body and soul as a precious jewel, and preserved it with jealous care. And how was this virtue regarded by the persons who surrounded him? It is well known that amongst the Hebrews the very name of virgin was a term not of honour, but of reproach, even when applied to men. Under the Old Testament dispensation the instances are most rare in which we find virginity to have been held in high esteem, as it was by Melchisedech, by Josue, by Jeremias, whom Saint Ignatius the Martyr ranks among virgins; as it was by Elias, Eliseus, and

Daniel, who, according to Saint John Damascene, were also such. Furthermore, amongst the number of the twelve Apostles, John is the only one known certainly to have been a Virgin, although he, of all others, was endowed by nature with those qualities which render the practice of that virtue most difficult: a vivacious disposition, an attractive exterior, a warm temperament. We do indeed find him following the humble calling of a fisherman, but we know that, according to the opinion of Saint Jerome, he was of a noble family, and as such had free access to the courts, as is shown by the fact that on the night of the Passion his influence there was sufficient to obtain admittance for Saint Peter, at a time when the followers of the Redeemer were, if not shunned as outcasts, at least looked upon as evil-doers. How great a thing it was to preserve his virginity so pure and so immaculate amongst all these dangers, that it entitled him to be admitted by Christ to continual intercourse and familiar intimacy with Himself! What more can be said in its praise, since it was on account of his virginal purity, as Saint Peter Damian opines, that Christ gave Mary to be the mother of Saint John, and that He chose this Apostle to fulfil towards Mary the duties of a son. And how, after the reception of so signal a favour, must Saint John have striven to perfect himself in the precious gift, which had constituted his claim to that favour? We learn from a tradition handed down by many of the Fathers, that it was enough to look upon the calm serenity of the Blessed Virgin's countenance, enough even to cast on her a single, an accidental glance, in order to banish from the soul every unclean thought and engender within it a desire for celestial purity. What must it have been then continually to behold her, to be beheld by her, to talk with her, to listen to her, to sit at table with her, to accompany her whithersoever she went, to hold with her such free and familiar intercourse as Saint John enjoyed not for one year alone, or for two, but for the uninterrupted space of twenty-three years, during which, according to the generally received opinion, he discharged the office of her protector and guardian! This is enough, exclaims Saint Peter Damian, to warrant me in giving to Saint John the first place among Virgins in the Church. Is not this the reason why the Angels did not consider him as inferior to themselves, why they refused, as we read in the Apocalypse, to accept from him any act of homage or adoration; because, as the same Saint proceeds to state, he was equal to the Angels in that very characteristic which forms the chief point of their superiority to mankind in general?

And now, what think you, my hearers? Supposing that the glory of his virginity were Saint John's sole title to distinction, would he not on account of this alone command our highest admiration? Would not the extraordinary lustre of this virtue prove us right in concluding that the magnitude of the graces and the rewards bestowed on him exceeded all that our imagination can conceive? We read of some, such as Cecilia and Valerian, deserving, as the reward of their virginal purity, to gaze on the unveiled countenance of Angels; others, such as Colomba and Daria, to daunt the fierce fury of wild beasts. We find the virginity of Stephen surnamed Arvernenses imparting to his chaste body, even during his lifetime, a most exquisite fragrance; we know that the pure Clodesinda was privileged for a considerable period to feed on the bread of Angels alone; that Flavia was clothed with miraculous light as with a rich mantle. If such signal favours were given as the reward of virginity alone, to persons possessing this virtue in a degree far inferior to Saint John, how glorious must his reward have been whose purity shone with a splendour sufficient to eclipse them all!

But to proceed: let us now contemplate Saint John exchanging the lily for the staff, about to set forth on his apostolic journeys. Does any one presume to assert that in this point he may perchance have been inferior to some of his brethren? In the dignity of the office, it was indeed impossible for him to rise above his colleagues, but he surpassed them all in the length of time during which he discharged its duties. He entered upon the work of the Apostolate at an earlier age than any of his fellows, and he was older than any when death gave him rest from that work. The other Apostles, after the death of Our Lord, laboured for ten, twenty, or at the most for thirty-five years, as is recorded of Saint Peter and Saint Paul, but the labours of Saint John extended over a period of no less than seventy. And is not the ardent zeal, the fervent love, which formed his distinguishing mark from the very commencement of his career, too well known to admit of the supposition that of all those long years one single moment remained unemployed, was not dedicated by him to the service of the Church? He first, after the Ascension of Christ, went forth in company with Saint Peter, to preach the truth in the public places and to defend it before the judgment-seats; he was the first to suffer imprisonment for the faith, he was the first to receive scourgings, he was the first to endure outrages. If we see him animated with such fervour in the early dawn of his apostolic career, is it probable that his love waxed cold as mid-day approached, and the sun of charity, rising ever higher as his merits increased, shed its rays more brightly upon his soul? Do we hear of Churches more numerous or more flourishing being founded in a single province under the administration of either of the other Apostles, than those which, according to Saint Jerome, Saint John himself established in Asia Minor? He founded the Church of Ephesus, the Church of Philadelphia, the Church of Laodicea, the Church of Pergamus, the Church of Sardis, the Church of Smyrna, the Church of Thyatira. The conversion of so many souls must have cost him vast labours, great fatigue, long journeyings, protracted vigils, much teaching and preaching, the endurance of hardships innumerable. Let us consider the pains he took for the ransom of one soul alone, and we may thence infer at how great a price he purchased the salvation of so many. Having met in one of the cities of Asia with a youth of good dispositions, who showed great aptitude for the service of God, he placed him with the bishop, in order that the latter might personally instruct him in manners and morals. But in the course of time, the young man, like an untamed steed, began to loathe the bit, and endeavour to shake off the guiding hand. He gave himself up to games and revels and amusements; and before long he fled into the country, and having constituted himself leader of a band of robbers, became the terror of the adjacent forests, making them the scenes of bloodshed, of robbery, and of treachery. After some years had elapsed, Saint John returned to the city, and heard from the lips of the bishop the sad story of the unhappy youth. Who can express the grief with which these sorrowful tidings filled his heart? Straightway he asked for a guide conversant with the country, and directed his course towards a mountain, well known to be the favourite haunt of those robbers. From afar he was descried and recognised by the young man, who, ashamed of his conduct, took to flight, hoping to conceal himself among the crags. The holy old man did not lose heart; following the fugitive as closely as he could, with mingled tears and entreaties, he called on him to pause and listen to him. "Stop," he cried, "my dearly-loved son! why do you fly from your unhappy father? what have you to fear from me? how can I harm you? Remember that you are young and I am old; you are strong and I am weak; you are armed to the teeth while I am entirely defenceless. It is usually the wayfarer who flies from the robber, not the robber from the wayfarer. Rest assured that I come hither in the sole hope of being of service to you. I will give account for you to Christ, I will take your guilt upon myself; I will bear the punishment you have deserved; I am ready to give my life to ransom yours, whether forfeited to human justice or divine." These touching words melted the heart of the young man; he stopped his horse, he leaped to the ground, and flung himself at the feet of the Saint, hiding in his breast for very shame that guilty right hand stained by so much bloodshed, polluted by so many deeds of violence. Saint John would not permit this; himself kneeling on the ground, he threw his arms round the neck of the young man, he pressed him tenderly to his heart, he raised him up, he kissed him, he possessed himself with gentle force of that right hand, saying: "Why withdraw this hand from me? Give it me, give it me, that if it is indeed defiled, I may cleanse it with my tears. Why do you hesitate? Am I not empowered by God to promise you eternal salvation? Come with me to the church, come now, come at once, that I may lose no time in making intercession for you; I will take no rest until with my prayers and sighs I shall have prevailed with God, until I am assured that I have regained you for heaven, and heaven for you." And now what is the sequel of my story? The heart of the young man was at once and so completely transformed by divine grace, that the Apostle on his departure a short time after did not hesitate to confide to him the care of a church, either because he saw him to be already fitted to govern, or because placing a man in a position of authority over others is often the most effectual means of making him watchful over himself. Now from this fact can we not argue as follows? If Saint John thought no toil too great to rescue one soul from perdition, if when old and weary, worn out and infirm, he hunted his prey through the thickets, like an eager greyhound in pursuit of game; if he shed so many tears and sorrowed so deeply over one wanderer from the right way, can we suppose that he would spare his exertions when the souls of multitudes were at stake, when youth and strength were on his side, and outward circumstances showed themselves less adverse? If he went in pursuit of those who fled from him, would he, think you, turn away from those who came to seek him? And furthermore, if he was able to make thieves into bishops, into what must he not have been able to transform his bishops? Into what did he transform them? Read the Apocalypse, and thence you will learn what name was applied to his bishops in heaven, in what estimation the bishops of those seven Churches of Asia mentioned above were held. To the Angel of the Church in Ephesus write; to the Angel of the Church of Smyrna write; to the Angel of the Church of Thyatira write; thus were they all in turn called by no other name than that of Angel. Some of them are, it is true, reproved on account of grievous failings, but, on the other hand, all are extolled for their rare virtues. The zeal of one is commended, the constancy of another, the fidelity of a third; this one is praised for the purity of his doctrine, that one for the depth of his humility; and one may almost imagine that the true object of these praises is to make apparent the transcendent greatness of the Apostle who not only founded such famous churches, but bestowed on them such exemplary pastors. I think all my hearers will agree with me, that had Saint John achieved nothing else of importance during the whole of his Apostolate, this alone would have sufficed to render it most memorable. But I have more to tell: not satisfied with having by his fervent eloquence effected the spiritual regeneration of Asia Minor, he journeyed into Phrygia, he went on into Parthia, he even penetrated farther to those tribes most abandoned by Nature, relegated by her to the remotest regions of the East. It would be too much for us to attempt to follow him in all his wanderings through those inhospitable climes, inaccessible almost even in our own day; and I am impatient to see him lay aside the staff, and assume the pen, in order that we may for a short time consider him in his character of a Doctor, whose achievements as an Apostle we have already sufficiently contemplated.

And in very truth, did not his doctrines win admiration in every seat of learning, Pagan as well as Christian? I do not mean to infer that the teaching of the other Apostles was not equally in accordance with the doctrines of the Gospel; but we know that when uttered by their lips, it fell upon the ears of the heathen philosophers as the ravings of madmen, and was derided as such. But Saint John possessed the gift of making it acceptable even to the proudest among them; for do we not find him gaining the applause and commanding the respect of the haughty followers of Plato themselves, so much so that they did not deem it beneath them to adorn their writings with his maxims? And who does not know that Saint John alone of all the Apostles has been distinguished in the Church by the name of Theologian? In the Church, do I say? It appears that in heaven, in heaven itself, he was openly acknowledged and honoured as such. Have you never heard what happened to Saint Gregory, who was surnamed Thaumaturgus on account of the wonderful miracles he wrought? He had, on leaving the Roman school in Pontus, been raised by Phedimus to the episcopal chair of Neocæsarea, a city at that time so buried in error and idolatry that it seemed almost impossible to distinguish between the Christians and the unbelievers. Wherefore, diffident of his own powers, Gregory humbly besought the Mother of God herself to vouchsafe to dictate to him the tenets of the

Catholic Faith which he ought to teach to the people committed to his charge. The Blessed Virgin heard the prayer of her devout servant and granted his request, since it was not proffered by one who, instead of adoring with reverent simplicity, asks reasons for the faith he holds, but by one commissioned to establish the faith of others, a task befitting the intelligence of an angel rather than a man. Yet she did not choose herself to play the principal part in imparting this instruction, perhaps because even from heaven above she wished to inculcate upon women those principles which she had enforced by her example on earth, in that she abstained from the exercise of all such functions as were less suited to her sex. "I suffer not a woman to teach" (1 Tim. ii. 12). And under such circumstances of whom do you think that she made choice? Truly in heaven there was no lack of eminent persons who had enjoyed a great reputation for learning in the Church; there were those who were well versed in the most abstruse religious controversies, who had taught the faith in the schools, argued about it in the councils, defended it before the tribunals, upheld it in their writings. And yet Our Lady passed all these by and chose John alone to accompany her; with him she entered the chamber of Gregory, radiant in her majesty, lovely in her modesty, and addressing her companion by name, spoke thus: "John, thou who didst rest upon the bosom of my Son, and drink of the fountain of uncreated wisdom at its very Source, infuse into the soul of this my servant some portion of that wisdom." And immediately the Apostle obeying, dictated to the holy bishop a rule of faith so lucid, so compendious, so sublime, that since that time no other has been equally famous throughout the East; and it served as a powerful antidote to preserve the cities of Neocæsarea free from the contagion of those errors with which at a later date so large a part of the world was to be infected. Hence, when called to receive his eternal reward, Gregory left this creed as his sole and most precious legacy to his children; for he could confidently affirm that by means of it he had so effectually rooted out the belief in heathenism from that portion of the Church committed to his charge that, whilst on first coming thither he had found but seventeen Christians, on departing thence he left but seventeen idolaters.

But does it not appear on first sight as if an Angel, endowed with loftiest intelligence, would have been more suitable than Saint John to accompany the Blessed Virgin on this occasion? What will you say when I proceed to tell you that the Angels themselves learnt of Saint John? Would you have her choose the pupil as her companion when the master stood by? and a master of such ability that even on earth he could teach the angels many things before unknown to them? For this reason they came down like docile scholars to learn from his lips lessons of loftiest sublimity, to be initiated by him into mysteries most hidden. And if by chance you may imagine this to be a mere figure of speech, an unwarrantable exaggeration on my part, before pronouncing me unworthy of belief, ask Saint John Chrysostom, and he will tell you that it is a certain fact that the Angels themselves listened with the greatest attention to John. Yes, indeed; he declares that the Angelic powers, even the very highest, the Cherubim and Seraphim, acknowledge themselves to be the disciples of John; and to this fact he asserts the Apostle of the Gentiles to be alluding when he speaks of the Church militant as being the teacher of the Church triumphant in respect to certain mysteries of the faith. "That the manifold wisdom of God may be made known to the principalities and powers in the heavenly places through the Church" (Eph. iii. 10). And if this be true, what more could possibly be said in honour of Saint John? It is indeed a well-known fact that mortals have often learnt from Angels things of no ordinary importance. It was from Angels that Daniel learnt various secrets in reference to the deliverance of the Hebrew people from the Babylonish captivity. It was from Angels that Manue learnt how to bring up his son Samson in the best possible manner. It was from Angels that Tobias learnt the means of restoring sight to his father, who was blind. It was from Angels that Gedeon learnt the artifices necessary for effecting his escape from the hands of his enemies the Madianites. But for Angels, the Apostles would not have known with what glory Christ would one day return to judge the world. It was Angels who taught Anatolia when a child to appreciate the inestimable beauty of virginity; they also stooped to make the shepherd Hermas acquainted with the correct day for the solemnisation of the Easter festival. But what are all these things which men have learnt from Angels in comparison with those which the Angels have learnt from one man alone, from Saint John? if it be indeed true that he revealed to them the sovereign mystery of the Incarnation, a mystery unknown to all preceding ages, transcending all human intelligence; such a mystery in fact (to quote Saint Chrysostom again) that not even the Angels knew it, until he announced it. And now, my hearers, are you not convinced that the first place amongst the Doctors of the Church belongs to none other than Saint John, both by reason of the sublimity of the doctrine he imparted, and also the dignity of those to whom he imparted it?

In proceeding to consider the character of Saint John under a new light, we need not as heretofore bid him lay aside the symbol of his office; he may retain the pen, and continue to employ it, although now no longer as a Doctor, but as an Evangelist. And, as such, let him for a short space unyoke from the mystic chariot of Ezechiel that proud eagle which, impatient to soar above the clouds, longs to bear with it in its flight the pure Apostle on whom Christ lavished such special marks of love. What say you to this, my brethren? will your sight be able to follow him, borne aloft on the pinions of that eagle? It cannot be denied that the other Evangelists likewise moved with exceeding swiftness, but they did not rise above the earth, as we may gather from the mysterious animals chosen to be their symbols; for these, although winged, are, notwithstanding, dwellers upon earth, not inhabitants of the air. The other Evangelists also, it is true, set our God before us, but they exhibit Him to us, either trembling in swaddling-clothes, fainting upon the cross, wearied with journeyings, exhausted by preaching, agonising in prayer, or sorrowful even to tears. Saint John upon his eagle was privileged to mount higher; leaving earth he penetrated the clouds, he rose above the heavens, and not above the first heaven alone, nor the second, not even above the third, as did Saint Paul (we quote the words of Origen), but above the highest of all, so that he did not stay his flight until he beheld God Himself in His essential being, until he gazed upon the sun in its meridian splendour, unobscured by clouds, untroubled by eclipse, unshadowed by change. Origen himself, in rapturous astonishment at this wondrous flight, exclaims, in words which might be deemed over-bold in a writer of less mark: "John surpasses all creatures, visible or invisible, and himself deified, participates in the divinity of God." Shall we wonder, then, to find Saint John distinguished by most signal marks of divine favour at the time when he was preparing to write his gospel? Of no other are we told that having called on the whole Church to unite with him in a solemn fast, he ascended to the summit of a lofty mountain, there remaining for several days and nights in unbroken contemplation, until through the mists and darkness which surrounded him, amid the lightnings and tempests there fell upon the ear of that second Moses a voice terrible as thunder, proclaiming truths as yet unrevealed to created intelligence: "*In principio erat Verbum;*" and "*Verbum erat apud Deum, et Deus erat Verbum.*" And if the spot in which he composed his gospel was at that time miraculously shrouded in storms, ever since it has been the scene of a miraculous and perpetual serenity. Saint Gregory of Tours tells us that down to his own day no drop of rain had been known to fall on that mountain top, but however copiously the clouds shed their showers all around, and the rivers inundated the land, they invariably spared that sacred spot; a spot far more wonderful than Olympus of old, for whilst the latter reared its summit above the clouds, the latter felt the tempests play about its head, and feared none of their fury.

Furthermore, my brethren, what can equal the esteem in which this Gospel of which we are speaking has ever been held by the Church? It has been the impenetrable shield wherewith she has been enabled to repel the attacks of the Cerinthians, the Ebionites, the Theodorsonians, and other like monsters, who issuing from hell, have dared to assault the Majesty of the Son of God, disputing either the eternity of His existence, the divinity of His essence, or His equality with the Father. Thus in those times of conflict when Arius, having thrown off his allegiance to the Church, enrolled under his fatal banner so many Monks, Bishops, Nations, Princes, and Emperors, it was the habit of those few courageous souls who stood their ground against him, to hang around their neck a copy of Saint John's Gospel; this they wore in sight of all, and I cannot say whether it was intended to defend them as a breastplate, to adorn them as a jewel, or to distinguish them as a badge alike honourable and uncommon. Not Catholics only, but Jews also and Pagans unanimously concurred to hold this Gospel in extreme veneration. Epiphanius tells us that the Jews preserved it amongst their treasures as a thing of utmost value. Saint Augustine relates that the Pagans extolled it in terms of the highest praise, as embodying the teaching of a wisdom more than human. So unbounded was their admiration, that we even find a Platonist suggesting that the wonderful words with which this Gospel opens should be inscribed in letters of gold above the portals of the temples, and should afford topics of discussion in the Lyceum. The lightnings fear those marvellous words, and beholding them, are seized with sudden alarm and fly from the towers they were about to strike; the earthquakes fear those words, and reading them, reverently forbear to overthrow the walls already trembling from their shock; the devils fear those words, and on hearing them abandon in mad fury the bodies which had too long been their prey. Much more might here be said, were I not impelled to hasten on, eager to behold in the hands of Saint John that mysterious volume inscribed with secret symbols, closed with sevenfold seals, on which he rests his claim to the title of a Prophet.

My brethren, do you hesitate to follow me? Do you perchance deem it scarcely possible that Saint John can here again be first as we have ever seen him heretofore? It cannot be denied that God has honoured all the Prophets with special confidence, in that He has revealed to them secrets concealed from the rest of mankind; but who amongst them has ever enjoyed confidence so unbounded as that bestowed on Saint John? To the other Prophets God did but make known some particular event in an especial manner; to Isaias He foretold the calling of the Gentiles, to Jeremias the destruction of Jerusalem, to Ezechiel the rebuilding of the temple, and so forth; but he to whom one secret was revealed, was not made acquainted with the others, or at least only privileged to know them partially. Of Saint John it can be said with truth that God concealed nothing from him; and if we believe this, we shall see the Apocalypse so full of mystery, written by him, to be nothing else but a full revelation of all that was to happen from the first foundation of the Church until the end of the world. Such is the unanimous opinion expressed by the holy Doctors. Must not facts like these justly fill the minds of all who hear them with wondering amazement? It was regarded as an act of the greatest condescension that which He manifested under the Old Testament Dispensation to Abraham, when, about to rain down fire and brimstone upon the guilty city of Sodom, He seemed unable to execute His design without having first communicated it to him whom He honoured with the title of friend: "And the Lord said, Can I hide from Abraham what I am about to do?" (Gen. xviii. 17). It must ever be an act of supreme condescension when a created intelligence, although of the highest order, is admitted to hold any communication whatsoever with the Deity, for when God speaks, a God alone is worthy to listen. But what is the revelation of the impending ruin of a few cities compared with the revelation of the convulsions of so many kingdoms, the destruction of so many nations, the overthrow of so many states? To Saint John God discovered the mournful occurrences which were to put an end at once to the kingdom and the royal line of a people formerly highly favoured; the persecutions which the Christian Church in its infancy would have to suffer at the hands of the Jews first and subsequently of the heathen, who successively would conspire to effect its overthrow; the confiscations, the imprisonments, the exiles, the barbarous cruelties, which would be employed by seven different Roman Emperors with a view to exterminate the faith of Christ from off the face of the earth. Nor was this all that God revealed to Saint John; He further permitted him to behold on the other hand the glorious victories, the rich trophies which the Cross was to win; He showed him Paganism overthrown and exterminated, the true Faith widespread and triumphant. He discovered to him also the new Empire which would spring from the ruins of an obsolete Paganism; the incursions of Barbarians, the rebellions of subject races, the discords amongst nations, the revolutions of states, each and all destined through the marvellous orderings of Providence to prepare the way for the evangelisation of the whole world. And then a new and more distant vista opened upon the sight of the Apostle; he beheld the wars stirred up by Antichrist in the latter days of a world decrepit and tottering to its fall; the confusion, the terror, the dismay prevailing among such nations as were spectators of the universal ruin; the signs of the final Judgment, the eternal state of the Elect and of the Reprobate, whose distinctive features, whose very numbers are recorded in the sublime book, which so many have vainly attempted to open, much more to read. No more need be said; it is enough that we proclaim, in the words of Abulenses, that "Every event that has marked the history of the Church up to the present time, and all yet in store for her, was revealed beforehand to Saint John;" this all the expositors of the Apocalypse explaining it piece by piece fail not to show: witness Saint Antoninus, the golden Doctor, Salmeron, Bellarmine, Ribera, and many others too numerous to name, not inferior to these in orthodoxy of belief, and not less well known to fame. Now, that the knowledge of events so momentous, so manifold, so various, should be imparted to Saint John at one and the same time, would of itself appear a confidence of no ordinary kind; but there is something which renders it more important, more extraordinary still, namely that the revelation was made so many ages before the occurrences predicted were to take place. To most of the other Prophets God only made known things which were to happen at no distant day; in which they themselves were often to bear a part, or of which at least they were to be spectators. Such was the case with the calamities foretold by Jeremias, Baruch, Ezechiel, and many others, whilst the events with which Saint John was made acquainted were not to occur until thousands of years were past and gone; and we know well that the communication of secrets destined to remain hidden for many ages is universally acknowledged to be of greater importance than the communication of those which the course of a few years will bring to light. Again, from the strictness of the concealment required from any one to whom a secret is intrusted, the importance of the secret itself may in a great measure be argued; now tell me, where do we find God requiring more absolute concealment than He did from Saint John? Read the whole Apocalypse and decide for yourselves if secrecy was ever more rigorously enjoined or more religiously observed? "In the Apocalypse of John, every word is a mystery," says Saint Jerome. All the authors who have sought, pen in hand, to decipher the abstruse characters of that book, have without a single exception been unanimous in agreeing that to hope to attain a full and clear understanding of every part of it would be nothing short of audacious presumption. Ribera compares this little volume to a vast ocean, abounding in rocks, in shoals, and in whirlpools, where all mere human wisdom must infallibly make shipwreck.

Were this not so, would it be possible that the Apocalypse should still remain a mystery to us, since for so many centuries the greatest intellects, intellects which were the wonder of their age, have busied themselves in striving to expound its few brief pages? Those must indeed be great secrets which God Himself guards with such jealous care, for we know that in this respect the divine secrets are widely different from those of men; prudence requiring that the projects of mortals should be kept hidden: "It is good to hide the secret of a king," as the Angel said to the aged Tobias; whilst no such reticence is necessary in regard to the designs of Deity; "it is honourable to reveal and confess the works of God" (Tob. xii. 7). For God fears not lest anything mar the success of His purposes, or interfere with their execution, should they be divulged before the time fixed by His eternal wisdom for their accomplishment.

And this leads me to consider another point on which Saint John strikingly differs from the other Prophets, viz., that the knowledge enjoyed by the latter was not conferred on them for their own sake, but for the sake of those to whom they were to reveal it; whereas acquaintance with the future was a privilege bestowed on Saint John for himself alone, not in order that he might communicate it to others. Wherefore Gagneius, in his "Commentary on the Apocalypse," takes occasion to remark that "this volume contains many mysteries which no man was to know, save John alone." This proves the sublime revelations made to Saint John to be favours bestowed on him exclusively, favours in which mankind at large had no share; such a privilege being granted to no other among the Prophets, who were indeed permitted to draw from the fountain of divine mysteries, but only in order to be a channel whence others might drink of those waters.

For my part, I no longer doubt that Albertus, Saint Thomas, and Hugo were justified in confidently affirming that the prophecies of Saint John should be ranked higher than the most celebrated prophecies of the Old Law; it has even been asserted further that the difference between the two may be compared to the difference between a servant and his master, between man and God. Nor can I fail to perceive that it was the good pleasure of God to bestow upon John the preëminence in every kind of grace. He treated him as a familiar friend, He treated him as a chosen favourite; He exalted him among his neighbours, not among strangers alone, but among neighbours; therefore, it is just and right for every inferior servant to give precedence to him. On one point, however, it is still possible for some to imagine that he may be excelled, if not in the favours received from God, at least in the sufferings endured for God. This leads me on to consider Saint John in his final character of Martyr; but before proceeding to do so, let us pause for a moment to gather courage to gaze on the cruel tortures to which he is about to be exposed, and to go to meet the awful spectre of Death himself.

SECOND PART.

IF God had not, in the case of Saint John, put forth His miraculous power, causing boiling oil to be for him a harmless dew, and glowing flames a sweet refreshment, it would not have occurred to us, for a single instant, to doubt his having as good a right as any other martyr to wear the crown and bear the palm. Nor must it be forgotten that he underwent his tortures not merely at an advanced age, but in the decline of life; when his strength was exhausted by toilsome journeys, by innumerable hardships, by incessant preaching. And, nevertheless, to the stupefaction of the whole city, gathered together in crowds by the celebrity of the victim, Rome witnessed a new spectacle, that of an aged man, more than octogenarian, scourged by brutal executioners, and then, naked as he was, cast into a surging caldron of boiling oil; yet confronting those torments with unruffled serenity, a serenity which none of those whose lot it was to inflict them could boast. However, God willed that His servant should receive no harm from this fiery immersion, but come forth from it rather with added beauty and fresh vitality, like gold from the crucible and the fabled phœnix from its funereal pyre. What must we believe to have been the intention of Providence in this? Could any one be so madly foolish as to imagine that God prevented His beloved Apostle from expiring under his sufferings, because He grudged the triumph they would have won for him? Surely not. Besides, it is an acknowledged fact that true martyrdom consists in the will, not the deed, so that it matters little if death fails to crown the desires of him who calls for it. But what unwonted timidity restrains my tongue to-day? Let us bid the executioners incontinently release Saint John from their ruthless grasp; let us bid them lay down their scourges, quench the flames, and empty the heated caldron; let us suppose that there is no more question of his being exiled, but turn the prow of that cruel barque which is bearing him to the barren Isle of Patmos, there to wear out his waning life in the mines and be buried alive in its desolate caverns. What say you to this? Do we thereby deprive Saint John of his claim to be a martyr? No, indeed; a martyr he shall be, and one of no ordinary kind; for to him shall be assigned the highest place, the proudest rank, the chiefest honour, in that noble army of which the Church so justly boasts. Listen whilst I show you why. Every one will be ready to allow that of all the Martyrs there is not one who can rival Mary. All will acknowledge her to have been "a Martyr, and more than a Martyr," as Saint Bernard and Saint Ephrem style her; "the very Sun of Martyrs," as Saint Basil of Seleucia entitles her; nay, "the Queen of them all," as the united voice of Christendom loves to proclaim her. And now tell me, what tyrant condemned her, what executioners put her to death? Certain strange writers have indeed affirmed that she met with a violent death, but they have been amply refuted by Saint Ambrose, Saint Isidore, and the Venerable Bede. How then can the Church award her the Martyr's palm, since it was not won for her by the sword of the executioner? How can she award it her? You already know, my hearers, how she can do this. Mary was, doubtless, a Martyr; although she did not fall a victim to the hand of a tyrant, she was a Martyr to Love; Love, which may perhaps be termed the greatest of all tyrants. Her martyrdom was fully accomplished when, standing on Calvary, she beheld her Son nailed to the wood of the Cross, hanging between two thieves; for she then endured in her soul the same Passion which He suffered in His Body. And if she did not die with

Christ, it was only in order to obviate the slightest suspicion of her help having been necessary to Him in the great work of the world's redemption; to this Saint Ambrose seems to have referred when he spoke of the Sorrowing Virgin in these glowing words: "She imagined by her death to add something to the public gift, but Jesus needed no helper." But to return to my former subject; would you know, my brethren, what was the nature of Saint John's martyrdom? Exactly the same as that of Mary. They alone remained standing at the foot of the Cross, both sharing in the sufferings of Christ, Mary as His Mother by nature, Saint John as His brother by adoption. By this public act they made open profession of being the followers of Christ, an act essential to true martyrdom. It was the portion of both these loving hearts to sustain the various pains received by Our Lord over the whole extent of His Body; they felt with Him the thorns, the nails, the cross, the bitterness of the gall and vinegar. And that thrust of the spear, which to no effect vented its cruelty on a dead body, transfixed it is true the Heart of Jesus, but it failed to wound save the hearts of Mary and of John; wounding perhaps most deeply the heart of John, standing as he did in the place of Christ, left by Him as a last legacy to Mary, in order that he might replace to the utmost of his power the Son she had lost. And now tell me, my hearers, was not this the very highest kind of martyrdom? Whilst the other Martyrs endured bodily torments, Saint John endured a martyrdom of the soul; and we well know the soul to be the part most sensitive to pain, since it can suffer without the body, but the body cannot suffer without the soul. Besides which, if the glory of martyrdom is proportioned to the greatness of the cause for which it is suffered, as is expressed in the words, "The cause, not the penalty, makes the Martyr;" who can in this respect surpass Saint John, who suffered such intense interior anguish in order to cleave to Our Lord at the time of His greatest desolation, when He was abandoned by those He loved best, and denied by those who had been foremost to profess their devotion to Him. Furthermore, it was Christ entering upon His glory, Christ risen from the dead, Christ triumphant over the grave, whom the other Martyrs confessed with unflinching resolution; but Saint John was not ashamed to confess Christ at a time when no such glory was His, when like a common malefactor, He hung naked upon the Cross, a companion of thieves. And this, too, occurred in open day, in a public place, in the midst of a vast concourse of people, so that the mocking taunts to which the fidelity of the Apostle could not fail to expose him from the vulgar crowd, must in themselves alone have been sufficient to constitute a martyrdom.

But putting all this aside, I will make bold to go still further, and to say that life was martyrdom to Saint John, not death, as is ordinarily the case; for what could be greater suffering to so ardent a lover of Christ than the mere fact of being compelled to survive Him? Perhaps, however, it was but for a short space of time that he survived Him? Let me remind you how the great Teresa, the glory of our age, regarded the few brief years during which she was separated from her Beloved. She was continually heard to exclaim: "I die, because I cannot die; I die, because I cannot die;" this was the ejaculation which fell most frequently from her lips. What then must have been the feelings of Saint John, who had enjoyed intercourse far more intimate and more familiar with that same Lord, and yet was not permitted to behold again His beauteous countenance until extreme old age, that is until the age of ninety-three years as some affirm, whilst other accounts extend the period to the age of ninety-eight, or even one hundred and six years. Must not this ardent lover have felt a separation like this to be truly a martyrdom, and a martyrdom all the more terrible because so protracted? Saint John might indeed have shed his blood as did the other Martyrs, but to suffer a violent death would have been impossible for him; it was so hard to him to live that he could not have found it hard to die. And we know full well that death did in fact cost him no struggle; for he descended himself into a grave prepared for him on the summit of a lofty mountain, and there having laid himself down as one about to die, he was shrouded in a mysterious light which hid him from the eyes of the astonished bystanders; they meanwhile weeping more bitterly than do the worshippers of the Sun, when the luminary they adore disappears below the horizon. I know that Saint Thomas believes John to have been taken up into heaven and to be dwelling there in body as well as in spirit; however this may be, one thing is certain, that in many of the celestial choirs his presence is ardently desired. The Virgins would fain have him amongst their number, because he is a mirror of purity; the Apostles, because he is a model of fervour; the Doctors, because he is a marvel of wisdom; the Evangelists, because of his keen discernment; the Prophets, because of his acquaintance with hidden things; the

Martyrs, because he was a living victim of charity. And now, my hearers, I appeal to you. What is your opinion? Cannot Saint John lay claim to the possession of all these titles, each one of which would merit a place in these separate choirs? And if, in order to set his merits in their brightest light, I have not only permitted myself to compare him to the other Saints, but even frequently to award him the foremost rank and highest place amongst them, be not in haste to condemn me; I am justified by the example of Christ Himself, who although so careful not to show partiality towards any of His disciples, broke through this caution in the case of Saint John, and without reserve and qualification proclaimed him to be His chosen favourite. Moreover if in speaking of him I have somewhat surpassed the limits of brevity assigned to me, I venture to hope that the nature of my subject will furnish me with an apology. One single Panegyric does indeed afford sufficient space to enlarge on the merits of almost any other Saint; but as the rays with which many Saints have severally shone meet in the aureole which surrounds the head of Saint John, so the Panegyric uttered in his honour must be manifold in its character and consist of many woven into one.

PANEGYRIC IN HONOUR OF SAINT JOHN BAPTIST.

THE ABSENCE OF MIRACLES A PROOF OF SANCTITY.

"John indeed did no sign."—JOHN x. 41.

ALAS for Sanctity! Unless supported by numerous miracles, which either like lightning-flashes reveal its true nature, or like thunderbolts confound its adversaries, Sanctity must perforce remain exposed to the undiscerning contempt of Ignorance, or the biting tooth of Envy. The Church herself, whose decrees are all regulated by consummate wisdom, refuses any longer to authorise such Sanctity to be worshipped in her temples, or to be honoured with incense and offerings; she bids it be satisfied with the tribute of private and individual homage, and not aspire to public veneration. Who is not ready to laud and admire Virtue, nay more, to bow down before her, when she is accompanied by an attendant train of miracles? In this case Ignorance suddenly learns to appreciate her worth, and the mocking tongue of Envy is speedily silenced; all with one voice hasten to praise her, every man finding it easy to persuade himself that God would not as frequently have set aside laws so rigid and so universal as are the ordinary laws of Nature, had not the request for these exceptions been proffered by a friend very dear to His heart. If this be so, I crave your pardon, O great Precursor! My esteem for you is most sincere, my reverence most affectionate, my affection most reverential; but how can I possibly form an adequate estimate of your merit when all the Doctors, and all the Fathers, and the very Evangelists themselves, attest that throughout the thirty years of your life (a life certainly resembling more closely that of angels than of men) you never achieved the performance of a single miracle? "John indeed did no sign" (John x. 41). I see before me no small number of Thaumaturgi, showing the lakes they dried up and the mountains they removed. I see a Benedict whose word is potent to arrest destruction, a Mucianus by whose command flames are extinguished. I see a Francis able to traverse on foot and dryshod the most stormy of Sicilian gulfs, bidding defiance alike to the treachery of Scylla and the ensnaring whirlpools of Charybdis. The dead raised to life through the power of a Martin, the dumb speaking at the command of a Dominic, the blind restored to sight through the intercession of a Laurence—these press around me and deafen my ears with their joyful clamours. On beholding them, what can I say of you, O great Baptist? Of you, when throughout the length and breadth of Palestine, it could not be said of you that you once gave sight to the blind, or cooled the burning of a single fevered frame? It is well for me that the audience I am addressing this morning is one composed of men of subtle intellect and well-trained mind. For I must own, my brethren, that were I speaking to less intelligent hearers, I should almost despair of making them duly appreciate the worth of a sanctity which is thus barren in miracles. I should be compelled to gloss over this fact, to put it aside with intentional neglect, if not to suppress it altogether. But in treating of the subject with you, so far am I, as you see, from allowing this difficulty to dishearten me, that I hasten to proclaim it loudly, saying in a voice which every one must hear : In the whole course of his life, John the Baptist did not work one miracle. What then ? Is his merit, is his holiness on this account to be less highly thought of ? On the contrary, I can assert the very fact of no miracle having been worked by him throughout his entire career to be the strongest proof we have of his rare merit and transcendent sanctity. I see this novel proposition strikes you as one somewhat difficult of demonstration; it is, perhaps, for the first time in your life that you hear a man exalted on account of the very thing which is apparently most calculated to abase him. But this need not dismay you; you have but to listen, the burden of proof rests with me.

There is no doubt that God, whenever He calls one of His servants to fulfil some charge, invariably furnishes him, at the same time, with the ability needful to sustain it, not only satisfactorily, but even with dignity. It was indeed ingenious cruelty on the part of Eurystheus to command Hercules to attack, now the lions of Erymanthus, now the hydras of Lerna, now the cerberi of Cocytus, without on either occasion providing him with any stronger weapon than a club, and that not one of bronze or of iron, but a club of weak olive-wood. Very different is the manner in which God deals with men. His consummate goodness compels Him always to give arms suitable to the enterprise He intrusts to any one; that is to say, with the office He bestows the power to fill it, with the burden the strength to bear it, with the undertaking the ability to execute it. Let us take the case of Moses. I know that God called him from keeping a flock to deliver His people Israel; but at the same time He endowed him with such a courageous heart, lofty intelligence, and power of speech, that his gifts as a leader of armies stand unrivalled. In a similar manner God acted when He chose Jeremias who was a stammerer, Eliseus who was a ploughman, Amos who was a shepherd, Daniel who was a mere child, to communicate His secrets to the great Princes of the earth. Into the workmen charged with carrying out the sublime plans according to which the Ark and the Tabernacle were to be constructed, He infused in a moment perfect understanding how to work "whatsoever had to be made of gold, and silver, and brass, of marble, and precious stones, and variety of wood" (Ex. xxxi. 4, 5). If you will pass the field of Scripture carefully under review, you will perhaps discover for yourselves that God has indeed sometimes given the strength without the burden, but never the burden without the strength. Seeing this, there can be no doubt but that Saint John, too, like all other servants of God, was abundantly endowed with the talents and gifts without which he would have been unable to accomplish the task laid upon him. But what was this task? tell me, my hearers, what was the charge committed to him? The most difficult, let us frankly own, that was ever confided to mortal man: "He came, that all men might believe through Him" (John i. 7).

He had to overcome the stubborn opposition and wilful incredulity of the Jews, to convince them that the Son of a poor working woman, a man whom they daily saw before them barefoot and indigent, subject to pain and weariness, liable to all the infirmities of human nature, susceptible of hunger and thirst, cold and heat, needing repose and suffering exhaustion, that such an one was in truth no other than God Himself. One would have imagined that in order to gain credence for so hard a saying as this, John ought to have been endowed with a power of working signs and wonders as great as it is possible for created arm to wield. Listen while I bring forward a few examples in support of this. When Elias wished to prove to the messengers of the king that he was truly a man of God, was not power at once given him to call down fire from heaven? Again, when Josue wished to show the Hebrews that he was Moses' lawful successor, was he not immediately empowered to divide the waters of the stream? And, a more signal instance yet, when it was needful for Moses to persuade Pharao that it was God's will that he should permit the oppressed and afflicted people of Israel to offer sacrifice in the desert, was he not authorised to reverse with his rod all the ordinary laws of nature? With a single motion of his hand he enrolled in his service countless multitudes of frogs, sciniphs, flies, locusts, caterpillars; he turned the rivers into blood; he obscured the light of day by thick and horrible darkness; he called in a moment from above thunders, whirlwinds, hail, tempest, and arrows of destruction upon all the land of Egypt; he brought disease on the cattle and death on the first-born; he ruled the fate of Egypt with a single word, as if he were, I will not say a despotic monarch, but rather an omnipotent Deity. If therefore those whose task of persuasion was so much easier received power to confirm their words by means of miracles alike stupendous in their novelty, sublime in their quality, vast in their number, should I not be warranted in concluding that John had power to work still more and greater ones, in confirmation of his more difficult mission? And yet when I look at the page of Scripture I find recorded there that John indeed did no sign. To such an extent did God keep the hands of His servant fettered, that John was never permitted to make a single flower of the field spring up miraculously, to arrest the course of a single river, or to call down a single thunderbolt from the clouds. And here I would have you consider: With what natural eloquence must not God have endowed his tongue, and with what efficacy his words, in order to compensate for such a privation! How great must have been the charm imparted to his manner and the fervour breathed into his heart! How apparent to the eyes of all men the virtue of his life and the superiority of his wisdom must have been made, that he might readily succeed in carrying conviction when he announced the marvellous doctrine, which, as I have said, he was sent to proclaim in the ears of persons who were uncouth, uncultivated, perfidious, and malicious! On the other hand, if you deny the fact of such compensation, you are compelled to fall back on the unworthy alternative of supposing God to act like Eurystheus; that is to say, that he gives the burden without the strength to bear it, and the duties of an office without the capacity to fulfil them.

Now, as it is evident that a supposition so derogatory to the character of God is on no account to be entertained for a moment, I will proceed to clinch my argument in the following manner. To persuade men of the Divinity of Christ, as it was the mission of Saint John to do, was a task far less easy then than it is now. We have the benefit not only of all the arguments then in force, but of a multitude of others besides, so potent that in our day persistent unbelief requires stronger intellectual coercion than acceptance of the truth. Does any one still refuse to believe? We close with him at once, we drive him into a corner. "Upon what other supposition," we ask him, "than that Christ was God, is it possible to account for the marvellous influence He exercised over men? How did He induce them to exchange feasts for fasts, riches for poverty, honour for contempt, a flowery and alluring path for an uninviting and thorny one? But perhaps it was in the case of a few individuals that He was thus successful? On the contrary, he found innumerable multitudes ready to follow Him; people of every age, every creed, every rank, every tongue; some of the wisest senators, the most learned philosophers, the most powerful princes. And, furthermore, with what facility He won them! Observe, He beat no drum, wherewith He might raise a small troop of soldiery. He neither unsheathed sword nor drew bow; He only summoned to His side twelve fishermen from the shores of the Tiberian lake, men of low birth, ignorant, poor, and despised. Of these He sent one to Italy, one to Greece, one to Armenia, one to Persia, one to Tartary; with them alone He entered on His vast conquests, and, so happy was His choice, that not the intrigues of a Tiberias, or the cruelty of a Nero, nor the angry contempt of a whole world, leagued together and armed against Him, could avail to arrest for a moment the career of His victories. Thus with no other aid, in an incredibly brief space of time He established a kingdom which, marvellous to relate, seemed to be furthered by persecution, increased by slaughter, glorified by contempt; now who that knows all this can doubt the divinity of Christ?" Thus one argues in the present day with any one obstinate enough to persist in denying this great article of our faith; and truly these proofs are clear as the noontide rays, so brightly are they to be seen, so plainly to be discerned, that however carefully it is sought to exclude them, it can hardly happen that some small crevice be not found through which they will penetrate even against the will of him who would shut his eyes to them. Does it not then appear incredible, that in spite of all this, unless the messengers of the Gospel are able to support their assertions by the performance of startling miracles, which may serve as authentic credentials in the eyes of unbelievers, they labour in vain to obtain credence even in our own day, although they be gifted with celestial wisdom, and endowed with extraordinary sanctity. The purity of the life led by Saint Francis Xavier amongst the heathen was notorious to all; the name by which they commonly called him being the great and holy Father. All knew that the bare earth was his couch, his undermost garment a rugged hair shirt; that he was accustomed to walk barefoot on thorny paths, over glowing sands, through frost and snow. Who was there amongst them who was not aware that he often passed nights without sleep, and days without food; and that even when prevailed on to relax somewhat from this rigid fast, he allowed his palate no greater delicacy than dried rice, slaking his thirst with insipid water? And here I must ask pardon of the Saint for saying that all this came short of what was required. How much had he not to toil, performing wonders never before seen or heard of, till he succeeded in tiring the idle curiosity of the Indian, and all this in order to convince him that the Redeemer he preached was truly God? Was it not necessary to restore to life more than twenty-five corpses, on some of which decay had begun its fearful work? was it not necessary almost every day either to make salt water sweet, to avert the coming storm, to recover lost vessels, or to put armed hosts to flight? And, if you look further, you will see the same to have been the case with Rembert when carrying on the conversion of the Danes, with Boniface when labouring amongst the Sclavonians, with Hyacinth when subjugating Poland to the faith; and do we not find that the efforts of the great Seraph of Assisi to win the Egyptians to the faith of Christ were more meritorious than successful, because, although he edified the barbarians by the saintliness of his life, he did not dazzle them by the brilliancy of his miracles? And now to return to my argument: If it was needful for men of such great wisdom and eminent sanctity continually to perform numerous and astounding miracles in order to prove the divinity of Christ to heathen nations, far less proud, malicious, and perverse than were the Jews, at an epoch, moreover, when heavenly mysteries are more easily discerned, when the Holy Ghost the Paraclete sheds His gifts in more abundant measure, what must have been the purity, what the wisdom dwelling in the breast of the Baptist, since he was able to persuade men of this truth without the aid of a single miracle, at a time when the work of the Holy Spirit was more limited in its operation, and heavenly mysteries less plainly comprehended? And if, finally, we consider, the character of those he addressed, we shall find them as a nation possessed of pride so arrogant that they assumed to be the sole arbiters of religious truth, of envy so malicious that they maligned all sanctity which surpassed their own, of perversity so obdurate that they condemned every opinion differing from that they had already formed. Do you believe, therefore, that in order to achieve such triumphs, it was enough for John Baptist to commit no sin, however venial? to refuse all pleasures, however innocent? to fast some days only in every week; to sleep upon the bare earth; to clothe himself with rough sackcloth; which are indeed generally regarded as limits which it is not given to human sanctity to surpass; no, it was necessary that his innocence, his mortification, his austerities, should be of a nature so marvellous as to produce on those who witnessed them a greater impression than the sight of men lifted above the earth at the voice of any other saint, or bodies already the prey of worms raised living from the tomb!

I am well aware of an objection that might here reasonably be urged, namely, that all this that I have said would be indisputably true, if the preaching of Saint John had been so persuasive as to induce men to believe the truths he proclaimed. But was it so? Had such been the case, Christ would have met with a different reception at the hands of the Jews; He would not have been treated as a malefactor, much less crucified as a thief. Since he failed thus to persuade them, his poverty of miracles cannot be said to argue an unusual wealth of sanctity. Bear with me awhile, my hearers; I am not striving to prove that Saint John succeeded in bringing home the much-contested truth of Christ's divinity to the minds of all the priests, all the scribes, or all the common people who flocked in eager crowds to hear him. It must, indeed, be evident to all that I should be foolish in taking this for granted, seeing that Christ Himself did not effect as much, after He had made all Judea and all Galilee resound with the fame of miracles so numerous that if they were written every one, the world itself would not contain the books which should record them. But I do say that if Saint John failed in convincing the Jews, this failure is not to be attributed to any fault of his,· but only to the obstinacy, the malice, the guilt of those who would not believe him. And this being granted, it is evident that the argument you advance against me, instead of weakening my position, tends the rather to strengthen it; for would the incredulity of the Jews, on a point of so much importance, have been thus inexcusable, had not the preacher possessed a superhuman sanctity, of eminence sufficient to compensate abundantly for the absence of miracles? Besides, I am prepared to assert that this incredulity was far from universal. Have you never read in the Gospel that many were led at his advice to take on themselves the yoke of Christ, to worship Him, to serve Him, to follow Him, and to bear witness to others of the truths of His divinity? We even find that the first disciples of

Christ were those whom the Precursor had sent Him from the banks of the Jordan, not those whom He had gained for Himself on the shores of the Tiberian lake. And I cannot help regarding this as the greatest wonder of all, for with what authority must not he have spoken, by whose mere word men were persuaded to acknowledge Christ as the only true Messiah, before He had as yet made Himself known throughout the world, either by the fame of His preaching, the report of His sanctity, or the reputation of His miracles? And yet it was by John's persuasion that Andrew, who became later the chief of the Apostolic college, was induced to follow Our Lord. And if many refused to believe John when he told them that Christ was their own Messiah, what, I would ask, was the reason of this incredulity? The reason was this: Because they rather took John to be himself their Messiah. Now, see in what a marvellous manner this clinches my argument; for how sublime, how unparalleled, how divine must that virtue have been, which could cause such an opinion to be formed with regard to the Precursor! Elias and Eliseus could, indeed, by their power recall the departed soul to the bodies of children already become the prey of death; Isaias could bid the sun return back, making a timid fugitive of that mighty giant who had never before been put to flight, whatever the monsters who met him on his steep course, or appeared amidst the rocky declivities of the Zodiac; Daniel could indeed repose safe and unharmed in the midst of hungry lions, and Jonas from the frightful depths of a whale's belly could in security cry aloud to God; nevertheless, in spite of all this, it never occurred to any one to suspect, much less to believe, that either of those we have just mentioned could possibly be the promised Messiah. And yet each and all of them had in their favour proofs of no ordinary sanctity; austere fasts, rough clothing, perfect uprightness of life, intrepid courage, apostolic zeal, and, above all, most intimate union with God. How much then must the Baptist have surpassed them in sanctity, since without the aid of any miracles he was taken for the Messiah, not by ignorant and illiterate persons only, but even by Scribes and Pharisees!

And now I am going to say a thing strange indeed, but none the less true; namely, that whilst to others the gift of miracles is generally awarded on account of supereminent sanctity, in the case of Saint John his sanctity was the cause why this gift was denied to him. For if even without such power he was generally supposed to be the Christ, and acquired such great authority and reputation, that, as Saint Augustine observes, he might easily have induced men to pay him divine homage, and offer him victims and sacrifices, what would have been the result had he united to the purity of his life miraculous powers in equal measure? I for one am ready to say that scarcely a single individual would have been found throughout the whole of Judea, who would not have preferred John to Christ, seeing that many did actually so prefer him even at the time when, receiving from John no possible aid of a miraculous nature, they on the contrary continually obtained from Christ sight in their blindness, health in their sickness, food in their hunger, life in their death. I do not know whether the observation I am about to make has ever occurred to the minds of any of my hearers; to me it appears so singularly appropriate that I will not hesitate to introduce it here. All the Apostles, not excepting even the traitor Judas (who, however unworthy of the honour, was nevertheless one of the twelve), all the Apostles, I repeat, were distinguished by the glorious appellation of Lights. "You are the light of the world" (Matt. v. 14); an appellation so peculiarly appropriate to the Redeemer, that the Evangelist Saint John, wishing to depict in a single word the sanctity of His life and the sublimity of His office, could find no more fitting terms in which to speak of Him than these: "That was the true light, which enlighteneth every man that cometh into this world" (John i. 9). And yet these very Apostles, not to speak of Judas, quickly fell into thick darkness, for you are well aware that one denied Christ, another forsook Him, another fled away; and, ere long, there was not one who had not abandoned this Good Shepherd, fleeing from Him in timid dismay and alarm when divine chastisements fell upon Him, as if scattered abroad by sudden thunderbolts from heaven. And, on the other hand, we may observe what scrupulous care is taken in the Gospel, not only to avoid giving this title to the Precursor, but expressly to point out that it did not belong to Him. The Evangelist takes special occasion to speak of this great man: "Take heed," he says, "take heed that you do not mistake this point: this man came for a witness, to give testimony of the light; he was not the light, but was to give testimony of the light." He was not the light? Oh! some will say, this is indeed an extraordinary proceeding! What! Shall we say of a perjured Peter, of an unbelieving Thomas, that they are lights, and not say the same of John the

Baptist? nay more, shall we take the greatest care to prevent all possibility of any one ascribing to him such a title? Was he perhaps inferior to either of the Apostles in the subtlety of his wisdom, the fervour of his zeal, or the spotless purity of his life, three points on which the Apostles shone with especial lustre? Without derogating from the others, I find recorded of him: "There hath not risen among them that are born of women a greater than John the Baptist" (Matt. xi. 11). How then can a title conceded to the lesser be denied to the greater? And yet it is unhesitatingly alleged of him that he was not that light; "he was not that light." Have patience, my hearers; this title, granted to the other Apostles because they are inferior to the Precursor, is denied to him precisely because he is superior to them. For with the name of Light, a glorious title peculiar to Our Lord, a Peter or a Thomas might safely be distinguished, who, notwithstanding the brilliancy with which they enlightened the earth, were afterwards veiled by such gloomy eclipses, plunged into such deep obscurity, that there could be no possible danger of mistaking them for the Christ. It is evident enough that they were not the true Light, and that between Him and them this essential difference must ever remain, that whilst He shone with a native and inherent light, they, on the other hand, shone with a borrowed and adventitious brightness. The same in a greater or less degree may be said of each of the other Apostles, whenever these words are applied to them: "You are the light of the world." But if these same words had been applied to the Baptist, to one whose advent had been foretold by the mouth of the same prophets who predicted the coming of Christ; to one whose conception had been announced by the self-same Angel who brought the tidings of Christ's birth; to one who, like Christ, had been sanctified in his mother's womb; to one from whose hands Christ had received baptism; to one from whose sermons Christ had deigned to borrow the theme of His own discourses; to one whose life at the first glance appeared even more saintly than that of Christ, at any rate more austere, more unprecedented, more likely to win the applause of the crowd; if, I say, to such a man as this the glorious title of Light, Christ's peculiar prerogative, had perchance been given, I tremble to think how terrible would have been the danger of confounding the true light with the reflected, the native with the borrowed; for in this way a parhelion would, so to speak, have been formed, two suns would have appeared calculated to deceive the keenest eye, the eagle's glance. And therefore it is said expressly of John: "This man came for a witness, to give testimony of that light;" he was not the light, but was to give testimony of that light; for truly it is the greatness of his merit that precludes him from bearing a title adequate to that merit. And now convince yourselves, my hearers, that his greatness was in fact the sole cause why he was condemned during his whole life to abstain from performing any miracles. For when any creature reaches a height of virtue, wisdom, or power so exalted as apparently to warrant the supposition that he is divine, God is compelled either to conceal or diminish the splendour of those gifts, in order to remove the risk of idolatrous worship being paid to their possessor. It is a thing of small importance for a man in whom human defects of word, deed, or intention are evident, to perform great miracles, since no one will be easily tempted to believe that he does these things by his own power and not by the permission of Heaven. But the case is different with a man in whom no fault is to be seen. In like manner the Blessed Virgin is known to have worked no miracle in her lifetime, for if to her immaculate purity and celestial sanctity she had united miraculous works, I think the great Dionysius, who all but worshipped her as a goddess, would not have been able to restrain his veneration within due limits.

But to return to John, before closing this part of my subject; it is clear that the danger with regard to him has always been that of attributing to him gifts superior to his merit rather than inferior to it. For not only did the Jews look upon him as the Messiah, whereas he was but His Precursor, thus taking him to be the Bridegroom who was in reality but the best man at the wedding; but besides this, Origen has fallen into a grave error on this point, considering Saint John to have been angelic in his nature as well as in his office; and other more recent heretics have stated that he had power to abrogate the Mosaic law, that he was the founder of the Christian religion, that he was the institutor of the Sacrament of Baptism; many of the Fathers even themselves putting forward propositions with respect to him, which require a mild interpretation to be put on them, else they would sound exaggerated, not to say erroneous. Such, for instance, is the passage in which Saint Cyril affirms that John reached the summit of human perfection: "*Ad eos pervenit, terminos qua natura humana aspirare potest;*" language which, if true, would not only derogate much from the merit of the Blessed Virgin, incomparably greater as it was than that of John, but also from the omnipotence of God, who, since His power is infinite, can always create men of greater perfection, and, in the language of the schools, never bestows upon any one so much as not to be able to bestow still more. Now what is my object in recalling these errors to your minds? I wish to demonstrate to you that all the false opinions entertained concerning the person and the office of this great man, do not consist (as is usually the case) in denying him all that he merits, but rather in ascribing to him more than is his due. Imagine, then, how much wider would have been the field open to erroneous conclusions concerning his gifts, whether of nature or of grace, if God had rendered him illustrious on account of his miracles. It was therefore most necessary, to guard against fresh occasion of error, that God should not thus exalt him; and, seeing this, I ask you now to tell me, was I not right in declaring at the commencement of my discourse that sterility of miracles was in John a proof of sanctity? Here let us pause awhile.

SECOND PART.

EVEN were all the arguments hitherto brought forward found fallacious, yet it was a most wise ordination of God that Saint John the Baptist should perform no marvellous works during his lifetime. And in what way? By teaching to all Christians a great lesson, one which I will discover to you in a few words.

A deeply-rooted persuasion is fixed in the minds of a large majority of mankind, namely, that to be a great

Saint consists in working great miracles; a persuasion equally false and pernicious, and consequently one which the enemy of our souls fosters with the utmost care. Now all may here see a Saint, the greatest perhaps of which the Church can boast, who passed his whole life without performing a single miracle: "John indeed did no sign;" and thus they may perceive that sanctity does not rest in dispelling the clouds with a breath, in quenching the lightnings with a word, but in fulfilling perfectly the duties of a Christian. The disciples of Our Lord thought it triumphant proof when they were enabled to say to the lame, stand upright; to the sick, be healed; to the possessed of devils, be delivered; and they returned with joy to Christ, saying: "Lord, the devils also are subject to us in thy name" (Luke x. 17). And, indeed, who would feel inclined to chide them for such joy as this? The gifts of which they boasted were bestowed by God for the good of their fellow-men, in the service of all; it seems, therefore, that they had good cause of rejoicing. Nevertheless, no sooner does Christ hear their exultation than He checks it, He reproves and rebukes them, as if they estimated wrongly the goods in their possession: "Rejoice not in this;" and He calls on them, at the same time, on the other hand, to rejoice in being numbered amongst the elect: "Rejoice in this, that your names are written in heaven." Hence I draw a conclusion, one which appears to me most obvious, namely, that to work miracles affords no certain proof of being numbered among the elect; for were it so, all must acknowledge that the Apostles would then have had as much occasion to rejoice as a convalescent on the recovery of his appetite, because it is a sign of returning health; as the countryman on affording shelter to the swallow, because its presence is a sure token of spring; as an anxious mariner, tossing on the stormy sea, on beholding the dolphins disporting themselves on the water, because it is a proof that calm weather is close at hand. Since, then, Christ bade His followers rejoice that their names were written in heaven, and not that they were empowered to work miracles, it follows that to work miracles is not a sure sign of our names being written in heaven. And, alas! how great is the number of those who for a long time illustrious on account of their splendid miracles, yet went astray, fell into sin and, after all, were lost! Look through the annals of the Church, and you will be dismayed to see how many of these sad examples meet your eye. Yet why should we give ourselves this trouble? Do we not know that in the last day many will come to Christ and say: "Lord, in Thy name we have foretold events to come, we have cured grievous diseases, we have delivered multitudes of persons tormented with evil spirits;" and, in spite of all, they will hear the answer: "*Nescio vos*, I know you not?" How, then, is it possible that any one can be found who values no other sanctity than that which brings hidden things to light, which heals sickness, which removes mountains and allays the storm?

Let us suppose, one of my hearers may say, that such an estimation be erroneous, yet why take up such a subject this morning, especially as this discourse is addressed to an audience which certainly is not composed of Thaumaturgi? The reason which has led me to deliver it is twofold. First I would remove a grievous abuse prevalent nowadays with regard to

the adoration of Saints, who may now be compared to
lakes, of which those count the greatest number of inhabitants on their shores whose waters abound most
plentifully in fish. Thus we find many persons when
about to choose a patron, seek him not from amongst
those who have left to the Church the brightest examples of humility, of mortification, of zeal, of charity,
such as Saint Peter, Saint Paul, or some of those first
Apostles, whose virtues rivalled in number and brilliancy the stars of heaven; they choose him rather from
amongst those who appear to be in the present day
most richly endowed with the power of working
miracles; that is to say, they choose their Patron
Saint amongst those who can do more for their temporal interests, not among those who have exerted
themselves the most to ensure their eternal welfare.
My brethren, is not this a poor, one-sided, interested
devotion, resembling the piety of the well-known
French King Louis XI., who confined himself to
enriching the altars and venerating the shrines of
those Saints who died at an advanced age, hoping by
their means to obtain for himself a long life? Far be
it from me, however, to condemn the excellent usage
prevailing in the Church, of paying homage and giving
honour to Saints for the sake of temporal benefits.
For when the thirsty earth after long drought opens her
hundred mouths in search of refreshment, let Paris have
its Géneviève who, in the time of need, dissolves the
clouds in gentle rain; let Avignon have its Agricolus,
Brindisi its Theodorus to avert the fierce hailstorms so
destructive to the autumn vintage; let the inhabitants
of Lingonia invoke their bishop Saint Urban, who is
generally represented as holding in his hand a fine

cluster of grapes; nor let the mariners shipwrecked in the Mediterranean hesitate to cry aloud to Saint Elmo; nor those who have been bitten by mad dogs fervently to invoke Saint Hubert, whilst those stung by venomous serpents should turn to Saint Amabilis. Let him who is tortured by gout have recourse to Saint Gebuinus, and the fevered patient to Saint Hugo; in fact whatever the disease by which the sufferer is afflicted, he will find some Saint to help his special need. But how great a mistake to let the worship of the Saints stop short here, else when these interested motives are wanting, they will remain neglected and forsaken, like bankrupt money-changers whose resources have failed. My second reason for thus addressing you is that in the present day there are not a few devout persons who make their whole devotion to consist—in what? In tasting in their mouths a sweet or savoury flavour when they return from the altar after Communion, as if they had partaken of honey in the comb; in obtaining from God all they ask, either for themselves or for others; in being rapt in ecstasy as soon as they kneel down to pray; or in having their cheeks bedewed with exquisite tears of consolation when hearing Mass, reciting the rosary, or meditating on some holy mystery, so that their countenance at such times may be compared to a dewy cloud, lit up with rosy tints and dissolving beneath the rays of the sun into gentle rain. And can all these things be put down as certain proofs of sanctity? No, my brethren. Sometimes under such external devotion a snare of the Evil One may lurk, like a venomous snake beneath flowers, or a poisonous herb in the green pasture. And if in some cases these gifts are indeed favours from Heaven, and not illusions of the devil, even then it is not in them that true sanctity consists. In what does it consist? It consists in this, that if perchance words of blame are addressed to you instead of eagerly seeking to justify and exculpate yourselves, as the imperfect do, you humbly bend your head, and listen to them in silence, glad to appear blameworthy in the sight of men, so long as you can thereby render yourselves all the more praiseworthy in the sight of God; in this, that you are ready to make peace with any one who has shown himself your enemy, nay, even endeavouring to render him good for evil, honour for contempt, praise for reviling; in this, that if it please God to make you poor, you are content with your poverty; if sick, you bless Him for your sufferings; if afflicted, you give Him thanks for your tribulations; that, far from envying the prosperity of others, you willingly give precedence to such of your fellow-citizens to whom God may have given superiority either of rank, wealth or power; and not only willingly give precedence to them, but also do all that lies within your power, if need be, to enhance their greatness, following the example of the little streams which contribute their small quota of waters to swell the mighty rivers which take their source in the same soil as they do themselves. In this and this alone, according to the opinion of all the truly wise, does real virtue consist. And what are we to think of those other superhuman, extraordinary, and special gifts, which we term *gratis datæ*? Here a distinction must be made. If you perceive them in others, you must for the most part, reverence them as excellent; if in yourselves, you must regard them with suspicion, and refrain from attaching great importance to them. Bear in mind the teaching of Saint Chrysostom, with which I will conclude my discourse. If, says that Saint, it was offered you to choose between two things, whether you would, by means of some supernatural alchemy, convert the dust of the streets into so much gold, or, on the other hand, tread riches under your feet as the dust of the streets, conformably to the teaching of the Gospel, on which of the two ought your choice to fall? The second, exclaims Saint Chrysostom; for although it is true that by your miraculous powers you would be enabled to relieve many poor, found many hospitals, enrich many churches, yet you might easily occasion serious harm, by awakening in others who witnessed your actions, love of money and envy of your miraculous gifts, leading them into strife and confusion, and causing them to soil themselves whilst endeavouring to possess themselves of that precious dust.

But if, for the love of Christ, you succeed in despising such riches as you possess, you will be infallibly certain to benefit others; you will put the bad to shame, you will encourage the good, and set an example which all may easily follow without envyings and contention. In the same way, if you heal the sickness of others you incur the risk of creating disturbance, but in bearing your own sufferings with cheerful patience there is no such danger; if you unloose the tongues of others, you may give occasion of grievous sin, but in guarding your own lips with jealous care no harm can be done; and this is true in all cases. Sanctity enables its possessor to walk with most security when it is unaccompanied by miracles; for miracles are like torches carried in the hand which shine on the face of the bearer, but cast no light at his feet; and whilst they render him plainly discernible to others even from afar, he is himself liable to stumble at every step, unless he proceeds with greatest caution. This subject is treated at great length by the golden-mouthed Doctor. If this be all true, O Christians! what excuse have we for not becoming saints? Which of us cannot with the help of God learn to despise riches? who cannot subjugate his passions? who cannot curb his tongue? Which is, in other words, to acquire that sanctity which, though the least apparent, is nevertheless the surest. God demands from us nothing which is beyond our power; hence it is that in heaven virtue is esteemed, not miracles; merit is rewarded, not gifts. It is indeed certain that there hath not risen among them that are born of women a greater than John the Baptist, and that the throne he occupies in Paradise is one of the loftiest, that the bliss he enjoys is exceedingly great, and yet it is no less certain that no miracle was ever worked by his hand: "John indeed did no sign."

PANEGYRIC IN HONOUR OF SAINT STEPHEN, THE PROTO-MARTYR,

THE FIRST WHO FOR CHRIST'S SAKE LAID DOWN HIS LIFE.

A GIFTED poet of antiquity, by name Martial, equally celebrated for the majesty of his graver works, the witticism of his jests, and the bitterness of his satires, is so struck with astonishment at the intrepidity of that generous but unfortunate Roman youth of whom we read that he burnt his own right hand in a slow fire because it had failed to accomplish a deed no less disastrous than magnanimous, that he exclaims in admiring wonder: "After such a glorious action it is needless to know what he did previously; for it is enough for me to see and know this hand." "What need," he asks, "what need for me to recount with useless prolixity the earlier feats of Mucius' prowess (such was the name of the youth)? Would you have me gaze on the rivers of blood he caused to flow, the mountains of corpses he piled up, the laurels his sword won for him, the trophies he erected in the Capitol? I tell you, I care to know none of these things. It is needless to know what he did previously. And why so?

Because when I see a man reach such a height of courage as not to hesitate to consume his right hand in the fire rather than imperil his reputation, I care to ask no more about him." So lofty a deed, even were it the only one of its kind, is enough to enable us to form an opinion of the whole man, because no one ever springs at one bound from the depth of cowardice to the height of valour; the weakness of human nature, timid at the outset, but gathering courage at every step, generally requiring many great deeds to be done before one of this nature can be achieved. I know, my brethren, that many pulpit-orators are wont to regret the sparing mention made by the inspired writers in Holy Scripture of the Proto-Martyr Stephen, a Saint held by the Church in such high repute and honour. They regret that whilst his death is related in Holy Scripture at considerable length, so little is told us about his life; and as if feeling their burning eloquence confined within too narrow limits, they long to be able to enlarge from the pulpit on the manner in which the Saint conducted himself when, as the scholar of Gamaliel, he disputed in the schools; when, as the disciple of Christ, he preached the Gospel in the cities; when, in his capacity of Deacon, he served at the altar; or when, as guardian of widows, he disposed of the alms of the faithful. But, for my part, were I to meet with any one who would give me information of this kind, I should nevertheless prefer to follow the example of the heathen poet whose words I have already cited, and profess my indifference to such details. I should in fact deem it a disparagement of the unequalled heroism exhibited by Saint Stephen in being the first to give his life for Christ, were I, knowing thus much, desirous of knowing anything more. It is needless after such a glorious action to know what he did previously. For can it be imagined that so grand an action was not preceded by other deeds of generous heroism, other splendid victories? since, as the holy Pontiff Saint Gregory says: "No one ever became perfect all at once, but in good conversation every one begins with the least, that he may attain to the greatest." Triumphs are not for the warrior in the outset of his career; his brow must wear the parsley, the fir, the olive, and the oak, ere he can claim the laurel for his own. If then you are anxious that I should acquaint you with all Saint Stephen's greatness, let me speak to you of this his greatest deed, namely, his death; thus I shall show all that is involved in his having gained for himself the title of the Church's Proto-Martyr.

Do not imagine, my hearers, that I am not well aware that the present time is one by no means favourable to the cause I have in hand; for how can we be expected to understand the great and special merit of giving one's life for Christ, now that the Church's annals tell us how vast are the number of men, women, youths, children, and even infants, who have succeeded in acquiring it? Do not deceive yourselves; already I hear those words of friendly warning addressed to me by Saint John Chrysostom, bidding us remember "that to walk on an old and well-worn track is one thing, and another to open a new and untried path." The difficulty is not the same in passing over a trodden and smooth road, after many travellers, and in passing over one which now for the first time is opened, which is rough, stony, full of wild beasts, and has never been traversed by any one. Nowadays, we can while away an idle hour on the sea-shore watching the ships about to set sail, talking gaily with the sailors, jesting with the crew, bidding a smiling farewell to the passengers, before setting out on the sea. But was it thus, think you, on the launch of the first barque which ever traversed the ocean? How different was then the case! Picture to yourselves how the relatives, the friends, the acquaintances of the celebrated Argonauts hung around them, full of anxious apprehension. "Where are you going?" (thus weeping children, doubtless, addressed their sires, and wives, with dishevelled hair, their husbands); "what are you going forth to encounter, O wretched men? A rock against which you will be beaten to death, a wind to destroy you, a whirlpool to swallow you up? Is your life such a weariness to you, that, instead of tranquilly awaiting at home that death which will surely come, you must needs rush madly out to meet a thousand deaths never meant to be your lot? What will you do when you witness the war of elements, the strife of Eurus with Caurus, of Aquilo and Auster, knowing full well that your lives are to be the victor's prize? Is it possible that in the midst of this fierce struggle yon frail barque will afford you any protection, solitary, forsaken, tempest-tossed, without means of escape from a host of insidious dangers and a crowd of foaming furies to whom compassion is a thing unknown?" In words such as these, perhaps, would the timid souls, with clasped hands and streaming eyes, give vent to their fears; and when they saw their dear ones persist with magnanimous daring in going forth upon the deep, with what vows would they besiege the stars to shine serenely upon the travellers, how would they entreat the waves to murmur gently, and petition the winds to breathe favourably on them! But now it is the exception to find a single prayer sent up to Heaven on behalf of the ship to which a man is about to intrust himself, or "the other half of himself," as a poet gracefully termed the friend of whom he was taking tender leave on the sea-shore. What is the reason of this vast difference between embarkations past and present, departures then and now? Do not our ships in the present day plough the same seas? are they not liable to strike on the same rocks? do they not expose themselves to the same tempests? Most certainly they do; but who would dream of instituting a comparison between the ship which sails where so many have sailed before, and the one which is the first to launch out upon the deep? The difficulty is not the same in passing over a smooth and beaten track, after many travellers, and in passing over one which is now opened for the first time. Where the first have waded through the waters in safety, they have shown the way for others to follow, as from the rocks where others have perished those that come after are warned off; and thus it becomes easy work for us to sail in regions where the failure of others serves to make us cautious, or their success to render us more courageous. Now, what we have been saying holds equally good in regard to all those who generously plunged into the red sea of their own blood for the glory of Christ or the good of the Church. It is, indeed, true that they all traversed the same road which the first Martyr had trod; but then they had a leader on that unknown path, but when we speak of any one being the first and foremost to enter on this hitherto untried road it is equivalent to saying that he was without a guide. "Stephen leads the host of purple-robed Martyrs." Such are the words in which Saint Peter Chrysologus expresses his admiration of the Proto-Martyr. Very different sentiments must have animated that breast. It is hardly credible how much encouragement is afforded by the mere sight of some one who goes before us. Soldiers advance more boldly to the assault when they see someone has already succeeded in scaling the walls; the pearl-fisher dives with greater confidence when he has seen another plunge below the waters. And, whether deceived by foolhardy presumption or inspired by reasonable hope, every one believes that what his fellow-man has done he too may do. Have you not heard of the alarm which seized on the soldiers under the leadership of Simon, the illustrious Machabean captain, when they reached the banks of the impetuous torrent which had to be crossed ere they could give battle to the enemy? Out of an army of 20,000, not one man at first possessed the courage to attempt the passage. But no sooner did they behold their undaunted general wading through the waters than they hastened to follow his example as eagerly as if competing for some prize. "He went over first; then the men, seeing him, passed over after him" (1 Mach. xvi. 6). So true is it that a single individual, who is willing to take the initiative, is able to give an impulse to a thousand hearts by the force of his example, making them despise dangers of the most appalling nature, although, if left to themselves, not one amongst all this number would have been found ready first of all to confront those dangers.

But you will be reminding me, my hearers, that, long before the time of Stephen, others had made the sacrifice of their life in defence of their faith; witness Isaias, who was sawn asunder; Zacharias, who was killed on the very steps of the altar; Eleazar, whose flesh was torn from his bones; besides very many more. This is true, but these men died for a creed which had the prestige of antiquity, which was widely spread, and held in universal honour; which could, looking back to distant ages, enumerate a long succession of Patriarchs and Prophets, of Leaders and of Kings; which from time immemorial had possessed temples, elected its own priests, offered sacrifices; whilst Stephen was, on the other hand, the first to lay down his life for a faith as yet in its infancy, which could boast no other lawgiver than one crucified as a malefactor, and quote no other authority than that of twelve poor fishermen. What unparalleled fortitude must have been required in order to go forth, as he did, to publish his faith, and at the same time to defend it; daring, almost alone, to brave the opposition of a crowd of furious and unbelieving fanatics, of whom an overwhelming majority, comprising all persons of any distinction, were hostile to him; whilst his sympathisers were few, and belonged, moreover, to the humblest classes of society. Furthermore, Saint Stephen had not been brought up in the despised Christian faith, which he was now called upon to defend; he had been educated in the time-honoured code of Moses, which he was then strenuously combating. There is a great difference between laying down one's life in defence of one's hereditary faith against the innovations of a new creed, and dying in support of new tenets as opposed to the beliefs handed down to us by our forefathers. It is natural to us to uphold the faith we have drunk in with our mother's milk. Birth, education, habit, all tend to confirm us in these tenets, and our adherence to them is, moreover, strengthened by the reverence due to our ancestors, who held them; our affection to our parents, who instilled them into our hearts; the teaching of our instructors, who imprinted them on our minds; the universal consent of past ages, who walked by their light; and the example of present times, in which their authority is universally admitted. But to act in direct opposition to those generally received opinions, in which one has been brought up; to assume a position of hostility, not only to the example of those around us, but at the same time to the universal consent of past ages, the teaching of the schools, our affection for our parents, our reverence for our ancestors, to custom, education, and family tradition, ah! this does indeed require mettle of no ordinary kind; it requires a lively faith, plenitude of grace, and a noble intellect! Most of the martyrs laid down their lives for the faith of their forefathers, which they had imbibed in their earliest infancy, and which they clung to with fond affection in their maturer years; at any rate they walked in the footsteps of others when they trod the path which led to death. Stephen alone was destitute of any such support, and deserves on this account to take precedence of all. "If any one can be preëminent among martyrs, he is seen to be the chief who is the first of all," as Saint Augustine writes.

Hence it is that I can bring forward a still more convincing argument in proof of his surpassing merit; for who will not acknowledge that the prospect of imminent martyrdom loses almost all its terrors when the eye is fixed on the glorious reward of those who have already suffered? Of this the Emperor Julian was well aware, and, therefore, during the time of his persecutions, the fiercest, in the opinion of Saint Gregory Nazianzen, ever waged against the Church, he strictly prohibited honours to be shown to the bodies of those Christians who perished for their faith. " He devised the most terrible persecution which the world had ever seen;" such are the words of the Saint in speaking of him; "and he even grudged to the martyrs the honours customarily paid to those who fell in battle." The impious wretch well knew that faith in a heavenly recompense was not so powerful in every breast as to render uninfluential the hope of earthly reward; and he knew moreover that for this reason Christianity had ordained that the ashes of her martyrs should be preserved as precious treasures, and their effigies receive such honours as are ordinarily decreed to the statues of conquerors; in order that these demonstrations might serve as an encouragement to all, not as an inducement to embrace that sort of death, but as a sure proof of the honesty of the cause for which they had suffered. Thus the wicked Emperor, by doing away with all posthumous honours, succeeded so far in cooling the general fervour, that the persecution he instituted may fitly be termed the most terrible of all persecutions, because, by depriving the Christian dead of their well-earned laurels, he weakened for a time the force and vitality of faith in the hearts of the living. Nevertheless, the proud Apostate could not impede the speedy revival and final triumph of religion, so that going to martyrdom was soon looked upon as equivalent to going to receive a crown of glory. Stephen alone, as being the first to lay down his life for our holy faith, was unable to gaze on the glories she bestows on those who suffer for her sake. Would he not naturally imagine that his name would be held in abhorrence, and his memory in contempt? He knew how hated was the creed he preached, and he could expect nothing else but that his friends, to screen themselves from any share in his disgrace, would erase the date of his birth from the family records, and would leave his body after death to be devoured by dogs, as in fact it was left exposed in the open country for a day and a night, before any one dared to give it suitable interment. Let death be stripped of those embellishments with which the piety of the faithful seeks to adorn it, and then we shall see how much greater courage is required to go forth and meet it. Here I must ask your pardon, sons of the great Dominic; and yours, children of the illustrious Francis; and, further, I crave your forgiveness, Fathers of my own Order, if I appear in any way to obscure the brilliancy of your virtue. It is true that many of you, forsaking the comforts of home, go forth cheerfully to encounter dangers in foreign lands; you cross the ocean, you battle with storms, you expose yourselves to all the perils of the deep; you land in unknown climes where you find a barbarous race, speaking a strange tongue, who have no conception of honour or honesty, whose customs are uncouth, whose laws are iniquitous; amongst a people such as these you labour, you suffer, you toil; and for what? To obtain from the hands of an Indian executioner a cruel death; to be crucified, to be strangled, to be burnt alive, to be thrust through with spears, or cut to pieces with an axe. Yet tell me, have you not been witnesses of the honours rendered to those whose example you emulate? Every day their names are read from the annals of sacred martyrology with encomiums and applause; their conflicts are related, their triumphs are extolled; their portraits are painted to adorn your walls, and, as soon as the voice of authority sanctions public adoration, splendid altars are erected to their memory, their bones are enclosed in costly shrines, tapers of virgin wax are burnt in their honour, whilst their names are uttered by every tongue, invoked by every heart. Are not all these alleviations calculated to render the horrors of their death less formidable to the weakness of human nature? And yet who is there but must acknowledge that unflinching courage and well-tested piety are indispensable to meet such a death? In how eminent a degree, then, must these graces have been possessed by Stephen, since he had witnessed none of these triumphs, and could expect nothing else but ignominy would cling to his family, and insults would be offered to his corpse.

And yet, consider awhile who Stephen was. For, had he been one of those Apostles who were admitted to a more perfect knowledge of the heavenly mysteries, so that, like John, he had reposed upon the bosom of Christ, or, like Peter, witnessed the marvellous transfiguration upon the mountain, the faith he manifested would not in such a case have been so wonderful. But that a simple disciple, one not privileged to receive from Christ a special vocation, not admitted to familiar intercourse with Him, nor singled out by a miraculous conversion, that such an one should have been the first to exhibit faith so remarkable does indeed argue in him merit most transcendent, incomparable, immense; so great in fact, that I, for my part, no longer wonder to find Saint Clement go so far as to declare the charity of Stephen equal to the charity of the Apostles themselves; I no longer scruple to unite with Saint Maximus in confidently asserting that in the present instance the disciple surpassed his masters, since in his glorious and triumphant death he outdid the Apostles themselves. Thus he who was inferior in degree was made the first in suffering, and he who ranked as a disciple rose to be a master in his martyrdom.

But I know not wherefore I have so long confined myself to arguments of a higher kind, reasoning *a priori* (to employ the language of the Schools), when I might easily prove my point with arguments more homely and familiar, reasoning *a posteriori*, as the Schoolmen say. How comes it that even the most unlearned know that to be the first in an honourable enterprise is a distinction greatly to be coveted? They learn this from the sight of the reward allotted to the foremost. The Roman soldier, having once seen that promotion and emolument became the portion of him who first cast himself into the trench of the beleaguered citadel, or first boarded the ships of a discomfited fleet, required no studied discourse to teach him to look on the foremost one with an esteem quite distinct from that in which he held those who came after. Why should not we apply this to our case? Does not the recompense which awaited the first martyr suffice to convince us of the magnitude of his merit? And oh! my hearers, that recompense was indeed of the sublimest order! Every one knows that the highest reward which a generous prince can bestow upon the subject who has deserved well at his hands, is to dispense largely of his best gifts to others, at the request of that subject. This power of impetration is the last privilege granted to a favourite, when, as far as he himself is concerned, he has received all that it is possible for his master to bestow on him; how much then must he have already received whose petitions can obtain much in behalf of others? Such, then, was the prize which Stephen won; the privilege of asking and obtaining for others the choicest gifts contained in the treasury of God. This was clearly seen when he succeeded in gaining the faith for Paul, and Paul for the faith. Did not this display his great power of intercession? Behold him converting a sinner into a saint, a bloodthirsty persecutor into a Doctor and Apostle of the Church. And what an Apostle was this one! One who, when scarcely converted to the faith, was caught up into heaven, to hear unutterable secrets, to enjoy the beatific vision of God; whose indefatigable footsteps traversed the whole earth, arousing the world with the thunders of his eloquence, enlightening it with the refulgence of his doctrine; who was admired by pagan philosophers in the Schools; who proved an invincible antagonist to the Jews in the Synagogues, a formidable enemy to superstitious heathen in the temples; whom his antagonists failed to convict in the tribunals, and Princes in the court were forced to respect. One, moreover, who endured shipwrecks, despised scourging, bore imprisonments; who toiled, struggled, suffered, wore himself out, for the sake of spreading the same religion, whose followers he had formerly terrified with threatenings, and persecuted with the sword. Does not the fact of gaining such an Apostle as Paul afford abundant proof of the power of Stephen? But why should I say the gaining of Paul alone? It is universally known and admitted that the blood of martyrs is the seed of the Church; therefore the blood of the first martyr was the first seed of Christianity, and a fertile seed indeed it proved. Saint John Chrysostom, contemplating the tender blades sprouting everywhere throughout the wide field over which the seed had been cast, exclaimed: "Stephen was uprooted, and Paul sprang up, and all those who believed through Paul." I call on you, inhabitants of Arabia, of Soria, of Lycaonia, of Cilicia, of Phrygia, of Galatia, of Macedonia, of Cyprus, of Malta, of Candia, of Rhodes; I bid you raise your heads and answer me. To whom were you indebted for your salvation? Was it not to the preaching of Paul? And if to the preaching of Paul, still more primarily to the blood of Stephen. And if we must give faith to the assertion of Saint Augustine, that if Stephen had not prayed, the Church would never have had Paul, who can tell what would then have been your sad fate, O ye nations? You would, perhaps, have continued to love your darkness; you would, perhaps, never have shaken off your former fetters; accursed, miserable strangers to the true faith, enemies of heaven, your fate would have been to feed the eternal fires of hell. Nor is this all; for if from the Epistles of the same Paul, as from an inexhaustible quiver, the Church has ever drawn new arrows, wherewith to strike down the monsters who, from time to time, rise up to wound and tear her anew, must she not confess that, after Paul who gives her weapons, she is principally indebted to Stephen, who gave her Paul? We see a Calvin trembling with rage in France; we hear a Luther roaring in Germany, pierced by the keen shafts of these unanswerable arguments. But if these heresiarchs, in their pride, rage against Paul, why do they not acknowledge the virtue of him who gave Paul to the Church? for, truly enough, but for Stephen's prayers, the Church would not have had such a champion to oppose them, and they would not have found a victor to defeat them so signally.

If, as we have already remarked, one who is able to impetrate so much for others, must already have received a yet larger measure of gifts for himself, how vast must the spiritual wealth of Stephen have been, since God made him the dispenser to multitudes of that choicest of all gifts, the knowledge of the true faith. Nor must we imagine that God acted thus only on one solitary occasion, when He granted the conversion of Saint Paul to the prayers of Stephen. No, in all times, under all circumstances, amongst all peoples, one of the most effectual means whereby to overcome the incredulity of unbelievers has been recourse to Saint Stephen's intercession. Although this observation has often struck me forcibly whilst bending over the pages of ecclesiastical history, yet I should scarcely have ventured to have proposed it to you as fruit of my own reflections, had I not afterwards chanced to meet with it in the writings of Lorinus, who is celebrated for his Commentary on the Scriptures. This learned man avers that as God has adorned each individual Saint with some special gift whereby they render themselves conspicuous, thus He has bestowed on Stephen the power of bringing to the knowledge of Christ souls most obstinately persistent in their rejection of the truth. I might bring many proofs in confirmation of what I say, but I would rather refer any one requiring further testimony on this point to the writings of Saint Augustine, where he will find recorded the marvellous conversion of the Jews in the island of Minorca, of the heathen by the waters of the Tibilitanus, besides numerous other instances. I will select but one. Who is there amongst you, my hearers, but has heard with astonishment of the wonderful transformation of Hungary, which from a stronghold of idolatry became a citadel of the true faith? Its earliest inhabitants, the Huns, taught the whole world to tremble at the mere mention of their name; they repeatedly laid waste Saxony, France, and, above all, our own unhappy country of Italy, in those days a sad scene of conflagration, plunder, slaughter, and captivity. And yet those very Huns, once the most ferocious of barbarous tribes, became in later times the most pious of Christian nations, remarkable for learning, distinguished for wisdom, eminent for sanctity; in fact, no inconsiderable portion of the hagiology of modern times is composed of the glorious records of their Saints. And to whom is due the honour of this marvellous transformation, if not to the Proto-Martyr Stephen? It was the will of Providence that to him in the first place the Church should owe the conquest of that famous nation, the moral regeneration of those benighted heathen; therefore he was sent to announce the approaching reformation to the wife of Geiser, Prince of Hungary. It was at a time when this princess, whose name was Sarolta, was near childbirth, that Stephen, in his deacon's habit, appeared to her, and with smiling countenance addressed to her these words of kind encouragement: "Know," he said, "that the hour of salvation for thy subjects is close at hand. To the child that shall be born of thee thou shalt give the name of Stephen; continually protected by my care, he shall bring peace to his nation, not only by governing it wisely, but by subjugating it to the true faith. He shall be the first to wear the regal crown in Hungary; but nobler by far than the diadem he shall wear on earth is that which is already prepared for him in heaven." The princess, astonished at this vision and at the words she heard, asked the Saint who he was; "I am Stephen, the Proto-Martyr," he replied, and so saying he disappeared swift and bright as the lightning-flash. The prophecy was speedily fulfilled, the princess gave birth to a son, who received at his baptism the name of Stephen, and afterwards became that first King of Hungary, equally renowned for his brilliant victories and his eminent sanctity; who was to earn from a grateful nation the name of Apostle of his country, and thus succeed in uniting for the first time in his own person two titles hitherto deemed so incongruous, namely, those of king and apostle. And now tell me, my hearers, why did God ordain that the Hungarian people should owe their conversion to the sanctity of their king Stephen, and that the royal Saint should in his turn owe his sanctity to the patronage of the Proto-Martyr; why, if not in order that both might see and acknowledge the true author of so memorable a change? We will not dispute the claim of others to the possession of various miraculous powers, such as restoring the sick, giving sight to the blind, raising the dead to life; but to prove the merits of Stephen it is sufficient if we can assign to him that highest privilege of all, the power of converting unbelievers to the faith. It would, I am well aware, be no difficult task to set before you a proud array of the infirm to whom he has restored vigour, of the lepers whom he has cleansed, of the dumb whose tongues he has unloosed, of the cripples who through him have recovered the use of their limbs. For we find Saint Augustine, when he wishes to confute those who deny the continuance of miraculous powers in the Church, bringing forward those miracles alone which had been wrought in his own day by the intercession of Saint Stephen; these he declares to be so numerous that many volumes would be required to record them all, and on this account he confines his attention to some of the most remarkable, narrating amongst these the history of the resuscitation of seven dead persons. I might repeat how, by the experience of a girl in Carthagena, it was discovered that devils did not dare to approach his relics; how, as the Huns saw in France, the devouring flames did not venture to injure his temples. I might, moreover, recount the numerous prodigies attendant on the joyful discovery of his hallowed remains, the supernatural light which dispelled the gloom, the earthquake which unlocked the grave, the bounteous rains which closed a season of drought and scarcity; so that all the world suddenly became anxious to possess at least some trifling portion of so great a treasure. Rome, the queen of cities, having obtained a royal share, was witness of the graceful courtesy which the body of Saint Lawrence showed to that of Saint Stephen, which was placed by its side, for the body of St. Laurence withdrew to the left side, as if he would, with courteous deference, yield the place of honour, on the right, to one so worthy of all respect. But it is unnecessary to multiply those proofs of sanctity which are common to other Saints; let me rather dwell on what is peculiar to Stephen, the power spoken of above, of converting a Saul into a Paul, stubborn heretics into orthodox Christians, pagans into Saints. Let others, if they see fit, employ themselves in searching out all the various graces bestowed upon Stephen; we are content to know that he received, as the guerdon of his heroic death, the highest gift of all. And when we wish to prove him to rank inferior perhaps to no one Saint of the Church, is it not enough to say that it was he who headed the white-robed army of her martyrs?

SECOND PART.

To proceed with my subject; it would be useless for me to remind you of the readiness with which God listens to the prayers of Stephen, were not Stephen on his side equally ready to turn a prompt ear to the petitions of his devout clients. And I would urge this as a powerful motive to induce you to have recourse to a patron so illustrious, so distinguished, as I consider Saint Stephen to be. For if, as we know, he showed such generous kindness towards his enemies, what will he not show towards his clients? If he pleaded so earnestly for those who stoned him, will he not intercede for those who invoke him, who reverence and worship him? If he prayed for those who had not asked his prayers, will he not do as much for us who implore them? To me this seems beyond a doubt, for in benefiting our enemies we perform an act of charity, whereas we are almost constrained by the very claims of justice to show kindness to our friends. One who is by nature so ready to perform them on behalf of those who, far from soliciting his favours, despised and rejected them, will assuredly not fail to confer them where they are not only desired but earnestly requested. In illustration of this, let me relate a very remarkable occurrence, in order that all whom my arguments have failed to convince, may yield to the resistless logic of facts.

In the year 1147, at the time when Spain was still under the dominion of the Moors, King Alphonsus advanced at the head of a large army against Almeria, a city of Granada. The undertaking being one of no inconsiderable difficulty, he had sought the alliance of several other Potentates and the assistance of other States, amongst them Catalonia, which furnished a large contingent of picked squadrons, both land forces and maritime, under the command of Admiral Galzerano dei Pini, Baron of Baga. The city was attacked by sea and land; but although the assailants displayed the utmost bravery, they were repulsed and routed; and the admiral himself, having ventured too far in front of his soldiers, was overtaken and made prisoner, to the great rejoicing of the Moors, who carried him into the city and confined him in a strong tower, heavily ironed. The news of his captivity soon reached the ears of his parents, who, overwhelmed with grief, sent immediately to entreat the King of Granada to name terms of ransom. This barbarian, for such indeed he was, demanded a large sum of money, a number of horses, a large quantity of cloth, and (the most important item of all) he further demanded one hundred maidens of rare beauty to be his slaves. Who can conceive the grief and indignation which filled the hearts of the unhappy parents, when they listened to this inhuman proposal? Seeing, however, no other way open to them whereby to obtain their son's deliverance, they set to work, and by dint of strenuous exertions succeeded in accumulating the required ransom, with the exception of the one hundred maidens. The great difficulty now was how to find these; Galzerano's father, therefore, convened his vassals, and having explained to them the state of affairs, asked if they could suggest an expedient. These vassals were greatly attached to their young lord, and, with a loyal devotion rare indeed, scarcely to be commended, and certainly not to be imitated, they offered to part with their own daughters, making the rule that whosoever had three should give up two, that he who had two should give up one, and that he who owned but one should draw lots with another similarly circumstanced. In this way the requisite number was at last got together, and the unfortunate girls were forced to quit their homes. I leave you to imagine their departure; the tears, lamentations, and confusion with which it was attended. The heart-broken mothers, weeping to see their innocent daughters thus sent among infidels, openly upbraided their husbands for delivering these tender lambs into the jaws of the wolf, these gentle doves into the talons of the hawk. They cursed the hour in which they had brought them into the world, they tore their hair, they wrung their hands, they disfigured their faces; but sighs and tears were unavailing, and, after giving their unfortunate children one final embrace, they were constrained to let them go. On the other hand, the victims could hardly speak through the very intensity of their grief, and amidst sobs their eyes implored that mercy which their tongues were unable to ask. Thus they proceeded towards Tarragona, on their way to the port of Salo, where the ship which was to take them on board lay at anchor. Meanwhile, the imprisoned admiral, in ignorance of the exertions being made elsewhere on his behalf, was all intent during his wearisome captivity in endeavouring to move Heaven to have pity on him; and addressed fervent supplications by day and night to the illustrious Proto-Martyr Stephen, the patron of his city and his state, to whom he had a great devotion. The Saint was not slow to hear him. One night, when the admiral was praying with more than his accustomed fervour and humility, Stephen appeared to him in a magnificent deacon's vestment; he cheered and encouraged him, and, taking him by the hand, bade him follow him. The rattling of chains and the sound of voices catches the ears of the jailers; hastening to the cell, they draw their swords, seize their halberts, and take their keys to unfasten the door, but all in vain; the lock resisted their most violent efforts, and they were at length compelled to burst open the door. But long ere this the Saint had, by means known only to himself, conducted his client beyond the confines of the prison, although, to make the wonder greater, the latter remained encumbered by his fetters and chains; nor did his protector leave his side until, at break of day, he found himself in safety in the seaport town of Salo. The morning of his arrival there was the very one appointed for the embarkation of the unhappy maidens, who were destined to purchase their master's freedom at the cost of becoming the slaves of a barbarian; and now, more disconsolate and dejected than ever, they filled the air with their cries as they advanced, and mingled their sobs with the murmur of the waves. The admiral, astonished at the sight of this mournful procession, inquired of a bystander what was the destination of the weeping band. In reply, the person addressed informed him that they were on their way to the King of Granada; and told him all particulars concerning the occasion and object of their journey. Deeply moved by what he heard, the young man could no longer contain his emotion; but, hastening towards the tearful company, he bade them pause, exclaiming: "He whom you go to ransom is no longer

a captive; he is at liberty, he is here before you; I am
that admiral. Look at me, O faithful subjects; behold
the master you love so well, who, though he still retains
his fetters, is now no longer a captive!" Where shall
words be found to describe the stupefaction, the amazement, the bewilderment caused by these words? Mistrusting the testimony of their ears, all crowded around
the speaker to convince themselves with their own
eyes that they were not deceived; and, though they
beheld and even touched him, they still feared lest it
were all a dream. But he dispelled their wonder, or
rather, he increased it, by relating in detail the story
of his deliverance through the interposition of Saint
Stephen; how, in answer to his prayer, the Saint had
so kindly come to his rescue, had led him out of the
prison and brought him to that shore. You can imagine how grateful and reverent were the ejaculations
that rose to Heaven! tears of grief were changed into
tears of joy, lamentations into rejoicings; the maidens,
falling on their knees, gave thanks to their heavenly
protector who, in saving one, had saved so many; and,
in bringing deliverance to their prince, had at the same
time preserved to them all home and country, reputation and freedom, innocence and even life itself. Galzerano was soon relieved of his heavy chains and
prison garments; once more suitably attired, he set
out with the others on the road to his ancestral home.
As soon as the church of the Proto-Martyr could be
descried, although at the distance of half a league, all
prostrated themselves in reverent adoration; and the
admiral persisted in accomplishing the remainder of
the way on his knees, although this was attended with
such pain and laceration that it resulted in a fresh cap-

tivity, the wounds thus produced rendering him unable to leave his house for a year afterwards. Meanwhile, the news of his approach had preceded him to the city; the inhabitants flocked out to meet him and welcome him with joy; and he had the satisfaction of restoring to the weeping mothers the daughters who had been freed ere they knew the yoke of slavery. Nor was this all; for he provided each with a liberal dowry, besides showing to their fathers his sense of the obligation he was under to them, by conferring on them many honourable distinctions. With his father's consent, he made over to the church of Saint Stephen a moiety of the tithes produced by his barony; and shortly after, wishing to consecrate entirely to God the life which had been preserved to him so miraculously, he withdrew to a Cistercian monastery, where, after leading an exemplary life, he died a holy death. How few other Saints are there, my brethren, of whom instances can be related of their having brought to their devout clients assistance so prompt, so efficacious, so extraordinary! It is not necessary that I should name the author from whom I have this story, because he is of modern times; he is, however, a learned and well-known writer, and a member of the Cistercian order; besides which he affirms the occurrence to be well-known in Catalonia, and mentions several old chronicles in which he had met with it.

What heart is there so cold as not to be inflamed with devotion to Saint Stephen, on seeing him to be equally willing and powerful to help his faithful clients? How kindly he condescended to come himself to the prison to take the captive by the hand, and lead him to a place of safety! But on this I will enlarge no longer, but rather repeat my former question: Have we not seen how merciful Stephen was to his enemies? Let this suffice to prove how generous he will be to his friends. And if, O our illustrious Proto-Martyr (for I venture, in all humility, to address you this morning in the name of those here present), if you requited the cruelty of your persecutors with such magnanimous generosity, will your heart suffer you to despise the tribute of our loving devotion? I remember how Joab, perceiving that on a certain occasion king David, in his exaggerated love for his rebellious son Absalom, was unduly harsh to his faithful soldiers and defenders, did not scruple to tell him that such conduct would alienate his best friends, as they would see that to injure David was the surest way to gain his favour. "Thou lovest them that hate thee, and thou hatest them that love thee; and thou hast shown this day that thou carest not for thy nobles, nor for thy servants" (2 Kings xix. 6). Far be it from me to presume to address you in such language, which on my lips would be nothing short of sacrilege or madness; but one thing I would fain say, and it is this: If it had been our unhappy lot to be amongst the number of those who stoned you, if impelled by blind fury and barbarous impiety we had taken up those missiles to cast at you, if we had been amongst the number of your murderers, we should then most assuredly have shared in the inestimable benefit of your prayers; prayers which obtained the conversion of Paul, and of many others at the same time, as Saint Peter Damian avers, saying that in virtue of those prayers your enemies were changed into so many friends. Shall it then be to our disadvantage, O holy martyr, that we were not among the number of your enemies? God forbid. Would you have it appear a thing to be desiderated by any one of us to have had part in a work of cruel persecution? You pledged yourself to a great deal, when you interceded for those who stoned you, for in so doing you laid yourself under a perpetual obligation to offer prayers no less fervent for those who venerate you, who invoke you; otherwise some might make bold to reproach you with loving those that hate you, and not caring for your adoring friends and servants. Surely it shall never be said of you who rewarded the injuries of your enemies, that you do not repay our homage with an equal liberality. Therefore we unanimously choose you this morning for our common advocate; I for my part gladly offer you my whole self. I shall rejoice to employ in your service, when occasion presents itself, my time and labour, my breath and being; in the hope that you may make me worthy to tread in your footsteps, and follow your example even by laying down my life.

PANEGYRIC IN HONOUR OF SAINT IGNATIUS OF LOYOLA, FOUNDER OF THE SOCIETY OF JESUS,

WHO CONTINUALLY SOUGHT THE GREATER GLORY OF GOD, AND WHOM GOD, THEREFORE, GREATLY GLORIFIED.

"Whosoever shall glorify me, him will I glorify."—
1 KINGS ii. 30.

SINCE it is an undoubted truth, my brethren, that the sons of an illustrious father must necessarily partake, to a certain extent at least, in the glory of their parent, you will understand the difficulty I feel in entering upon the subject I have to treat of this morning; for I am called upon to pronounce the panegyric of that illustrious Patriarch of whose family I gratefully own myself a member, the least worthy, it is true, but not the least loving. Is there not, on this account, reason to fear that the lofty deeds and splendid achievements which I shall have occasion to relate to you will be received with some degree of suspicion; for if the glories of Saint Ignatius are of so transcendent a nature as to savour of exaggeration, even when recounted by the lips of a stranger, how much more will this be the case when one of his own sons undertakes their recital? Would not any one be pardoned for imagining that filial affection might lead me to represent them as greater than they really are; or self-interest might, perhaps, prompt me to solicit the aid of rhetoric to dress up the truth and render it more imposing. Behold then the dilemma in which I am placed; either I must, with despicable cowardice, conceal the merits of the Saint, or, with affected humility, strive to depreciate them. To act thus would be to betray my trust, and wilfully withhold the truth from a morbid fear of appearing to display it in too ostentatious a manner. You see, then, the painful alternative before me; I must either be false, whilst endeavouring to seem truthful, or seem false whilst trying to be truthful. I know not, in fact, my brethren, how I should contrive to extricate myself from this embarrassing position, were it not that the character of the audience I have the happiness to address is such as to solve every doubt, relieve all my anxieties, and, far from diminishing my courage, serve only to augment it. My fears would, I own, be but too well-founded, had I to speak of Ignatius to persons possessing small knowledge of his work, and little affection for his person; I know, however, that in the present instance, I speak to those who gladly assemble year by year to celebrate his festival and listen to his praises. The unusual numbers present here to-day, the devotion which beams from every eye, the attention depicted on every countenance, all these things concur to bid me open my mouth freely and fearlessly; confident that, how great soever may be the marvels I have to relate of Ignatius, they will create no surprise, for either you will have heard wonders yet greater, or you will be desirous of hearing such. Thus encouraged, then, I will proceed to speak of him rather with the freedom permitted to a stranger than with the reticence becoming a son; taking as my own the words uttered by Velleius under almost similar circumstances: "I will not, whilst relating the truth, suffer the ties of relationship to induce me, through modesty, to withhold anything that is glorious:" Thus laying before you a brief summary of the great merits of Ignatius, I hope to show how amply and how royally in his case the promise was fulfilled by which God bound Himself, in the hearing of all the earth, to render glorious in their turn all who should contribute to promote His glory: "Whosoever shall glorify me, him will I glorify." And since by first acquainting ourselves with all that Ignatius did to glorify God, we shall the better be enabled to understand how he merited that God should do so much to glorify him, we will begin, if you think well, by directing our attention to that part of our subject; for it belongs to the due order of things that the service should ever precede the reward.

I feel myself constrained to acknowledge that ofttimes when I reflect on all the Saint did for the glory of God, I cannot refrain from doubting whether it was indeed one man alone, and not many men, who accomplished so much, since it appears almost inconceivable that one single individual should have been able to act so many parts, to endure so many labours, to gather in so rich a harvest, and to present in his solitary person different types of sanctity of so opposite and apparently contradictory a nature. For, glancing at his life, I see him now a silent anchorite, now an eloquent preacher; at one time a pilgrim wandering through many lands, at another a student rooted to a single spot; now instructing children, and anon framing the constitutions of a Religious Order. One year I found him in Spain, and the next in France; one year in Italy, and the next in Jerusalem. I meet with him in desert caves, and in crowded thoroughfares; in prisons and in Universities, in hospitals and at Court; until bewildered and amazed, I doubt his identity, and ask myself: How is it possible for one and the same individual to be in so many places, or rather how is it possible for one and the same individual to be in so many persons, for he who undertakes labours of so different a nature, is surely not one and the same man? But here a thought strikes me, which tends greatly to lessen my wonder; I remember that these characteristics are precisely those which invariably distinguish one who has devoted himself to the greater glory of God; such an one is ever to be found without country of his own, without will of his own, without habits of his own; ever ready to hasten thither where he discerns an opportunity for advancing the great object he has in view, transforming himself into every possible shape, suiting himself to every imaginable style of person, and like a Proteus of charity, making himself at the same time all things to all men, if by this means he may gain all to God. And would that it had pleased Heaven to call Ignatius earlier to His service, ere thirty whole years, half his life-time, had been wasted in the pursuit of military glory, and the follies of love! What might he not have accomplished for God when his youthful energy and vigour were at their height, since even in maturer years, and with enfeebled health, he achieved so much. But let us not give way, my hearers, to regret; let us rather remember that the noble racer loses nothing through being somewhat late in leaving the starting-place; for in consequence of the delay he is urged on to traverse the course with more rapid strides, and far outstripping all competitors, he wins for himself a more brilliant victory.

Ignatius was no sooner converted than he immediately resolved to leave undone no great thing which he might feel inspired to do for the service of God; and this practical determination to aim in everything at the greater glory of God, which you will perceive to have been the crowning act of sanctity in the case of others, was formed by Ignatius, in the very outset of his conversion. Hell must have been aware of this, for at the same moment when Ignatius, looking up to Heaven, first offered to God this holocaust of himself; the powers of darkness trembled with affright and dismay, and forthwith sought means of encompassing his destruction. And to what means did they resort? They caused a terrible earthquake to shake to their foundation the walls of the apartment where he was, threatening to bury him alive beneath the ruins; but the rage of the demons could only prevail to wreck the walls and shatter the roof of the building, restrained as they were by a strength greater than their own. The newly-enlisted soldier of Christ was not to be daunted by trifles such as these; on the contrary, he viewed them as signs of happy augury, warning him to abandon the frail shelter of such perishable habitations, and it was not long before he bid farewell to the world. But let no one wrongly deem that to have been a cowardly flight which was, in fact, a triumphant victory.

I do not indeed forget that in all ages there have been some who, like Ignatius, have unflinchingly turned their back upon the world, abandoning a high military position and brilliant prospects, to stoop to Christian humility. But could not these men, for the most part, in this very abasement, discern the reflection of their glory, for is it not esteemed a glorious thing to despise honours, when they are voluntarily renounced with magnanimous resolution, not abandoned from motives of pusillanimity? With Ignatius the case was widely different; for he quitted the world immediately after the unfortunate loss of a fortress which he had defended with more valour than success; and under these circumstances who would not have attributed his unlooked-for determination either to cowardly fear, mortified vanity, or brooding melancholy? He himself at least, as we learn from his own lips, anticipated that this and no other would be the judgment universally passed on his conduct; he already imagined that it would be the topic of every letter, the talk of all military men, at their meetings, how this Ignatius Loyola, who was so anxious for distinction in his profession, after having surrendered Pampeluna to the French, had retired in despair to hide himself in lonely caves; and in order not to expose his life again to such terrible risk, had adopted the safer course of retreating to a Hermitage, in whose peaceful shelter he might spend his days singing psalms, instead of facing the artillery of the enemy on the walls of a fortress. These fears of public opinion rose like gloomy phantoms on the threshold of the world he was about to quit, as if to deter him from leaving it; such considerations, however, were powerless to induce him to postpone the step he had resolved on taking until a time when it would be less injurious to him in the eyes of the world. Intent as he was on offering to God a complete and unreserved sacrifice even of his reputation, he would allow of no delay; but ere the wounds received in the last deadly fray were fairly healed, he secretly fled from his home, and having bestowed on a beggar his costly raiment, and hung up over the altar of a church the sword which he had loved so dearly, he provided himself with a garment of sackcloth, girt himself with a cord, and with unsparing self-immolation went about barefoot and bareheaded, with unkempt hair, and untrimmed beard, his whole appearance denoting poverty and neglect; moreover he did not blush to be seen begging his bread from door to door, as if he deemed himself unworthy to enjoy life, except in the character of one dependent on the bounty of others. Now what do you say to this, my hearers? Was it possible for Ignatius, in his desire to promote the glory of God at the expense of his own reputation, to go to greater lengths in his humiliation, abasement, annihilation of self? And who was he, do you think, who did such great things? What rank did he occupy in Biscay, his native country? that of an ignoble peasant? Quite the contrary; he came of the illustrious race of the Ognes, the members of which noble house had distinguished themselves equally in times of peace and war. His childhood had been passed among the Pages of the Court of Ferdinand of Castile; his youth was spent in acquiring knightly accomplishments, whilst manhood found him intrusted with the command of armies. His spirit was haughty, his heart intrepid, his temper vindictive, and his ideas of honour so overstrained that he would gladly have avenged an insult at the cost of his life, as the bee, some would have us believe, is content to pay the penalty of death for the satisfaction of burying its sting in the body of its adversary. It was therefore no small thing for such a man as this, out of love to God, to stoop so low that the roughest peasants of Montferrat and the filthiest beggars of Manresa could insult him with impunity, treat him with contumely and contempt, and count it a disgrace to be seen in his company.

When Ignatius, with lowly self-abasement, had, as we have seen, immolated to God the highest part of himself, his spiritual nature, it remained for him to bring into subjection his lower nature, his flesh, by a series of most painful mortifications, and thus prepare himself, by mastering domestic foes, to battle successfully against the two formidable antagonists which must ever be encountered by those who seek to spread God's glory throughout the world; I mean humiliations and sufferings. And if you imagine that he treated his body with tenderness, listen to me, and listen, if you can, without shuddering. If we inquire into the manner of life he led in the cave of Manresa, we shall see him wearing a garment of sackcloth over a rough hair-shirt, binding around his loins a girdle composed of prickly nettles, sharp thorns, or points of iron; fasting on bread and water every day, except Sundays, and then allowing himself no other indulgence than a dish of bitter herbs mingled with earth or ashes; passing sometimes whole days, three, six, or even eight at a time, without partaking of any food at all; scourging himself five times a day, and always to blood; cruelly beating his bare breast with a heavy

stone, and resting his weary limbs on no better couch
than the hard ground, a stone serving him for a pillow.
Seven hours daily he spent in profound contemplation; his tears were unceasing, his mortifications continuous; nor did he relax anything of the austerity of
this, the unbroken tenor of his life, on account of the
tedious and painful infirmities it soon brought on;
languors, swoons, paroxysms of pain, attacks of debility,
and even dangerous fevers; and now tell me, do you
not think that, reduced to such a state by the excess
of his fervour, he is fit to be placed on a par with
those austere recluses, who at one period of time
peopled so thickly the groves of Nitria and the moun-
tain-caves of Palestine?

But yet, if the truth must be confessed, I own I am
tempted to fear lest this early fervour, so impetuous in
its outset, should be like the mountain torrent, whose
waters dash wildly past us and are gone. Surely this
ill-advised penitent has begun with too much ardour;
he will infallibly break down, and be obliged to give
in, for an overstrung bow cannot fail to break. And
did it not happen as I have said? After a short time
passed in severe mortifications, Ignatius left Manresa,
quitted the grotto, abandoned his solitude, laid aside
the iron girdle he habitually wore; and if he still
retained the hair-shirt next his skin, he at least exchanged his outer garment of sackcloth for an ordinary
one of cloth, of a very poor description it is true, but
not such as to excite remark; he no longer went about
with his feet bare, his head uncovered, his hair un-
dressed; he relaxed the inexorable severity of his
fasts, he began to show himself among the habitations
of men, to mix in their society, to visit them at their

homes, and even to frequent the schools. What may we conclude from this? That the ardent desire which burnt within his breast ever to advance the greater glory of God, at the expense of his own convenience and of his own honour, had already died out? For if his thirst for suffering had really been so intense, would he not have manifested more constancy, persevering unto death in his painful solitude? how was it that his austerities were not augmented rather than diminished? why did he change his dress and alter his manner of life? why did he assume a different character? I am well aware, my hearers, that the situation is one of no small difficulty. For I am absolutely convinced that if Ignatius had spent the remainder of his life in those first practices of mortification and self-inflicted torture, there is not one of you but would have entertained a far higher opinion of his sanctity; for sanctity is in this respect like the stem of an oak, whose external ruggedness is supposed to be in proportion to the vigour of its growth. But let us for a moment suppose Ignatius to have gone on as he began, to have continued in the grotto of Manresa that life which might more fitly be termed death. Had he done so, where would now be all those children of the Church whom he ransomed from the tyranny of vice, or delivered from the darkness of heathenism? Where would be all the souls which he alone converted by his private instructions or public preaching, by his edifying example or excellent institutions? Moreover can we imagine that all those numberless souls would have been saved, who, down to our own day, have owed their conversion to the instrumentality of his sons? Would the millions of barbarians whom Saint

Francis Xavier baptised in the Indies with his own hand, have received the Gospel? Would their idols have been broken in pieces, and consigned to the flames? Would so many new churches have been erected, so many old ones restored and decorated afresh? Would history have had to record the celebrated embassy sent from the unknown shores of remote Japan to offer homage to the Holy Father? Would China have been opened by Ricci to the glorious triumphs of the Cross? Would Brazil have been subjugated by Anchieta, Tonquin conquered by Baldinotti, or a great part of Ethiopia won by Oviedo? Would England have been able to boast a zealous Campion, Germany an indefatigable Canisius, Poland a learned Possevin, France an eloquent Coton, Italy an admirable Bellarmine? Where would have been these able champions whose gifted tongues inflicted on heresy such memorable defeats? Many of the volumes which enrich our libraries, many of the learned doctors who have filled the professor's chair, many of the martyrs who throng the courts of heaven, would have been lost to the world had Ignatius remained in his solitude occupied in weeping over his own faults, instead of issuing forth to correct those of others. I will not deny that as much might perhaps have been done by other Religious Orders, boasting a greater antiquity and enjoying a greater reputation than our own, who have ever toiled and are still toiling to advance the cause of Christianity. But it has been a glorious privilege for us to coöperate with these our elder brethren in their lofty enterprise, to bear a part at least of their burden, to lighten their labours, to share their toils, and to send out additional reapers into the field when the harvest was seen to be most abundant. I should, indeed, lay myself open to the charge of false humility or criminal fear were I to pass unmentioned a well-known truth, one to which successive Pontiffs have borne their solemn testimony, namely, that in those unhappy times which gave birth to a Luther in Germany, a Calvin in France, a Henry VIII. in England, God, Who on the appearance of every new Goliath sends forth a David to slay the giant with the very sword in which he trusts, raised up our Society—a whole phalanx of intrepid warriors—to combat those foes of the Church with the weapons of learning and eloquence; the same weapons of which those foes had already made use with such disastrous effect.

But to return to Ignatius. Surely he does not appear less worthy of admiration as we next behold him, a man of thirty-four years of age, sitting with children on the benches of a grammar school, than he did when we last saw him absorbed in the contemplation of celestial mysteries within the lonely cave of Manresa. And by what was he in both instances inspired, if not by the same desire of spending himself for the greater glory of God? At his mature age, with broken health and opposite inclinations, it must have cost him no small effort to take his place amongst little children, and with them learn concords, recite tasks, stammer out exercises; until, after having passed through every stage, from a pupil in a grammar school he became a Doctor of Theology. One thing, at least, is certain: that the devil busied himself much more with Ignatius the student than he did with Ignatius the contemplative; and gladly would he have bargained to allow him to return unmolested to the grotto, if only he could have induced him to abandon his seat in the school. If you do not credit this, listen to the cunning arts he employed to bring about such a result. Each time when the new scholar entered the class-room, the crafty foe, transforming himself into an angel of light, threw open to him, as it were, the very gates of Paradise. He would bring vividly before his mind the heavenly visions, the ecstasies, the raptures, the ravishments enjoyed in Manresa; he would cause sweet tears to stream from his eyes, and when he saw him open his book in order to learn by heart the first conjugation, he stopped him at the outset, allowing him to go no further than the first words, *amo, amas;* suggesting indeed no impure thoughts, kindling within his breast no unchaste desires, as he might have done in the case of any other man, but inebriating him with ardent desires to love God, he whispered to him words such as these: " O Ignatius ! close the book open before thee; if thou wouldst learn to love aright, then God, Whose love sought thee out when thou wast ungrateful and rebellious, will be Himself thy best teacher. The birds of the wood, who at break of day pour forth glad songs of praise to the Most High, will teach thee how to love; the stars of heaven will teach thee, while by silent night they pay to God the tribute of unceasing homage; even the flowers of the meadow and the herbs of the field, and every stream, together with the wild denizens of the forest, all will in their mute language teach thee to love, by the example they give of submission and obedience to their Creator." Such were the suggestions of the wily tempter; and gradually he succeeded in arousing within the mind of Ignatius so intense a longing for his former solitude, that at last he openly urged him to exchange his noisy surroundings for the charms of solitude, to abandon study and return to contemplation, to leave the classroom, and seek once more the hermit's cell. And, in truth, the Saint, not discerning at first the hidden snare, was on the point of setting out on the way from Barcelona to Manresa, of resuming his garments of sackcloth, of reloading himself with his chains, when a ray of heavenly light discovered to him the precipice yawning at his feet; filled with confusion, he forthwith pledged himself by a solemn oath to pursue his various studies with unwearied energy; and having asked his master to meet him at a certain church, fell at his feet, and confessed to him the temptation which had assailed him, humbly asked forgiveness, and entreated that thenceforth, if he failed to fulfil his tasks in a satisfactory manner, he might be subjected to the penalty of stripes. An act of such deep humility sufficed to prevent the baffled tempter from venturing to repeat his former attack: from that day forward ecstasies and raptures no longer intruded themselves on Ignatius during the hours set apart for study; and you will readily believe that he, striving daily to render himself a more useful instrument in advancing the greater glory of God, not only in his own person but also in others, neglected the use of no means which appeared likely to prove conducive to this great end. For as the sun, when it appears above the horizon, does not successively light up one place after another, but sheds its rays over a whole world, so Ignatius began to spread abroad the light of divine truth at once in the churches and public squares, in the halls of Universities, in the homes of private citizens, and in the neighbouring villages; making it his endeavour everywhere to root out abuses, to reform Convents, to abolish evil customs and dangerous amusements, above all, to revive the salutary practice of frequently approaching the Sacraments, which at that time had fallen into general disuse.

And certainly it appears almost incredible that one who was neither a religious nor a priest, who lived in circumstances of such destitution that he was fain to beg his daily bread, should in a short time have become so influential that a word from his lips was enough to throw into excitement cities of note, such as Barcelona, Alcala, Salamanca, Paris, Venice, and Rome. The conversions he effected in these places were so wonderful, so numerous, and so important, as to cause this bewitcher of hearts (I am using no exaggerated terms) to be cited before the supreme court of each city, and accused of dealing in enchantments. His innocence, however, was on all occasions so evident as invariably to procure for him an acquittal, although the prodigious ascendancy he exercised constantly brought him under fresh suspicion.

And what had he not to endure on account of his zeal for the glory of God? He was attacked by calumny and defamed with insults, he was thrown into prison, bound with fetters and loaded with chains; indeed, upon several occasions he nearly fell a martyr to his zeal, being found half-dead in consequence of the blows he had received from men living in open sin, the partners of whose guilt he had been the means of converting to God. After hearing all this, you will readily believe that no dangers of the road, no inclemencies of the weather, no bodily weakness or mental suffering ever caused him to relax his exertions, or sufficed to check the ardour with which, like an eager sportsman, he was wont to press forward over rocks and precipices, through briars and thickets, whenever the least chance offered itself of gathering some prey into his net. In proof of this, let me relate to you an incident which occurred during his residence in Paris. After having in vain employed exhortations, entreaties, and menaces, in order to induce a young man addicted to immoral practices to change his course of life, Ignatius, as a last resource, determined to lay wait for him, one dark night in the depth of winter, standing in a frozen pond beside the road by which he knew the evil-doer would pass on his way to his sinful indulgences. On seeing him draw nigh, the Saint exclaimed in a voice of thunder: "Go on, unhappy man, pursue thy guilty way; meanwhile, I shall stand here naked, praying and doing penance for thee. Know, moreover, that until thou dost forsake thy sin, every night thou wilt find me here as thou goest, and here I shall be as thou returnest; each time offering atonement in my body for the licentious gratifications accorded to thine." These words fell like thunderbolts on the ears of the young man; appalled and conscience-stricken, he threw himself on the ground. He had surrendered, he was vanquished! A torrent of burning tears streamed from his eyes, a proof of the sincerity of his repentance, which by the warm consolation it imparted to the heart of Ignatius proved the best possible means of restoring animation to his half-frozen limbs. My brethren, does not such conduct evince zeal worthy of an Apostle? It is, I am aware, likewise related of a Bernard, a Cuthbert, an Anselm, a Henry, a Peter Damian, and related as a marvel of fervour and charity, that they plunged their naked bodies into ice and snow; but this they did, let me be permitted to add, in order to extinguish the fire of concupiscence within their own breast, not in that of another. Ignatius alone, as far as I know, performed this last act of heroic charity. Therefore, it was only just that his burning zeal, instead of being cooled by contact with the ice, should be thereby all the more inflamed, and desire more ardently to impart to others its own glowing heat, to kindle the whole universe. And truly, as it was his to bear a name signifying fire, so it was his also to possess that property peculiar to fire, the power of transforming everything into its own substance. For all those who were privileged to stand in intimate relation to Ignatius, not only forsook their sins and aspired to sanctity, but learned moreover to share his zeal for the conversion of all mankind. And this is how it came to pass that he was able to enrich the Church with a new body of religious, all whose members, however widely they might differ as to the country to which they belonged, the language they spoke, the rank they had filled in the world, should yet in spite of all this, be of one mind, one heart, one soul; and all be animated with the self-same desire of kindling everywhere the fire of divine love.

Here it becomes impossible for me, in treating of what Ignatius did for the glory of God, any longer to refrain from speaking of what God did for the glory of Ignatius; for it appeared that God purposed, in reward for the great number of conversions he had made, and the great store of merits he had acquired, to bestow on him in the early years of his conversion, the honour of being the founder of such an Order as the Society of Jesus. Do not imagine, however, my hearers, that it was not till then that God began to exalt him. Such was far from being the case; we know, as an indisputable fact, that even before Ignatius left his bed of sickness, whilst he was still at home, reposing on a luxurious couch shaded by rich canopies, God sent from heaven His Vicegerent and Chief Minister, the Apostle Saint Peter, in bodily form, to restore him to health, and heal the wound he had received at Pampeluna; an honour apparently intended to show how desirous God was of gaining him for His own. But Ignatius was now thirty years of age, the time when a man's passions are often hot and untamed, and they would not allow him to yield altogether to the divine call. What was the result? The Blessed Virgin came down in person from heaven, bearing in her arms the Holy Infant; she entered the chamber where he lay, she showed herself openly to him in all the beauty of her virginal purity, a sight which had so great an effect on Ignatius that concupiscence was completely lulled to rest, or, perhaps, even extinguished within him. From thenceforth he was not only free from all temptations to sensual pleasures, but he became utterly deaf to their voice and insensible to their attractions; as if that lofty and celestial joy had produced on him the same effect which wine made from palms is known to produce, for the man who has once partaken of it finds all other wines insipid, and he himself becomes abstemious. Ought not this favour alone, my hearers, to be held in great account? I know that God has often granted similar favours to persons of eminent sanctity, grown hoary in the pursuit of perfection, consummate in the practice of virtue; but that He should bestow them upon one who not only had not as yet reached the meridian of his career, but had as yet hardly started in the race, this has an appearance of partiality, if one may so speak, which might well excite the envy of the most favoured of God's servants. And if God was pleased to exalt Ignatius by giving him such signal marks of His love, whilst he was as yet a beginner in virtue, as yet a layman, as yet living in the world, and attached to it, what may we not conclude to have been his portion at a later period? You will scarcely be surprised to hear of the marvellously familiar intercourse with God which the Saint enjoyed until the close of his life. He saw Christ face to face about forty times during the period of his retirement in the cave of Manresa; and so many were the visions there vouchsafed to him, so many the secrets unfolded to him, respecting the mysteries of the creation of the world, the redemption of man, and, above all, concerning the most holy Trinity; that if, on emerging from his seclusion, he had found the whole aspect of the world changed, the Holy Scriptures consumed by fire, the records of the Sacred Councils destroyed, churches profaned, pictures burnt, crosses broken, altars overthrown, and all men united in open rebellion against the faith of Christ—nevertheless, on the strength of what had been revealed to him at Manresa, he would, as he said, have been ready to enter the lists single-handed to shed his blood, and, if needs be, lay down his life in defence of the truths so dear to him. And he went even further than this, alleging that the only effect produced on him would be to make him more devoted to the cause of religion; just as the Nile pours into the sea a fuller and more generous tribute of waters at the time when the drought universally prevailing around has dried up all other streams.

And after hearing this, who will wonder that a man so destitute of all literary acquirements, should notwithstanding compose that small but wonderful book, "The Spiritual Exercises?"—a book in praise of which enough is said when we are told how all modern heretics are transported with fury at the very mention of its name; they hesitate not to denounce it openly as a work of the devil, a forge of enchantments, a handbook of the black art. But if we would tell the truth, my hearers, and give the credit where it is due, we must ascribe the composition of this book rather to Mary than to Ignatius, whose whole learning at that time consisted in being able to read and write, and who, as we are informed on the authority of a trustworthy tradition, did no more than transfer to paper the instructions delivered to him orally by the Blessed Virgin, on her frequent and familiar visits to him. Thus he contributed nothing of his own; but merely acted the part of the shell, which receives into its cup the precious drops of heavenly dew, and preserves them for our perpetual benefit. But what would not be the glory accruing to Ignatius could we relate that which the humility of the Saint ever led him to conceal with scrupulous care, namely, all he was privileged to behold during a miraculous ecstasy lasting eight entire days and nights, in the cave of Manresa? It is, at all events, highly improbable that the wondrous revelations he then enjoyed in anywise fell short of those vouchsafed to him later on, when Our Lord repeatedly manifested Himself to him, on different occasions and under varying circumstances. At one time He appears to him on the road to Padua, to cheer him in a time of great dejection; at another time to console him, when, on the voyage to Cyprus, Ignatius was labouring under severe mental anguish; and now, again, at a spot not far from Rome, with a view to encourage him by the promise of a favourable reception in that city. And this last, indeed, is the well-known vision which forms, as it is only right that it should do, the pride and consolation of each member of our Society, whenever he recalls to mind the circumstances I am about to relate to you. Ignatius and his early companions were on their way to the Eternal City, where he contemplated uniting with an indissoluble bond his little band of followers, already one in heart. They had almost reached the gates, when, before entering, Ignatius turned aside to pray in a little secluded chapel on the wayside. His prayer soon became an ecstasy: he beheld the Almighty Father, and heard Him warmly recommending to His Divine Son the projects conceived by Ignatius. And what answer could Our Lord return to this supreme Advocate? In response, He turned towards Ignatius a countenance of kindly love, He beckoned to him to approach, He clasped him to the heavy and blood-stained cross He bore in His arms, and with a gentle smile: "Go on thy way," He said; "I will be propitious to thee in Rome." It appears to me that, unless I am greatly mistaken, both these tokens—the sad cross, indicative of approaching suffering, or the gracious countenance of Christ, promising future success—were intended to show that Our Lord would take the Society as His own, and watch over it with especial care; providing for it in the time to come such a wise combination of persecution and success, of honour and dishonour, as should be for its truest good, by preserving it from the danger of being unduly elated by prosperity on the one hand, and from being too much cast down by adversity on the other. And now I bid you tell me whether it were possible for God to honour any man in a more signal manner than by thus showing that He vouchsafed to take to heart the success of his projects, by appearing to him, speaking to him, bidding him draw near, embracing him and treating him with such gracious condescension? Not, indeed, that signs like those were necessary to convince Ignatius of the divine protection; for this he had already experienced on many happy occasions. If proof were needed, he had but to recall what occurred when, arriving in Venice late one night, he was unable to procure either food or shelter, until a voice from heaven called upon the Senator Trevigiano to rise quickly from his sleep, and seek the wanderer in the streets, and offer him hospitality under his own roof. And was this all? Did not God bid the winds fly to his succour, when, on the voyage to Cyprus, the sailors attempted to cast him away upon a barren rock? Each time they turned the prow in that direction, their vessel was forcibly driven back and their wicked design frustrated. Were not the storms commissioned to avenge him on the pilot who ungenerously refused him a free passage on his return from Palestine? It is well known that the gallant vessel in which the unhappy man sailed one morning was, before nightfall of the same day, a mere wreck. Once when a daring miscreant, brandishing a naked sword, advanced to kill Ignatius, he was struck suddenly with paralysis, nor did he regain the use of his arm until Ignatius restored it by his touch. On another occasion, a citizen of Alcalà, who affirmed that Ignatius ought to be burnt alive, was himself overtaken by that terrible fate ere many hours had elapsed; and an inhabitant of Cordova, who proposed to drown him, before long met with a watery grave. Thus, we see the very elements themselves uniting as one to defend the cause of this holy man; although, otherwise, they are ever found at variance, and at war amongst themselves.

And if, in my enumeration of the glories which fell to Ignatius's share during his lifetime, I am also to include the high esteem in which, notwithstanding the calumnies of the wicked, he was held throughout the length and breadth of Christendom, what a long series of honours, of distinctions, of plaudits, opens upon our view! I shall have to tell you of the great opinion entertained of him by four Sovereign Pontiffs, Paul III., Julius III., Paul IV., and more especially Marcellus II., who in fact generally designated him by the name of Saint; they gladly listened to his advice, they consulted him frequently, they admitted him to the most intimate familiarity; at his instigation they promulgated wise laws, they founded convents, established seminaries, and provided for the needy; they responded promptly to his every request, giving way to the slightest indication of his wishes more quickly than the snows of the mountain summit melt away before the warm breath of the southern breeze. I shall have to tell how the King of Portugal, John III., wrote to Ignatius as to a father, and employed every exertion in order to bring about his elevation from the particular government of the Society to the headship of the universal Church. I shall have to show you the clergy of various cities coming out to meet him at the head of a solemn procession of their flocks, while the bells peal joyously from every tower, as was the case at Aspezia. I shall have to bid you listen to Saint Charles, who, in his humility, was accustomed to state that the marvellous sanctity to which he attained owed its origin to the spiritual exercises of Saint Ignatius, or, again, to Saint Philip, who, with a like edifying humility, attributed the acquisition of his wonderful powers of contemplation to intercourse with Ignatius. And if you object that the testimony of those who lived in intimate familiarity with him cannot be received as impartial, let Saint Francis Xavier speak, and declare to you, as he often did, that he not only ascribed to Saint Ignatius every step he had made in virtue, and also every conversion he had been enabled to effect in the Indies, but that even during the lifetime of the Saint, he had worked many striking miracles by means of papers signed by his hand; that it was his habit to write letters to him on his knees, to invoke him in litanies, and that the last epistle he ever penned to him bore this superscription, dictated either by enthusiastic affection or by a prophetic spirit: "To my Father in Christ, Saint Ignatius."—But for the aggrandisement of such an one as Ignatius, I care not to dwell on the patronage bestowed on him by the great, the testimony borne to him by Saints, or the splendid encomiums lavished on him by his children, for all of these are liable to be regarded with more or less of suspicion. I will call upon Lucifer to come forth from his infernal abode and confess facts which, constrained by resistless force, he will be powerless to withhold.

And if Saint Jerome is right in asserting that the witness given by the lips of an enemy is infallibly true, I am content to see all other testimony set aside, and that given by Lucifer alone regarded as worthy of credence. We know that during the lifetime of the Saint, the sound of his name proved sufficient to constrain the foul fiend to abandon the bodies he was tormenting. And what did he say of him, not once, but three several times? "I will not hear of Ignatius," he exclaimed, in a transport of fury, "his name is hateful to me, for he is the greatest enemy I have in the whole world." This is enough; we need look no further; we have heard Lucifer declare Ignatius to be his greatest enemy. We may now forget all that has been said hitherto; we can afford to leave out of sight every other fact, to ignore all his other triumphs. Is it a small thing that while he lived, hell knew no more formidable foe in the whole world? although, surely, at that period, it did not lack foes alike numerous, powerful, and determined. I will not weary you, my hearers, by indulging in comparisons which cannot fail to be invidious; read for yourselves the annals of that age, as fertile, perhaps, as any other in illustrious Saints, and let each one form for himself his own conclusions. To all, however, it must be apparent that God purposed to glorify His servant in a signal manner by this memorable confession, which He not only extorted from the unwilling lips of the demon, but which He compelled him to reiterate three several times, using the same words, and displaying the same signs of frantic rage.

One individual alone there was who hated Ignatius, with so deadly and persistent a hatred that in no way could he be forced to contribute the smallest quota to fill up the measure of his glories. This was no other than Ignatius himself, who, indifferent to the fear he inspired in hell, to the veneration paid him on earth, and to the favour shown him in heaven, set himself resolutely to contend against all that could serve to exalt him. What was the sole privilege he asked of God upon earth, as the reward of all he had done and suffered for His sake, if not that he might be despised by all men during his life, and forgotten by them after his death? The same motive led him to dissemble the favours received of Heaven, burying them deeper from sight than earth does the gold she hides in the mine, or ocean the treasures she conceals in her unfathomable bed. So jealously did he guard his secret, that on hearing that his confessor, the sole recipient of his confidences, had expressed a hope that he might be permitted to survive Ignatius, if only long enough to disclose the unheard-of marvels which he knew concerning him, the Saint made him expiate with his life this incautious remark. For his humility immediately took alarm, and not only did he forthwith choose another confessor, but he also asked of God that his own death should be preceded a day or so by the death of his former confessor; a request which was granted, to his great consolation, but to our greater loss. And this is the reason why, although I have been able to unfold to you many of the glories of Ignatius, I have, nevertheless, been unable to speak of what were in reality the most important of them all. Such was the wish of our Founder; of him alone we have to say, and to say with sorrow, that, while his lesser glories are known to us, the greater must ever remain beyond our ken. But if Ignatius whilst on earth used his utmost efforts to elude honours, and was to a great extent successful in those efforts, he at least failed in attaining the same object after his death. He did indeed several times express the desire to have his dead body exposed on a dunghill; but, in spite of his wishes, not only do gold and silver adorn his shrine, but even the stars fell from heaven, apparently desirous to pay their tribute of respect to his remains. This occurred on the second translation of his sacred relics, when it seemed as if heaven would descend to receive those relics, unable to await the time when they would be carried up to its starry courts, there to enter on the eternal and blissful existence in store for them. It was owing to Ignatius' earnest prayers that the miracles he performed while on earth were so ordinary in their nature, when compared to those he wrought after death. He brought to life again an unhappy man who had hung himself in a fit of fury; he restored the use of their limbs, both to a woman whose arm was paralysed and to a man whose hand had been severely burnt; his blessing cured a patient in the last stage of consumption; he delivered persons from epilepsy, fevers, and contagious diseases. Again, he was seen at one and the same time in different places, in cities far removed from each other, as, for instance, Rome and Cologne. But when once he was dead, he could no longer put a limit to the marvels God willed to work through the instrumentality of the Saint; and he was employed to perform prodigies of daily occurrence, as startling in their nature as they were abundant in number and widespread in notoriety. Indeed, so frequent were the apparitions of Ignatius on earth after the time when he took what seemed to be his final separation from it, that he may almost be said never to have quitted it, but still to abide amongst men, as truly as he did whilst his spirit was confined in the prison of the flesh. He appeared in the Gulf of Genoa to a young girl, and saved her from shipwreck; in the forests of Peru to a young man whom he rescued from robbers; in the city of Lecce to a woman on the point of death, restoring her at once to health and strength. Again, he showed himself in the province of Toledo to console a maiden in deep affliction; in the convent of Macerata to deliver a nun from death; in a valley of Piedmont to cure the sick child of a weeping mother; in a city of Gascony, to inspire affection for our Society in the breast of one who declared himself its bitter foe; in Florence, to preserve the person, house, and belongings of a certain nobleman from a disastrous fire raging in the immediate vicinity of his home. We hear, moreover, how he granted the prayers and calmed the grief of two bereaved mothers, by restoring to life the infants they had lost; how he raised from the dead a girl, twelve years of age, living at Pardos, in Spain; or how in Ferrara, when an unfortunate mother, whilst leaning over a balcony, had allowed the child she was nursing to fall from her arms into the street, he promptly came in person in answer to her call, and returned the infant, unharmed and smiling, to her eager embrace. But is it not a greater and higher thing to snatch souls from the very verge of hell than to rescue them from the jaws of the grave? Yet this too Ignatius did; he obtained the grace of repentance for two miserable youths who had made over their souls into the power of the devil, by means of a formal document subscribed by their own hand, and in their own blood. In spite of hell's furious opposition, he caused the two youths to repent of their sin, the deed of gift to be annulled, and the document given up; thus achieving a triumph far surpassing that of the fabled Orpheus; for the souls he rescued from the dark abyss were won, not by dint of insinuating entreaties, but by the exertion of imperious command.

I should indeed exhaust your patience, my brethren, were I merely to classify the various miracles wrought by Ignatius; for to enter upon each individual miracle would be of course utterly impossible, and I trust enough has already been said to show you that however much Ignatius may have done to glorify God, God certainly did not do less to glorify Ignatius. There only remains for us to do our part, to glorify his memory by every possible expression of homage and devotion. And if we are bound to honour those Saints who have made it their primary object to accomplish their own sanctification, as merchant ships plough the deep in order to bring home a precious cargo to their owner, how much more honour is due to Saints who have sacrificed themselves for the good of others, like ships of war which are destroyed in the service of their country?

Wherefore, my brethren, if you owe aught to the toilworn sons of Ignatius for benefits received, during the last hundred years; if youth has found in their academies some advantages as regards their training and instruction; if holy souls have within their churches met with spiritual directors to help them somewhat along the path of holiness; if any of you, in the course of many years, have ever perchance derived profit from their eloquent discourses and relief from their solutions of intricate questions of conscience; if you have experienced their aid when death has cast its shadow across your path, you must own that for this you are indebted to their Father Ignatius, and that to him alone your thanks are due.

PANEGYRIC IN HONOUR OF SAINT FRANCIS XAVIER,

IN WHOSE CASE MIRACLES WERE THE RULE INSTEAD OF THE EXCEPTION.

"Lift up thy hand over the strange nations, that they may see thy power. Renew thy signs and work new miracles. Glorify thy hand and thy right arm."—ECCL. xxxvi. 3, 6, 7.

AMONGST all the glorious attributes of God, it is His power of working miracles which conveys to the finite intelligence of man the fittest idea of His infinite greatness. So long as, without departing from those laws which He solemnly proclaimed from the beginning as regulating nature, He continues to give to the stars their accustomed light, to impart to the fire its accustomed heat, to guide the spheres in their accustomed orbits, the winds in their accustomed course, and the streams in their accustomed channels, few among His creatures are found to praise Him, many know nothing about Him, whilst some even go so far as to raise serious doubts as to the very fact of His existence. But when, setting aside the laws which He has made, He performs in the sight of men one of those wonderful acts which are termed miracles, not so much on account of their magnitude as on account of their rarity, all raise their eyes to heaven with reverent awe, and acknowledge the hand of that Deity on whom they were previously so slow to believe. Hence on the first occasion when God communicated to another the power of working miracles, He gave him at the same time permission to bear the name of God, so inseparably connected is the idea of divinity with that of miracles. "Behold," thus God says to Moses, "I have appointed thee the God of Pharao" (Ex. vii. 1). Wherefore, since this power causes man to appear in the light of a God, the reason becomes at once apparent why God deals it out to him with so sparing a hand. And truly, as Saint Paul asserts, when God vouchsafes to impart His gifts to man, He does not make a single individual the recipient of them all, but to one He gives power to heal grievous sickness, to another discernment of spirits, to a third unknown tongues; thus amongst various chosen servants He allots to each a share of His power, as the sun, with like jealous thrift, does not communicate to one planet the whole of his light, choosing rather to admit many to partake in his refulgence. Nevertheless, it seems to me that for some reason or other, God made an exception to this general rule in the case of Saint Francis Xavier, the illustrious Apostle of the Indies; for, on due consideration, it seems that he united in his person all the extraordinary gifts which are usually divided amongst a number, so that the achievements of Francis' unwearying arm made him appear among the nations as the vicegerent of Omnipotence, endowed with that immeasurable and illimitable power which the wise man ascribes to God in these words: "Lift up thy hand over the strange nations, that they may see thy power. Renew thy signs and work new miracles.

Glorify thy hand and thy right arm." Happy, therefore, is your lot who have put yourselves under the protection of a Saint so dear to God! I can safely promise you that Francis will never lack power to help and defend you. Is not the possession of power so exalted and superhuman the first and most essential qualification desired in a protector? And must not that man be acknowledged to be endowed with extraordinary power, of whom it can be alleged without fear of untruth or even of exaggeration, that his every action was a miracle?

Now listen to the unusual restraint I am about to lay upon myself for your sake; in the whole of my present discourse I propose solely and simply to place before you a sketch of the life Francis led upon earth after he gave himself to the service of God, in its beginning, its progress, and its end (an end of which we know so little), and, nevertheless, I shall relate nothing concerning him but an uninterrupted series of miracles. Before entering upon the subject, let me ask you, my hearers, for once to lay aside that indulgent kindness with which you are accustomed to listen to me: to-day I desire an audience, not tolerant, but critical. Examine all I say with stern rigour, weigh it well, judge it severely; this is what I desire and request of you. And why do I desire it? In order that you may decide whether I am exact in keeping my promise I have just given you, to speak of nothing concerning Francis but that which is of miraculous nature, or whether I fail to fulfil my engagement. I cannot indeed promise to recount all his miracles, for that would be a task far beyond my strength; but I do promise to recount nothing else but miracles.

Having said this, I will at once proceed to open my subject.

And truly, when we hear that the appearance of a man upon the stage of the world has been foretold ages beforehand by miraculous signs, there is no difficulty in believing such an one will himself be a worker of miracles; for it is only when an individual is destined to promote in no common degree the glory of God and the good of his fellow-men, that God is accustomed to announce him to the world a long time previous to his actual appearance. And for how long a period had not Francis been promised to the Indies? We know upon good authority that when the Apostle Saint Thomas first caused the light of gospel truth to dawn on those benighted lands, he planted a cross at some considerable distance from the sea-shore, telling the barbarous natives that when the waves should reach the spot on which it stood, then some one should come from Europe to succeed to his office and teach his doctrine. And on the arrival of Francis in the Indies, this prediction was fulfilled; for the sea, which by little and little had gradually been gaining on the land, was seen to wash the foot of the cross, like an humble pilgrim, who, his journey over and his vow accomplished, reverently kisses the sacred threshold which was the goal of his weary steps. What need of further testimony to the greatness of Francis than the eulogium bestowed on him fourteen centuries beforehand by so eminent a Saint, an eulogium couched moreover in the words of so remarkable a prophecy? Cannot this saying of Saint Maximus be rightly applied to him? "Who would not feel the most intense admiration for one who has received so much from God that his merits are lauded even before his birth?" For, if the coming of Francis to the Indies was announced by miracles, does it not follow that his life there should likewise be attended by miracles? And, indeed, the existence of Saint Francis subsequent to his conversion can be termed nothing but one perpetual miracle. Knowing nothing as yet of the destiny reserved for him in the secret counsels of Heaven, and regarding his life as useless, if not pernicious, to the world, he well-nigh put an end to it altogether, so severe were the persecutions which, in his newly-awakened fervour, he inflicted on his body. He denied sleep to his eyes, relaxation to his mind, and the necessary sustenance to his exhausted frame. He ventured to prolong his fasts for four or five consecutive days, sometimes even for a whole week, refusing to listen to the importunate demands of famished nature; and, when he at length condescended to heed them, the scanty pittance of bread and water reluctantly dealt out to them served rather to increase than appease their clamours. The frozen ground was the only couch on which he suffered his wearied limbs to rest, until they, seeing that even after excessive toil nothing better was prepared for them, in very self-pity preferred a continuance of their labour to such repose as that. Every night he more than once scourged himself to blood; and by day, in order that no moment might be exempt from suffering, he wore either a rough hair shirt or a garment studded with sharp points of steel, so as to make his life a continual martyrdom. And finding that nature was able to bear up even against ill-treatment such as this, Francis, enraged with himself for not being able to invent more tortures than his body could endure, devised a new species of torment, by means of which he literally realised in himself that which was written in the life of Saint Zenon as a rhetorical hyperbole, that in one single body there were to be seen as many kinds of martyrdom as there were limbs. He bound his thighs, legs and arms so tightly with cords, that the knots gradually cut into the flesh, which, closing over them, hid them from sight. And now, at last, Nature gave way, overcome by excessive pain, and acknowledged herself fairly vanquished; and since the skill of surgeons and the help of art alike proved vain, that precious life, on which the salvation of a whole hemisphere depended, seemed trembling in the balance. What was to be done? Francis had been promised to the Indies, and for the Indies his life must be preserved even at the cost of a miracle. We are told that in the space of a single night, the cords dropped off, every wound was healed, and all pain was at an end; in a word, it was plain that Heaven itself had intervened to loose those fatal knots, to which such disastrous consequences seemed attached.

It is true that, meanwhile, Heaven was continually compelled, in order to satisfy the insatiable desire for suffering felt by Francis, to reveal to him by miraculous signs the future which awaited him, giving him an occasional foretaste of that suffering which, some time hence, was to be his in long and undisturbed possession. In his dreams he sometimes felt as if staggering under the burden of frightful monsters, sometimes tottering beneath the weight of heavy crosses; when he was serving the sick in the hospitals of Vicenza, Saint Jerome appeared to him, and showed him in a vision the whole course of his future weary wanderings. The venerable Saint, taking Francis under his special protection, displayed to his mental sight stormy seas and rocks of an almost inaccessible approach; he showed him alternately populous cities and desolate solitudes; and then addressing him, with a beaming smile: "Why do you weep, O Francis?" he said; "why do you weep? Behold those oceans, those islands, those deserts, those plains, those mountain ranges; all those ere long your feet must tread, your steps must traverse. Be of good heart, labours and sufferings will not be wanting to you. Poor and unknown, you will have to pursue your way, without provision for your journey; your habit, your Bible, and your Breviary being all you will take with you on your weary pilgrimage of so many miles; a pilgrimage which will lead you round the world, not once, or even twice, for you are destined to make its circuit as many as five times. At every step you take on that unfriendly shore your bare feet will be scorched by the burning sand; on the steep paths the stones will cut them; in the thickets the thorns will pierce them. Rice and brackish water will be the only refreshment awaiting you there; sometimes you will have to seek shelter for the night in caverns when darkness overtakes you in pursuit of the heathen, whose souls you would fain save; sometimes your rest will be taken in the hospitals, where you will expose your life in the service of plague-stricken sufferers. On your shoulders will rest the whole burden of a world's conversion. Your arm will grow weary with baptising, your feet will be tired with going to and fro, your lips will be parched with long preaching. Are not these sufferings enough for you?" What think you, my hearers, was Francis content with so little? Whilst those miraculous visions passed before his mental sight he unceasingly repeated the words, "More, O Lord! more, more!" and ever and anon his groans, his sweat, bore witness to the agitation of his spirit. Thus did he resemble the gallant warrior who displays his real valour even when the conflict he is engaged in is but a mock fight.

Such prowess could not fail ere long to find an arena worthy of itself; and, as the limits of one hemisphere seemed too narrow to contain a heart so vast, it was necessary to discover to him a new world. The voice which called Francis to the Indies was no ambiguous one; and no sooner did he arrive there, than all the wondrous gifts usually distributed amongst many were found united in his single person. I invite you to gaze on them all, and if they appear to crowd on one another, like the myriad gleaming stars which form the Milky Way, do not be discouraged, deeming it difficult, if not impossible, to distinguish any one amongst such vast numbers. For will you not acknowledge the gift of tongues granted to him, in order that he might effect the conversion of nations remote from one another, differing widely in their religion and their customs, to have been a most glorious prerogative? In the different provinces of India alone, not to speak of Japan, he discovered at least thirty languages in use; and, since no human skill could possibly have enabled him to master so many in the course of a few years, God bestowed on him the marvellous privilege of making himself understood by all his hearers simultaneously, whatever their varying nationalities, whilst he addressed them in his native tongue. But of this power instances may be met with elsewhere. There is another gift which appears to me more special to Francis: the power of answering various objections with one and the same reply. For we are told that when, as was frequently the case in Japan, a great number of unbelievers, learned alike, and desirous of information, came together in great numbers to question him on religious subjects, he, first of all, made each in turn state his special difficulty, and then returned one single answer, of a nature to solve the doubts and satisfy the mind of each individual questioner; a prodigy which may be compared to the mysterious manna from heaven, in itself the same, but differing in flavour, according to the taste of every one of the thousands who partook of it. But what marvel that his words possessed such wonderful efficacy, since by means of signs alone he was able to effect so much? Incredible as it may appear, it is nevertheless true that in Socotra, an island with whose language he was entirely unacquainted, he preached by signs alone; by signs he touched the hearts of its inhabitants, by signs he converted them, by signs he was able to instruct and baptise a great number of them. These graces were, it is plain, bestowed on Francis to gratify his ardent desire of saving as many souls as possible in the shortest period of time; for this end, had he been able, he would gladly have made himself all voice and all tongue, and therefore God not only multiplied as it were his one voice, making it do the work of many, but imparted moreover to his other members not only a silent language, but even eloquence.

It is certain, also, that in order to satisfy the longings of His servant, God granted him the further power of rendering himself present in more places than one simultaneously. For was not Francis' person eagerly coveted at the same time by the people assembled in the church to receive his instructions; by the sick in the hospitals needing his consolations; by the warriors on the battle-field demanding his protection; by the storm-tossed mariners craving his succour, all of whom strove, so to speak, to divide him amongst them; if indeed it can be said that they divided him, when all these several classes seemed to enjoy his undivided possession at one and the same time. Indeed, so frequent was his exercise of this rare gift, that it almost ceased to appear miraculous. Yet it is true, the incident I am about to relate to you excited the greatest astonishment. Saint Francis was returning from Japan to India, when his vessel, overtaken by a sudden storm, was carried into an unknown sea, which even the bold daring of the Portuguese had not hitherto explored. The crew used every exertion to secure the safety of the ship's boat, so indispensable in those long voyages, but in the darkness of night the winds and waves rose high in their fury, and carried it far out to sea, where it appeared as if it must fall a victim to their violence. In the boat were fifteen persons, amongst them a nephew of the captain; all these, being entirely lost to sight, were mourned as dead; the sobs of the afflicted passengers mingling with the roarings of the typhoon. Then Francis, pitying the deep grief of the captain, consoled him with the assurance that in three days' time the lost child would of his own accord return to his parent, that is to say the little boat would come back to the ship. Nor did he fail in the fulfilment of his promise. Towards the close of the third day, when the others had given up all hope of seeing the skiff again, concluding that it had been long ago either dashed to pieces on the rocks or swallowed up in a whirlpool, one of the crew, who was on the look-out, suddenly shouted: "A miracle, a miracle! Here is our little boat again!" Hearing this, all hastened on deck; and behold the boat, having braved many a storm, came proudly on its course, now borne aloft on the crest of the foaming billows, now disappearing from view in the yawning gulfs which separated them. The sailors wished to throw out a rope, but Francis would not hear of this, in order to let them see the fulfilment of his prediction, that filial love would suffice to bring the child back to its mother's bosom. Who can describe the astonishment, the tearful joy with which the missing comrades were welcomed back, rescued as they were from the very jaws of death? They had already been taken on board, when, observing that one of the sailors was thrusting off the empty boat, they all cried to him first to help out Francis, who had been left behind in it. "What do you mean?" replied the man; "Francis has been all the time in the ship with us." "That cannot be," rejoined the others, "we have had him with us in the boat." "On the contrary, he was here assuring us of your return." "We again had him there directing our course." And this strife was only put an end to by their perceiving that the Saint, in order to lend his aid to both parties, had during those three days been present in both places. To this prodigy was due the immediate conversion of two Saracens, who were among the rescued mariners; and, did not time forbid, I might relate to you many other interesting incidents of a similar nature.

And now, seeing, as we have done, that Francis, for the sake of helping others, was able to make himself present in body at the same time in more places than one, we shall surely have no difficulty in believing that he could even more readily make himself present in spirit by the knowledge he had of what was passing in remote localities. His power in this respect seems to have been unlimited. Were proof needed, it would suffice to pass in review the innumerable occasions on which he made known occurrences distant in time or distant in place, and sometimes distant in both time and place. Thus, whilst himself in the Indies, he was able to give a minute account of the proceedings of King John in Portugal, and of the enactments of Saint Ignatius in Rome, and to shape his conduct accordingly. When about to sail for Malacca, he refused to embark on the vessel provided by the king, although it was far better equipped and more commodious than his own; foretelling the opposite fates in store for the two vessels, namely, that the better ship would be shattered upon the rocks, whilst the frailer craft would reach port in safety—a prediction which was shortly accomplished. He foretold the shipwreck of the bark which had brought him to the Indies, as also of that which escorted him to Cochin, and that which preceded him to Sancian; not to mention many others. At sea, he frequently predicted to the pilots that the ports to which they were bound would be reached in safety; and often he would point out the direction towards which they ought to steer when mists and darkness hid the pole star from view, or the charts by which they were wont to guide their course had been lost in some storm. It would be a lengthy task to enumerate all those persons to whom he announced the near approach of death, or even the exact hour of their decease; let it suffice to take the instance of Peter Veglis, who, in recompense of an alms given to a child, received from the lips of the Saint this valuable warning of his approaching end. Although at the time in perfect health, he at once arranged all his family affairs, made his confession with scrupulous care, fortified himself with the sacraments, took leave of his friends, and—what seemed the strangest thing of all—invited them to accompany him, with sad solemnity, to the church where his funeral obsequies were about to be performed; there he laid himself out upon his bier, crossed his hands, closed his eyes, and, having been covered with a black pall, while a solemn requiem Mass was being sung for the repose of his soul, he calmly expired, to the extreme astonishment of all present, and the great grief of his friends, who could no longer refuse to credit the truth of the Saint's prophecy. But although this incident, if it stood alone, would be quite sufficient in itself to prove what I have asserted, being of so novel, unheard-of, and exceptional a nature, many others might be adduced, somewhat less marvellous perhaps, but of a very similar description; in fact, Francis received the surname of the Prophet, because in him resided habitually that gift of prophecy which, in the case of others, is generally but a transient favour. He foretold the different destinies in store for two young men, one of whom was for a considerable period the companion of his travels. To him he promised a happy death, but announced that the other, who attended him on his death-bed, would come to a miserable end. And events proved the truth of his words; for the former became a Religious, and died a holy death; whereas the latter took to an immoral course of life, and was killed by the chance shot of an arquebuse. Upon several occasions, when preaching in one place, he interrupted his discourse in order to recommend to the prayers of his hearers the soul of some individual at that time expiring in another; thus, when preaching in Amboyna one day he commended the soul of James Gilio, then dying in Tournai, to the charity of the faithful; and when preaching in Tournai he asked prayers for John Galvano, perishing by shipwreck off the coast of Amboyna; these two places being two hundred miles apart. But most wonderful of all was what he did in Malacca. He was preaching in the church there to a large congregation of the faithful, when, in the midst of his sermon, he suddenly stopped, as if his attention had been attracted to something else. And then, breaking off his subject, he began with marvellous eloquence, and more than his usual fervour, to depict in glowing terms a fierce naval engagement, just as if he were present at it. The audience were amazed, unable to conceive what the Saint was aiming at, when he, as if he saw the battle grow hotter, and trembled for the combatants engaged in it, clasped his hands, and fixing on the crucifix his tearful gaze, began to pour forth impassioned supplications for the Christians, at that time in deadly conflict with the Moors, three hundred miles away. Then, as if weary, he leant his head on the pulpit for a short space; at length, rising to his feet with a serene countenance, he joyfully exclaimed: "He has conquered, my brethren; Jesus has conquered for us; at this moment our forces are putting their foes to final rout." And he proceeded in this manner to describe minutely the issue of the fight, the numbers of the slain, the nature of the booty taken, the very time when the victorious fleet would return home; all of which was verified by the event. But it is no matter for wonder that Francis should have foreseen this victory, since he himself was the means of its being gained. He it was who in the first place encouraged the Portuguese captain to give battle, although he had only eight small and badly equipped vessels wherewith to engage twenty-five large and well-armed ones; and but two hundred and thirty men, deficient alike in arms and in courage, whereby to oppose a force consisting of several thousand daring and confident warriors. He promised them a calm sea and favouring breezes; he promised them a glorious victory; and a glorious victory they did indeed obtain, for whilst the enemy lost as many as four thousand men, only four of the Christians fell in the combat. Do you think it marvellous that a handful of men were able, with Francis' help, to prevail against such heavy odds? I can tell you something yet more wonderful. Francis himself, alone and unaided, without shield, without helmet, without cuirass, ventured to confront a whole army of barbarians; he reprehended and threatened them, he routed them so completely, that, bewildered, they took to flight in hasty confusion, their great numbers only rendering more ignominious the precipitation of their retreat.

In ascribing to a single individual prodigies so wonderful, I am well aware, my brethren, that their very number and magnitude makes them difficult of belief. You shall nevertheless hear greater things than these. Is it marvellous that men should tremble before one of whom the very elements themselves stood in awe? Was not each one of those elements ready to obey the slightest indication of his will? Do you ask if the earth obeyed him? How many times it quaked before him, as if smitten with sudden fear! Do you ask if the fire obeyed him? How often did the devouring flames stay their progress at his command! And when he saw fit to punish the city of Tolo which had apostatised from the faith of Christ, did not the arsenal of the air furnish him with the necessary weapons? Lightning and tempests, darkness, deluges of brimstone and ashes, showers of sharp stones and fiery bolts; and as if the keys of the dungeons where the winds are enchained had been committed to his custody, at his mandate they issued from the abyss to overthrow houses and lay walls low, and give to impenitent sinners a foretaste of the day of judgment. But the waters more than either of the other elements were subject to his control. Innumerable were the occasions on which Francis sweetened their bitterness, or appeased their fury; once, when on his way to Malacca, he allayed a storm by dipping a reliquary belonging to him into the sea; another time when sailing amongst the Molucca isles, he assuaged a tempest by touching the billows with his crucifix. It was this crucifix which, as all know, when carried away by the impetuosity of the current, was miraculously restored to him by the agency of a crab; that creature having, as it appears to my mind, been selected from amongst the denizens of the deep as the one to perform this singular act of reverence, in order to enhance the marvellous nature of the occurrence; since the formidable claws of the crab might rather be expected to rob a man of what he already had than to restore to him what he had lost. But it would take too long to recount half the stories of this description which I might tell you; it is enough to know that storm-tossed mariners knew no name more powerful when invoked than that of Francis. Traders used to contend for the privilege of having him on board their ships, confident that thus the security of their merchandise would be ensured. And not only since his death has it been the practice of mariners to invoke him; they were accustomed to do this while he was yet alive, and with most happy results. For scarcely had their lips breathed his name ere he would appear, hastening over the waters to their succour; as was the case with one John Arangi, who, clinging to a plank in time of shipwreck, commended himself to Saint Francis; and forthwith he beheld the Saint standing upon the plank, who reassured and consoled him, accompanying him moreover for five days and nights until the perils of the deep were safely past, and the port of Meliapore was reached. And we find sickness and death yielding him a no less implicit obedience than did the winds and waves; the instances of cures effected by him were so many, that the Bishops charged with preparing the process of his canonisation were appalled at the work before them, despairing of ever finishing their investigations. The Saint did not usually visit the sick at their own homes; they were mostly brought in multitudes and laid at his feet, that he might sprinkle them with holy water, and thus restore them to health and vigour. But he only adopted this course in cases of ordinary sickness; when he met with a sufferer afflicted with any malady which he might turn to his own profit as an opportunity for penance and mortification, he acted otherwise. Thus on one occasion, in Comorin, falling in with a leprous beggar, he first embraced him, and then cleansed his sores, and, after drinking the water in which they had been washed, he left him perfectly whole. Many he healed with a touch, others again with his passing shadow; and when the calls upon his aid were too numerous and too remote to be answered by him in person, it was his habit, like a modern Eliseus, to send children in his place with his staff or rosary, a device in which his humility rejoiced to find a pretext for attributing the marvels wrought by their agency rather to the innocence of the youthful messengers than to his own personal sanctity. What miracles were not worked, alike on Christians and heathens, by means of a discipline left by him with an old man in whose house he had lodged? As a great favour the old man used to allow sick persons to discipline themselves with it, and two or three blows invariably proved efficacious in causing the most obstinate diseases to flee away in terror, leaving their victims in peace. But why do I enlarge on the frequency with which Francis restored health to the sick, when I might rather relate the numerous times when he restored life to the dead? Of this we find no less than twenty-five cases amongst the miracles authenticated in the acts of his canonisation. Some he raised up from the funeral bier, others from the depths of the waters; some from the very grave itself, in one instance after an interment of three days, a miracle almost equal to that wrought by Our Lord in Bethania.

These, then my hearers, are some of the prodigies which were habitual to Francis during his life on earth. And now let us listen to Saint Paul while he makes his famous division of miraculous gifts. Let him tell them to us one by one. To one, diverse kinds of tongues; truly Francis was not wanting in the gift of tongues. To another, interpretation of speeches; Francis did not lack the knowledge of secret things. To another, the discerning of spirits; in truth Francis was gifted with power of reading the inmost thoughts of the heart. To another, prophecy; again, Francis was rich in prophetic gifts. To another, the working of miracles; here also we find Francis endowed with ample power over nature. To another, the gift of healing; yet Francis possessed dominion not over disease alone, but over death itself. It is certainly impossible to call to question the truth of the Apostle's statement that there are diversities of gifts. Nevertheless for once God has departed from His own laws, choosing to manifest concentrated in one individual that power which is His custom to divide amongst many, as the sea shares among many rivers the treasures of its waters.

But you will perhaps conclude that I have now come to the end of my subject, or that the miracles I have recounted to you comprise, if not all, at least the most remarkable of those for which Francis was so justly celebrated. On the contrary, let me assure you that I have only mentioned the least, both in number and importance. Do they seem to you so striking, so astounding, so unparalleled? They are far from making this impression upon me. Pardon me if I say that there are other miracles which I admire more in the life of this Saint. And what are these? In my opinion it is a far greater wonder that a man capable of working these prodigies should preserve such profound humility as to stoop voluntarily to render the most menial services to his fellow-men; that we should find him at sea washing the clothes of the lowest of the crew, in the hospitals making the beds of those afflicted with the most revolting maladies, in the inns grooming the horses belonging to the lowest of the serving-men. He had, moreover, been appointed Apostolic Nuncio to the Indies, a dignity of which he refused the title, whilst accepting the onerous duties attached to it. Besides the miracles I have related to you above, is it not truly wonderful that he should have journeyed on foot over more than one hundred thousand miles, that he should have baptised with his own hand more than one million two hundred thousand persons, that he should have overthrown with his own arm more than forty thousand idols and false deities, avenging thus the outraged dignity of that God whose throne they had usurped? Surely these must appear great miracles, the more so when we consider that they were all wrought within the space of ten years. How wonderful, moreover, to see a man, come, so to speak, from another world, a man whose dress was strange, whose language was unknown, whose customs were foreign; a man who had no riches to recommend him, for he begged his daily bread; whose external appearance was not imposing, for his garments were worn to tatters; who did not command respect on account of his birth, for although he came of royal race, yet he concealed the fact even from his servants with greater care than that with which some

noble river hides its source; is it not a wonder, I say,
to see this man, a wanderer and unknown, attracting
to himself whole nations as if by a magic spell, and
with the might of his single word overturning cities,
upheaving kingdoms, subjugating haughty princes,
uprooting ancient customs, deposing dynasties, exterminating national religions, and substituting, in the
place of all these, new rites, new laws, a new creed?
And new indeed were the laws he promulgated; laws
which claimed to establish a fresh code throughout the
universe, to make shame appear as glory, poverty more
desirable than riches, hardships than ease, weakness
than power, insults than honour, tears than smiles,
sufferings than enjoyment. This same law he succeeded
in planting firmly in the centre and stronghold of
heathendom; in Goa, the metropolis of the East; in
Mozambique and Melinda; on the barbarous coasts of
Cochin, Comorin and Coromandel; in the kingdom of
Travancore, in Ceylon, Malacca and Amboyna; in the
savage isles of the Moor and of the Moluccas; in Japan
with its six principalities; in Malay and Acheen;
amongst the aborigines of Mindanas, of Celebes, of
Canavar, besides many other wild and barbarous
peoples. How countless are the numbers who in these
remote regions under the influence of this law despised splendid inheritances and repudiated brilliant
alliances, endured wearisome exile, lengthened captivity, or agonising death! I can go yet further.
Alone and unsupported, Francis dared to oppose the
teaching of three celebrated and flourishing oriental
schools, those under the direction respectively of the
Brahmans, the Imans and the Bonzes; by his wisdom
he confuted their learning, discredited them, and

gained over the minds of five royal monarchs, who, humbly kneeling at his feet, laid aside their proud diadems to receive the holy sacrament of Baptism at his hands. The same was done by the wise Mona, consort of the King of Ternates, and other queens, besides many members of royal families and persons of distinguished rank. What are to be called miracles, my hearers, if not things like these? If we consider the subject closely, we shall perceive them to be the most admirable of all, for the miracles hitherto mentioned were but signs and tokens of sanctity, whilst in these sanctity itself is embodied; the former cost the Saint nothing, whilst on the latter he expended his whole self; on them he spent his toils, he spent his blood, he spent his health, he spent his life. What was there indeed that he did not expend? I appeal to the remotest corners of the earth, I bid them answer me. Did not this strange sight fill you with astonishment, the sight of a man who, with absolute self-oblivion, sacrificed himself for others, and died at last of exhaustion on a desert shore, with no other shelter than a mud cabin, with no other couch than the bare ground, unprotected and uncared for, cruelly betrayed and abandoned by those very men who were most indebted to him? Thus we may see a vessel, shattered and broken by its struggle with the winds and storms, stranded on the shore, and left to its fate by the ungrateful crew for whose sake it fought so gallantly, and whose lives it succeeded in saving from the fury of the waves and from the hungry monsters of the deep. These are the miracles which I hold in highest esteem, and yet I almost regret having spoken of, or rather alluded to them, for some may be led to imagine that I have already failed to fulfil my promise of relating nothing concerning Francis but the miracles he wrought.

And yet, even did we designate those events only as miraculous in which God seems to play the part of the principal actor, still I should never be able to relate them all. Indeed, I may truly affirm that were I to attempt to narrate them all, it would be necessary for me to ask the Saint to lend me awhile those marvellous powers which some writers ascribe to him, when they assert that the sun was known to stand still at his command. For surely a Saint who wrought so many wonders during his life, would not have been less prolific in this respect after his death, since Heaven is seldom as liberal in permitting the former as in granting the latter, in order not to expose the sanctity of the individual, while still on earth, to the danger ever attending such signal favours. Did not the dead body of Francis perform a perpetual series of miracles? In vain did the Portuguese enclose it for six whole months in a chest filled with quicklime, thinking that the bones, if separated from the flesh, could be transported with greater facility from the island of Sancian to the city of Malacca; even up to this very time that original body has remained incorrupt, having lost nothing of its beauty or life-like colouring; so that the beholder gazing on it might fancy speech alone was wanting; nay, only close observation would convince him that speech was wanting, and those silent lips were closed for ever. On the sacred remains being brought into Malacca, a plague which was ravaging the city immediately ceased its work of destruction. And when its removal to Goa was announced, although the vessel chosen for this purpose was old and unseaworthy, merchants having declined to intrust their wares to it, yet on hearing of the honour to be conferred on it, all hastened to secure places for themselves or their merchandise at any cost, confident that it would be preserved from all misfortune. Nor were they deceived in their expectations. In the course of the voyage the vessel went aground upon a reef, and stuck so fast that it could not be got off again. In their extremity the crew resolved to expose the sacred body upon the deck, when the rock, as if terrified at the sight, cleft apart with a loud noise, leaving free passage to the ship. This latter, having reached her destination and landed cargo and passengers in safety, suddenly foundered close to shore; either because no one else was worthy to make use of it, or because it had now nothing left to hope for, or because the sea claimed it for her own, to rival, as some have pleasantly remarked, that which shines resplendent in the heavens above. However that may be, we know that not only Europeans and Christians, but barbarians and unbelievers, flocked in crowds to honour the venerated relics, and all without distinction offered him then, as they offer him now, the homage of their prayers; they made vows to him, they lighted tapers, they kept lamps burning before him; all uniting to practise so great devotion towards him that the King of Travancore, although a Mohammedan, was led to erect a sumptuous temple in his honour. But it was not the will of God that the glory of Francis should be confined within the limits of the Indies, between which countries and our own so many mountains rise and seas roll. The number of miracles performed by him in Europe is, in fact, almost incredible. Nor is this without good reason, if I judge aright; for since Francis for the glory of God voluntarily forsook the land of his birth, which he loved so well, to bury himself in a new world, in an unfamiliar and uncongenial clime, God on His part was graciously pleased to compensate His servant for the honours he had chosen to renounce in his lifetime by those which He bestowed on him in rich abundance after his death. Francis is now present amongst us, with all his gifts and graces, just as if he had spent his life for us and died in our midst.

I do not intend to relate these graces, for, even though I were not to touch on them all, to do so would be to return to the starting-point when the goal is almost reached. Nevertheless, I cannot omit mentioning what happened to Marcellus Mastrilli, for this most remarkable occurrence attracted the attention of all who witnessed it, and aroused astonishment in the farthest corners of the world. Who has not heard of the glorious end of our missioner, Mastrilli, in the island of Japan, whither, a few years ago, eager to preach the faith, he had penetrated, despite the fury of the storm and the rage of persecutors, where he triumphed victoriously over prisons and snares, over fire and water, and finally over the cruel steel of the barbarians, who little knew that the hand which dealt the murderous blow, at the same time culled for their victim a martyr's glorious palm! And who obtained for him the grace to make such a glorious end as this? who, moreover, foretold it, and animated him to meet it, if not Francis? He it was who, when Marcellus lay sick in Naples, seemingly at the point of death, appeared at his bedside, in the dress of a courteous pilgrim, a staff in his hand and a wallet on his shoulder; he it was who conversed a long time with him, encouraging him, and exhorting him to renew the vow he had made not long before, of dedicating himself to the missions of the Indies; he it was who dictated to him the very words in which to frame his vow and urge his request for martyrdom; he it was who cured him in a moment, and restored him to strength, healing his wounds so that they left no scars behind. And finally, throughout the perilous voyage the Saint continued to make his protection felt by delivering him from the dangers of the deep, from the horrors of war, from the attacks of a fierce soldiery; even causing the balls aimed at his breast to fall harmless at his feet. And now, my hearers, I would ask you, if in all Europe Francis had performed no other miracle, would not this alone have sufficed to establish the fact of his great merit? For where in the annals of the Church do we find a miracle containing within itself, if I may so speak, so many miracles as did this one worked on behalf of Marcellus? In it we meet with apparitions which cannot be called in question, wonderful cures, prophecies of a new order, the unmistakable fulfilment of the same, favours and protection hitherto unparalleled. Then it was that all Europe beheld a missioner go forth in quest of martyrdom with the absolute certainty of finding what he sought; and could revere Marcellus while yet alive as a martyr, applying to him the words spoken by the Bishop Zenon of the martyr Arcadius: "Arcadius, whilst yet tarrying in this world, is already proclaimed a martyr in heaven." And if this one miracle is not enough to satisfy the mind of any one, he may see at a glance how abundant are the favours which the Saint continues to shower upon Europe by the number of those who choose him for their patron. How many cities of Italy alone have placed themselves under his protection! Witness Bologna, Messina, Naples, Perugia, Turin, Parma, Piacenza, Aquila, Cremona, besides many others; and from the fact of finding instances so numerous in one country, may it not be inferred that they are no less numerous in those countries which were the scenes of Francis' birth or conversion, as France, Portugal, or Navarre? What does all this teach us? In his lifetime Francis was in no way connected with the majority of these Italian cities which now own him for their patron; he was perhaps never seen in their streets, his very name was unknown there. Hence we may fairly conclude that from Heaven above he has gained their esteem and won their affection, by means of favours bestowed on them; for alas! in the present day devotion appears to be more or less interested in its nature, and the Saints are regarded as those fountains to which no one has recourse when congealed by winter frost, or reduced by summer heat, and thus rendered useless for practical purposes, though they still continue to charm the eye. And has not Francis, indeed, bestowed upon Italy a sure pledge of his continual protection, by permitting her to possess an important portion of that body over which corruption has had no power; the right arm which baptised so many idolaters, threw down so many idols, raised so many dead from the grave. That same arm now reposes in Rome, like a conqueror taking his rest at the foot of the Capitol; there it may be seen and touched, still incorrupt, fresh and pliant. May I not now turn to Francis with grateful affection, and, in concluding my discourse, address to him the words which formed its commencement, bidding him arise and show forth his might? "Lift up thy hand over the strange nations, that they may see thy power. Renew thy signs and work new miracles. Glorify thy hand and thy right arm." Was it for naught that your right arm returned to dwell amongst us? Lift it up, lift it up over the nations; over this country, yours, not by birth, but by the strong tie of a most cordial affection. Renew amongst us those prodigies which excited the astonishment of so many barbarous tribes; and remember that if death snatched you away whilst still far from us, this was our misfortune, but by no means our fault. Our holy father Saint Ignatius, whom you so deeply revered, had already chosen you to relieve him of the heavy burden of the Generalship of his Order. The letter recalling you was already written, it was even despatched on its way to you, when your death frustrated his intentions; otherwise, you would have crowned all your past miracles with a fresh miracle inferior to none. The whole world would have seen that, at the behest of that simple *I*, written by his hand beneath the letter, with unhesitating obedience you would have immediately undertaken (in ignorance of its purpose) a long and wearisome journey, crossing once more the same oceans, confronting once more the same dangers, traversing the same zones; and, what is more, leaving others to reap the fruit of your toils, and enjoy the glory won by your labours. This was the lot Saint Ignatius certainly intended for you. And oh! what a welcome we should have prepared for you on your return to our shores, the conqueror of a heathen world, a second Apostle of the Gentiles! Your triumphant reception should have surpassed all Rome ever saw during the long course of many centuries; for, unless I am greatly mistaken, whole cities with their entire population would have gone forth to meet you, contending for the honour of carrying you upon their shoulders; you, the teacher of many nations, the prophet of such great renown; you, who preached in so many tongues, who put to flight so many diseases, who raised to life so many dead. But if envious death deprived us of all we hoped thus to gain from you, it is for you now to restore it to us; and this, as we know full well, you are even now doing, manifesting your presence in our midst by daily recurring wonders of love and power. Grow not weary of this course of munificence. "Glorify, glorify thy hand and thy right arm." Let each day witness some fresh deed calculated to make your arm more glorious, by pouring fresh benefits on your devout clients. And if to-day your blessing is to descend anywhere with especial efficacy, oh! let it be upon the inhabitants of this noble city; bless the walls which surround them, the air which they breathe, the earth which nourishes them; bless above all the pious congregation assembled here this morning; who, indifferent to those rhetorical embellishments, which might perhaps tend more to obscure the truth than to elucidate it, have patiently borne with the unvarnished simplicity of my discourse, bent only on acquiring a perfect knowledge of your surpassing deeds.

PANEGYRIC IN HONOUR OF SAINT ALOYSIUS GONZAGA.

THE INNOCENT RANKING HIMSELF WITH PENITENTS.

He was perhaps not far wrong who compared this world to a stormy ocean, temptation to the rocks which endanger navigation, and those who fall into vice to the shipwrecked. There is one thing, however, which always remains to afford hope of salvation to many, one plank to which the drowning man may cling, and this is Penance; and on this account some persons have grown so confident, so presumptuous, that trusting to find safety at the last upon this plank, they actually (incredible as it must appear) allow their vessel to drift upon the shoals and strike against the rocks, until it is split to pieces. What boundless folly is this! What a mad and wicked scheme we have here, one unworthy to be entertained for a moment by any generous heart! "Penance is, as it were, a saving plank to the unfortunate after shipwreck," thus wrote the eloquent Jerome to the Virgin Demetrias, "but by a virgin the ship is preserved entire." Base and ignoble is he who parts with his innocence without a pang, because he can yet save himself by penance. The truly courageous man aims at bringing his vessel into port safe and sound, having braved the whirlwinds and defied the tempests. Let him hand over penance to whoever may wish for it so long as he remains the possessor of innocence. It is one thing to seek what thou hast lost, another to possess what has never escaped thy grasp. And yet it appears to me that a loftier height and greater beauty might be attained by the soul who should unite at once in itself both these fair virtues, preserving the spotless innocence of an Angel whilst practising the penance of a sinner. I know that penance necessarily presupposes guilt, and that on this account it can form no closer union with innocence than iron can with silver, or lead with gold. But then again, if, as we learn from the celebrated saying of Gregory the Great, it is peculiar to holy souls to see sin in themselves where no sin exists, why should it not be possible to live a blameless life and yet never cease to bewail one's guilt? And this indeed is what Aloysius did, that Saint to whom, upon his throne in heaven, we offer our homage to-day. I think that in very few instances could greater purity than his be met with; and yet, on the other hand, where can instances of greater penitence be found? It is my intention to set before you on this occasion these two qualities harmoniously united in his person. And do not imagine that this union is not in every degree worthy of admiration; for since the Communion of Saints is divided into the two companies of the innocent and the penitent, ought we not to award a high place in our esteem to him who, not content with the glories of the former, can likewise claim the merit belonging to the latter, and who resembles the wondrous Angel beheld in Patmos standing with one foot upon the earth and one upon the sea? I ask you to lend me your kind attention while I proceed to show you that this is precisely what Saint Aloysius did.

And truly how small is the number of those who can boast with truth that they have preserved inviolate that innocence which they received in their infancy at the sacred font! It cannot be denied that all the Saints who form the Church's brightest ornament, whom she has raised to her altars, whom she year by year commemorates, are heroes of sanctity, proposed to us as admirable patterns for our conduct, like eagles who teach the lesser birds to soar. But how few are those whose every action affords an example for our imitation! The Church herself is constrained to admit that in the case of some there is much to condemn, much to blame, in the case of others it is only for the sake of the deaths they died that she condones the life they led. Far be it from me, my brethren, to diminish the glory of any one by means of an invidious comparison. But who is not aware that amongst those Saints who are our models, many have only been distinguished for their continence after having for a long space of time given rein to their lusts; or for their humility after having freely indulged their ambition; and of those who have made themselves worthy of imitation on account of their piety, how many had previously yielded to abominable license! In some we admire their temperance, but it follows upon years of debauchery; in others we admire their wisdom, only attained after a period of folly; we marvel at the voluntary poverty of others, but those very same persons were formerly remarkable for their gorgeous apparel; and those who afterwards became models of recollection could look back on years of distraction; those who are now patterns of compunction on a long series of amusements. Thus, even Seneca, speaking of Augustus, extols his piety and moderation, but adds that in bygone days he had often swelled the ocean with rivers of blood, filled the land with slaughter, the islands with exiles, and the strongholds with prisoners. Nothing of this kind can be alleged respecting the subject of my present discourse. He did not begin to practise virtue after having, so to speak, wearied himself out in the service of vice; on the contrary, all his actions may be justly regarded as worthy of our admiration, praise, and imitation, and they are all of such remarkable merit that each might be pronounced supereminent, were not the rest found to be in no way inferior to it. My hearers, if you reflect for a moment, you will perceive this to be sanctity of no ordinary stamp, for it has been the privilege of very few, even among the holiest of mortals, never to do anything during the whole course of their life which could cause them even a blush, much less fill them with confusion. "This," exclaims Saint Jerome, "is a special glory; this is a boast which can be rarely made."

And if you proceed to tell me that the life of Aloysius was cut short at the early age of twenty-three years, I state in reply, that he lived long enough to pass through the most dangerous stage of life. Who does not know that childhood, youth, and early manhood are the periods when the tendency to vice is strongest, and when a hasty tongue, hot blood, want of experience, and weakness of purpose, make it especially difficult not to run upon some one of the many rocks which lie concealed beneath the treacherous current of such a world as ours? And yet Aloysius kept himself so free, during those perilous years, from any serious fault that Cardinal Bellarmine (a man whose learning and integrity are of world-wide reputation), after having carefully considered, searched, and passed in review the conscience of the holy youth, who was his own spiritual child, unhesitatingly gave it as his opinion that Aloysius had been confirmed in grace. This privilege is known to have been conferred upon the Apostles, and after them, according to the teaching of the same Cardinal, upon some few other chosen and highly-favoured souls, whom God in all ages preserves for Himself in the Church, in order that He may delight Himself in them as in a garden enclosed. Can we for a moment doubt that the soul of Aloysius was one of these when we see how speedily God claimed him for His own? His mother, the Marchioness Martha, during her pregnancy, underwent such sufferings and experienced such peculiar symptoms that the doctors agreed in thinking that no hope remained of preserving the life of her offspring; therefore, she made it her sole object to secure to him at as early a period as possible that heavenly life, the acquisition of which alone gives importance to man's entrance into this world. On this account the zealous nurse hastened to confer on him the sacred rite of Baptism almost before he had left his mother's womb; no sooner had she done so than all danger was at an end. So that I have no hesitation in affirming this to have been nothing else than a wise scheme, a loving artifice of divine grace, anxious to take possession at the earliest possible period of so fair a soul. Those of you, my hearers, who follow the chase must know well the pleasure a sportsman experiences when able to take from the nest the birds he requires for his sport; knowing as he does the ease with which he can attach these young fledglings to himself, can feed them, teach them, train them, and make them in everything obedient to his will. And here I am reminded how Christ, that valiant huntsman on Whom it was enjoined that He should hasten to take away the spoils, "make haste to take away the prey" (Is. viii. 3), gathered of all kinds and in all places. He caught Andrew, James, Peter, and John by the shores of the Galilean lake; He hunted down a publican, Zaccheus, from among the boughs of a tree; He captured a prostitute, the Samaritan woman, beside the well of Jacob; He snatched the soul of a thief, hanging upon the cross, hovering between heaven and earth. But of all the prey He took, none was so dear to Him as the soul of the Infant Precursor, his own ere it quitted the nest, that is to say, the maternal womb; in this case above all He proved Himself no dilatory hunter, but made haste as he was bidden, to take away the prey. We see, moreover, that none was a more successful capture, for this one surpassed all others when arrived at its maturity in gifts, in talent, and in value. And now behold (if I may be permitted to express myself thus), behold what God did in the case of Aloysius; He took him from the nest. And if He did not use as much speed in making this capture as in that of the Baptist, yet He showed to this child a special mark of favour, in that He vouchsafed to make him His own ere he set foot upon this earth.

Hence, who can unfold aright the marvellous training in virtue which Aloysius received, even in his tenderest years, from his illustrious captor? When reason's first ray fell upon his infant mind, he was as one who awakes from a deep sleep; for he awoke to a full and unclouded knowledge of God, to an ardent resolve to consecrate himself to His service. In after-life he preserved so distinct a recollection of this self-dedication, which took place at the age of seven years, that he used to term it his conversion; and amongst the most precious reminiscences confided by him to those who had the charge of his soul, one was that he had begun to love God from the very first moment in which he first knew Him. May we not rather say that he began to revere his Maker even before he began to know Him? for whilst yet a mere baby of four years old, a secret impulse urged him to so close a union with God that, to the extreme astonishment of his attendants, he was often found on his knees in prayer in some lonely corner or deserted garret. Nor need this seem incredible to us. For as nature teaches the sunflower to bend towards the sun, which it cannot discern; the loadstone to follow the attraction of that planet, which it does not know; and the flame to tend towards the sphere it fails to detect: thus certain souls, specially favoured by God, are usually found to possess a secret and indescribable impulse by which they are led, in some hidden manner, to seek Him before they know Him, and to invoke Him before they have learnt by what name to address Him. On the other hand, Aloysius no sooner began to know the world than he began to despise it. Occasionally he was obliged to be present at entertainments and sights, such as tournaments, feats of horsemanship, and games; but even whilst yet a child he disdained to gaze on them, and either fixing on the ground his modest eyes, or covering them with his hand, he preserved amidst the hubbub of the theatre a spirit of recollection which others have barely attained in the silent cell of the hermit. His attire was always indifferent, and sometimes even torn; his words were few, and uttered with reluctance; he never sought the company of others, but, on the contrary, frequently shunned it. What marvel is it, therefore, that he kept his innocence unspotted amid the temptations of the world and the snares of the court, in which he lived until he reached the age of seventeen years; like the solar ray which, rather than contract any stain itself, purifies the objects it rests upon? And if in the world he remained so pure, think what he must have become in the cloister. We know that, in the natural order, everything possesses greater power, achieves far more, lasts much longer, in its own native element than elsewhere. See yonder fish as it lies inert and panting on the river bank; moved by compassion, perhaps, you restore it to the stream; immediately it revives, swims away, darts hither and thither, and is itself again. There are some roses which when reared on our soil have neither vigour nor fragrance, and yet in their native land of China they form the delight of the fairest gardens. The cedar in our clime is stunted in growth and barren of fruit, while beneath its own Eastern heaven it constitutes the glory of the far-famed Libanus. It is in their own sphere and region that the fire is brightest and the air purest; it is from the bowels of the earth that virgin soil is dug; and we find water which if kept even in a silver vase becomes foul and putrid, springs up clear as crystal from its bed, though this should be of mud. And why is this? Because each locality is possessed of qualities peculiar to itself, and admirably adapted for the preservation of whatever nature entrusts to its safe-keeping. Now who is there but knows that piety finds in the world an uncongenial soil, that its true home is in religion? And if Aloysius preserved his innocence untainted in the vitiated atmosphere of a court, how must it have flourished when transferred to the pure air of the cloister?

Notwithstanding his great purity, he yet followed a course of penance so rigid, so unintermitting, so inexorable, that it can scarcely be recalled to mind without tears of tender compassion, especially if we consider the illustrious station of the child who practised it and the delicacy of his youthful frame. Listen while I tell you how Aloysius taxed his ingenuity to invent mortifications severe even to imprudence, stopping short only of what was prohibited, for such were those which the courageous youth imposed on himself. From the age of eleven he entered on a course of fasting so austere, so rigorous, that one would hardly believe it possible for him to have borne it, did not facts assure us that he did so. Whenever he eat a whole egg at a meal, he thought that he had indulged his appetite to an excess; and the strictest, most dreaded fast on bread and water was to him so ordinary a matter that although in the first instance restricted to Fridays, he gradually extended the practice of it to one day after another; and even from this penitential fare he would rise with unappeased appetite. In vain did hunger clamorously urge its claims, in vain did it gnaw his entrails and cause its pangs to be keenly felt; it was forced to content itself with three small slices of bread

steeped in water of a morning, and one perhaps at
night, as the utmost concession to be obtained. Even
on those days when he did not fast (and which can they
have been?) he gradually retrenched much from his
ordinary food, so that the amount of bread and other
things he eat at any meal being weighed was found
not to exceed an ounce; a thing so unheard of that
many were led to entertain the firm belief that as the
manner of his birth had been miraculous, so the preservation of his life must be a continuous miracle. For
what more could he have done in the deserts of Egypt
or the caves of Palestine, had he been sitting at table
beside a frozen fount with such hermits as Hilarion or
Macarius, as Zozimus, Onofrius, or Serapion? But in
my opinion it was a far greater thing that he should
act thus in his father's house, sitting daily like a voluntary Tantalus at a well-spread board, which groaned
beneath exquisite viands, tempting wines, appetising
condiments of all kinds. For if a perfect self-control
with regard to food and drink is accounted by Cle-
machus as admirable and very rare even in an aged
anchorite, how much more wonderful was it in a boy
of twelve or fourteen, at the very age when all children
show an avidity for food, since they are not as yet
capable of appreciating anything better? No wonder
then that in a short time he became so pale, so emaciated, so fragile, as to remind all who beheld him of a
fair lily, to which both cloud and stream had grudged
their fertilising stores. What an incessant struggle
had he not, think you, to sustain with his parents, his
attendants, his medical advisers, who were alarmed for
his life? But, taking his excessive fervour for his only
counsellor, with pious craft he disguised under an

alleged aversion to food the ardent desire of penance that consumed him. That such was in fact the true nature of his desires we need not hesitate to affirm, since to Penance, as to a sweet spouse, he had dedicated his whole being; hers he was in body and soul, in his sleeping and his waking hours. The house he dwelt in afforded far more inducements to self-indulgence than opportunities for the practice of austerities. But what availed this? Till he succeeded in obtaining a more fitting hair-shirt, he used to wear next his skin a belt composed of sharp spurs; so great was his thirst for suffering even in these tender years! In vain did his servants prepare for him a luxurious bed beneath a rich canopy, Aloysius would stealthily possess himself of half-burnt firebrands or rough boards, and secrete them under the soft linen, partly to render his slumbers uneasy, partly to enable him the more readily to awake. For after a short period—I know not whether I ought to say of suffering or of repose—courageously springing from his bed he would kneel upon the bare ground, clad in nothing but his shirt, on the coldest winter nights, when all around was wrapt in thickest darkness and most profound silence. Thus he would remain, persevering in prayer for four or six consecutive hours, until he became from head to foot benumbed and almost stupefied with cold; until the blood seemed to freeze in his veins, and his powers gradually to forsake him. But when was his strength ever known to fail him so completely as not to leave enough for the purpose of self-torment? Full well could that right hand of his attest how, though frozen with the bitter cold, it was ever ready to handle pitiless scourges. Cords, collars, spikes, chains, all were used indifferently in chastising himself to blood; as it was his habit to do three times between night and day. Week by week his linen stained with blood was shown to his tender mother; and she, sorrowfully gazing on it, would say amidst her tears: "O my son, why dost thou thus throw away the blood which was my gift to thee? Perhaps because it was mine thou dost deem it unworthy to flow within thy veins? Have pity on me, son of my heart, if thou wilt have no pity on thyself! I did not give thee life in order that thou shouldst spend it in tormenting thyself. Thou knowest full well how nearly I lost my own life in giving birth to thee; it had been better for me if I had lost it, for then I should not have been compelled to die daily, as now I do, fearing to behold thy death." Thus would she lament from time to time, and thus would she discourse with her son. And he, with bashful modesty, would answer: "Hinder me not, my mother, from doing this little in atonement for my sins!" "In atonement for your sins, O Aloysius! and at what age did you first urge this plea? When scarcely thirteen years old; at a time when, although the life you led might have awakened the envy of the angels, you were nevertheless habitually practising penances from which the very anchorites themselves might shrink!" Is not this enough, my hearers, to fill us with the deepest confusion? Add to the innocence of which I spoke above the penitence I have just been describing, and tell me, when did union more uncommon meet your eye? Even in one who has been a great sinner, great penance must ever excite our admiration, although experience teaches us that a consciousness of guilt forms the strongest motive for self-torment; when frightful phantoms of the past rise up in unmasked hideousness before the mind of the startled sinner, and show him a heaven that might have been his, a hell yawning to receive him, a crucified Saviour despised, a God trampled under foot! What wonder, then, that man, indignant with himself, should take justice into his own hands and call for blood in expiation of his crimes? But how is it possible that a youth so perfectly innocent as not to have a single fault deserving of chastisement should treat himself with, one might almost say, ferocious cruelty, so that, as Saint Bernard says: "Let one who has not been guilty of actual sin assume the feelings of the penitent, and he who has in himself no cause for doing penance, may have reason for sorrow.

But let us see what were the faults with which Aloysius reproached himself, and for which he wished to make atonement with his blood. Had he, perhaps, defiled his body with sins of the flesh? God forbid: never did a gardener show more assiduous care in protecting his jonquils and jasmines from the malignant breath of the north wind than Aloysius did in preserving the delicate flower of his purity. At the age of nine years, whilst living in this very city of Florence, he consecrated himself to the service of Mary by a vow of perpetual chastity. How loyal he was to that Mistress, and how untarnished and immaculate he kept his chastity it is superfluous to add; for he practised admirably that jealous circumspection commended by Saint Gregory, the circumspection of a man intrusted to carry gold through a wood known to be the haunt of thieves. Thus he was ever on his guard in the company of others, mistrustful of every recreation, suspicious of every pleasure. I need not tell you that feminine art never succeeded in leading him to bestow on any beauty a curious, much less an amorous, glance. We find him solicitous on all occasions to avoid the sight of women, which incautious youth in the present day no less eagerly seeks; and it is further recorded of him that even at home, when sitting at table or engaged in conversation with his mother, he rarely ventured to fix his eyes on her countenance; as if he had heard, from the lips of Saint Jerome, that not even at home is there anything which it is safe to look upon. You will readily perceive that so angelic a youth could have no carnal sins to expiate in his body. What, then, had he to avenge? Perhaps outbursts of uncontrolled anger? We read of him, on the contrary, that the greatest annoyance he ever displayed was when one day, after he had entered into religion, some person in the course of a discussion loaded him with praise. Perhaps he gave way at times to immoderate laughter? We do not read that he ever indulged in greater signs of joy than once when during his religious life he was insulted and abused at an inn. But why prolong this examination? At last, my hearers, I have discovered the truth; at last I have discovered what it was which Aloysius sought to expiate by all this self-inflicted suffering. Now I apprehend the object of those facts, the aim of those flagellations, the meaning of those hair-shirts; I know, if I mistake not, the purport of these and all his other strange modes of torture. Shall I tell you his intention? To atone for certain sins which he thought he had committed before he reached the age of seven years. These words may perhaps sound in your ears as a jest; but Aloysius himself acknowledged that, as far as his subsequent life was concerned, he had nothing of any consequence on his conscience. His chief sorrow arose from the remembrance of two childish failings of which he had been guilty when about five years old; childish failings we call them, but Aloysius himself gave them a very different name, and never ceased to deplore them as long as he lived. One was having appropriated to himself some gunpowder by stealth, and the other was having inadvertently repeated some indecent expressions learnt of the soldiers with whom his father intentionally allowed him to mix, in the hope that he might acquire a taste for the profession of arms. Such were the two greatest faults he had ever committed; and these he took so much to heart, that, going on one occasion after he was seven to accuse himself at the feet of the priest, so intense was the agony of his mind, so great the compunction of his conscience, and so extreme the confusion he felt at the remembrance of these imperfections (which really did not deserve the name of sins) that on opening his lips to confess them he fell down in a dead faint. O pure and tender heart! not human indeed in thy nature, but angelic! If such were thy greatest stains, what can the lesser ones have been? Did these call for such pitiless expiation at thy hand? was it to wipe out these thou didst shed thy blood, and ever wound thyself afresh? If this was meet for thee, what beseems a guilty wretch such as I am? How can I atone for offences, alas! but too real, if so much expiation was due from thee, for faults more apparent than actual? Hand over to me the cruel instruments of torture thou didst wield with so relentless a hand; mine should be those chains, mine those scourges, for what punishment will be severe enough to wipe out my sins, if thine demanded such penance as this?

But I perceive that the subject presents another aspect. It may be said that Aloysius practised all these rigours rather with a view to prevention than to expiation, directing them to this end, as has been done by other innocent souls, such as Bernard, Francis, and Benedict, who cast themselves naked into freezing water, or on to a bed of thorns, not in order to atone for sins they had committed, but to blunt the edge of temptation. Is it so? Let me tell you, my hearers, that now my astonishment reaches the highest pitch. It is indisputable that Aloysius was distinguished by great natural vivacity, by gentle manners, a pleasing exterior, and a high spirit; of which latter he gave proof whilst yet a mere infant, displaying such dexterity and daring in the use of arms that with his tiny hand he would put the match to small pieces of artillery, never flinching for a moment, although his life was in great danger. Yet we are solemnly assured by those most intimately acquainted with his heart that never, in the whole course of his life, did he experience the least movement repugnant to modesty, never did the least desire of carnal gratification stir within him, never a passing shadow of impurity flit across his soul. Such an effect is utterly beyond the powers of nature to produce; it is, moreover, exceptional in the order of grace, as is plainly shown by the instances quoted above of Bernard, Francis, and Benedict. How much the more admirable, then, is this thirst for penance of the severest kind in a soul so highly gifted as that of Aloysius? That a penitent like Jerome, who, as we hear from his own humble confession, even while imprisoned in body amongst the caves of wild beasts, was, despite himself, present in spirit in the halls of the Roman ladies; that such an one as he should chastise his flesh with thorns and stones I can readily conceive; nor is it to be marvelled at that he should choose the frozen earth for his couch, and slake his thirst with pure water. But that all this should be done by a mere child, by one, too, who constantly dwelt in spirit amongst the Choirs of Angels, not so much to pay them homage as to join in the homage they pay, this is an instance of penance to which I think it would be difficult to find a parallel. Perhaps, however, temptations of a different nature leagued together to assail the holy youth? May we not suppose that the peace of his heart followed upon the tumult of passions, as the sea enjoys a period of calm after a storm, halcyon breezes succeeding the fierce struggle of wintry winds? I have recounted to you the greatest faults into which Aloysius fell; now listen while I relate to you the severest temptations which assailed him during the course of his whole life; and having told you in what the greatest consisted, I will leave you to draw your own conclusions as to what the lesser ones may have been. From his earliest years he habitually entertained a most lowly opinion of himself, and after he went into religion, this humility having increased in proportion to his increasing sanctity, one day he began seriously to confer with his own heart, and to ask himself: What will my Order do with such a worthless wretch as I am? The devil, seeing in this dejection an opportunity for assailing that soul which had hitherto proved invulnerable on every side, directed against it a last and most formidable battery; and, well aware that vice is never so insidious as when it wears the mask of virtue, he carefully fostered that pernicious humility, in the hope that it might degenerate into pusillanimity, mistrust, and despair. But the practised warrior quickly perceived the astute devices of the enemy, and, in order to repulse his attack, had recourse to his accustomed weapons of penance and tears. Such, then, by his own confession, was the greatest temptation he ever had to encounter. And was so much needed to overcome it? O Aloysius, why was I not at your side when you asked yourself over and over again that melancholy question: What will my Order do with me? for, had I been there, my heart would have foretold what was in store for you; and not even the risk of displeasing you could have deterred me from uttering words calculated not only to dispel your discouragement, but to afford matter for self-complacency. What, I should have said, you ask what your Order will do with you? Listen, and I will tell you what she will do with you. She will mention you with joy on her greatest feasts, as one of the most distinguished persons who have ever worn her habit and shed lustre on her name; she will exult to think that for her sake you relinquished the rich domains of the house of Gonzaga, that you spurned your illustrious parentage, your splendid prospects; that you extorted the permission so long denied you to number yourself among her members, not like others, by dint of tears and of entreaties, but at the cost of your own blood.

What will your Order do with you? She will hold you up to all posterity as an angel of manners; she will propose you as a model of obedience; she will exhibit your portrait, traced on a thousand canvases, to those distant nations, who having heard of your fame, desire to gaze on your features; and moreover, for your greater glory, those portraits will depict you as conquering the waters, when the whirlpools of the Ticinus, though they already had you within their grasp, were fain to yield up their prey unhurt; or as triumphing over fire when, in Castiglione, the devouring flames enveloped your couch and left you unscathed. Nor will they fail to record that memorable moment when, like the bow in the cloud, a harbinger of fair weather after long storms, you brought peace to your troubled country; when a few words from you were efficacious to appease an implacable feud existing between your cousin the Duke of Mantua and your brother the Marquis of Castiglione—a feud which the Archduchess Eleanor of Austria, aunt of the Emperor Rudolph, and the Archduke Ferdinand of Austria, brother of the Emperor Maximilian, besides other royal personages, had long laboured in vain to extinguish. What will your Order do with you? She will select you (in preference to many of her sons highly distinguished by learning or sanctity), she will, I say, select you as the illustrious Patron of all those colleges in which she is wont to impart instruction to the young and train them in piety. And she will have good reason to congratulate herself on the happy choice she made, when she sees how many youths whose mental powers were naturally of a low order, and whose education had been neglected or defective, after having had recourse to you, excelled all their comrades in acuteness. She will hasten to erect splendid altars in your honour, and when nought but your ashes remain to her, the possession of these alone will suffice to make her an object of envy and to establish her fame. For the least morsel of those ashes will be deemed the most precious gift that Princes can receive at her hands; and Duke Vincent of Mantua, your cousin, after having by their means twice been miraculously restored to health, will employ his interest with other magnates in order to gain for you public honours in the Church. What will your Order do with you? She will preserve you as a precious relic within tombs of silver and urns of gold; she will surround you with magnificent trophies, with glorious spoils, the votive offerings of multitudes of her children who have not invoked your aid in vain. She will commemorate you as one before whom demons tremble, since in Rome the invocation of your name was all-powerful in compelling them to let go the victims they were tormenting; she will mention you as giving sight to the blind, for when your portrait was publicly exposed in Siena, many eyes were opened long closed to the light of day; she will show you as healing the sick, for in Perugia the touch of your bones proved efficacious in dispelling the malignant fevers by which many were laid low; finally, she will exhibit you as restoring those hovering on the brink of the grave, for in Poland did you not frequently appear to persons whose life was despaired of, and obtain for them a prolongation of their days? You ask what your Order will do with you. Behold what she will do with you. Do all these great things appear as nothing in your eyes?

Thus I would fain have answered Aloysius, and in some such manner (to return to the point whence I originally started) I would have endeavoured to persuade him that if he was beset by no temptation more grievous than this, it behoved him to lay aside his disciplines, to put off his hair-shirts, to abandon his fasts, or at least relax their severity; since truly there was more danger of pride than occasion for despondency. However, you must plainly see that my efforts would have been fruitless. Death alone was able to bring repose to the body he tormented so mercilessly; and indeed (if the truth must be told) he contrived to inflict suffering even upon death itself. For after he had received the sacred Viaticum, and his departing spirit, hovering upon his lips, was about to spread its wings for its final flight, he conjured his Superior by the mercies of Christ, to permit him to be severely scourged from head to foot, as an atonement for the too great tenderness he had shown his body when in health. What more could Aloysius have asked, if he had humoured and indulged his feeble frame, instead of treating it with such severity? And now, let the sinner draw near and hear the last request of an expiring angel! Was it nothing that throughout the many months of his fatal illness, he habitually drank his medicines slowly and by degrees, in order the better to taste their bitterness? Was it nothing that he intentionally continued to lie on one side, until a putrefying sore was formed, which greatly aggravated his suffering? Was it nothing that when enduring intensest pain he would not accept the least alleviation, refreshment or comfort? It would seem as if all this were indeed nothing, when we hear him entreat for that last and final chastisement. O my hearers, let this recital fill us with confusion; us, miserable sinners, who although guilty of innumerable misdeeds, can yet enjoy our ease, and dream of purchasing a happy death at the price of a single sigh!

But what was in fact the real object of your desire, O Aloysius? Did you hope to obtain at the hands of your friends something akin to that martyr's death which you had long but vainly wished to receive from strangers? Reassure yourself on this point, for the martyr's crown, apparently denied you on earth, will certainly be yours in heaven. How so? my hearers will exclaim; what is this we are told? Aloysius a martyr in heaven? Yes, truly, my brethren; Aloysius is a martyr; in heaven he ranks as such. And whence do we know this? We know it on the authority of one whose testimony admits of no question; you have often heard of Saint Mary Magdalen of Pazzi, that flower of Carmel, the glory of this city of Florence, the pride of our century. She it is who assures us of the fact. In one of the most wondrous visions with which that holy soul was favoured, she was caught up in ecstasy to heaven, and there beheld the bliss enjoyed by Aloysius. The glorious sight filled her with astonishment, so that in her rapture she exclaimed aloud: "Oh, how great is the glory of Aloysius, the son of Ignatius! Had I not witnessed it, I could not have believed in it! Oh! how great is the glory of Aloysius, the son of Ignatius! It appears to me" (mark, these are her very words) "it appears to me that the glory which Aloysius possesses is such as I should not have thought possible to be found among the blessed in heaven. I tell you he is a Saint of no ordinary merit; would that I could proclaim his greatness throughout the whole world." Here she paused awhile, and then resumed: "Aloysius was a hidden martyr; he himself made a martyr of himself." And thus she went on for a considerable space, using various expressions to magnify and exalt both his past merits and present reward. What do you say to this, my brethren? Is not this a weighty confirmation of my assertion? Moreover, who can doubt that Aloysius was judged worthy of a martyr's palm in heaven, since his death may be more fitly termed a violent than a natural one. Impelled by ardent charity, he courted death in the most crowded hospitals, wherever infection was at its height; for, when the plague was raging in Rome, he asked and finally obtained the permission of his Superior to succour its victims at the risk of his life. And so freely did he expose his life that he lost it, offering himself as a voluntary holocaust for the salvation of his fellow-citizens. And if on this account you will not award him the title of martyr, he can yet claim it in virtue of his self-inflicted torture, which in the case of a sinner we term penance, but in the case of one who is innocent we may reasonably designate as martyrdom. But, however this may be, you must at least acknowledge that his merit must be of no common order, who in heaven shines with a two-fold lustre, who ranks both with the innocent and the penitent, in one or other of which two classes all the Saints must range themselves.

Nor need you wonder that one of your fellow-citizens, a Florentine, was chosen by God to proclaim the glory of Aloysius, for the city of Florence was especially dear to the heart of that Saint. Here he passed several years of his life, attached to the service, and enjoying the favourable protection of a Prince, equally illustrious in character and in name, who unites in his own person the glories of all those noble houses with which he is connected by blood. Here it was that he carried on his studies, that he made rapid progress in piety, that he consecrated his virginal purity to heaven by an indissoluble bond, as we have already stated. In after-times he always remembered this city with feelings of grateful tenderness; and whenever in the company of his intimate friends mention happened to be made of it, he used affectionately to term it his dear Florence, the place where his spiritual life took its birth, where any childish piety he might have possessed was confirmed and strengthened. And shall we think that a city which was so dear to him during his sojourn on earth is not still dearer to him now that he is in heaven? Does not the seraphic Virgin, your distinguished fellow-citizen, of whom I have just spoken, amongst other revelations respecting Aloysius, tell us that in Paradise he is constantly engaged in interceding for his earthly benefactors, especially those his obligations to whom are of a spiritual nature? If this be true, may we not conclude that he offers earnest and unremitting prayer for the city which he himself calls, not merely the nurse of his interior life, but its mother? It is only necessary for you on your side to approach your loving Advocate with confidence and security; to redouble your expressions of homage; to present more costly pledges of your devotion. Why should you hesitate? Do you fear, perhaps, lest your Patron should prove less powerful than he is kind? But let me here remind you of a secret (one certainly of no trifling importance) which during his lifetime he confided to his confessor, namely, that he never (and I am adding nothing to his words) that he never had commended to God any affair, great or small, without obtaining the result he desired, although to others the difficulties might appear inextricable, and the obstacles insuperable. If on earth he was thus all-powerful, what must he be in heaven? If he does such great things for others, how much the more will he do for you, O Florentines? And of this he has already given you abundant proofs; for was not that a Florentine, the child of the noble Ridolfi, who, thanks to his intercession, was freed from the power of a fearful spell which left no repose day or night to his tormented spirit? And was not that pious maiden also a Florentine, the daughter of the Carlini, who, through invoking him, obtained the cure of a malignant gangrene, which was, in the opinion of physicians, past all remedy? And I might name many others, Florentines likewise, were it not that they are still living, are perhaps present here in our midst, who, as we learn from their own lips, have in various ways experienced his assistance; one having been delivered from imminent danger of drowning; another healed of incurable tumours in his knees; another relieved from severe internal spasms; others having, when prostrated by fatal illness, been snatched by main force, as it were, from the relentless jaws of death. How, then, can you do otherwise than confide in so illustrious a Protector, in one who gives you such continual pledges of his patronage? Look down upon us, O Aloysius, from your place in heaven, wherever that place may be; behold us who call upon your name, who turn to you with holy confidence and trustful love. Receive our vows, accept our offerings, listen to our prayers. Forget not the Mother of your piety, your dear, your beloved Florence; and, above all, remember the illustrious Princes whom on earth you disdained not to serve, and in heaven you cannot fail to protect.

PANEGYRIC IN HONOUR OF SAINT THOMAS OF AQUIN.

"To him that giveth me wisdom, will I give glory."
Eccl. li. 23.

How well would it be for many persons in the present day if, instead of applying themselves with so much diligence to the cultivation of their intellect, they were rather to direct their studies to the improvement of their heart! The number of proud Lucifers who rebel against God would not then be daily on the increase, as it is now. For what does the Christian want with so much learning, since faith alone is enough for him? Will any one of us, when summoned before the dread tribunal of Christ, receive condemnation because he has not mastered the writings of Aristotle and Plato? Shall we be lost because we have not soared on eagle's pinions to the summit of Libanon, there to gather the pith of those giant cedars, the sacred books of which so vast a forest stretches before us? What folly on our part to forget that what God requires us to give Him is not our understanding, but our heart: "My son, give me thy heart" (Prov. xxiii. 26). Furthermore, how plainly He shows us that it is His delight to converse with the simple, that He loves to receive little children?

Why should we spend our strength in poring over books, seeking to become wise beyond our years, since, should it be our lot to reach an advanced age, would not the object of our endeavours then be to return to the simplicity of childhood? Such, my brethren, is the foolish language of some persons, who, in order to depreciate those gifts which they do not possess, use arguments true in themselves in proof of false assertions, as, for instance, that ignorance is to a certain extent a necessary element of sanctity; as if the archer who drew his bow in the dark was more likely to send his arrow straight to the mark than one who took aim in broad daylight. But, thanks be to God, to-day the example of Saint Thomas, that great Angel of the Schools, will confute all such false reasoning. In him the most fervent devotion of heart was united to the most rare intellectual acuteness; he was a Lucifer among men, without a Lucifer's pride. And greatly will it redound to his glory in the last great day, that he studied Aristotle and mastered Plato; that from his very infancy he devoured the sacred Scriptures with the relish of a famished man. Did not Christ love to converse with him, though He knew him to be so wise? Did not Christ delight in his society, though he was so advanced in all sciences? How then can one possibly allege that it ought to be enough for us as Christians to believe with childlike faith, when we have it in our power even to teach others to believe? That without learning we can please God is certain; let not, therefore, the ignorant and illiterate disquiet or distress themselves on account of their lack of erudition, for all that God *requires* of us is our heart. But, on the other hand, let the man of intellect rejoice, let him take courage and aim high; for what great things may he not accomplish if he consecrates to God the powers of his mind as well as the affections of his heart! "To him that giveth me wisdom will I give glory." It seems to me that God addresses these words to each and all of us, inviting us to give Him so great a gift. I know that these words are usually taken in another sense, for they are often applied to man addressing his God, Whom we acknowledge to be the sovereign Giver of all wisdom; but who can find fault with me if, on this occasion, I put them in the mouth of God, in the sense in which they are applied above? That great glory will accrue to all who dedicate their talents to the service of God, is a fact so indubitably certain that none will be tempted to call it in question; and this is the reason why Saint Thomas now wears so glorious a crown. Behold then, my hearers, one equally eminent as a scholar and saint, held up for your imitation. Behold him, the living Eden, in which the tree of knowledge and the tree of life flourish side by side in rival luxuriance; behold the Ark, in which are laid up both the pot of manna and the tables of the law; behold the nest, where the simple dove and the wise serpent can abide together in peace. Learning and sanctity are not at variance; on the contrary, they mutually help one another, if, instead of employing it for his own profit or his own pleasure, man will but give his intellect to God. This our Saint did most fully; and since he thus so distinguished himself, who can blame me if, for this very thing, I look on him with admiration?

And in fact, what great things might not Saint Thomas have achieved, if, instead of exclusively devoting his powers to the service of God, he had chosen rather to employ them in the furtherance of his own interests. How many there are in the world, who have made letters a source of gain, and have cultivated them for the same end, as the alchymists of yore who sought to change mercury into gold. Antisthenes is a prominent instance of this mercenary spirit among orators, Pythagoras among sophists, Aristippus among philosophers, Simonides among poets. Trebonianus among lawyers; all were so intent upon pecuniary gains, as actually to introduce avarice among the liberal arts. Now I am well aware that gains such as these had no attraction for Thomas, since his family was a noble, wealthy, and illustrious one, and he would have scorned to degrade his intellect by employing it for the purpose of accumulating gold, gathering together a heap of glittering dust. But if with his brilliant mental gifts he had sought either for preferment in the Church or a high place at court, what a splendid position might not his illustrious connections have secured for him! Before he had fully reached the age of fourteen years, he had already completed his philosophical studies under Peter of Ibernia, a professor of note, and had left his fellow-students so far behind him, that the eyes of all Naples were fixed upon him, and he met with universal applause and renown; like the gallant courser, who not only has none to contend for the prize with him, but none even to follow him from afar off. Who can tell what might have been the result, had he given a ready ear to the flattering breath of fame? But did he do so? By no means; quickly perceiving that worldly honour is but a fleeting breath, he judged it unworthy of his aspirations; and his attention having been attracted to the Order of

Preachers, then in its infancy, without informing any one of his intention, he went to hide himself within its sacred shelter; laying aside his titles and stripping himself of all his possessions, casting off everything that might hinder him from immersing himself in the ocean of divine contemplation, an ocean which knows no shore and which no mortal intelligence can ever fathom.

It will perhaps surprise you, my brethren, to hear of such generous courage in one so young; but from his earliest years, to know God had been Thomas's most insatiable desire. You know what a natural avidity for information may be remarked in very young children; if they see a butterfly fluttering in the sunshine, if a glow-worm sparkle in the darkness, or the shrill cry of a locust is heard, they importune one with ceaseless questions as to what everything is. But of what description, think you, were the questions in which Thomas displayed his childish curiosity? He interrogated every one concerning the nature of God. All his thirst for knowledge centred in this one point; he repeated his inquiries, he insisted on them with troublesome importunity; and these sublime thoughts possessed such absorbing interest for the simple mind of the child, that all who witnessed it were astonished and touched; beholding in him an exemplification of the truth of Anaxagoras' words, that man does not come into the world in order to gaze on the glory of the sun, but on the glory of Him Who made that sun. Wherefore take heart, O Thomas! and be of good cheer; for if in your day any mortal man shall be privileged to comprehend the divine nature, you shall be that one. It shall be yours to discover the errors into which

Chrisippus fell, when he presumed to call in question the liberty of God, as if without liberty of action dominion were a thing possible; it shall be yours to expose Epicurus, who denied the Providence of God, or Cleanthes, who disputed the simplicity of His being; and then, having refuted one by one the errors of others, you will discourse upon the divine attributes in so sublime a strain that men, awestruck at your vast wisdom, and reluctant to acknowledge their own great inferiority to one formed of the same clay and made of the same nature as themselves, will agree to pronounce you to be more than human, to call you an Angel. Withdraw then to the shades of the cloister, and there let it be your occupation as it is your desire, to mortify yourself, to humble yourself; for in the valley of self-abasement may be found the surest and nearest path to the mountain of the Most High.

Our Saint has already set off on his road; but of what use is it for him to do so when there are so many ready to oppose his entrance into the cloister? Fiery is the ordeal through which he will have to pass, terrible is the onslaught that will be made upon him, numerous are the outrages he will have to endure. Come down, ye angels, from your starry heights, hasten to his succour: protect the innocent young man from the cruel attack made on him in the public highway. Soldiers, hired for the purpose, suddenly surround him; he is covered with blows and cuffs, and finally, like a criminal, he is confined in a tower, where he must either retract his purpose or languish in misery. But who are they who have ventured to treat him thus? Are they Moors, perhaps, or the barbarous inhabitants of Tartary or Thrace? Alas! that

I should have to call them Christians, and thus bring shame on all who bear that name! Those who ill-used the pious youth so cruelly were his nearest relatives; they were his brothers, his sisters, his very mother herself. As is commonly the case, they could not bear to see the destruction of the lofty hopes or grandeur and glory to their house which had been raised by the early career of so promising a scion; they were maddened by anger, and, rather than relinquish one of the supports of their family, they sought to rob Christ of one of His followers. And to what length did they not go, carried away by rage? Not content with cutting him off from all intercourse with religious persons, whom they dreaded as ravenous birds of prey, not content with forbidding him to speak of spiritual things, and putting an obstacle in the way of all his pious practices, they proceeded to an action, the mere thought of which makes my blood run cold. They sent an abandoned woman to his room to tempt him to sin. Could ingenious malice and treacherous cruelty go further than this? And what, O unhappy youth, were you to do in such a position? It had been less dangerous for you to find yourself shut in your room, face to face with one of the fiercest lions of Erymanthus, than with this shameless daughter of Eve! David slew lions with his own hand, but he was overcome by the deceitful beauty of Bethsabee; Samson strangled lions in his might, but he was powerless to resist the enticing words of Dalila. And what will you do, who are so far from equalling them in years and in experience? Are you trembling for Thomas, my hearers, seeing him in such peril? Fear not; he is unconquered, he is unconquerable; nay, more, he is already triumphant; he has put to flight his tempter. And with what weapons has he done this? with a club, or a sword, or a spear? No; our youthful Saint could not, had he wished it, have wielded those weapons. A burning brand was the weapon he made use of. With such contemptible arms was she chased away; a brand plucked from the hearth put this brand of hell to flight. And then, the combat ended, was it not due to the youthful athlete that the angels should come down to reward him, that they should bind around him a girdle far more glorious than the soldier's cingulum, because it is given, not to him who is about to enter on the battle, but to him who has conquered in the fight. Now I understand wherefore you refused the aid I asked of you for him, when he was assailed on the highway. The laurel is only for the victor's brow; without labour the reward cannot be won; nor could this second Jacob be admitted to the close and undisturbed contemplation of his God without having first proved himself a successful wrestler.

I must here answer an objection which some of you may probably feel disposed to make on witnessing the entrance of our Saint into the cloister; namely, that if, as has just been affirmed, he was desirous of concealment and abasement, he ought not to have selected an Order which comes so much before the public as it is the vocation of Saint Dominic's sons to do. For in this Order, professedly a very learned one, the greatest minds find a theatre on which to display their talents, and steps whereby they may reach distinction; they are candles placed upon a candlestick, not hidden under a bushel. This is most true. But the very fact alleged by you as an objection, afforded the strongest reason why Thomas, in his profound humility, preferred this Order to any other. For, to conceal one's powers in a sphere where, even were they known, they would not be valued or appreciated, and would bring no honour to their possessor, is, as all must agree, a small thing; but it is a great thing to conceal them there, where talent is valued, where it is held in much esteem, and where the highest honours are unanimously accorded to it. And now I ask, what was the intention of Saint Thomas in dedicating himself to God in the Order of his choice? Did he wish to shine, to put himself forward, to become famous, to throw others into the shade? Such a supposition would indeed wrong him. We are told that, when sent by his superiors to Cologne, to pursue his theological studies under Albertus Magnus, at that time the Oracle of the Schools, the youth, who was soon to be the chief glory of his age, appeared at first so dull of understanding, was so backward in asking and so slow in answering questions, that he received the contemptuous appellation of the silent ox. And so far was he from any shadow of ostentation, that he accepted the offer kindly made by one of his fellow-students to rehearse with him daily the lecture they both had attended; this was done for a considerable time, Thomas listening attentively, thanking his instructor, and apparently profiting by his assistance.

What are we to think of such conduct? Does it seem to you probable that one who, not for one month or two, but for three long years, concealed the most brilliant gifts from the keen glance and discerning wisdom of such a master as Albertus Magnus, could have been led to enter this illustrious Order from any motive of ostentation? Could he have deluded the eyes and deceived the ears of so many persons? Would he have been able to endure the taunts of his jocular fellow-students, always ready to amuse themselves at the expense of another's stupidity? Experience alone can teach how hard it is to bear an undeserved reputation for folly patiently, for the love of Christ, even for one day. To promote God's glory by acting the part of the Lion or the Eagle of the mystic chariot, is no difficult task; but oh! how difficult and how irksome to personate the humble Ox, especially for one who might fill the place of the Angel; and who more worthy to fill that place than the Angelic Doctor himself? At length, a paper he accidentally dropped led to the discovery of his secret; for this paper having been picked up and shown to his teacher, Albertus was so astonished and delighted at the vast erudition which it contained compressed into a small space, like a princely fortune in the compass of a single gem, that on the following day he put the powers of his pupil to a severe test. He engaged him, in fact, in a learned discussion; at the close of which he acknowledged him as victor, expressed the greatest admiration and respect for his talents, and, addressing those who had made this more than human intelligence the object of their jests, predicted that ere long the *dumb ox* would utter bellowings which would resound not only on the banks of the Rhine and the Seine, but would re-echo throughout the whole world. Thomas was, however, soon obliged under obedience to repair at once to Paris, and there, having read Aristotle with that reputation which soon made him celebrated throughout Europe, he publicly took his

Doctor's degree; for his superiors had the wisdom to perceive that they would be the losers were they to permit the treasure so long hidden to remain in obscurity. This decision caused great grief to our Saint, for, strange as it may appear, it was only then that he could not bring himself to yield and embrace the opinion of others, when that opinion was one which would fain have made him appreciate his own merits. Hence it was that considering himself unworthy of the distinction, he was so distressed at his appointment that for several days he never ceased weeping. In the midst of this mental disquiet there appeared to him a venerable old man, who consoled him, exhorting him not to fear incurring any danger from an honour which was not sought after by ambition but accepted by obedience; intimating to him at the same time that it was the will of God that he should receive it. In this way Saint Thomas was restored to his former serenity; and who can doubt that whilst employing his brilliant intellect, as he did from that time forward, in composing, arguing, lecturing or teaching, the glory of God was his sole aim, the one end he had ever in view?

And now I ask you to examine his writings, and tell me if he ever penned a single word dictated by ambition or vainglory. He discourses, it is true, with authority, but without ostentation or wanton display. Nor did he strive after originality for its own sake, since he knew full well that truth is like the offspring of a noble house, all the more illustrious the further back its pedigree may be traced. Therefore, he was careful that all his decisions should be supported by the authority of the Fathers, or by the doctrines universally received by the Saints. And yet no man could accuse him of plagiarism because he thus borrowed from others, any more than the bees can be accused of theft when, without injuring the flowers of the field, without in the least impairing their beauty or diminishing their perfume, they extract from them a hidden juice; doing this not for their own enjoyment, but to part with it again when converted into honey. Similar was the use Thomas made of the treasures he gathered from the teaching of the Saints. And if on any point he felt himself constrained to differ from them, he expressed his opinion with respectful modesty and rare moderation; not seeking to expose the faults of their writings, but only bringing them to the surface, like sea-weeds, for the sake of disentangling the corals the weeds entwine, and the pearls they hold in concealment. But is it wonderful that he should be courteous to his allies, when he dealt so gently with his opponents? Most of the Saints, when writing against heretics, consider themselves at liberty to employ vehement and bitter invective, holding them up to ridicule and sarcasm; Saint Thomas, however, was merciful towards his adversaries, he carefully refrained from vituperation while refuting their errors, content to be a beacon in the Church, to bring to light the dark designs of her piratical foes without having recourse to violence. And is it possible to overrate the great and widespread good his beneficent pen was the means of effecting? To him the religious Orders especially owe it, that they survived the terrible storm raised against them by William de Saint-Amour, by Desiderius, Gherard, and others such as these; and, more than this, that each succeeding year saw them in a more flourishing condition, their rights more clearly defined and their privileges more firmly assured to them. He it is whom Christian Princes have to thank, if they seek the true principles of government, set forth in a work of great erudition, which he dedicated to the King of Cyprus. Philosophy is indebted to him for showing that the teaching of Aristotle is not antagonistic to Christianity; theology has to thank him for reducing to method the writings of Saint Augustine. What more can I say? If we believe Pope Pius V., not a single heresy has arisen since his day which does not find its refutation in his writings. He foresaw every doubt that might arise, every objection that might be put forward against the doctrines of Catholicism, and he removed and refuted them; in this unlike those troublesome planets which know well how to gather clouds and attract exhalations, without having the power to restore serenity to the atmosphere they have disturbed.

And now, as I am endeavouring to prove how entirely Saint Thomas consecrated to God the whole of his vast intellect, it behoves me to show the glory that accrued to him as the reward of his holocaust. "To Him that giveth me wisdom will I give glory." What glory, my hearers, could surpass that of being universally esteemed a Sun amongst Doctors, and as such represented bearing that orb upon his breast? What should this denote if not that, as when the Sun rises the wild beasts quickly retreat to their dens, the pirate takes to flight, the thief hides himself, and those who carry on evil deeds under the cloak of night, ashamed of themselves slink away to their homes; so error and deceit must vanish before the writings of Saint Thomas, bright rays of this unrivalled luminary of the schools. It has been affirmed by one who was no Dominican himself, I mean Pope Innocent VI., that after the canonical books, the Church has no surer foundation on which to rest her doctrines than the teaching of Saint Thomas; that no one, moreover, who keeps close to this guide can ever wander from the straight path of truth; and finally, that he who ventures to attack him cannot do so without incurring grave suspicion of error. Countless universities vied with each other in drawing from the crystal spring of his pure lore, just as we are told that at the waters from which the unicorn has been seen to drink all other animals hasten to quench their thirst, certain that such waters are free from all taint of poison. And these honours, usually a tardy tribute, only paid when the grave has already closed over him who is the subject of them, were given to our Saint during his life-time. Those who attacked him were men whose blame ought to be held in far greater esteem than any praise, they were exclusively heretics; all good Catholics united to magnify him, they contended for the honour of his presence among them. Therefore, after having lectured during a considerable period in the University of Paris, he lectured in Bologna, in Naples, and in Rome; indeed, it would not have been right for any city to enjoy exclusively the benefit of his teaching, or any individual nation to claim him as her own, since he should be of cosmopolitan nationality who, as we have already seen, was called the Sun of Doctors. It was esteemed no small honour to offer him hospitality, to render him a service, or to boast of acquaintance with him. On one occasion when he was detained by illness at the well-known monastery of Fossanuova, the monks would not even allow the wood for his fire to be transported from the neighbouring forest by beasts of burden, or carried by the servants; the great reverence they felt for their guest leading them to take upon themselves this laborious office. Saint Louis of France paid him the honour, but rarely accorded to any one, of inviting him to his table; nor did the royal host take umbrage on seeing that the Saint, forgetful of time and place, remained absorbed in seeking arguments wherewith to refute the Manichees; on the contrary, this circumstance had rather the effect of increasing Louis' respect for him, since he appeared so completely dead to the world as to be unconscious of the distinction between the royal palace and the convent cell.

And it need occasion us no surprise that God rewarded Saint Thomas, even in this life, with so much glory; for, in surrendering to Him his intellect, did he not freely give Him his whole being? There is nothing more difficult for a man than to submit his intellect to God; it is the last thing he can give up. His intellect is that which distinguishes him from the lower animals, which makes him equal to the Angels, which renders him, as Saint Augustine observes, like unto God Himself; moreover, in this he is usually most impatient of all control. And here we may observe that when the Holy Scriptures would ascribe greater glory to God, He is spoken of as sitting upon the Cherubim. "Thou that sittest upon the Cherubim:" thus David addresses him in the Psalms; "Thou that sittest upon the Cherubim:" thus Ezekiel speaks in his prophecies; "Thou that sittest upon the Cherubim:" thus the three children sing in their sublime canticle. But in the sacred pages God is never said to sit upon the Powers, to sit upon the Principalities; and because in the

Church there had been introduced, I know not at what period, the custom of singing, "Thou that sittest upon Seraphim," it was forbidden by an express decree. "They do wrong," as Saint Jerome says, "they do wrong who are accustomed to say in their prayers, 'Thou that sittest upon Seraphim,' there being no warranty for this in Scripture." But why is this ? Is not God lord also of His Seraphim ? Doubtless He is so. Nevertheless, it is a small thing to rule those who love one much, it requires no extraordinary power, no special might; but to subject to one's sway those who are distinguished for their vast science, is a work reserved for the arm of Omnipotence alone. How many, alas! are the men of intellect who refuse to pay, even to God, this homage of which we speak! Tertullian brought the appetites of his body into subjection to his Maker by protracted fasts; but he would not submit to Him the powers of his mind. Origen, by a strict vow of celibacy, offered to God his chastity; but he could not yield to Him the tribute of his understanding. And in like manner we meet with countless instances of men who, rather than submit to some decree of the Vatican, have not hesitated to throw away a rich store of merits, accumulated either in the hermit's cave or the monastic cell ; the sad list of whom contains such names as those of Palladius, Rufinus, Didymus, Evagrius; all men possessing a high degree of intellectual power, but a no less degree of pride. But one who, like Saint Thomas, reverently dedicates, first of all, his intellect to God, is not likely to withhold from Him the homage He demands, or to refuse to believe what He enjoins. Was the Saint required to forego the pleasures of the senses? No one could have been more completely a stranger to them; rapt as he habitually was in God, he became indifferent to and oblivious of the things of earth; and if he descended awhile from the celestial heights where his spirit loved to dwell, it was only on some errand to which an angel might have stooped, to comfort the afflicted, to direct the wandering, or to perform some similar work of charity. The unhappy Democritus went so far as to put out his eyes, in order that he might not be diverted from the study of wisdom by the sight of external objects; others again, while condemning such excesses, retired to sequestered valleys and lofty mountains, or, at least, imitated the Ephori, the sages of Sparta, who, when they met to deliberate upon the affairs of the State, assembled in a room bare of every ornament, where were neither pictures, statues, nor ornaments of any kind, lest the sight of such objects might distract their attention from the business in hand. But the Angelic Doctor stood in need of no such industries and precautions. The control he exercised over his mind was so complete and continual, that nothing which did not tend immediately to God's service had power to attract him; at table he was unconscious what he ate and drank; when out of doors he took notice of nothing that met him on his way; moreover, he possessed the power of going into ecstasy at will, a gift which is not known to have been conferred on any other Saint. Truly, a marvellous power this, my hearers; yet one which all who knew our Saint, or had any intercourse with him, agree in acknowledging to have been his when sickness rendered necessary the application of painful remedie; she had but to recollect himself in prayer, and immediately he became passive in the surgeon's hands, insensible to all suffering, unconscious alike of incisions made by the knife or the painful application of red-hot iron. Pliny tells us of a man named Hermotimus, whose soul possessed this rare faculty; that it was able suddenly to quit the body whensoever and for what period soever it pleased, so that he visited in this way remote countries, becoming acquainted with various nations, learning new customs and strange usages; until at one time when desirous to return again to the body, he found that it had in the meantime been consumed on the funeral pyre. But what, when read for many years in the pages of Pliny, had provoked a smile, as being a mere fable or foolish fiction, must in the case of Saint Thomas be believed with admiring wonder. Frequently when the spirit that had been absent from the body came back to revivify it, it found the latter had been cut, torn or burnt, without having experienced the least sensation of suffering; for the emancipated spirit had meanwhile roamed among the starry spheres, there holding intercourse with the Angels, and conversing with the souls of the Blessed.

And now, my hearers, do you think it possible that a man who thus long and frequently made heaven the place of his sojourn, could find any happiness on earth, could regard the things of earth as other than most vile and contemptible? No wonder indeed that they appeared to him in this light, nor that he regarded all titles with scorn, all dignities with abhorrence. And here let me meet a grave objection which has doubtless occurred to the minds of some amongst you this morning. How, you will ask, was it possible that, if, as we have seen, Thomas was in his lifetime held in such high esteem, if he was so beloved by Princes and so much thought of by Popes, he should nevertheless have been left to end his days in the cloister, a poor and humble monk, neither having been promoted to the purple, raised to a bishopric, nor distinguished by any ecclesiastical preferment whatsoever? This too is the more strange since it would seem that to no better guardians could the care of the Church, the earthly Paradise, be committed, than to the Cherubim, that is to say her most learned Doctors. This need cause you no surprise, my hearers; the reason is this, that the principal favour which Thomas earnestly besought of God day by day was to be permitted to die in that safer and humbler state he had chosen during life, that of a fervent religious. Therefore when Clement IV., desirous of raising him to the highest posts in the Church, proposed to dispense with all intermediate steps, and create him at once Archbishop of Naples, offering at the same time, if such were his wish, to increase the revenues and importance of the see, the humility of Saint Thomas would not allow him ever to consent to the proposal. As a proof of his small esteem for all earthly grandeur, it is related of him that on hearing the great city of Paris extolled on account of the number of its population, the splendour of its palaces, the reputation of its schools, and the pomp of its court: "For my part," the Saint remarked with the utmost sincerity, "if some one offered to make me a present of either the city of Paris or the homilies of Saint Chrysostom, having to choose between the two, I should certainly prefer the homilies of Chrysostom to the city of Paris." O noble heart! Heart most truly wise! must not all admire the generous scorn, the holy contempt with which thou didst tread under foot all vain and transitory things! Earth could find nothing wherewith to ensnare thee; nothing, less than nothing was all she could offer, since even God could find no treasure capable of contenting thee unless He gave thee Himself. You doubtless remember, my brethren, how on one celebrated occasion Our Lord, grateful to Saint Thomas for the admirable manner in which he had written of Him in the third division of the Summa, spoke to him from the crucifix, and encouraged him to ask some special favour as the reward of his labour. What was the Saint's rejoinder? Did he ask time to deliberate, to form a decision? No; without a moment's hesitation he turned to Our Lord, and replied in words dictated by ardent affection, "I ask none other than Thyself, O Lord, I desire none other than Thyself." This request was abundantly granted; for shortly afterwards he was called to dwell for ever in heaven, even before the completion of his great work. And incomplete that work must ever remain; for more easily could some one be found to find fault with the masterpieces of Timanthes or of Phidias, than to take up the pen which dropped at death from the fingers of the Angelic Doctor.

And now we understand the true meaning of those words, "To him that giveth me wisdom will I give glory." They do not refer to earthly glory alone, for that is as nought; they refer to heavenly glory, heavenly glory of the loftiest and sublimest order; for we learn from the testimony of one who was privileged to gaze into heaven, that Saint Thomas there fills a place equal to that of Saint Augustine; equal indeed in degree, though differing in kind, for by reason of his Pontifical dignity Augustine ranks higher than Thomas, whilst he on the other hand surpasses Augustine by virtue of his virginal purity. How must he now rejoice that from his earliest years he consecrated his whole self to God! He is reaping the fruit of his toils, enjoying the reward of his labours. These words sum up all which I have to tell of him, or which you, my hearers, have to ask. Perhaps some of you may wonder that in speaking of so great a man, I have not, as is usual on occasions like the present, made mention of any miracles worked by him; but what end, I ask, would have been attained had I done so? Should I thereby have confirmed your belief in his merits, or made his sanctity more apparent in your eyes? No, my brethren; on the contrary, I should do him great wrong. But if even the Pontiff who raised him to our altars judged such proofs unnecessary and superfluous, how should I presume to deem them requisite? The most remarkable miracles worked by Thomas during the latter years of his life were two thousand six hundred and fifty-four in number, equivalent to the sum total of the articles contained in the Summa. And who can enumerate all which he worked at an earlier date? They are, so to speak, without number and without end. All these were, moreover, pronounced in full consistory to be miracles of the highest order, and as such were lauded and extolled by John XXII. Wherefore then would you have me seek for miracles of a different nature? Do you suppose me unaware that hardly had Saint Thomas closed his eyes in death, when he opened those of the Prior of the Convent where he died, who had long been blind? That he delivered ten persons from acute sufferings, and healed as many more suffering from ulcers? Have I never heard of the little child who fell into a river, and on invoking the name of Thomas, immediately felt himself drawn by his hair to the bank? Am I ignorant of the number of fevers, even of the most malignant description, which he interposed to cure? Do I not know how many baneful spells he was the means of breaking? Full well I know it all; and in the case of any other Saint I should perhaps have dwelt at length on such wonders, but in the case of Saint Thomas I count them unworthy of notice, since it may truly be said that Thomas himself was a living miracle, far greater than any of those which he wrought. Was it not a miracle in a few short years to be able to master so many and such abstruse authors; to solve in a few short years so many and such intricate questions; and, notwithstanding the numerous and weighty occupations inseparable from the public post which he filled, to write more volumes than other persons in the same space of time could contrive to read? No mortal could ever have accomplished so much, had not God imparted to him supernatural powers. It would not have been enough for him to possess, as he did, an intellect capable of grasping the meaning of all that met his eye, or a memory capable of retaining all it ever received; nor would those vast powers have been enough which enabled him to employ at one and the same time the pen of four secretaries, whilst dictating, not letters on familiar topics or political affairs, as did Cæsar, but arguments on subjects as abstruse as any which formed matter for debate in the halls of the Peripatetics. I say all these gifts together would not have sufficed, had not God vouchsafed to illuminate the mind of His servant with a ray of celestial light. Wherefore since I have this morning dwelt at so much length on the greater miracles of Saint Thomas, would you have me strive to place the lesser before you, instead of hastening the rather to pay to him the tribute which highest excellence ever has the right to demand at our hands, the tribute namely of silent adoration?

SECOND PART.

IF, as we have seen in the case of the eminent Saint of whom I have been speaking to you, great glory is awarded to those who employ their intellect in the service of their Maker, how great must be the confusion awaiting those unhappy persons who, far from rendering this homage to God, make use of their mental powers in directly opposing His will! Instances of this are, alas, not infrequent. Too often do we see God's creatures turning against Him the very intellect He has graciously bestowed upon them, or employing their talents only to execute more successfully their designs, of however guilty a nature those may be, to overthrow their rivals at Court, to secure for themselves some match on which they have set their heart, or to gratify their evil passions with greater impunity. "They are wise, they are wise to do evil" (Jer. iv. 22). Thus we read in Jeremias. And who can imagine aright how terrible is the punishment reserved by Heaven for such daring offenders?

The sacred historian, speaking of David in terms of the highest eulogium, says that in all things he faithfully fulfilled the law of God, without ever deviating from its injunctions or violating its restrictions, except in putting Urias to death. "David had done that which was right in the eyes of the Lord, and had not turned aside from anything that He commanded him all the days of his life, except the matter of Urias the Hethite" (3 Kings xv. 5). This passage has occasioned much difficulty to commentators, for is not David known to have been guilty of other crimes, crimes too of no trifling magnitude? Was he not carried away by anger when he marched against Nabal? Was not the sentence which he passed on Miphiboseth one of gross injustice? Did he not revenge himself on the Ammonites in a manner not merely cruel but absolutely brutal? Why, then, is everything passed over in silence except the murder of Urias? I am not unacquainted with the various and learned explanations which might be given here; but one amongst them will suffice for our present purpose; namely, this, that all the other faults into which David unhappily fell, were due to thoughtlessness, inadvertence, or the frailty of human nature, whilst with regard to Urias, the case was far otherwise. In order to accomplish that murder, he applied his mind, and applied it with singular acuteness and elaborate premeditation. Not knowing how to rid himself of his faithful servant, in whom could be found no faults worthy of punishment, only virtues deserving reward, to what plan do we find the crafty monarch having recourse? He sent Urias to Joab, the general in command of his forces, with a sealed letter, containing instructions to place him in the foremost ranks of the storming party, and, when the fight was at its hottest, suddenly to abandon him in such a position that he could not fail to fall beneath the enemy's sword. This plan was successfully executed, and a messenger despatched to acquaint David with the result; whereupon he carried dissimulation so far as to send to cheer and condole with Joab, as if the recent occurrence were a disaster both unfortunate and deplorable, no less unexpected than severe. Is it matter for wonder that God should take strict account of such a crime as this? For what purpose did David on this occasion employ his mental powers? For what did he plot, and study, and contrive? In order to sin more cleverly. Alas! such ingratitude cannot be lightly passed over. This is what the great prelate Paulinus ably expressed when he wrote that "It is worse to plan sin than to commit it." Doubtless sin is ever a great evil, but it becomes doubly heinous when the mind is exerted in order to sin more successfully, to sin more craftily, to sin more maliciously; for to do so is to employ against God that very gift which beyond all others makes man like unto Him.

And yet how many are there who, not content with prostituting their intellect to their own sinful ends, make use of it to lead others into sin! They compose impure songs, they pen stinging satires, they make themselves public centres of infection, spreading on all sides false dogmas, pernicious maxims, heretical doctrines; to one they suggest an easy means of corrupting innocence, to another some quibble whereby to obtain a favourable verdict in an unjust lawsuit, to a third some underhand method of acquiring unrighteous gains. It is not enough for them to point out to their fellowmen the way of perdition, they are, moreover, careful to indicate to them the shortest road. Oh what tremendous judgments are awaiting these unhappy sinners! how terrible will be the vengeance demanded by Justice! how fearful their lot for all eternity! But I need enlarge no more on so painful a subject, for I speak to an audience whose piety is as well known as the refinement of their intellect. Rather will I rejoice that the spirit of Saint Thomas has been infused into you after such a manner that you may all justly hope from God one day to be made sharers in His glory.

PANEGYRIC IN HONOUR OF SAINT PHILIP NERI,

WHO PRACTISED THE VIRTUES OF THE CLOISTER WHILST LIVING IN THE WORLD.

"He obtained glory in his conversation with the people."
ECCL. l. 5.

Is it possible that no other means could be found to effect the deliverance of Israel, the chosen people of God, from the cruel bondage in which Pharao held them captive, except that of a hasty nocturnal flight from the land of Egypt, undertaken at their peril? Is it possible that Jacob could not elude the rage of his brother unless by escaping into Mesopotamia? That it was necessary for David to take refuge on Mount Carmel, in order to avoid the fury of Saul? "This flight was indeed indispensable," Saint Jerome was wont to answer, when these questions were addressed to him by your noble ancestors, O Romans: "because in flight from the world is safety alone to be found." And therefore he frequently, when writing from Palestine, invited one or other of them to come to that Holy Land, whither he had preceded them, there to kiss the sacred stones where the Infant Saviour was laid in the cradle, to dwell amongst those rocks where Amos fed his flock, and caused his herdsman's pipe to send forth prophetic utterances; to drink of the stream into which Sisara cast himself, when he leapt from his chariot in craven fear after his crushing defeat. But Saint Jerome is far from being the only one who urges the wisdom of such a flight upon those who live in the world. With what warmth do we not find Saint Bernard continually inviting them in the most affectionate terms to seek the shades of his far-famed Clairvaux, promising that they would there enjoy a lasting peace, complete immunity from all danger. Francis invites them to the caves of Auvergne; Bruno to the mountains of Grenoble; Walbert to the forests of Valiombrosa; and from the heights of the Appenines the voice of Romuald calls on them to share the holy austerities of the Camaldolese. But what do I behold? A Philip Neri commending and approving such invitations, exhorting multitudes to their acceptance, although, as far as he is personally concerned, himself turning a deaf ear to all, remaining steadfastly resolved to accomplish his sanctification in the very heart of Rome itself; not shut up within a cloister, or bound by vows, or even entirely secluded from the world; thus to prove by his bright example that neither place, nor companions, nor dress, nor state of life, affords a plea sufficient to excuse any one who has refused to give his whole heart to God. And what shall I say at the sight of so astonishing an example? I say that Philip had the wonderful courage to attempt a most difficult and wonderful undertaking, one, indeed almost surpassing our powers of belief. I will say (and I crave your pardon, O holy Anchorites!) I will say that, in this undertaking he succeeded; and succeeded so well that the same sanctity which holy hermits in their seclusion attained by withdrawing from intercourse with men, he attained whilst remaining in their midst. Can any one who is desirous of becoming the Panegyrist of such a man find terms of greater praise to apply to him than those which may be borrowed for this purpose from the Ecclesiasticus? "He obtained glory in his conversation with the people." These words appear to contain the highest and most fitting eulogy, and it is from the point of view they offer that we will consider his character on the present occasion.

And in the first place let me observe that I am well assured that there is no one here present who does not fully understand how solitude tends to promote the growth of sanctity. Behold the tree planted by the wayside; the soil may be good, the climate favourable, running water close at hand, careful culture not lacking; and yet, how seldom does a tree thus situated bring its fruits to maturity! The more pleasing they are to the eye, the more grateful to the palate, the sooner it will lose them, exposed as they are to be snatched by the greedy hand of the passer-by, or to fall a prey to the tooth of any chance beast who may browse on the foliage. How is it possible to do otherwise than admire Saint Philip, whom we see planted, so to speak, on the world's highway for a period of eighty long years, living amongst seculars, amongst worldlings, "in conversation with the people;" and preserving, nevertheless, his virtue free from the least blight. Never did he lose a single fruit, nay, more than this, not a single flower or even leaf; that is to say, he preserved that exterior modesty which are the first to drop off as years go by. Every one who looked at Philip, even in his advanced age, could not help saying that his appearance was that of an angel. His eyes shone with so bright a lustre, and his countenance beamed with a light so radiant, that no one could keep his eyes fixed on him for long together, much less succeed in taking a satisfactory likeness of him, whether a mere sketch or more finished portrait. And if in his later years his exterior was still so attractive, what must it have been in the bloom of his youth, when he won the love of the Angels themselves, so that they came down to visit him; one, disguised as a beggar, asking of him a kindly alms; one under the form of a child opportunely supplying him with sugar, of which he happened to stand in need; another in the semblance of a noble youth, interposing to withdraw him by the hair of his head uninjured from a deep pit into which he had fallen. Indeed, it is no easy task to express in words how courteous were his manners, how fascinating and winning, how affable and kind; God having singled him out by these gifts as one destined, evidently, to shine as a great huntsman, who should take many souls. But yet, O Philip, lovely and chaste as thy exterior was, it were almost to be wished that thy countenance were less beautiful, thy manners less pleasing; for thou wilt not always be in the presence of Angels. Remember, thy dwelling will not be with Macarius in the solitudes of Soria, with James in the groves of Palestine, or with John in the rocky caves of Monserrat; thy lot will be cast in the midst of a dissolute age, "thy conversation will be with the people," thou wilt live among effeminate men, scoffing youths and vain women; alas! how great indeed is the danger that instead of taking others, thou wilt thyself be taken!

But what did I say? "Philip taken!" Listen! listen! and recognise in him virtue so sublime that, like merchandise brought from far-off climes, it will, unless I am greatly mistaken, fill you with amazement. Even among the solitaries of the desert some have been found unable to resist the enticing snares of women; they have even yielded at the first assault, although their brow was furrowed by age, and their hair had grown white. As such I might cite Macarius in the deserts of Soria, James in the forests of Palestine, and John in the caverns of Monserrat. Philip, on the contrary, was a youth whose chin was barely covered by a glossy down; yet three times was his valour tried, by night and by day, by open attack and hidden wile, and each time he triumphed; defending himself either by prayer, by reproofs addressed to his tempters, or by recourse to a timely flight. Thus he preserved his virtue like Joseph of old, whom he may be said to rival in the glory of that heroic deed which has won the untiring praise of all succeeding ages. What shall we say then? The only fear that need be entertained on behalf of Philip is lest, like Noah's dove when absent from the Ark, he should find hardly a single spot on the face of the earth whereon to rest, without incurring manifest danger of pollution. You will readily imagine that after such victories over his lower nature, all rebellion of the senses would be quelled in him for ever, as was the case with Saint Thomas and Elzearus; but far more than this, it was given to his body to exhale, even during his lifetime, so peculiar and exquisite a fragrance, perceptible to all who approached him, that it was termed by them the odour of virginity; it was, moreover, the experience of some of his penitents that a breath of this odour sufficed to extinguish in them every carnal desire, just as the smell of myrrh proves fatal to worms, that of amber to vultures, and that of cedar-wood to the serpent. We are told, besides, that he was endowed with a subtle sense of smell, by which he was immediately made aware if any persons with sins of unchastity on their souls entered his presence, whether they came to obtain absolution, or merely for the purpose of transacting business. He could, with the greatest ease, dispel from the minds of the tempted the impure phantoms which disturbed them, by simply laying his hand upon their head, putting his arm around their neck, or by giving them a piece of some cast-off garment of his own to wear; indeed, he inspired the impure spirits with such terror, that having instructed a woman to cry out when she should chance to be tempted: "I shall complain to Philip of you;" the demons used to take flight more swiftly than goat or stag on hearing the lion's roar. To this lofty height of virginal purity Philip succeeded in raising himself, not among the hardships and solitude of the desert of Thebais, but in the midst of the refined enjoyments of Florence, and the luxurious pleasures of Rome. And now, while closing this part of my subject, let me ask: If we consider it a great thing to preserve snow unsullied and unmelted even in rocky caverns, that is to say, in the fittest place for its preservation; what shall we say of one who keeps it similarly pure and unchanged beneath the burning rays of the sun?

But some may be inclined to think that there is, after all, no great merit in abstaining from sensual pleasures; for, in this respect, Nature herself does much for many persons, as lilies spring up in fields and meadows without the fostering care of the gardener. Some will deem it far more difficult not to yield to the unworthy suggestions of self-interest, nor be caught by the glittering baits of ambition, which few indeed are capable of withstanding. Granted that this be true, what then? Did Philip show less courage in combats of this kind? We hear how a Roman noble, who was deeply attached to him, determined upon his deathbed to make him sole heir to all his property. This news, which to most men would have been a cause of rejoicing, so distressed Philip that he privately informed the sick man of his resolution not to attend him any longer, or even to see him again, unless he altered his purpose. But this expression of disapproval remaining ineffectual, he went once more to visit him when the last Sacraments had been administered, and death appeared imminent; with arguments, remonstrances, and entreaties, he endeavoured to induce the dying man to cancel his will. All was in vain. The Saint, with a look more divine than human, then said to him: "Do as you will, in spite of your efforts you shall not have me for your heir." Then, withdrawing aside, he recollected himself in prayer for a short space; after which he returned to the bedside, and, taking the hand of his friend, said to him: "Thou shalt not die." Wonderful to relate, at these words death fled affrighted from the couch, all pain ceased, and every weakness disappeared; and after a short sleep, he, whose obsequies had been already arranged, rose perfectly cured. What think you of this, my hearers? Did ever any one take as much pains to become rich as Philip did to remain poor? What a strange aversion he must have had for money, how he must have abominated, detested, and abhorred it, since he even employed miracles to avoid its possession ? Do you not think that conduct such as this would surely have excited astonishment in the breast of Solomon himself? For if he was surprised to see a man indifferent to the acquisition of that wealth which is more difficult of capture than the prey of the hunter, what would he have said to one who, when pursued by riches, refused to stretch out his hand and make them his own ? And it was not on one occasion alone that Philip acted in this manner; three several times he firmly refused to accept large fortunes from his relations; and when, as it sometimes happened, the title-deeds of various legacies made to him by some affectionate penitent were put into his hands, hardly had he glanced at them, when he either tore them across or threw them aside; and at times, not deigning to look at them, he used them as so much waste paper.

But why should I lay stress on his refusal of these lesser things? It is evident from the authentic records of those times that Philip over and over again rejected the offer of a splendid canonry or rich see, and even had the magnanimity to refuse a cardinal's hat. I should not think of mentioning such conduct to you as anything very remarkable in one animated by ardent love of God, did I not know what strength of virtue is required in order to live continually at Court (as Philip did for the glory of God) without being in the least dazzled by the enticing splendours of the Court. When the Prophet Eliseus embraced for the last time his beloved master Elias, and with sorrowful reluctance suffered him to mount up to heaven in a fiery chariot amidst storms and whirlwinds, he entreated him that, as soon as he arrived there, he would obtain for him a double portion of his spirit: "I beseech thee that in me may be thy double spirit" (4 Kings ii. 9). At the first glance this appears indeed a bold request; for why should not Eliseus content himself with possessing the same spirit as his master, the same purity, the same zeal, the same constancy, the same charity, the same faith? Why should he aspire to more? The most ingenious explanation of this passage is in my opinion one which is taken from the writings of Saint Augustine. He says that the circumstances in which Eliseus was to be placed were very different to those of Elias; he was not, like his master, to be a persecuted and hated fugitive prophet, but one held in universal esteem; foreseeing the dangers to be dreaded in the position he was to occupy, he desired to provide himself with extraordinary graces to aid him in encountering them. In proffering this request, therefore, Eliseus seems to say, "Those who are placed in the greatest danger are in need of the greatest assistance. Thou, O Elias, hast spent nearly thy whole life in wild solitudes, wandering over mountains and through valleys, finding with difficulty any one to give thee the bare necessaries of life; such will not be the case with me. My lot will be to pass my days in cities, beloved by the people, a favourite with the great, and, therefore, how much more virtue shall I require in order to avoid being led astray by the rich gifts of a Naaman, corrupted by the offers of a Benhadad, or elated by the honours paid him by a Hazael!" My brethren, had Philip spent his life in wild solitudes, unknown to the world, despised and neglected, I should not have esteemed it a proof of uncommon virtue in him to regard with indifference the riches and greatness which were never likely to come within his reach. Would it be much for any one under such circumstances, with feelings of sovereign contempt for the world, to offer to God dignities his only in imagination? I do not deny that such an act would be good, meritorious, praiseworthy; but it would not be of a nature to excite any ardent admiration. But to have continually before one's eyes objects so magnificent, so splendid, and yet feel no affection for them; to be surrounded by wealth, and all the pleasures it brings in its train, and yet prefer poverty; to have greatness and its attendant glory offered to one, and yet choose a lowly state, this appears to me the highest virtue, and such was the virtue of Philip.

And yet we can hardly wonder that earth had no attractions for him, because his spirit dwelt continually in heaven. Even in his youth, before he was admitted to Holy Orders, he was known to spend forty consecutive hours in contemplation. The sweetness, the consolations, the raptures he enjoyed on such occasions were so delicious, that unable any longer to bear the arrows of love wherewith he was transfixed, he was heard to entreat God to desist and withdraw His hand, and in pity on his weakness put a stop to these favours. In midwinter he was obliged to bare his chest by reason of the ardours of love by which he was inflamed. In the night he was at times compelled to call upon some one to divert his mind from a strain too great for nature to endure. Oh! happy you, were I able to relate to you what used to take place in that lonely chapel where he frequently spent the whole morning at the altar! But it must suffice you to know what his own lips confided to a friend, namely that several times after the consecration, God vouchsafed to reveal to him the glories of Paradise. Hence his ever-flowing tears, hence his deep-drawn sighs and ardent aspirations, hence the impetuous longing of his heart to quit the earth altogether; so that his body, insufficient to outweigh the upward tending of his soul was constrained to rise above the earth, as though it were rid of its grosser and weightier element; as the waters when powerless any longer to retain within their embrace the Sun, eager for departure, follow him on his course in clouds of vapour. And I will relate further a thing most wonderful, but yet wholly true. Absorbed as he was in the things of God, on more than one occasion the very act of preparing the sacred vessels, finding the places in the Missal, or touching the amice, was enough to send him into an ecstasy. When visiting churches he used to curtail his devotion as much as possible, indeed hardly had he entered and knelt down than he went out again, so great was the danger he felt himself exposed to of being suddenly overtaken by an ecstasy in public, if he did not seek safety by a timely flight. This precaution was nevertheless not always availing, for on one occasion he fell into a rapture whilst praying in the famous Vatican Basilica, in broad daylight, before a large assembly of people, and remained suspended in the air in a kneeling posture, as the compass which points steadily to the North Pole and is motionless because it has found the Planet to which it is wedded. Look down from the starry spheres, Antony, Arsenius, Pacomius, Onuphrius, and Hilarion; I call on you to witness a new and unwonted sight; behold a man who without concealing himself in your solitudes was able at will to enjoy at public oratories, in frequented churches, the closest union with his God. You deemed this union so difficult of attainment that you must needs seek it in lonely caverns, remembering that only in the desert was manna rained down from heaven for the Jews; to the deserts you resorted that you too might gather that manna, might draw honey from the stones, and nectar from the rocks. But see, Philip enjoys all these, even amongst the habitations of men. From heaven above you will agree with Saint Bernard, who, speaking of the communications God vouchsafes to make to His creatures, says, "That voice does not resound in the market-place, it is not heard in public, it loves to be heard in secret." With Philip this was otherwise. Neither the tumult of the busy crowd, nor the distractions of surrounding objects nor the multiplicity of cares could ever distract his attention from that divine voice; so that when walking the streets or waiting in ante-chambers it was necessary for some one to be always at hand, to pull his cloak and recall him to himself, to make him recognise those whom he met, and return their salutations. But was there one amongst you all, O holy Anchorites, who could exhibit to the world a prodigy so startling as that which Rome beheld in the person of Philip? and did the love of God so expand your heart that your breast throbbed and beat again by reason of the vehemence of its agitation? And here I almost hesitate to speak of a fact which, though one of the best authenticated and most widely known, may yet appear to some of my hearers as surpassing belief. One day Philip, ravished in a transport of divine love, heard his Beloved knocking at the door of his heart. In his eager haste to open without delay to the celestial visitant he broke the strong bars of its prison. But let us speak in plain terms. Two ribs on the left side of the Saint were broken and raised up, never again to be united (as if Christ had wished to keep a way open to enter at pleasure into the heart of His servant); thus they remained until his death, which occurred fifty years later; and what is still more wonderful, not only did these broken ribs occasion no suffering to Philip, but they afforded him on the contrary immense relief, enabling his heart, as if it were a volcano, to unbosom its inner flames. O sublime mystery! O wonder unheard of! But you will doubtless imagine Philip, at the time he was favoured with this supernatural visitation, was secluded with Abram beneath the oak at Mambre, alone with Moses by the bush of Horeb, or sleeping like Jacob, pillowed on a stone in the inhospitable desert of Soria. Far from this, my brethren; I must again repeat: "He obtained glory in his conversation with the people." In noisy thoroughfares, in the houses of seculars, in places where we find such difficulty in keeping our minds fixed on God for a single hour, Philip, although engaged in continual intercourse with his fellow-men, attained to those sublime degrees of contemplation enjoyed by the Stylites on their lonely pillars, where like bold eagles, they built their lofty nests, in order, far from all that could disturb them, to fix their gaze on the Sun they loved so tenderly.

But admirable as all this is, I can go a step further, and add that if Philip is to be so highly esteemed because he was holy in his conversation with the people, we ought perhaps to consider it a yet higher proof of merit that in his conversation with the people he was held as such by all; for, not only did he raise himself to sanctity, but he further attained to the glory of sanctity. Now I will explain my meaning somewhat more clearly. All of you, doubtless, well understand the truth of the saying, "Proximity lessens fame." For when men discourse in our presence on the eminent virtues of some cloistered Saint or far-off hermit, it is incredible what an amount of reverence we forthwith feel for him; we almost envy the very ground he treads and the air he breathes. But if we are brought into familiar and daily intercourse with this Saint, if we meet him in our walks, frequent the same houses as he does, and sit with him at the same table, how soon our idea of him is unconsciously lessened! For either we discover some defect in him, or he does something we do not quite like, or perhaps we merely alter our opinion in virtue of that law which holds good in all cases, as it does in that of those brawling streams, which, judging by the noise they make at a distance, one might almost fancy equal to the falls of the Rhone or the cataracts of the Nile; but which, when approached, are found to be so insignificant that the traveller disdains the use of a bridge, and scornfully fords them, hardly condescending to bare his feet. But to return to our subject. There is no doubt that Philip, as we have already said, spent his whole existence in conversation with the people, going in and out of shops and dwelling-houses, and frequenting the Court; in a word, he lived under the very eyes of Rome, that is to say, in a city more given to criticise and more difficult to please than any other. And now, would you know what opinion was there entertained of his sanctity? Listen, and you will be astounded. Cardinal Gabriel Paleotto, in his elegant and learned work, "*De Bono Senectutis,*" describing what the ideal old man would be, who was formed on the maxims he lays down, passing by all others, chooses Philip, although still living, without heeding the obvious objection to be made, that no pilot is to be congratulated until his vessel has furled her sails in port. Cardinals Fredk. Borromeo, Cusano, and Palavicino, all three men of no ordinary merit, who were united to the Saint by such close bonds of affection that they were called his "soul," being his constant companions in health, and nursing him in sickness, did not hesitate openly to affirm that, as far as they could see, Philip had attained to the highest point of perfection possible in this life. Cardinal Bandini, moreover, has left the following splendid testimony: "Philip," he says, "enjoyed such a reputation for sanctity, that not only was he held in universal veneration, but a large majority of persons used to imagine that they could make no spiritual progress unless they placed themselves under his direction; so that he was consulted on all sides as an oracle." We hear that the Pontiffs Gregory XIII. and XIV., and in an especial manner, Clement VIII., besides habitually consulting him on important matters relating to their sovereignty, used furthermore to show the veneration they entertained for him by obliging him to remain covered in their presence, by embracing him, and lavishing upon him every mark of affectionate regard; even condescending reverently to kiss his hand with those sacred lips which are the medium whereby God promulgates to the Church His infallible decrees. After bringing forward such illustrious witnesses, it were useless, my brethren, for me to appeal, in addition to the unanimous testimony borne by a multitude of Religious of all Orders and all ranks, who used to call him the living relic. Of what use would it be to tell you how, even during his lifetime, the smallest thing belonging to Philip was cherished as a relic; the hairs off his head being preserved as precious treasures, and the very blood he had voided in an attack of illness; how many persons hung his portrait upon their walls among the pictures of the Saints, and, with an ill-regulated devotion too common in those days, presumed to prostrate themselves before it in adoration, invoking him day by day in the words, "Saint Philip, pray for me"? How, when he passed through the streets, crowds pressed around him to kiss his garments, and when he entered any house, some devotees were sure to come forward to cast themselves at his feet; the common voice publicly proclaiming him to be at one time an Apostle, at another an Angel, or a Prophet. It is well that I should remind you' of these things, for we know moreover upon indisputable authority, that even the highest nobles at Court vied with each other for the honour of sweeping out his room, cleaning his boots, and, with the hope of obtaining from his hand a passing blessing, performing for him menial services of a humbler nature than those which, with a like object, were rendered to the aged Isaac by his sons. My brethren, was it not a new, wonderful, and unheard-of thing to live for sixty years beneath the eyes of a city so critical as Rome, seen and known by all men in daily and familiar intercourse, and yet enjoy universal admiration? And in this very city of Rome which aims at nothing short of perfection itself, are things of common occurrence, and where, as in the bosom of a vast ocean, not only the smaller streams, but even royal rivers, as the Tagus and the Ganges, are swallowed up; in this city I say, Philip was, even in his lifetime, acknowledged to be a saint.

But perhaps he gained this reputation for sanctity with comparative ease by his ascetic appearance, by wearing sackcloth, girding himself with a rope, putting ashes upon his head, and going barefoot in the most inclement seasons? I know full well how much attention these penances are calculated to attract; they drew many disciples to Elias on the rocky heights of Carmel, they won many admirers for the Baptist on the banks of Jordan; in all ages those who practised them have been regarded as saints, so that, in the popular mind, the very woods they inhabited have been invested with something of the sanctity of those who dwelt in them. But let no one imagine that austerities of this nature, however admirable they may be, were the means of raising Philip to so high a place in public esteem. I am far from intending to deny that he treated his body with great severity; that the hours he devoted to sleep were few, his disciplines most severe, his hair-shirts of the roughest description. But so completely did he contrive to conceal his penitential practises that scarcely any one knew of them; in everything he followed the rule binding on his own beloved sons, with a single exception, and that was that he did not ordinarily dine with the community, to prevent any one from observing with admiration his great abstemiousness; for he invariably abstained from eating cheese or butter, rarely took fish, and still more rarely meat, often fasting the whole day on bread and water. How then did it come to pass that, whilst apparently doing in every respect as others did, and conforming himself to the common usage with regard to food, dress, habitation and general tenor of life, he was yet accounted as a man quite out of the common? The reason is this: however anxious he was, like Saul in his days of humility, not in any way to appear conspicuous amongst the crowd, he could not possibly remain concealed, because he was a head higher than all those around him!

I know well what you will answer me here; you will say that he probably owed his great reputation to the miracles he worked. And, in fact, it is impossible to deny that even during his lifetime his miracles were not few in number; I should be deceiving you were I to pass them by in silence for the sake of making my statement appear more wonderful. But do not for a moment imagine that I would resort to any such ungenerous artifice. We find recorded seventy-six miraculous cures performed by him whilst still living; cures of sick or wounded, paralytics, such as were suffering from fever or any other kind of malady. To many persons who were in perfect health he foretold the near approach of death; to many who were hovering on the brink of the grave he announced a prolongation of their days. To Baronius, Tarugi, Diatristano, Aldobrandino, Del Bufalo and Panfilio, who were afterwards raised to the Cardinalate, he predicted the dignity which awaited them; and in general the gift of prophecy was so habitual to him as to be scarcely distinguishable from the gift of speech. He could as well discover at a glance the hidden thoughts, secret temptations, and interior trials of the heart; and in very many cases he was able to draw from the unwilling penitent the confession of some hidden sin, as easily as the wind brings to the surface of the troubled water the weeds which lie concealed in the depths of the ocean. But all this, and much more besides, you can, if you please, read in the annals of his life; where you will frequently find it remarked as a singular circumstance how very few of the miracles wrought by Philip were noticed before his death, because he performed them all as it were in sport. Prophecies sounded on his lips like playful sayings, and his hand worked cures as if for amusement. Thus when, after his death, the survivors sought to console themselves by calling to mind his most striking and remarkable actions, they were often heard to exclaim:. "How astonishing that when we had such obvious, brilliant and undeniable miracles before our eyes, we thought so little of them!" The only conclusion they could arrive at was that most probably the Saint in his humility, had, like Simon Salus, asked of God to permit men to fall into temporary blindness and indifference, since, although he truly desired to possess these healing powers for the good of all, he desired to possess them in the same way as do the stones and herbs, which, notwithstanding their medicinal properties, are nevertheless carelessly trodden under foot. Wherefore, if we attentively consider the subject, we shall perceive that it was not the miracles Philip wrought, numerous and great though they were, which gained him renown, it was nothing more or less than his virtue and his virtue alone.

Moreover, who has not heard of the strange expedients to which Philip resorted, and the ingenuity he displayed, in order to make himself contemptible in the eyes of others, in spite of his famous miracles? Hence we are told that in his old age he was frequently seen to jump about in the street, or perform extraordinary antics in public, sometimes in the crowded halls of the great, sometimes in the midst of the market-place. Thou, O Philip of Cantalicio, glory of the illustrious Order of Capuchins, tell us how he snatched up the flask hanging at thy side, and amid the derisive laughter of the bystanders, pretended that he would not give it thee back till he had drained it. Sometimes he would slowly walk, or we might almost say, strut, through the streets of Rome, arrayed in the most eccentric attire, a white satin waistcoat, perhaps, or a mantle trimmed with costly furs; another time he would appear bearing a bunch of broom; again, he would purposely commit strange solecisms, proclaiming in public the most trivial tales, reciting fables or nursery stories; and when invited to the table of Cardinals he would take with him under his arm the earthen vessel from which it was his custom to eat, and placing it before him, persist in celebrating its praises, and refusing the use of any other. This latter device, like all the others for which Philip was noted, had for its aim to obtain for him at Court the reputation of being half-witted, or at least a silly, thoughtless fellow. And yet, in spite of his efforts, not only did he fail in attaining his object, but the only result of these artifices was to spread and increase the fame of his sanctity. This sanctity must indeed have been supported by proofs of the clearest and most indisputable nature, in order to outweigh the effect produced by such extravagances. But we shall find in this no matter for wonder when we consider how many souls were brought to God through Philip's instrumentality, either from the hardened unbelief of Judaism, or the obstinate blindness of heresy; how many convents were, by means of his salutary exhortations, peopled with saintly inmates; how many worldlings were by him induced to attend the services of the Church, and approach the sacraments; how many priests were by him stirred up to celebrate with greater frequency; when we consider, moreover, the splendid hospital of the Holy Trinity, erected and endowed at his expense for the reception of pilgrims; the naked whom he clothed, often stripping off his own garments for this purpose; the hungry whom he fed, frequently bestowing on them the food provided for his own consumption; the widows, the orphans, the afflicted, the students, whom, to the number of thousands, he maintained for years with such unparalleled liberality, that Cardinal Bellarmine (who was, as all the world knows, so cautious and sparing in his praise) did not hesitate to compare him to John the Almoner. But, beyond the testimony of all these, we have the further witness afforded to his sanctity by many pious and excellent devotions originated by him with a view to detach men from the pursuit of dissolute amusements, from godless revels, and the unbridled license of the Carnival; of the villas converted by him into schools of spiritual edification; of the country districts changed by him into homes of devotion; and, above all, of many members of the aristocracy, who, under his direction, attained to a high degree of sanctity amid the pleasures of the world, amid luxury and dissipation of every kind; a matter of greater difficulty than would be that of making the fir-tree flourish in a soft and marshy meadow.

And indeed, the accomplishment of his personal sanctification in conversation with the people was far from being the only object Philip proposed to himself as the aim of all his endeavours; he strove furthermore to furnish persons living in the world with a model by imitating which they might succeed in becoming saints without quitting the position assigned to them by Providence; and he has left you, my Fathers of the Oratory, to carry on the difficult task which he had the courage to undertake. Therefore it is only right that, in conclusion, I should address you, at whose request I have to-day ascended this pulpit, and represent to you how weighty is the obligation laid upon you. Philip is now no more to be seen in the streets of Rome, he has long since been taken from us, death having suddenly, and as it were almost furtively, snatched him away at a moment when his end was least looked for (except by the few persons to whom Philip, with his habitual playfulness, had revealed it half in sport), Heaven seeming to fear lest, were its designs made known, the people of Rome would hold their beloved Saint in an embrace so firm that, in answer to their earnest supplications, it would be compelled to spare him to them. But although Philip is now lost to Rome, you are left to take his place in the public veneration and regard; to you, as to his heirs, all may come to gather from your example and your teaching the inheritance you have received from your illustrious Father. Is it not then your bounden duty, in imitation of your great Founder, to make sanctity attractive in the eyes of the world? For this purpose your dress is not conspicuous by its outward show of austerity, your manners are polished, your courtesy is invariable; that thus you may the more effectually win the confidence of all, as the shepherd when wrapped in a sheepskin, more easily overcomes the timidity or obstinacy of the most fearful and indocile of his flock. Do you not see what happened to God Himself? When He thundered from Sinai, amidst clouds and fire, he displayed the majesty of an omnipotent ruler; but did He thus win any hearts? On the contrary, he lost a great portion of the people who worshipped Him. But when, assuming the form of man, He conversed with men, appearing in their garb, speaking their language, then He drew unto Himself multitudes of followers; and this is the portrait you are called upon to copy. It is incumbent upon you to conform yourselves as far as you consistently can to the customs of the world, in order that the world as far as possible may conform itself to your customs. I know that this is a point of great nicety, and that it requires no ordinary skill to combine the useful and the agreeable, the wholesome and the palatable. And do you perchance fail in fulfilling it? Why ask a question which is evident? It is not to you, my Fathers, that this question should be addressed. Speak, O my hearers, if any such doubt be raised, speak, I say, you who day by day frequent this house and church, who throng to this beautiful Oratory and assist at services where pleasure and piety seem to vie with one another. How splendid is the ceremonial, how exquisite the music, how interesting the dialogues, and attractive the discourses. And on the other hand, what shall I say of the exemplary models you have before your eyes? what of the instructions you hear to such advantage? Is it not fitting that you should pursue sanctity when it stoops to your level, and comes amongst you as one of yourselves? The Persians long held aloof from their Macedonian conqueror, until at last he dropped his own nationality, spoke the Persian tongue, and followed the Persian customs, appearing with turbaned head and flowing beard, a scimitar at his side. Seeing Alexander thus, they were as much attracted as they had previously been repelled, and were never weary of crowding around him. Philip has acted in like manner with regard to you, he has brought sanctity within your reach, he has shown it to be a thing that can be attained without such great exertions. And even now it is set before you in this light by the sons of Philip, who in the sight of God and men daily acquire glory in their " conversation with the people." They prove to you that the highest sanctity may be attained without the restraint of vows; that the strictest interior recollection may be preserved without the seclusion of the cloister; they teach you that the pleasures of religion afford enjoyment far greater than any which can be found in licence, dissipation, and intemperance. After all we have seen, my brethren, can there be any excuse left for those who persist in abhorring sanctity as something repulsive?

PANEGYRIC IN HONOUR OF SAINT ANTONY OF PADUA.

SANCTITY RECEIVES A WORLD-WIDE HOMAGE IN THE PERSON OF SAINT ANTONY OF PADUA.

"There was not found the like to him in glory."
ECCL. xliv. 20.

IT has been said by one of old that if the sun were merely to pursue its wonted course through the heavens, adorning them, it is true, by its radiance, but remaining otherwise useless and inoperative, it would yet find many enthusiastic admirers, and devout worshippers of its splendour. My opinion on this point differs, I confess, from that of Seneca, who is the author of the observation I have just quoted. To me it appears that whatever glorious display the sun might make of its light, were it to cease to produce as it has ever done, gold in the mines, fruit on the trees, corn in the fields, and flowers in the meadows, men would soon weary of admiring it, and would turn away from it with careless indifference, we should behold its temples in Syria desolate, if not entirely demolished; in Persia its sacred fires expiring upon the altars; in Egypt its sacrifices contemned; whilst those northern nations of whom Solinus speaks, would no longer go forth, as was their wont, to greet its rising with jubilant songs of applause and melodious strains of music. I know how deeply-rooted self-interest is in the heart of man; indeed in ancient times the sun and all the heavenly bodies would not have been held in such high veneration, had they not been ever in motion, toiling for us mortals whilst we rested, and watching for us whilst we slept. And is there matter for wonder in this when we see how in the case of the saints themselves, the amount of homage and adoration paid to them is proportioned to the gifts and graces received from them. In order to excite in the hearts of the faithful devotion towards any saint, who, however admirable he may be for his virtue, is not liberal in his gifts, it is necessary, I own, to employ powerful argument and skilful rhetoric; but none of these are required in order to kindle devotion towards one who distributes his favours with a lavish hand. And seeing this is so, I need anticipate no difficulty in awakening within your breasts this morning a fervent devotion to Saint Antony, that Antony to whom already so many have concurred to give the glorious title of wonder-worker. It does not occur to me to lay before you according to the custom of some orators, the difficulty of the task I have undertaken, in order to increase the credit that will accrue to me if I acquit myself of it well, or diminish the blame I shall incur, should I fail to do justice to my subject. On the contrary it behoves me rather to acknowledge candidly that nothing can be easier in the present day than to win for Antony a high place in popular favour. In fact it can scarcely be said to be a matter of choice whether or no we venerate this Saint; we are, as it were, compelled to do so, because it is most evidently our interest to take him for our protector. It is a well-known saying that it is difficult to petition him for a favour which he will not grant. And even if the public voice did not abundantly confirm this opinion, enough might be gathered from daily experience to prove most convincingly that God has ever shown Himself, not only desirous, but I might almost say eager to see this His servant highly esteemed amongst men. And truly, my hearers, I have at times meditated deeply on this subject, and I have invariably found myself compelled at length to exclaim in wonder and amazement. "There was not found the like to him in glory." The care with which God employed every conceivable means of rendering him illustrious almost surpasses belief, whether we consider the natural gifts with which he was enriched, the supernatural virtues which were infused into him, or all the other many and marvellous gifts bestowed on him; and seeing that to grant at this Saint's intercession all that is petitioned for is the surest means whereby to spread the devotion to him, to increase his reputation, and to make all nations hasten to pay homage to him, can it be thought that God will deny any favour asked through his intercession? What I propose to myself to-day is to direct your attention to the loving and anxious care with which God has always shown Himself intent on magnifying His servant; it will be for you to gather from the consideration of this subject, how profitable must be the devotion towards a Saint who was so eminently pleasing in the sight of God.

From the first moment of his birth it was apparent

that it was God's Will to render Antony illustrious in no ordinary way. With this view Providence ordained that he should be born in the famous city of Lisbon, that he should be the offspring of noble ancestry, and endowed with a generous disposition, an acute intellect, a gentle character, a pleasing exterior; so that even whilst still a child his behaviour won the admiration of all who knew him. It seems, however, that in one quarter God encountered opposition in carrying out to the full His glorious purposes with regard to Antony; and from whom, think you, did this opposition arise? It arose from Antony himself; for, despising those honours which he might confidently have reckoned on obtaining in the world, and which he might have enjoyed without offending against his conscience and with much advantage to the Church, he was intent on nothing else but discovering the surest means of remaining entirely unknown. The solitude of the cloister, the seclusion of the monastery, alone had attractions for him; and to these he did not fly, like Elias, to escape from the persecutions of his enemies, but to elude the applause of his friends. At length, he sought admission into the Order of Saint Francis, at that time in its infancy, thinking there to find as sure a place of concealment as was afforded to the Prophet by the lonely summit of Oreb. Like him, he dwelt in a cave, hiding under the rough habit of the monk the gentle blood which flowed in his veins, and avoiding in the solitudes of the hermit that fame which was already busy with his name. This was, however, but a small part of what he did. In order to appreciate the zealous efforts he made with a view to complete concealment, we must see him hiding under the cloak of a common ignorant man, the eminent learning of which he was in reality possessed. You already know, my brethren, that he entered the Franciscan Order as a simple lay-brother, and in this capacity employed himself in performing all the most laborious work of the house, cleaning the kitchen utensils like a common scullion, and carrying loads like a very beast of burden. Strange as it may appear, he attained his object; for every one thought him stupid and incapable, and rather shunned than sought his society. My brethren, it is impossible for me to express the wonder with which this fills me, for we know that of all gifts, wisdom is the most difficult of concealment. Clothe a king in rags, and no one will know him from a common peasant, as Cyrus learnt by bitter experience. Place a strong man amongst timid women, let him follow their occupations, and he will appear to have lost his strength; and as such even Hercules was scoffed at. Load a free man with ignominious fetters, and nothing will distinguish him from a slave; was not Sinon taken for such a one, and pitied accordingly? But wisdom cannot be thus concealed; it is like a blazing torch, which makes its bearer conspicuous from afar, although his desire to elude observation may cause him to choose the darkest paths, and the thickest shades of night. Was not Ulysses the prince of dissemblers? and yet he could feign everything except madness. For when he was ploughing the sand of the sea-shore as a proof of his folly, the ingenious idea occurred to Palamedes to place his infant Telemachus directly in his path; whereupon Ulysses, instead of going on recklessly with his furrow, stopped short, and to avoid trampling upon his child, skilfully turned his plough, thus betraying his secret. But, oh, how differently did Antony act! With uniform indifference treading under foot his relatives and friends, his acquaintances and companions, as well as all the attractions the world placed in his path to induce him to violate the gospel precept, and withdraw his steadfast hand from the plough, he succeeded in disguising his talents so completely that for a long time he was considered wanting in ordinary intelligence. Thus on one occasion when he was compelled to attend with his companions a General Chapter of the Order held at Assisi, he did not proffer a single remark, or even utter a syllable, although he was without exception the most learned man present; in fact so false an impression of himself did he produce on all who were there, that when the Superiors had to make choice of subjects for their respective houses, it was with difficulty that one was found willing, even from motives of charity, to receive him into his community. And what may we imagine his secret reflections to have been, on finding himself rejected by one after another in so ignominious a manner? Is it possible that no rebellious thought stirred within his breast, that no interior voice whispered to him: O Antony, what are you doing? Do you not observe how every one despises your company? How long, pray, are you going to bear this neglect? If you chose to show yourself in your true light, you might do so with a word. Think how many years you passed in the Schools, how many nights you spent over your books! Show but a portion of the learning you thus acquired, and you will see those who now avoid your society show equal anxiety in seeking it. Thus we may fancy his conscious talent pleaded for an opportunity of displaying itself. But if such suggestions presented themselves to him, they must have come from the natural man, and doubtless grace enabled him speedily to overcome them.

At length God, apparently grown weary, if we may so speak, of this protracted concealment, inspired one of his superiors to bid him deliver a discourse on spiritual subjects before an assembly composed of his religious brethren. Antony was more terror-struck at this command than a wealthy traveller stopped by highwaymen and compelled incontinently to discover to them all the gold he has about his person. On the one hand obedience urged him to comply, and on the other humility held him back; after a long struggle, humility was forced to yield to obedience, and the lips of Antony were unsealed at length. Who can describe how the devils must have trembled at the first sound of that voice whose utterances were to inflict on them defeats so numerous and so crushing? How many losses they must at that moment have foreseen and deplored! Yes, Antony speaks at length; he speaks, and the confidence hell founded on his long silence is overthrown at a blow. Sinners, heretics, Jews, unbelievers, Atheists, that tongue is at length unloosed which is destined to triumph over you all. Wait but awhile, and ere long, one will hear himself put to shame from the pulpit; another will find his erroneous tenets confuted in the Schools; conviction will strike home to the worshipper in the synagogue, whilst others will be worsted in discussion and reduced to silence by the pen of controversy. Never has a protracted silence brought forth aught but a great power of speech. And the words of Saint Peter Chrysologus may be fitly applied to the instance before us, when he exclaims: "Of how great silence is this voice born!" For if it appeared to him a thing most wonderful that the voice of the Baptist should be born of the silence of his father, may we not perhaps deem it no less surprising that out of his own long silence the voice of Antony should be thus born? But enough of this. My brethren, we know that when those religious heard the extraordinary eloquence with which Antony spoke, they threw themselves at his feet, overwhelmed with shame at not having discovered him before, and asking him to forgive the ridicule and wrongs so often received at their hands. They admired him as an oracle of heavenly wisdom, an oracle, moreover, whose previous silence tended rather to augment than diminish the estimation in which it was held.

At this point it appeared that God made it His own especial care to promote the exaltation of His servant. He caused the report of Antony's great merit to reach the ears of the Patriarch, Saint Francis, who appointed him to direct the studies of his fellow-religious; thus Antony was the first who opened a school of learning in that Order which until then had been only a school of sanctity. And, indeed, I do not think any more weighty argument than this fact could be brought forward in his praise. Who is not aware of the reluctance Francis ever manifested to allow scholastic subtleties to intrude upon the simplicity of his religious? He knew full well how rare a thing it is to find learning and humility dwelling under the same roof, and feared, if science were once permitted to take up its abode in his monasteries, it would bring in its train love of display, contentions, emulation, rivalries, and desire for pre-eminence; unwelcome guests, whom it is easier to refuse to admit than to expel when once admitted. By entrusting to Antony's keeping the key of a door so jealously guarded, Saint Francis gave the greatest possible proof of the high opinion he entertained of his worth; the more so since he had then barely attained the age of twenty-seven years, an age at which such remarkable learning is a possession as dangerous as it is uncommon. But, thanks be to God, the event proved how wise a choice this had been. Succeeding ages have testified how admirably adapted Antony was to carry out this undertaking, as he perfectly understood how to introduce into his illustrious Order all that is beneficial and useful in learning, and at the same time to exclude from it all that was detrimental and pernicious. Let the Church speak, and tell us, if indeed it is possible for her to come to a decision on the point, whether, during the last four centuries these Religious have rendered her more illustrious by the splendour of their virtues, or by defending her with the aid of their erudition. For my part, I cannot look without astonishment on the sons of Saint Francis, when I see them after they have worn themselves out by long and fervent preaching, seeking no other means of recruiting their exhausted strength than the repose afforded by a hard pallet. I see them after bending over their studies with close application, content to refresh their wearied nature with the fragments of broken meat supplied by the charity of others. I see them in the schools engaged in subtle controversies, and yet satisfied with such opportunities of mental recreation as they can find within the limits of a narrow cell. It is the sons of Francis who, in so great a number, have expounded Scripture, explained science, spread the faith, uprooted heresy. And what reward have they claimed in return for such important labours? Are they not content, even in our own day, to live in the strictest poverty, to wear the coarsest habit, to renounce all exterior refinement, and to shun anything in the shape of honour? To whom do they owe this rare combination of the highest learning and the deepest humility, if not to Antony, who was the first in his Order to teach the art of uniting the two? How great, then, is his glory, since every time that the Church joyfully commemorates a Bonaventure, a Bernard, a Scotus, an Aureolus, or any other of the many names equally illustrious for learning and for sanctity, she cannot fail to acknowledge how greatly she is indebted to Antony, who showed to all who came after him that learning and humility were, in truth, sisters, although for so long they had been regarded as irreconcileable enemies.

But God, desirous of bestowing still greater glory upon His servant, would not permit his teaching to be confined to the classroom, where it could only profit those who dwelt under the same roof with himself; He desired that his voice should resound from the pulpit for the benefit of those who lived in the world. He gifted him, in fact, with powers of so high an order that I do not hesitate to say hardly ever has any orator, religious or profane, been listened to with greater attention and advantage. I will state in a few words what time forbids me to enlarge upon. Wherever Antony was announced to preach, not merely villages but whole towns turned out to hear him; his pulpit for the most part was placed in the open plain. Not unfrequently would people set out from their homes directly after midnight, in order to make sure of obtaining a place; on every side, one party after another might be seen wending their way down the hill-side, the upper classes attended by torch-bearers, the common people carrying lanterns, all pursuing their path in so quiet and orderly a manner, that the stillness of night was not broken, although its repose was disturbed. The bishops and clergy, the magistrates and governors of the various cities, came in order of rank, as if walking in a procession; law courts were closed, shops were shut and audiences were suspended, as on festivals of unusual solemnity. Thus to some ten, twenty, or even thirty thousand persons used Antony to preach, as well as to a considerable guard of soldiers, by whom, when the sermon was ended, he was escorted back to his monastery; in order to protect him from the crowds who, with pious importunity, eagerly pressed around him, to kiss his garments, or surreptitiously abstract some portion of them as a relic. Can any of the orators of antiquity boast of triumphs to compare with this? Hortensius, Tullius, Demosthenes, must you not own yourselves surpassed? What would you have said had you chanced one night to find yourselves on those vast plains, had you seen so many thousands of human beings, young and old, high and low, learned and unlearned, assembled there to await the coming of an orator. "Who," you would have enquired, with unfeigned astonishment, "who is the talented individual whose voice seems to possess such uncommon power? Long experience has taught us that no little skill is required to carry with one the sympathies of even a

small audience and hold their attention; what must
the gifts of that orator be who can draw together such
countless multitudes of hearers, belonging to all classes
of society and coming from so great a distance, at so
unseasonable an hour, to so inconvenient a place?" Yet
all this Antony was able to achieve. I do not deny,
my hearers, that on these occasions God vouchsafed to
assist him in no ordinary measure; He endowed him
especially with two singular prerogatives, of which one
was that when preaching in his accustomed gentle voice
he was audible at any distance, however great, and the
other, that when speaking in his native tongue he was
intelligible to any foreigner who might happen to be
present. To my mind, however, this does not in any
way detract from the glory due to the Saint, but, on
the contrary, rather enhances it; for what must not
have been the worth of that teaching, in favour of
which the ordinary laws of nature were suspended?
Think, moreover, how numerous must have been the
conversions he effected amongst those vast masses of
people, by all of whom he was regarded as a Saint. I
call on hell to come forward, and bear its witness; I
shall rejoice to hear it, for the most valuable of all
eulogiums are the confessions extorted from a panic-
stricken enemy. What efforts we find the demons
making to counteract the effect of Antony's glorious
labours! what stratagems they employed! what hin-
drances they interposed! what machinery they set in
motion! Sometimes with a view to create a disturbance among the people, they broke the supports of the
platform which served him for a pulpit; at other times,
for the sake of distracting the attention and diverting
the minds of his hearers, they appeared on the scene

in the guise of messengers, bearing despatches of importance; or again, they would gather together dark clouds, raise whirlwinds, and, by means of thunder and lightning seek to terrify and disperse the assembled multitude. But all these various devices came to nought; they were easily frustrated by the Saint, who needed only to exert his supernatural power to avert the impending catastrophe, to expose the deceits of the Evil One, and to arrest the threatening storm. Still, from the efforts made by the spirits of darkness to disturb those assemblies, it was only too evident how greatly they dreaded the effect produced by his discourses. And is it surprising, my brethren, that they thus feared them? We hear that by one single sermon Antony converted twenty-two notorious brigands. This was no inconsiderable victory; Saint John Chrysostom declares men of that class to be especially difficult of conversion, mentioning, in support of this assertion, that, of the two thieves to whom our Lord preached from the Cross, only one repented. Can it then be otherwise than matter for astonishment, that of the twenty-two brigands who went to hear Antony, everyone without exception went away converted? But why do I speak of twenty-two only? It is a well-authenticated fact that the voice of the Saint did far more to rid the forests of Italy from the bands of robbers with which they were at that time infested, than the arm of the law had done, or could do; just as the terrible roar of the lion, resounding through the woods, is a more sure and speedy means of driving out in panic-stricken flight the wild boars, the deer, and the goats who have made it their home, than the spear and arrows of the huntsman. Heretics abounded at that period in almost every city, and Antony extirpated them; feuds disturbed the peace of families, and Antony reconciled the parties at variance; churches were desecrated by sacrilege, and Antony caused them to be consecrated anew; the sacraments were dishonoured and profaned, and Antony put a stop to those abuses; convents were deserted, and Antony peopled them once more; he inspired in general so great a desire for penance in the hearts of the people, that it was no uncommon sight to see his hearers returning home, not only smiting their breasts (as the Jews did on leaving Mount Calvary), but applying the scourge to their shoulders with merciless severity. The practice of public penance, subsequently so widespread, is universally believed to date from the time of Antony's preaching; and it is certainly no small proof of the great influence he exercised over the age in which he lived, to find that it was owing to him that open and voluntary flagellation first became a spectacle of ordinary and frequent occurrence.

But we need not wonder that men should have hung breathless upon his lips, and have been struck to the heart by his words, when we read how even the brute creation at times contributed its eager quota to the ranks of his listeners. You have already heard, my brethren, of the memorable occasion when certain contumacious heretics, in order not to yield to his forcible arguments, chose, not indeed the best, but the only alternative left open to them, that of not listening to what he said. Antony, unaccustomed to such repulses, and burning with holy zeal, went to the sea-shore, and lifting up his voice, "O fishes!" he exclaimed, "come, and listen to the word of God, that word to which these men, or, to speak more truly, these vipers, refuse their attention." Scarcely had this bold appeal been uttered, ere the waters, but a moment before so calm and tranquil, were seen to become ruffled and agitated, and, gradually, all the finny dwellers in the deep, both great and small, rose to the surface of the water, and ranged themselves in marvellous order, according to their several species, close to the beach, presenting thus a numerous and attentive auditory. Whereupon the Saint addressed to them a lengthy discourse, recounting the benefits which God had conferred on this portion of the animal kingdom; reminding them how they alone had been spared at the time of the universal deluge; how they had been at one time singled out to receive and shelter a storm-tossed prophet, at another to restore sight to a just man who had become blind, at a third to furnish the tribute money demanded of an Incarnate God. After having by these and other arguments incited them to praise and glorify their Maker, he finally dismissed them with his paternal blessing. Surely never before did the mute fishes more keenly regret their inability to utter any sound than at that moment; fain would they, had it been possible, have made use of their fettered tongues. This being, however, out of the question, they bowed their heads in lowly reverence and quickly dived once more into the ocean depths. And now, perchance, the fabled glories of Arion may recur to the mind of some here present, of Arion, who, with the melodies of his tuneful lyre, moved the very dolphins to compassionate his lot. Away with such fanciful tales; no fables and no fiction are needed to obtain credence for the miracle I have just related.

When, even in imagination, did the sons of boastful Greece perform feats equal to the wonders Antony performed in reality! The famous Demosthenes may, perhaps, have ventured to hope for a similar triumph when, as Valerius relates, in elation at his youthful talents, he paced the sea-shore to test his powers, almost as if expecting the foaming billows and monsters of the deep to pause in astonishment at his eloquence; but never did the meanest of them all vouchsafe to bestow on him the slightest sign of attention. His words were heedlessly carried away by the winds, and the waves of the ocean continued their native course. Imagine, then, what glory Antony must have acquired in the presence of that great concourse of people, who, having flocked together to witness this novel sight, beheld the inhabitants of the sea positively hanging on his lips, and heard him convoke and disperse at will this unwonted but obedient assemblage! After this it can excite no fresh astonishment to learn that this wonderful achievement was followed by the conversion of a large number of heretics.

There is only one thing which renders it a matter of difficulty to believe in the miracles Antony wrought, and that is the fact that they were of so frequent occurrence. For it appeared as if God, desirous of magnifying his servant more day by day, had entrusted to his hand the rod of Moses, that thus he might humble the haughty, conquer the rebellious, and by force of miracles cause even proud Pharaos to fall prostrate before him. As an instance of this, we may take the case of the fierce Eccelino, kneeling humbly at Antony's feet, a rope round his neck, entreating pardon of the Saint, and submitting to his reproofs. This man was by nature so indomitable in his pride, that when wounded and taken captive in a battle near Milan, he would not condescend to make terms with the enemy, refusing moreover to allow his wounds to be dressed, to take any food, or to exchange a word with any one; preferring to die despairing and alone rather than accept any alleviation at the hands of his captors, much less endure their taunts. What triumph could surpass that of having tamed such a spirit as this? Let those who will gaze in wonder at a Humbert, who could make the savage bear forget her nature and follow gently where he led; at a Simonides, in whose presence the lion became a lamb; or at Antony himself, when on holding up the Sacred Host before the eyes of a mule, he caused that animal to kneel in lowly reverence before its Maker; in my opinion, however, to have brought an Eccelino as a suppliant to his feet is a victory far more glorious than those I have just enumerated. And if we proceed yet further with our investigation, we shall discover that of all the rarest, choicest, and most brilliant gifts Heaven has to bestow, there is not one which Antony did not possess in full measure. Do you ask if he could foretell future events? I have only to remind you how, with holy envy of so glorious a lot, he predicted in one instance of a child as yet unborn, and in another of a man already grown up, that they would both one day bear the palm of martyrdom; a privilege in the hope of winning which he himself had formerly sought the vast forests of that Moorish land, where so many Christians had already found the prize he strove in vain to acquire. Had he power to discern the hidden thoughts of the heart? Let a certain Bishop of Bruges answer this query, since the Saint read at a glance and as speedily solved doubts which were agitating the mind of the prelate. Could he discover the war of passions waged within the soul? A novice of his own Order will tell us how the temptations by which he was at one time cruelly tormented were disclosed to him by Antony, who gently lulled them to rest. Did he possess the supernatural faculty of appearing in places whence he was absent in body? Have we not heard that he frequently appeared by night to hardened sinners, rebuking them for their obstinate rebellion against God, placing before them one by one the sins of which they were bound to accuse themselves, and naming the priest to whom their confession was to be made, thereby displaying alike the marvellous flights his spirit was capable of taking, and the untiring, active zeal for souls by which he was animated. May he not on this point be fitly compared to the Sun which, when we fancy it has sunk wearily to rest in its ocean bed, has but gone elsewhere on its way to enlighten other climes and rouse other nations from their slumber? Nor must I omit to mention the dominion God gave to him over the elements, over disease, and over death itself. To heal cripples, give sight to the blind, restore the paralysed, were with him common-place actions of every day occurrence; to recall to life those who were not merely laid out for burial, but who were already decaying in the grave, was indeed a proof of greater powers, but yet this is far from closing the list of all his glorious gifts. We find that the angels themselves were subject to him; for he could command

and dispose of their services at his will, summoning them at his pleasure, sending them hither and thither at his bidding. But it is not enough to say that the angels were accustomed to await his commands, for they anticipated them. Thus it happened upon one occasion when Antony, desirous of sending a letter to his absent Superior, was searching in vain for some one to whom he could entrust it, behold an Angel suddenly appeared before him, and this winged visitant, without waiting for a word of entreaty or request, volunteered to become his messenger, and having taken the letter, executed his commission with wonderful alacrity and speed, swiftly returning with the desired answer. But ought this to astonish us, my hearers? When those about a court perceive any one to be the object of special affection on the part of their Sovereign, they esteem it a privilege and not a burden to serve the favoured individual. With what feelings then must the Angels have witnessed the extreme familiarity with which God treated Antony! Often did they behold their Lord lay aside His Majesty, and under the form of a little child, repose in the arms of the Saint, playing gently and sporting with him, as if oblivious of His own transcendent greatness! They perceived the looks of love, the tender embraces, the sweet smiles and fond endearments which were mutually exchanged; and how could such a sight fail to inspire them with feelings of profoundest respect for one who was raised to the enjoyment of these signal favours? They waited on him continually, accustoming him to such habitual intercourse with Heaven that the things of earth becoming utterly distasteful to him, nothing remained but to let him bid farewell to this earth at the early age of thirty-six years. I know not indeed whether this privilege was granted in answer to his own earnest desires, or in order to satisfy those blessed spirits who were eager to see him admitted into their ranks; one thing at any rate is certain, that Jesus and Mary came down in person to receive into their loving arms his triumphant spirit, and thus anticipate the welcome awaiting him in the celestial country. And even here in this world the name of Antony became more glorious than ever, for whilst his brethren in religion were striving to conceal for a short time the immense loss which earth had just sustained by the death of one of her greatest sons, little children began to publish the decease of the Saint throughout the streets of Padua, weeping aloud and refusing to be comforted. Moreover, a new grave was miraculously prepared (as some say by angelic hands) for the reception of the sacred remains, and no sooner had the Saint been laid there than he began to work miracles so numerous, so surprising, and so notorious, that at the end of one brief year, the reigning Pontiff found himself compelled, in accordance with the prayers of nations and the request of their rulers, to raise Antony without delay to the altars of the Church. This decision caused such universal rejoicing, that simultaneously with the solemn promulgation of the wished-for decree in the immediate neighbourhood of Rome, the bells of distant Lisbon, to the astonishment of all who heard them, began to ring of their own accord, pealing forth a joyous echo. Such then, and so glorious were thy triumphs, O Antony! No other tongue but thine own, which is even now incorrupted, could magnify them as justice demands. But at least grant me stength that I may not grow weary of proclaiming thy praise as best I can in the ears of a people who will never grow weary of listening to the story of one they love so much.

And now, my hearers, you will perhaps think that my subject is exhausted, and that I have at length finished my recital of the long series of Antony's glories. This surmise would indeed be correct, might we judge of him by the example of other saints, whom, as we well know, God is wont to distinguish by extraordinary gifts and graces for the first few months or years after their death. Then all hasten to bring gifts to their shrines, to burn tapers and incense upon their altars, to address to them numerous supplications; in their praise a thousand tongues grow vocal; in their honour fasts on bread and water are voluntarily undertaken; in their honour weekly confessions and communions are made. How many persons keep lamps ever burning before their images, and offer the Holy Sacrifice day by day on their altars! Fresh panegyrics of their virtue are continually heard; new records of the miracles wrought by their hand daily issue from the press; whilst objects of devotion can scarcely be manufactured quickly enough to keep pace with the ever-increasing demand. And are these demonstrations confined to a single city, or perhaps to one country alone? Generally they are so, and if you judge by the ordinary rule, you will expect to find this to be the same in Antony's case. For as the same constellations are not seen in different climes, so every saint is not equally honoured in all places; each city each country has its own peculiar patron, of whose protection it specially boasts, and towards whom it is accustomed to display special veneration. But the very same names which are incessantly invoked in one land, are almost unknown in another; how many Polish and Hungarian saints are there, for instance, of whose existence we are hardly aware! And God permits this to be so, as a concession to human weakness; our devotion being so poor and limited a thing, that unless concentrated upon a single object, it would be lost altogether, like the waters of some shallow brooklet, if diverted into several channels and dispersed through several meadows. But when we turn to Antony we have a very different tale to tell, for where, throughout the length and breadth of Christendom, is any spot to be found in which devotion to him does not abound and flourish? I do not speak of Portugal, the land of his birth, of France, the scene of his labours, of Italy, the place of his burial; I speak of the whole continent of Europe, and even of the far-off Indies, both East and West, where his fame has spread to such an extent, and where his miracles have produced so great an impression that there is scarcely a city which has not placed itself under his protection. Furthermore, to descend to individuals, we shall find few persons who will not acknowledge Antony for one of their favourite saints and most cherished patrons. What house is there, what workshop, what cottage but is adorned with some portrait of him? Even the very beggar, whose humble dwelling is barely provided with necessary furniture, not to speak of anything in the shape of ornament or decoration, contrives to hang by his bedside some representation of the Saint, if it be but a sorry woodcut, utterly devoid of all pretensions to artistic merit. The varying circumstances of need or danger in which we may find ourselves are wont to determine our choice of a special patron upon whom to call for help and protection; but to Antony recourse may be had at all times and under almost all manner of circumstances. To him we may turn alike in mental anguish or physical suffering, when threatened by loss of life or property, in moments of perplexity, or when commercial difficulties weigh upon us; so that his altar might fitly be compared to that famous pond of Bethsaida, in which every disease found its remedy, were it not for one important difference, namely, that whilst those who sought their cure from the healing waters had to wait many a long and uncertain hour, Antony is ever at hand to hear and help.

And now, my hearers, let me ask, do any of you deem me wrong in applying to Antony those words which escaped my lips on the contemplation of the many glories united in the person of this favoured Saint. "There was not found the like to him in glory." What could God do which He has not already done to show more plainly His great love for His servant; to make him more widely known and universally honoured? What more powerful allurements could He hold out in order to induce us to devote ourselves to his worship and enrol ourselves amongst his clients? Happy, indeed, are you since you have had the wisdom to make choice of so great an advocate; let it be your constant endeavour to co-operate in His glory as far as lies in your power, confident that from his throne above Antony will behold your efforts, and will be much pleased with them. But why do I say from his throne above? Before he passed from this life he saw them all presented to his mental vision;

for we read in the story of his life that to the dying Saint, when he was stretched upon the ground on a bed of sackcloth and ashes, God revealed with marvellous clearness the honours that would be paid to him by all posterity; and among these can you doubt that those you have paid him in times past will be numbered, and especially those which you are rendering to him on the present occasion? How must he rejoice to witness the warm piety which has drawn you together in crowds this morning to celebrate his Festival, heedless of the call of worldly business, deaf to the voice of worldly amusement! I am well aware that in the solemn hours, when ages yet unborn were revealed to his gaze, there were but few cities where he did not behold a numerous band of his future worshippers; but I do not know whether in many cities he beheld, as here, worshippers not less conspicuous for their rank than for their piety. It behoves you, therefore, to persevere with constancy in your pious practices, never doubting that you also will derive as much benefit from your good works as others have derived from theirs. And now let me conclude with one practical observation. The saints, as you well know, are the trusty guardians of our cities, and therefore with consummate wisdom you have confided to them the care of your gates, the protection of your walls, as to watchmen who, as Saint Basil says, afford security against the incursions of the enemy. Nor need we have any apprehension, lest treacherous slumbers should close their eyelids, and render them oblivious of our danger. But if you wish for a special defender of that liberty you prize so highly, to preserve which all hardship is light, and no vigilance is excessive, then I would bid you chose Antony as your champion. Do not imagine that I speak without sufficient warranty for the truth of my words, or that I am deceiving your ears with promises alike specious and delusive. God forbid that I should do so! Open the pages of history and you will see by whose help it was that the Paduans recovered their liberty, when, after the death of the Saint, the cruel tyrant of whom I have already spoken, growing bolder in his arrogance and pride as years went on, laid an iron yoke on the necks of his unhappy subjects.

The Papal forces, allied with the troops of Venice, sought in vain to break the fetters which held the unfortunate people captive; but what their united efforts failed to effect was readily accomplished through Antony's instrumentality. For on the night of his Feast, whilst a religious, prostrated before the tomb of the Saint, was interceding for the deliverance of his oppressed fellow-citizens, he heard a voice issuing from the tomb, and saying: "Be of good courage; on the octave of my Feast your city shall regain her former liberty." And so, in fact, it came to pass; for when the eighth day came round, Eccelino was suddenly seized with a secret and mysterious terror which impelled him to fly in panic-stricken fear from the city, the gates of which he flung open with his own hand; escaping with as much haste and precipitation as if a band of armed foes, sword in hand, were following close upon his footsteps. Now, if Antony showed himself thus able and willing to restore liberty to those who had the misfortune to lose it, is it not likely that he will be even more willing to preserve it to you who know so well how to maintain it?

But his task in this respect will be an easy one, for, thanks to admirable laws, vigilant administration, the concord and loving harmony prevailing amongst your citizens there is but little fear that your freedom will not be successfully defended. Nevertheless, it seems to me that it is one of the first laws of christian policy to employ all human means with as much diligence as if superhuman assistance were beyond our reach; and at the same time to entreat the aid of heaven with as much importunity as if we were incapable of making any effort of our own. Do not, however, for a moment imagine that I wish to convey the idea that because Padua has been privileged to lend its name to Antony, it may on this account lay claim to a monopoly of his favours, or to the exclusive enjoyment of his protection. All nations have an equal right in Antony, each one may assert that he is wholly hers. Wherefore, whether we consider the wide-spread homage paid him, or the gifts he freely distributes to all alike, we shall in either case be justified in giving him a new and more glorious title—namely, no longer the title of Antony of Padua, but Antony of the entire Universe.

DISCOURSE IN HONOUR OF THE BLESSED SACRAMENT.

TO PROVE THAT GOD CONFERS ON US GREATER BENEFITS BY REMAINING HIDDEN BENEATH THE SPECIES OF BREAD, THAN HE WOULD HAVE DONE HAD HE OPENLY SHOWN HIMSELF.

"Verily thou art a hidden God."—ISAIAS xlv. 15.

I DO not think he would be far wrong, who wishing to designate the present age with an appropriate name, should assign to it the appellation of the lover of display. For what is nowadays studied so universally and with such eagerness how to make an imposing appearance in the eyes of the world? Some men are even to be found who, though barely able to provide themselves with the necessaries of life, will yet pinch themselves in the use of those necessaries in order to procure rich apparel, to keep carriages and horses, to surround themselves with a retinue of liveried attendants; nor, in their anxiety to appear wealthy, do they shrink from incurring immense debts, and thus rendering themselves vastly poorer than they originally were. And if we visit the mansions of the great, we shall find their chief aim is to have long suites of reception rooms, abounding in the most superb decorations; we shall behold costly tapestries, splendid furniture, elaborate ornamentation, magnificent services of plate. But on the other hand, we shall find the inner rooms, appropriated by the owner of the mansion to his own private use, to be small and dingy apartments, the walls of which are bare of any hangings save such as the undisturbed spider chooses to weave there. And what shall I say of the gardens and parks, of the woods and villas? Everything is contrived so as to give an impression of grandeur above the reality, by means of false perspective, imitation marbles, fictitious metals and a thousand other ingenious and delusive inventions, in which now-a-days well-nigh every art excels. The manner in which God acts is indeed very different to this. He steadfastly shuns all empty ostentation, and follows a rule directly the reverse of that ordinarily followed by men, for whereas they endeavour to display the best outside, and keep the meanest within, He lets what is meanest appear on the surface, and keeps the choicest out of sight. And if any one inclines to call this to question, let him turn his eyes for a moment upon the Sacred Host which we venerate upon our altars, and tell me, where can we find anything of which the form is more simple, more insignificant, more contemptible? Nevertheless that which constitutes the joy of Paradise is present there. Well were it for us could we understand aright all that is comprehended in that truth; we should not then allow the evidence of our senses to mislead us into attaching so low a value to the priceless gift we receive in the Blessed Sacrament, as if God were not there really present in all His splendour and majesty because our senses fail to discern Him. But what would you have, my hearers? Would you have God manifest Himself there under a form of external beauty? Believe me, this would be out of keeping with His character; it would be at variance with the manner in which he loves to act. "Verily thou art a hidden God:" it is His delight to dwell disguised amongst the sons of men. This answer would in fact suffice to satisfy the mind of those who ask wherefore, since Christ was pleased for our sake to remain amongst us in the Blessed Sacrament, He did not further enhance the benefit bestowed upon us to its utmost limits by remaining visible to our sight. But it would be a mistake to suppose that the promptings of His own nature alone led Him to conceal Himself; He did so for our sakes, because He was thus enabled to confer on us far greater benefits than would have been possible had He not hidden Himself from our view. I do not deny that this statement at first sight appears paradoxical; but if you will follow me with attention, I shall be able to establish the truth of my assertion.

The world may be divided into two classes: the friends of Christ, and His enemies. And by choosing to remain hidden in the Blessed Sacrament, He has bestowed upon both of these classes of men the greatest possible benefit. Who does not know that weak eyes cannot endure the light of the sun; that even any light whatsoever, be it but the faint glimmer of a rush light, causes them suffering, so that it is the greatest kindness to leave them in obscurity? Judge for yourselves, then, what great scandal would have been occasioned, if the wicked, whose spiritual sight is so weak, were to see our Lord giving Himself to the faithful for their sustenance in His own proper form and substance.

What ignorant criticisms, what unseemly jests, what profane blasphemies would they not utter; for they would imagine themselves witnessing, not a miracle of divine power, but some triumphs of the magician's art. We are told by the Evangelist Saint John that no sooner did Christ proclaim the inestimable favour He was about to bestow on mankind by giving them His flesh for their food: "The bread that I will give is my flesh for the life of the world," than sinister murmurs arose among the crowd. Some disputed among themselves, forming conjectures as to how it could be possible to fulfil that promise: " The Jews therefore strove among themselves, saying: How can this man give us His flesh to eat?" Some blamed it as foolish and rash; others rejected it altogether as absurd: "This saying is hard, and who can hear it?" Others, again, still more scandalised, did not hesitate to turn their back on Christ, and forsake Him completely: "After this many of His disciples went back and walked no more with Him" (John vi. 52, 53, 61, 67). Wherefore, if so great a commotion was excited amongst the followers of Christ, on merely hearing that at some future day He would Himself become their food, what would have been the effect produced upon His opponents had they beheld this promise visibly fulfilled? Surely the only result possible would be the eternal death of their souls, and not of their souls alone, for in such a case it would appear almost inevitable that their bodies should perish likewise. For since those unhappy persons of whom I speak are reprobates, it is certain that Christ could not regard them otherwise than with anger; and how could they look upon the face of an angry God, and not forthwith perish, overwhelmed with terror? "They shall perish at the rebuke of thy countenance" (Ps. lxxix. 17); thus the Psalmist speaks of them in addressing the Lord; mark, he does not say the rebuke of thy *lips*, but "the rebuke of thy *countenance;*" for the sight of this countenance alone would be enough to slay a number greater than the number of the Bethsabites who fell before the Ark of God, upon which, without the covering of its veil, they had gazed.

But why should I spend so much thought on the lot of the wicked? Let us leave them to their fate, and turn our attention to the just; the just for whose sake alone Christ ever abides in this Divine Sacrament: "Eat, O friends" (Cant. v. 1). And, therefore, if He has willed to remain concealed, He has done so only out of love for them. For although they would not as the wicked fall down dead, horror-struck, yet I know not whether they would not expire with amazement. My brethren, it is indeed one thing to contemplate the face of Christ glorified as it now is, when He reigns in heaven; and another to see His Sacred Humanity as it appeared on earth. Which of us possesses an eye so keen as to be able to gaze upon the Sun of Justice without losing our sight? The illustrious Virgin Saint Teresa tells us that "if once privileged to behold Christ, nothing in this world would ever after appear pure in our eyes." And why is this? Because were true beauty once revealed to us, all things else would seem in comparison to it as fictitious imitations, deceptions and illusions; we should go on our way absently, like men walking in a dream; we should see and not perceive, we should hear and not understand, we should deem all earthly objects unworthy of our notice: "I said in my excess:

Every man is a liar" (Ps. cxv. 2). Nor is this all, for how would a miserable sinner, such as I am, dare to draw nigh, if such awful Majesty were unfolded to my sight? Should I presume to receive Communion? to feed on this heavenly food? to receive such a Guest into my heart? Happy those among you, if any such should be found, who would have the courage not to draw back; for my part, I doubt whether I should be amongst their number.

We cannot but wonder when we hear the well-known story of Judith, when we are told how a woman of such surpassing beauty went alone into the midst of an army composed of proud, daring, dissolute, and licentious men, without one of the soldiers to whom she had occasion to speak venturing to offer her [the slightest insult, to cast on her an immodest glance, to address to her a single unseemly word. And nevertheless it is a matter of notoriety that besides the splendid attire with which she had adorned herself, God Himself had contributed an additional charm to her loveliness, by imparting to it a radiance more than human. "Therefore the Lord increased this her beauty, so that she appeared to all men's eyes incomparably lovely" (Judith x. 4). How came it then to pass that of all that lascivious host no one spoke an amorous word to the peerless beauty? I know that this may principally be attributed to the watchful care of Providence, Who inspired her to take so unusual a step, but there was another cause, namely, the very fact that she was so surpassingly beautiful. It belongs to a low type of beauty to enkindle the passions of those who look on it; a beauty so elevated and so sublime astonishes and bewilders, it causes the beholder involuntarily to draw back in respectful reverence. What was the first feeling awakened by the sight of Judith in the hearts of the licentious soldiery amongst whom she found herself? was it delight, was it desire? No, my hearers, it was wonder; "and when the men had heard her words, they beheld her face and their eyes were amazed, for they wondered exceedingly at her beauty" (Judith x. 14). Notice the words of Holy Scripture, they do not speak of longing, or of love, but of amazement; for the tribute of astonishment is the first tribute we pay to what is great. And now to return to the subject under consideration: if the sight of a mortal countenance, such as that of the celebrated Judith, could not fail to strike awe into the minds of even the most audacious of the bold soldiers who looked upon her, is it possible that we could bear to look upon the countenance of Christ without being, I will not say awestruck, but rather stunned; and as it were deprived of our faculties and almost of our life. And granted that this be true, who would be found bold enough to venture to approach our Lord; to confide to Him the secret of his love, however pure that affection might be; to speak of union with Him, to think of receiving and embracing Him, of preparing a resting-place for Him in the interior of the heart! Our eyes would then be amazed; and, dazzled by such resplendent beauty, we should be obliged to shut them, like bats, who, issuing from their lurking-places at noonday, should attempt to gaze upon the sun. "He that is a searcher of Majesty shall be overwhelmed by glory" (Prov. xxv. 27). Thus we perceive how great is the benefit conferred upon us by our most loving Lord, Who, in order to place

Himself entirely at our disposal in the Blessed Sacrament, is pleased to veil His countenance as Moses did on coming down from the mountain, and to veil it so closely that not a single ray of His glory can pass through. "In order to spare our weakness," says the learned Hugo of Saint Victor, "He does not manifest Himself in the brightness of His Majesty, but hides it as it were, under a veil." The appearance of one Angel, coming down from heaven to impart wisdom to him so overwhelmed Daniel, whose powers of sight were in general strong and clear, that by his own admission he not only fainted, but nearly expired. "I fainted away and retained no strength" (Dan. x. 8). Tobias, Josue, Gedeon, Manue, and many others, were struck to the ground by a similar apparition, their swoon being so heavy and prolonged as almost to resemble the sleep of death. And what think you was the cause of the unaccustomed sensations of coldness experienced by King David, of whom we are told that in the latter years of his life he felt constant and intense chilliness, all coverings proving ineffectual to restore the natural heat of his frame? "When he was covered with clothes, he was not warm" (3 Kings i. 1). In the opinion of several distinguished writers this state of things arose from the terror inspired in him on seeing the Angel standing by the thrashing floor, sword in hand, although about to return it to the scabbard. Wherefore, if in all these instances the mere apparition of an Angel produced such strange tremors, what would be the effect produced upon us, weak and miserable as we are, were we to see, not an Angel, but the very Lord of Angels in all His inherent loveliness? Do you think we could then speak freely to Him, acquaint Him with our concerns, expose to Him our needs, pour forth to Him the inmost desires of our hearts? I leave you to form your own conclusions on this point. He is with us in a familiar form under these accidents of bread. When a king chooses to disguise himself, his subjects are not bound to address him by the same titles, to observe the same strict etiquette, the same rigorous ceremonial which it is incumbent on them to observe under ordinary circumstances. And therefore, since our Lord, as we have just said, sees fit to conceal Himself, he gives us mortals courage to approach Him, provided it be in the appointed manner, and proves His willingness to hold intercourse with us more as an equal than as a king. Now tell me, has not this Divine Sacrament been given to us under the most familiar and ordinary form possible? The most ordinary, I say, and for that very reason at the same time the most useful; since it is a treasure which differs from all others in this respect, namely, that the more complete its concealment, the greater and more wide-spread are the benefits accruing from it.

But let us suppose for a moment that it is possible for us to look with unfaltering gaze on the brightness of the divine countenance, to draw near to God in His unveiled glory, to receive Him within our breast, to converse with Him, to feed on Him; suppose, I say, such a thing to be possible, tell me, in what then would our merit consist? If we desire to be numbered amongst the faithful, we must in all things live the life of faith. Now Faith, if the Apostle is to be believed, "is the substance of things to be hoped for, the evidence of things that appear not" (Heb. xi. 1). "Faith," says

Saint Augustine, "is to believe in what one cannot
see;" for things visible to our outer eyes are made
known to us by experience, by the evidences of our
senses, not by faith. What was the greatest praise
Saint Peter could bestow on those recent converts to
Christianity to whom his Epistle was addressed ? It
was that in the Christ, whom he with his own eyes
had seen they believed, without having seen Him.
"In whom also now, though you see Him not you
believe" (1 Pet. i. 8). And on attentive consideration, we shall perceive the merit of faith in the Blessed
Sacrament to be still far greater; because in that we
are not merely required to believe what we do not see,
but furthermore to believe the direct opposite of that
which is apparent to our sight. Here we are called
upon to receive the testimony of our hearing alone,
and reject the evidence of all the other senses, which
conspire together to persuade us that that is bread
which is not bread, but the body of Christ. And I
shall not be far wrong in comparing the delusive appearance of this substance to the ingenious deception
practised upon the aged patriarch Isaac, when instead
of blessing Esau, as he imagined himself doing, he
blessed Jacob, disguised as Esau. Listen to me attentively, for the parallel is striking, though somewhat
sublime. In Isaac sight, touch, smell and taste were all
deceived, his hearing alone was not deceived. His sight
was deceived, for he believed he saw before him the
true Esau, whilst Jacob was there instead, clothed in his
brother's dress. His touch was deceived, for he thought
he was feeling Esau's hairy hand, when in fact his
fingers touched only the soft hairs of the skins of the
kid. His smell was deceived, for he imagined the

fragrant odour which greeted his nostrils to emanate from Esau's person, while in reality it proceeded from his garments alone. His taste was deceived, for he thought he was partaking of venison prepared by Esau, when instead of this, he was eating the flesh of kids of the flock, which Jacob had caused to be dressed as if it were venison. But was Isaac's hearing deceived, like all his other senses? No, my brethren, on the contrary, he continued to reiterate persistently: "The voice indeed is the voice of Jacob" (Gen. xxvii. 22). So that if the good old man had but been willing to give more credence to the testimony of his hearing than to that of his other senses, this famous artifice would have proved a failure. And now let us see how this may be applied to the Blessed Sacrament. When the priest officiating at the altar, extends his hands, like a second Isaac, over the consecrated Host in the act of blessing it, let no one deem that which is before him to be bread, although apparently it is nought else. Christ is as truly present under the accidents of bread, as Jacob was himself present when clad in Esau's garments. The whiteness which is seen, the hardness which is felt, the odour which is smelt, the flavour which is tasted, these are the accidents of bread, they are indeed bread in appearance, but not in reality. Yet the four senses by which these qualities are discerned, namely sight, feeling, smell and taste, naturally infer from the accidents the nature of the substance, as they are wont to do; and what is the consequence? With one voice they unanimously declare: "This is bread." But hearing asserts itself in opposition to them all, and boldly proclaims: "This is no bread, it is Christ Himself." Of these two conflicting decisions one must be wrong; where is the deception? That man is deceived who like Isaac believes the testimony of his palate, of his nostrils, of his hands, or of his eyes; whilst the true Christian accepts the evidence of his hearing alone, and believing the words of Christ when He says: "This is my body," corrects the evidence of all his other senses and refuses to be led astray by them. And now, returning to the point whence we started, I repeat that the chief merit of faith in the Blessed Sacrament consists in this; namely that not merely does our faith come from hearing, as we know to be the case with regard to other mysteries of religion, for "Faith cometh by hearing" (Rom. viii. 17), but that in this instance we are called upon to believe our hearing in despite of each and all our other senses, since their unanimous testimony is directly at variance with our belief. But if the presence of Christ were made openly manifest in this Sacrament, without doubt all our other senses would concur to recognise the truth, and thus our faith would lose its merit, being no longer that faith spoken of by the Holy Pontiff Saint Gregory, when he says: "That faith has not merit, to which human reason affords experience."

And now let me bring before your notice an excellent observation made by one to whom, on account of his lofty intellect all have ungrudgingly awarded the title of the Angelic Doctor. "How was it," he asks, "that the human race incurred in the first instance the sentence of eternal death?" Everyone knows that it was through our first parents believing the words of the enemy of mankind, when, in the terrestrial Paradise, he gave them to eat of a food seemingly incorruptible, but in which death lay concealed. "It is therefore just," says Saint Thomas, "that our work of reparation should begin by the faith we attach to the words of Christ, when, under the form of perishable food, He gives us the bread of eternal life;" and in this God has had in view nothing else but our interest, and to furnish us with an opportunity of eliciting acts of virtue, every time that we receive Communion, in a more perfect degree, by forming acts of more lively faith, deeper humility, and more adoring homage. Do you not now see what great things our Lord has done for us by remaining concealed in the Blessed Sacrament? Truly, "it is good to hide the secret of a king" (Tob. xii. 7), for in this disguise He is more familiar with us, and more useful to us. And in any case how enviable is our lot, since we are hereby enabled to give our Lord a more touching proof of the sincere affection we bear Him!

And here, my brethren, another thought occurs to me; it is this, that if it were possible for the Seraphim to envy us, they would do so because we can love the Lord Whose presence we have amongst us without ever seeing Him. You are aware of the posture in which the Seraphs stood before the throne of God, when the prophet Isaias was privileged to behold them with his mortal eyes; two of their wings they kept in perpetual motion, as a sign of rejoicing. And what did they do with the other four? With them they endeavoured to shut out the sight of their Lord; "with two they covered His face, and with two they covered His feet" (Isaias vi. 2). And do you ask their object in doing so? With all due deference to the many ingenious explanations put forward by learned doctors, I confess that the meaning of their action appears to my mind no other than this, to try whether their love of God would be equally ardent were they no longer to enjoy the privilege of contemplating Him. O blissful portion, and thrice happy state! This lot has been assigned to us, in preference to them. And who can say how rich a store of merits we might acquire, did we but know how to avail ourselves constantly of the precious opportunities thus placed within our reach?

But some, alas! instead of spending their time in loving this Lord, Who for their greater good vouchsafes to abide here veiled from their sight, allow the very fact of His being thus veiled to embolden them to treat Him with contempt. They think no more of Him than if He were not there at all; they show Him gross neglect, they offer Him reckless affronts; and if they enter there where He is present in the Blessed Sacrament, it appears to be with the express purpose of insulting Him. Can it, therefore, be imagined that those who exhibit so little respect to His hidden presence would behave in the same manner were our Lord to reveal openly to them His divine countenance, kindled with just wrath? What terror, what trembling would then seize upon those miserable beings! You know what befell those daring soldiers who approached Jesus in the garden of Gethsemane for the purpose of arresting His sacred person; a single ray of majesty emanating from His countenance caused them to fall prostrate on the ground. And yet, as Saint Thomas observes, on that occasion Christ appeared as a malefactor, a servant, a slave; nay, more, He was on the point of being led to judgment. Now picture to yourselves what would be the effect, if He were to appear here in His character of Judge. As I said before, the wicked would in that case experience a foretaste of the awful terrors reserved for them on the day of final judgment, when they will in vain entreat the mountains to fall on them, in order to exclude the sight, not indeed of the devils who are to be their tormentors, nor of the lost souls who are to be their companions, but of the countenance of their angry Judge, in all its awful beauty: "They shall say to the mountains, cover us; and to the hills, fall on us," (Osee x. 8); "and hide us"—from what? "From the face of Him that sitteth upon the throne" (Apoc. vi. 16). You will all agree that, were He thus openly manifested here, none would dare to despise Him, but it is not so, He is hidden; His look was as it were hidden (Isaias liii. 3), and hence comes the audacity of these unhappy sinners: His look was as it were hidden and despised.

"O earth, earth, earth, hear the word of the Lord" (Jer. xxii. 29). Listen, O sinner, to the words God addresses to you by my mouth, unworthy sinner that I am. I tell you, God will not for ever bear with the insolence of those who do not scruple when in His presence to talk, to joke, and to laugh, and even to indulge in foolish lovemaking. Is He not truly present in the Sacred Host, although our eyes cannot behold Him? How can you act as if you did not believe this, if you bear the name of Christians? Remember how the famous Athenian judges, when seated in the tribunal, were shut out from the view of the criminals on whom they were about to pass sentence, by a thick curtain, which effectually concealed their persons. Did the guilty, think you, on that account feel less trepidation?

Were they inclined to smile in derision or contempt? Were they inspired with less respect for their judges? Reflect awhile, and you will see how similar is the case with us. We stand before Christ our Judge; a curtain conceals Him from our sight; He is, I own, a hidden God; but is it therefore permissible to treat Him with a scorn which would be impossible if He were openly manifest? Alas! I fancy that I hear already the sentence of eternal condemnation, which is even now being issued from behind that veil! I seem to hear God speak as He spoke of old to Jeremias, asking: "Have you perchance met together in a haunt of thieves, or are you assembled in my house? Is this house, then, in which my name hath been called upon, in your eyes become a den of robbers?" (Jer. vii. 11). In vain can any one attempt to deny the outrages I receive there; "I, I am He; I have seen it, saith the Lord." Do you pretend to assert that many do not ply their tongues with unblushing effrontery? I have seen it. That many an amorous glance is not exchanged? I have seen it. That no laughing is carried on? I have seen it. That no frivolity is displayed? I have seen it. That no love-making is freely indulged in? "I, I am He, I have seen it, saith the Lord." I am hidden here, it is true; but this is no reason why anything can be hidden from My eyes. I will do here the same things I have done elsewhere: "I will do to this house, and to the place I have given you and your fathers, as I did to Silo" (Jer. vii. 14). I will destroy you, I will scatter you, I will send down judgments upon you from heaven, disasters public and private, disasters in ever-increasing numbers and severity. Yet more, after your death I will expel you from My Presence, that Presence for which during your lifetime you showed so little regard: "I will cast you away from before my face" (Jer. vii. 15). "Have mercy, O my God! in the midst of this Thy just wrath remember Thy mercy and spare Thy people! May it not be urged, in extenuation of this sad conduct, that it is held in abhorrence by the greater number of Christians; and that the transgressors themselves for the most part have been led into it rather through natural heedlessness and want of thought than by any deliberate intention of offending against Thy Majesty." But, alas! O sinner, I am but wasting my time; God refuses to accept my intercession. Dost thou not hear what he answers me: "Do not thou pray for this people; and do not withstand me, for I will not hear thee"? No, thus God seems to speak to me; I will not hear thee, for the disease is now so widespread and so firmly rooted that, if naught else avails to cure it, I Myself must at length apply the remedy; Seest thou not what they do? Seest thou not that at the very time thou art speaking of their evil practices, there are some present who can hardly restrain themselves from interrupting thee? seest thou not how they murmur, how they whisper amongst themselves? how far they are from any purpose of amendment? And if, perhaps, human respect keeps them silent for the moment, in a day or so they will return here to talk, to joke, and offend Me more than ever. Seest thou not, seest thou not? But the end has come: "Therefore, thus saith the Lord God, Behold, my wrath and my indignation is enkindled against this place, it shall burn and shall not be quenched." The fire of my fury waxes hotter day by day, at last it will burst forth. "Thus saith the Lord of hosts, the God of Israel" (Jer. vii. 20, 21).

But what am I doing? What are these predictions I have been declaiming whilst I am handling a subject of so different a nature? Whilst treating a subject breathing but peace, see to what an opposite point I have arrived. Nevertheless, do not be in haste to condemn me, my hearers; it is not I who have been speaking to you, this proves all the more that it is God Who has put into my mouth the words I have addressed to you; let them not fall upon your ears in vain. At all events, you cannot deny that the sight of our Lord hidden here upon our altars ought to induce you to love Him more, rather than to treat Him with disrespect. It would be a matter of no difficulty for Him to reveal Himself openly; indeed, He has done so already to more than one. And if He does not do so habitually it is, as I said, because in so doing he is actuated by a desire for our greater good. His design is to render this Divine Sacrament less unapproachable to us, and the same time more profitable; and, with this view, He has not shrunk from subjecting Himself to all the outrages to which the very fact of His being concealed could not fail to expose Him. And, I grieve to say, the completeness of our Lord's concealment in the sacred Host emboldens some miscreants, not only to behave with irreverence in church, but to commit the most horrible sacrileges; to treat the sacred Host with a profanity of which I hardly dare to think, much less to speak; they even venture to make use of them in those diabolical incantations which are the supremest insult a Christian can offer to his Maker. And yet God has regarded all these unparalleled offences as things of no moment, because by concealing Himself He is enabled to confer greater benefits upon us! O love incomparable and unspeakable ! who shall be found able to comprehend it ?

Is it not, then, at least, incumbent on us to endeavour to make some return for this great love ? Shall we allow ourselves to think less of the priceless blessing God bestows on us in the Most Holy Sacrament, because it is ever presented to us under so simple a form ? Let us not be guilty of such madness; for the unpretending exterior under which this benefit is bestowed upon us is in itself a proof that the gift is divine, and thus furnishes us with an additional reason for prizing it most highly. When men confer benefits on one another, they love to do so with as much ostentation as possible; but to the nature of God all such outward display is intensely repugnant. He is ever wont to give far more than he appears to give. Let us, then, my beloved hearers, look upon those accidents of bread, beneath which the Lord of glory lies concealed from our sight, as a cloud, which, though it may hide the sun from our view, cannot in any way deprive us of its glorious and life-giving influences.

DISCOURSE IN HONOUR OF THE HOLY WINDING-SHEET.

IN WHICH IT IS SHOWN THAT WE OUGHT TO LOVE CHRIST ON ACCOUNT OF THE DISFIGUREMENT PRODUCED IN HIS BODY BY CONTINUAL SUFFERINGS.

"We have seen him, and there was no sightliness that we should be desirous of him."—Is. liii. 2.

Most persons doubtless know what it is to have had their affections strongly moved by the sight of some picture, even though that sight may have been but a passing one; they have become enamoured of a Proserpine, depicted as wandering in the meadows gathering flowers; of Europa, straying on the sea-shore in search of pearls; or of the simple Narcissus, absorbed in the idle amusement of contemplating his own countenance mirrored in a fountain. But if you consider awhile, you will find this only to have been the case when the object represented in the picture was one of great beauty and external attractiveness, (such as those I have just mentioned) but never if unsightly or in any way displeasing to the eye. It is one of the characteristics of ugliness that, far from winning men's love, it alienates and repels. On this account Agesilaus, the famous Spartan king, whose face was as hideous as his soul was noble, gave orders when on his death-bed, forbidding under severe penalties that any portrait of himself should be preserved, lest perchance in after-ages, the sight of features so frightful should tend to diminish the admiration and affection excited in the minds of posterity on hearing or reading of his heroic deeds. How then, if this be really true, can I hope to kindle within your hearts on the present occasion a fervent love of our Blessed Lord, since I cannot depict Him to your gaze otherwise than with features disfigured, with beauty marred, if not effaced, as He Himself left His sacred impress on the holy Winding-sheet which here is held in so great veneration? Nevertheless, my hearers, you may, unless I am much mistaken, rest assured that this strange deformity will prove the very quality of all others most calculated to inspire His love in our breasts; and I am encouraged to speak thus confidently on this point by the testimony given by some holy souls in the writings of Isaias: "We have seen Him," (such are their words in reference to the Saviour as He appeared thus disfigured) "and there was no sightliness that we should be desirous of Him." What a strange paradox we have here! It would seem that, viewing Him under such an aspect, expressions of abhorrence and aversion would rather have been elicited from them, that they would have turned from Him in disgust; but no, on the contrary, they were enamoured of Him; because the very unsightliness of Christ, if attentively considered, possesses this peculiar characteristic, namely that it engages our affections. You will now perceive how lofty is the point I am proposing to reach on the present occasion; and I must therefore ask you to assist me with kind and indulgent attention, since it is always easier for an archer (more especially for one so unskilful as myself) to discern the object at which he is to aim, than to send his arrow home to the mark.

And truly we should be in a great measure excusable in refusing our love to Christ, in turning from Him in abhorrence on account of His unsightliness, if when He first loved us, we had been beautiful, and not most vile, more vile than words are adequate to express. For though a sinner paint his face, adorn his head, array himself in choice raiment, employ every device to beautify his person, in spite of all he may do, he must inevitably remain hideous in the sight of God, so that in comparison with him the countenances of witches, furies and gorgons would appear pleasing; since on closer consideration we shall find that he who is under the dominion of sin is not distinguished like those monsters, by one deformity alone, but all their several deformities are present in his person, and present there in an aggravated form. And this, as we all know, was our miserable condition when Christ in His great love, accepted death for us. "He loved us," these are the words of Saint Augustine, "and in doing so whom did He love but those who were hideous and deformed?" Have we not all read with extreme astonishment of the extravagant fancy taken by the Emperor Tiberias to a loathsome reptile, which he brought up with as much care as if it had been a pet dog or rabbit, feeding it with his own hand, stroking and caressing it, keeping it at his side in his royal apartments, and at length going so far as to weep bitterly over its loss, when this strange favourite met its death surrounded by a swarm of cruel ants? And yet it is far more wonderful that Christ found it possible to love us; for neither Lernian marsh nor Stygian lake ever produced anything more foul or abominable than the unregenerate heart of man; and surely if He loved us so tenderly in spite of the deformity of our souls, we in our turn may love Him notwithstanding His unsightliness, which after all, is only that of the body.

But I am wrong in speaking of unsightliness as appertaining to Christ, for none of us can really be of opinion that such unsightliness is essentially His own. Let him undeceive himself if there be any one labouring under such a delusion: the form and features of our Lord were indeed of a beauty so rare and superhuman that King David, being permitted on one occasion to behold Him from afar, could not refrain, even at that distance of time, from exclamations of ecstatic admiration at the surpassing grace and loveliness revealed to him. "Thou art beautiful above the sons of men, grace is poured abroad in thy lips" (Ps. xliv. 3); you remark he says *poured abroad*, as if to tell us that the beauty ordinarily doled out in measured drops to the children of men, was in this exceptional instance poured out in lavish abundance. And yet personal beauty was no unfamiliar sight to David in his own day; not only was he the intimate friend of Jonathan, a youth exceeding beautiful, but his own sons, Absalom and Adonias, were both remarkable for their striking beauty; the splendid hair of the former being estimated by weight, and a glance from the eyes of the latter being reckoned as a favour. I know that some take the words I have quoted as referring to the spiritual loveliness of Christ, and not to His personal beauty. But such a conclusion is no true one. Christ did indeed manifest a sovereign contempt for all external attractions, that is to say, instead of displaying that vanity and self-conscious pride which so generally accompanies their possession, He was ever lowly in His deportment and mean in His dress; His features were, moreover, probably worn and emaciated by privations and fatigue, but to pronounce Him destitute of beauty is quite another thing. No indeed, Christ was not destitute of beauty; He certainly did not appear so to the heathen Lentulus, who whilst our Lord was still living on earth wrote a minute description of Him to the Emperor Tiberias, describing His appearance as one which could well justify his being termed a thief, but in a different sense to that in which this epithet was applied to Him by His calumniators, since He seemed to rob all men of their hearts. Nor did He appear destitute of beauty to Saint Thomas, the great Angel of the Schools; nor to Saint Jerome, Saint Ambrose, and Saint Chrysostom, not to enumerate many other writers, whose unanimous testimony I might bring forward, since they all concur in affirming that a beautiful body must needs have been prepared for a soul so surpassingly beautiful as was that of Christ. A most perfect body belongs of right to a most perfect soul. If costly jewels ought to be set in pure gold, if precious balsams ought to be preserved in rare crystals, surely the vase destined to hold so choice an exotic ought to be worthy of the treasure it is privileged to contain. But if this be so, whence come the blemishes which we perceive in those sacred members as we find them impressed on the holy Winding-Sheet? Are they natural to Him, inherent in Him, do they appertain to Him as His own? No, my hearers; believe me, those blemishes belong altogether and entirely to us. Remember what Isaias tells us so plainly, "that the Lord laid on Him the iniquity of us all;" that "He hath borne our infirmities and carried our sorrows" (Is. liii. 6, 4); that, as Saint Peter says, "His own self bore our sins in His body" (1 Pet. ii. 24); that, as Saint Paul declares in still stronger terms, "For us He hath been made sin" (2 Cor. v. 21), "being made a curse for us" (Gal. iii. 13). What matter have we then for wonder in finding Him thus disfigured? Terrible indeed is the sight of the wounds wherewith He is wounded, terrible because they are the penalty due to our sins; His back is lacerated with scourges, His countenance is marked with bruises, His breast is seamed with hideous gashes; this pallor, these livid hues, these stains and discoloration wherewith his virginal flesh is darkened and disfigured, are terrible, most terrible to behold; for we know full well that, as Saint Jerome says, He has suffered for us what we ought to have endured for our evil-deeds; that He alone was typified by the victim of the old law, on whose head were heaped all the guilt, the reproaches, the ignominy due to the iniquities of a whole nation. How then could this unsightliness, however appalling it may be, produce upon our minds any other effect but that of rendering more dear to us the Saviour, Who, out of intense pity and commiseration for us, of His own free will took it all upon Himself?

And now there will be no difficulty in comprehending the reason why Christ, in leaving us His portrait, would not leave us an image of Himself in His beauty; but chose rather to be pourtrayed in that state of disfigurement and unsightliness of which we have just been speaking. Can we imagine that this arose from accident, and not from choice? that it was the result of necessity, and not of deliberation? No, the reason is apparent; it was this; our Lord wished to exhibit Himself to us in the light of the most devoted of lovers. For let the lover enrich his beloved with whatever gifts he may will to bestow; let him give corals, pearls, or gold, no other gift can be so sure a proof of his affection as a portrait of himself, painted from the life. This you will all acknowledge to be undoubted truth; but tell me further, what would it be if the picture had, in addition, been painted by the lover's own hand; if it represented him, moreover, as languishing and fainting for his beloved; as having in his yearning for her love grown pale and wan, lost his vigour and his life? Would you not term the affection of such a lover ardent, impassioned, nay, more than this, almost bordering upon insanity? And yet such is the nature of the image Christ has given us of Himself, so that we may venture boldly to proclaim, as Saint Chrysostom did, both in word and in epistle, "There exists no lover so madly enamoured of his beloved as God is of the soul of man." In olden times it was the custom for great men to have their most remarkable or successful achievements, those best calculated to shed lustre on their name, depicted on canvas, and publicly exhibited with elaborate ceremony, in one of the most frequented thoroughfares of the city. This, as I remember to have read, was done by Lucius Emilius the younger, after the victories he gained in Liguria during his first consulate. It was done by Sempronius Gracchus, after he had defeated Hanno at Beneventum; it was done by Valerius Messala, after he had subjugated Hiero in Sicily; it was done by Lucius Scipio after the great victory in Asia, which brought him into such high repute, and made him at the same time the object of such bitter envy, that almost inevitable attendant on glory. Finally, the same was done to a still greater extent by Hostilius, for, not content with exhibiting to the gaze of all Rome a magnificent painting, representing the taking of Carthage, into which city he had been the first to enter as a conqueror, he stood by it in person, to give minute explanations as to each part of the great picture. "In this spot," he said, "the first assault was made; here the scaling-ladders were planted, there the battering-rams were brought to play; here I first mounted the battlements, shouting death to the foes of Rome; in this place the standard was unfurled, yonder the walls were occupied, there the greatest number of our enemies were laid low." But oh! how differently did the Redeemer act when he left His image impressed on the sacred Winding-sheet! Scenes of glorious triumph were not wanting in His career, had He hungered after applause, as we miserable worms of earth too often do. He might have depicted Himself in that memorable moment when, a child of but a few days old, seated upon His mother's lap as upon a royal throne, He received the homage of three kings, the wisest men of their age, who had come from the far-off East, to prostrate themselves at His feet. He might have depicted Himself after His entrance on His public life, when, on the heights of Tabor, His countenance was seen to shine with a refulgence which almost caused the sun to hide itself for shame, seeing itself eclipsed in the brilliancy of its light. He might have depicted Himself when, as He journeyed barefoot through the scattered cities of Palestine, whole towns followed in His footsteps, amazed at the unheard-of wonders wrought by His hand; for they saw the blind, the lame, the dumb, the deaf, the lepers, the sick, the possessed, healed by Him with a word. He might have depicted Himself rebuking the winds, and waves with imperious authority, and bidding them cease their raging; or walking upon the waters, and awing them by His presence. He might have depicted His descent into hell, where He bound with fetters the rebellious spirits; He might have presented to us a sorrowful picture of the fruitless efforts of the lost souls to move Him to take compassion on them, their groans of misery, their cries of despair. He might have shown us the proud Lucifer panic-struck at His majestic presence. Finally, He might have shown us the joyous deliverance of the souls He freed from Limbo, or the triumphant resurrection of the bodies who with Him left their sepulchres, which had been forced open. Each and all of these scenes Christ might with the greatest ease have pourtrayed on the sacred Winding-sheet, had He made it His chief object to gain glory for Himself. But since, as a devoted lover He desires nought else but our love, since He prefers this to any tribute of admiration or applause which might be His, He has set aside all else, and only chosen to represent Himself here, wounded, blood-stained, disfigured, as He was for us, when for our sakes He delivered Himself up to a cruel death. How ungrateful, how undiscerning then should we be, were we to love Him less because of that which most forcibly proves the greatness of His love for us!

But am I right in alleging that the portrait Christ has left us of Himself is not such as to gain glory for Himself? No, indeed, my brethren; for of what greater glory can He boast than that of having suffered for our sakes? Conquering heroes generally rest their title to fame on the number of enemies they have slain, a boast which, it appears to me, might with greater reason be made by a lion or a bear. Lucullus vaunted himself on having slaughtered twenty thousand in a single day; Sylla on having put to death twenty-four thousand; whilst Mithridates could pride himself on having caused eighty thousand of the Romans who had settled in different parts of his kingdom, for the purposes of trade, to be massacred in the space of a single day, by means of letters which he had despatched in various directions. But the course of action pursued by our loving Redeemer was of a widely different nature. He counted it His greatest glory, not to have put His enemies to death, but to have been put to death for them; and therefore it is no wonder that He should have chosen to record this fact in the likeness He left us of Himself in preference to any other. You may, then, my hearers, if you so choose, speak of His sacred Body in terms of contempt and derision; you may say that there is in it neither form nor beauty; "There is no beauty in Him, nor comeliness;" you may say that He wears the semblance of the most wretched leper the world has ever seen, of one smitten by the hand of God, and humbled by Him: "We have thought Him as it were a leper, and as one struck by God and afflicted"

(Is. liii. 1, 4); you may say that from the crown of the head to the sole of the foot there was no sound spot in Him: "From the sole of the foot unto the top of the head there is no soundness therein" (Is. i. 6); that His countenance is so marred and disfigured as to have almost lost the likeness of a man: "Whereupon we esteemed Him not" (Is. liii. 3); you may, in short, heap what contumely you please upon that vanished beauty, and yet, unless your nature be more cruel than that of the tiger, you will love Him all the more for being thus unlovely. What tender emotions the sight of this sacred Winding-sheet ought to awaken in your hearts! what sighs it should draw from your breasts! what tears from your eyes! what holy indignation should fill your soul on seeing such unrivalled beauty brought into unsightliness and abjection!

I can hardly express the indescribable confusion that comes over me on reading of the great sensation produced in the Roman people by one of the adherents of Cæsar, immediately after the death of that hero; for wishing to create a reaction in his favour, we are told that he employed no eloquence, no declamation, no agitated words or violent action, he merely held up to their gaze the unsightly picture of the man they formerly delighted to honour, falling under the blows of his murderers, whilst he pointed out one after another the twenty-three wounds wherewith they failed to subdue his indomitable spirit, though they succeeded in depriving him of life. So great, indeed, was the emotion immediately excited in the hearts of all who witnessed this spectacle that they rose up as one man against the conspirators, forced them to take hasty flight, pursued them to death, and, with the rage of furies, rushed hither and thither bearing lighted torches to set fire to their houses and burn them to the ground. But was not Cæsar nevertheless one of the worst enemies Rome had ever known? Had he not forcibly usurped the supreme authority? Had he not sought to impose upon her inhabitants the yoke of servitude, and, actuated by insatiable ambition and thirst for glory, led them as sheep to the slaughter? And if it be true (as Cæsar himself boasted) that, during the course of his life, he had put to death more than 1,190,000 of his enemies, how many of his friends must not this heartless tyrant inevitably have sacrificed in ridding himself of so great a number of his foes? And yet the sight of twenty-three wounds inflicted on his body aroused to such a point the dormant love of him in Rome, that, like a too fond mother, she allowed the remembrance of every injury she had received from him to be at once effaced from her mind. What ought we, then, to feel on seeing Christ, our beloved Redeemer, bearing in His body, not twenty-three wounds only, but wounds so numerous that no human eye could trace them all, could tell their number or descry their form? And we must also remember that other pictures of this description are open to the suspicion of being overdrawn; the painter having, perhaps, permitted himself to exaggerate the reality—it might be from ignorance, or from design, or from an affectation of the wonderful (knowing what an attraction the marvellous possesses for us)—in virtue of the licence artists claim to indulge their fancy, either with a view to their own interests, or to serve some ulterior end. But in the case of our Lord no such unworthy suspicion can possibly intrude itself. Not only has He never shown Himself desirous of magnifying the sufferings He bore for our sake, but, on the contrary, He has ever striven to depreciate them. And yet, what terms do we find the Prophets, who were chosen to foreshadow in their person the Passion of Christ, employing to describe those sufferings? They most frequently spoke of them under the figure of inundations, billows, and tempests: "The waters are come in even unto my soul, I am come into the depth of the sea, and a tempest hath overwhelmed me" (Ps. lxviii. 1); thus we find David lamenting in the sixty-eighth Psalm; and in another he says: "All Thy billows have passed over me" (Ps. xli. 8); and, again: "All Thy waves Thou hast brought in upon me" (Ps. lxxxvii. 8). In the Lamentations of Jeremias we find the prophet complaining: "Waters have flowed over my head; I said, I am cut off" (Lament. iii. 54); and, in his canticle, Jonas speaks in still stronger language: "All Thy billows and Thy waves have passed over me; the waters compassed me about, even to the soul; the deep hath closed me round about, the sea hath covered my head" (Jonas ii. 4, 6). And, truly, there is abundant cause to justify the use of such expressions, for all the sufferings which ever afflicted the sons of men met in the person of Christ, as all the rivers meet in the bosom of the ocean. Nevertheless, when did Christ, in referring to His Passion, employ imposing comparisons and high-sounding metaphors, such as those we have quoted? Under what terms does He, in fact, speak of it? He calls it a baptism; that is to say, a cleansing process of so delicate and careful a nature that a new-born infant may be subjected to it. "I have a baptism wherewith I am to be baptized, and how am I straightened until it be accomplished" (Luke xii. 50). And, as if even this comparison seemed too strong, on another occasion He calls it a chalice: "Can you drink the chalice that I shall drink?" (Matt. xx. 22); and again: "The chalice which my Father hath given me, shall I not drink it?" (John xviii. 11); as if desirous to make us believe that sea of bitterness to have been nothing more than a few drops in His opinion. Thus we need have no apprehension lest Christ, with the licence claimed by some daring painters, should have allowed Himself to exaggerate and magnify the sufferings here depicted; on the contrary, the fear is lest His humility should have led Him to underrate the severity and magnitude of the pains He endured for our sakes. What emotions the sight of them ought to awaken in our hearts! What tender love! What agonising grief! Ought we not, on beholding them, to feel greater compassion than did Saint Gregory of Nyssa on contemplating Isaac, a patient victim beneath the uplifted knife of his father? or that which Saint John Chrysostom experienced when considering the beheading of Saint Paul, by order of a cruel tyrant? or that which Saint Asterius, bishop of Apamea, felt when gazing on a life-like representation of the Virgin Euphemia, dragged along by the hair of her head by her brutal torturers; for he paid her that tribute of tears which is the only tribute Love can pay, when to render practical assistance is out of her power.

I certainly must confess, my hearers, that I feel no small envy of the privilege you possess of preserving in your midst this holy relic, when I consider the opportunity thus afforded you of evincing the love you bear to our Lord. You may, like eagles, gather around this body, than which, surely, no other could present a more touching aspect; hovering over it, you care no longer to fix your gaze on the Sun, which, although a fair image of the divine countenance, is not so true and lifelike a representation as that which you are able to contemplate. You may, moreover, rest assured that such proofs of affection cannot fail to be most pleasing to the Redeemer, since, instead of turning aside from Him when He appears under a form so marred and uncomely, you are rather stirred up to desire Him more fervently. "We have seen Him, and there was no sightliness that we should be desirous of Him." Cease not, then, to value this high privilege, rejoice in it, congratulate yourselves on its possession; and, above all, give thanks to God for having chosen you to be the guardians of this sublime product of His pencil. In one of his discourses Saint Augustine earnestly counsels us to keep ever before us the image of Christ, but of Christ in His unsightliness. And who but will acknowledge that to your share has fallen a most admirable and advantageous opportunity of acting in conformity with this counsel? Christ in His unsightliness is consigned to your care; He has been placed in your midst, and it is His hope that by the practice of long and habitual contemplation, every soul, without exception, will become enamoured of Him. But what response can you make to all this? Can you be said to love the unsightliness of Jesus, O ladies of fashion, who daily spend so many hours in planning fresh devices whereby you may enhance the effect of your charms? Do you love the unsightliness of Jesus, O young men, who deck yourselves in finery in the hope of attracting universal attention? I tell you all, without distinction, that those who seek their delight in worldly pleasures, in luxury, in show, in dress and amusements, cannot be said to love the unsightliness of Jesus. Alas! how rarely do we find anyone to whom it is given to understand that the beauty after which the Christian should aspire ought to consist in the pallor produced by the use of disciplines and hairshirts, in chains and other austerities; that every wound thus occasioned should be valued by him as a precious jewel! But however that may be, let those who will, be enamoured of a beauty which will disappear as quickly as hoarfrost beneath the Sun, as snow before the south wind, as the flower of the field under the mower's scythe; for my part, I desire to be ever more and more deeply enamoured of that unsightliness which has to-day been the theme of my discourse, although my eyes have never as yet been privileged to gaze upon it.

DISCOURSE UPON THE ANGEL GUARDIAN;

IN WHICH HE IS PROVED TO BE THE TRUEST FRIEND
OF MAN.

"Blessed is he that findeth a true friend."—Eccl. xxv. 12.

Who will deny that among all nations the penalties inflicted by law on falsifiers of the current coin of the realm have been of the severest description? The Lombards used to condemn any one found guilty of this crime to lose the hand which had been his instrument in carrying out the vile scheme of deception; amongst the Sinopeans the usual penalty was banishment; amongst the Athenians decapitation; whilst one more closely connected with the crime itself was invented by the inhabitants of Suevia. Hear what they did to some dishonourable Muscovite traders, who, coming to their country for the purposes of commerce, took advantage of the simplicity of the people, and gave counterfeit coin in exchange for the goods furnished to them; as much of the false coin as could be collected having been got together, it was melted down, and the delinquents were plunged into the boiling mass of molten metal as into a bath, wherein to wash away the stains of their guilt. The Egyptians were wont to strike off with one blow both the hands of any one venturing to forge seals or signatures, to falsify weights or measures, or to adulterate cloth. We know, moreover, the horrible torture inflicted by Alexander Severus on one of his ministers, who, arrogating to himself a power to which he had no claim, fed a credulous populace with wild hopes and fallacious promises. The miscreant was hung up by the heels to a high beam in the public market-place, and a fire composed of damp straw, vine shoots dipped in water, and green boughs, having been kindled beneath his head, the smoke arising from it gradually stifled him; and whilst he was suffering this painful death, a herald proclaimed with a loud voice: "Behold he who traded in smoke is punished by smoke." The Romans and Greeks went yet further, for they would not even allow a false cognomen to be assumed; in fact, any one who was convicted of having changed his name for a fraudulent purpose was sentenced to exile if a freedman, and to the gallows if a slave. Philip of Macedon carried his abhorrence of dissemblers to a still greater length; for, on hearing that one of his judges, a man of great merit, whom he had raised to the bench on the recommendation of Antipater, was in the habit of artfully colouring his hair to impart to it a golden hue, he immediately deprived him of his office, alleging in the words of Plutarch that "he who would deceive as to the colour of his hair, was not likely to prove trustworthy in more important matters." What then shall we say of false notaries, false witnesses, false reporters? It is notorious that the laws of every nation without exception have ever with most stringent laws endeavoured to free the world from such offenders; and on this account I am much amazed to observe that no chastisement has anywhere been decreed for the punishment of false friends. What is there in the whole world so precious, so useful, so sacred as friendship? And yet those who counterfeit it abound in every country, in every district, under every roof. Are you credulous enough to believe that all those are true friends whom you see constantly conversing with one another? Whatever may be your opinion in this respect, one thing is certain, that the greater number of them are false. Their salutations are false, their smiles are false, their bows are false, their gifts are false, the expressions of extreme cordiality which fall from their lips are false; all, my brethren, all is false. And why, in the name of Heaven, since they sin so grievously in falsifying a thing of such priceless worth, are they allowed to do so with impunity? My hearers, it is for this simple reason, because there are so many of them. Let us, for a moment, suppose a law decreeing the extermination of all false friends; how quickly would the most crowded cities be depopulated, how soon would their busy thoroughfares be changed into lonely deserts and solitary wastes! Hear what the wise man declares in Ecclesiasticus, and declares too in no ambiguous terms: "Blessed is he that findeth a true friend" (Eccl. xxv. 12). It is as if he would say: To find a true friend is a thing so uncommon in this world, that he who succeeds in so doing may count himself most fortunate; just as, in another place, a like encomium is passed on the man who has not sinned with his tongue: "Blessed is the man that hath not slipt by a word out of his mouth" (Eccl. xiv. 1); and also on him who has not run after gold: "Blessed is the man that hath not gone after gold" (Eccl. xxxi. 8); to denote how extremely rare both the one and the other are. But notwithstanding all this, my brethren, I rejoice to tell you that, unless I am much mistaken, each one amongst you possesses one such faithful friend. Would you know who this is? It is your Angel Guardian. Believe me, Christian hearers, did you but know this friend and value him aright, no other friend in all the world would stand so high in your esteem! My task this morning will be to show you how fully he deserves the title I have given him; so that we may together deplore our error if perchance we find that we have denied to this true friend the regard which we not unfrequently lavished on false friends.

But to me it appears that the counsel to be obtained from a friend in time of need is the thing for which, above all others, he is to be prized and loved. Nothing is more profitable than good counsel, as Menander said of old. But generally among the number of our friends, how few are there to whom we can turn in difficulty, of whatsoever nature, with the certainty of obtaining wise advice! Some err through ignorance, some deceive from motives of self-interest, of some envy makes traitors, and oh! how many are those who, if they do no worse, out of weakness speak words of flattery, condoning the profligate excesses of an Ammon under the name of a natural vivacity of character, extolling the rebellious outbreaks of an Absalom as feats of valour, and terming the oppressive acts of a Roboam glorious triumphs. "No one," says Seneca, "persuades or dissuades out of the conviction of his own mind; it is with all a strife of adulation, a contest who can flatter in the most pleasing manner." And even preachers themselves seem to imitate bird-catchers, whose greatest fear is lest they alarm the prey they seek to ensnare; and it is not he who shouts the loudest, but who whistles most sweetly that entraps the birds on his decoy. No such suspicion can possibly attach to the Angel who has us in his custody. Not only is he most solicitous at all times and under all circumstances to suggest to us that which is most conducive to our real good, but he never fails to tell us the truth with the utmost sincerity; in fact, the secret voice which speaks within our heart, checking and reproving us so freely and so frankly when we fall into sin, is for the most part his alone. When Moses, accompanied by his wife Sephora and his two infant sons, Gersam and Eliezer, was going down into Egypt at the divine command, to fulfil his important mission, an angel met them, at a turn of the road, threatening to slay them with the drawn sword he held in his hand. What did the terrified mother do at the sight? She forthwith took up a sharp-edged stone, and with it circumcised the younger of the children she carried in her arms; thus appeasing the wrath of the angel, who immediately vanished, leaving the travellers to pursue their journey unharmed. Now, according to the opinion of the best writers, the most simple and obvious of the many ingenious explanations of this strange incident is this: Eliezer was born only a short time before his parents set out on their way down to Egypt, and his father, apprehensive lest the hardships and fatigues of the long journey might render it impossible to take due care of the child, postponed his circumcision until a more convenient time and more suitable place should be found. For, appointed as he was by God to the post of supreme lawgiver, there was no occasion to fear lest any of the people should venture to call Moses to account for his conduct; on the contrary, he imagined himself at liberty to put upon the law such a construction as best suited his own interest (as those in authority are apt to do), setting it aside or relaxing it at his will, instead of observing its rules with all the more rigorous precision. But here his Angel Guardian interposes: "From my lips, O Moses, shalt thou hear the reproof none other will dare to address to thee;" and hence that apparition which, whilst striking terror to his heart, served to open his eyes to the error into which he had fallen, and induced him forthwith to return to the path of duty.

"An angel stretches out his sword against him (thus Isidore Pelusiota writes) to reprove him for having transgressed the law for the carrying out of which he had gone forth. For when he had been appointed a legislator by God, and was bound to observe the law all the more closely, he himself was the first to violate it." It is true that it is not our lot to be visited with such apparitions of our Angel Guardians; but I would ask you, my brethren, whence arise the acute feelings of remorse and sharp stings of conscience, those unbidden guests which visit us when we have sinned? Are they not so many swords which he holds to our breasts, in order, through the alarm thus excited, to lead us to think seriously of our transgression, thus giving that correction and reprimand which no single one of our friends is willing to give us? But I am wrong in saying that we are not favoured with visible apparitions. At times our faithful Angel Guardian performs his task even in a visible manner; this fact is attested by St. Frances of Rome, who, upon one occasion when she allowed her relatives to carry on frivolous conversation in her presence unchecked, received from her Angel Guardian a smart blow upon the cheek, which recalled her to herself, and induced her to withdraw in confusion to her chamber. We may also bring forward the testimony of that young German, who, having been drawn on by his companions to join in unseemly conversation, was struck by his Angel so sharply that he fell apparently lifeless to the ground; and the following incident which I will relate to you has the same purport. A certain monk of Cologne, named Liffard, being assailed by a violent temptation to leave his monastery, was on the point of yielding to the evil suggestion, when his Angel Guardian, interposing with wise counsel, withheld him (by means of a moral compulsion far more effectual than any material fetters could have been) from executing his fatal design. For one night, when the monk was preparing to make good his escape, this faithful friend appeared before him, and, with a gesture of authority and voice of command, bade him follow where he led. Whereupon he conducted the unhappy youth into the public cemetery, into which they had no sooner entered than all the graves opened and disclosed their dead, to the intense horror of the young man, who turning was about to make a hasty retreat, when his conductor, taking him by the hand, thus addressed him: "Stop, and gaze with me on the corpse of this man, who died but a short while ago. Dost thou recognise him? Behold his hollow eyes and discoloured lips; reflect that ere long thou too wilt resemble him. And yet, forgetful of thy latter end, thou art actually scheming how thou mayest cast off the yoke of religion and return to the world!" Then the Angel dragged the youth to another tomb which exhibited a yet more revolting spectacle, and in this manner would have led him from grave to grave, until he had completed the ghastly round, had not his companion implored him to desist. "For pity's sake," he cried, "show me no more; spare me, Lord, spare me; I have not the heart to look any longer, and my eyes refuse to fulfil their office." But the Angel turned a deaf ear to all these entreaties, until at length his victim solemnly vowed to persevere in religion until the day of his death; upon which the Angel courteously led him out of the cemetery, and having reconducted him to his cell and placed him on his couch, left him free from all his former feelings of discontent. And now, my hearers, what do you say to this story, which we have upon the authority of Cæsar? What manner of reproof could possibly have been devised by the Angel more open and at the same time more intrepid, more courageous, more uncompromising than this? Is not Gregory right in boldly asserting that he esteems that man alone to be his friend, by whose tongue his moral stains are removed? And if this be so, what truer, what surer friend can we have than our Angel Guardian? There is no fear lest he deceive to please us, or lest he touch our sores with a timid hand, instead of courageously pressing out the venom which is destroying us.

But counsel and correction, proofs as they undoubtedly are of a friend's fidelity, are both of them proofs which require little or no sacrifice on his part; a moment's reflection will render it apparent that in the exercise of them he is raised to a position of authority, and fills the office of a superior. It is a much greater thing to accept toil for the sake of a friend, and unhesitatingly to render him any service, whether high or low, brilliant or obscure; for true friendship as Saint Ambrose says, knows no pride. Our Guardian Angel is at all times ready to stoop for our sake to the lowliest offices. But speak yourselves and say in what employment you would wish to see your Angel Guardian humbling himself in order to benefit the mortal committed to his care. I can show him to you in turn as a physician, curing the fevers of a Timothy; as a surgeon, healing the wounds of a Christina; as a valet, sweeping out the room of an Aurelius; as a messenger, carrying the dispatches of an Antony; as a herdsman, tending the flocks of an Isidore; as a pilot, guiding the course of Basilide's bark; as a gravedigger making ready the last resting-place of Landrada; as a cook, preparing refreshment for Huthbert; as a domestic-servant, cleansing the garments of Vandegisilus with his own hand, and laying them ready for use with equal humility and affection. You are, my hearers, doubtless fully aware that the prosperous are apt to forget and despise friends of low degree; you remember the well-known story of Pharao's butler, who, when recalled to the palace and restored to favour, lost all recollection of Joseph, his former companion in captivity, who still lay bound in prison. "When things prospered with him he forgot his interpreter" (Gen. xl. 23), as if it were altogether beneath him to waste thought on a servant languishing in want and misery. He was ashamed, as a commentator observes, to remember the captive Joseph, and whilst occupied in the royal court, was oblivious of what went on in the prison. How highly then should we value our Angel Guardian, who notwithstanding the greatness, the glory, the dignity, the happiness of his state, not only designs to hold converse with friends so inferior to himself, but is even willing to serve them; to serve them too in the most menial offices, the humblest occupations! How few human friends, my brethren, are capable of such devoted fidelity as this!

Nor is there any ground for apprehension lest one who loves us so much should desert us in the moment of danger, fail us in the hour of affliction, or leave us when want presses sorely upon us. Unhappy indeed is he who, in the time of adversity, rests his hope on any mortal friend! The majority of such friends may be compared to the pilot fishes, which accompany the vessel while, with canvass spread, she speeds on her prosperous way over the high seas; they sport and gambol around, they follow closely in her wake with assiduous attention, and appear to be her inseparable companions; but let the vessel be stranded in shallow water, and the faithless pilot fishes quickly disappear, leaving her to her fate. The counterpart of this often happens in the world. As long as your course is prosperous, how many will rejoice to bear you company! but beware lest you drift on the sandbanks, that is to say, beware lest you lose favour and position, and are reduced to poverty; how soon, in that case, you will see yourself forsaken by your friends and left solitary and desolate! "There is a friend for his own occasion, and he will not abide in the day of thy trouble" (Eccl. vi. 8). This is what the wise man says of the faithless friend, he will not abide in the day of trouble. How does he then act? He acts like the swallow, which, when ruin threatens the roof that has long sheltered her happy nest, readily takes flight elsewhere; or, like the gull, which retreats inland when it perceives a storm gathering over the sea it is wont to cherish so fondly. How different is the conduct of our Angel Guardian! He resembles the loving vine, which continues to cling as closely to the elm, and embrace it as tenderly, when its branch is withered; to him the well-known expression of the Proverbs applies: "He that is a friend loveth at all times" (Prov. xvii. 17); for our Angel Guardian loves us at all times and in all seasons, whether prosperous or calamitous, stormy or serene. But this is not enough; I ought to say that if there is one time at which he loves us more than at another, it is rather in the time of calamity than of prosperity, rather when clouds gather thick around our path than when the sun shines brightly overhead. From this I wish to conclude that the Angel Guardian loves to bestow his most signal favours on those who are in distress, affliction or tribulation. And have you never remarked to what description of person the Angels appeared, when first of all they began to hold converse with mortal men? Was it perhaps some prince of high degree? was it to Abram or Isaac, both individuals of no small distinction, to whom the heavenly visitant first came? By no means; he showed himself to no other than a weeping slave, the fugitive and desolate Agar, in order to comfort her under heavy domestic affliction. Again, under what circumstances did an Angel vouchsafe to place himself at the disposal of Elias? When the prophet was revered by Achab, when he saw that monarch tremble at his threats, and all the grandees of the court stand in awe of him? No, my brethren; it was when he was wandering through the forest, a persecuted man. When did the prophet Daniel experience the opportune assistance of an Angel friend? When he stood high in Darius's favour, when he saw the king depending on his counsel, and every one in the palace regarding him as an oracle? No, my brethren; it was when, a victim to calumny, he had been cast into the lion's den. And was it not the same in the case of the Apostle Saint Peter? Although the Angel found him loaded with chains and fetters, a companion of malefactors in the dungeon of Herod; it was then, as we know, that he performed for him that most friendly of offices. So true it is that, far from abandoning a friend in misfortune, our Angel Guardian is at such times all the more anxious to show him affection, afford him protection, and treat him with every mark of respect: "He that is a friend loveth at all times." Nor need this excite our wonder; for his affection being without admixture of self-interest, he is not among the number of those who look on friendship as a field to which, unless it be fertile, the seed is not to be confided. Our Angel friend has no object in view but our good; let me remind you how he rejected the homage paid him by Saint John, as we read in the Apocalypse; how he refused the sacrifice offered by Manue, as we read in the Judges; how he declined the gift Tobias would have made him of the half of all his goods, in recompense for watchful care over his son throughout the journey undertaken by the latter. He desired only that all praise should be ascribed to God: "Bless ye the God of Heaven, give glory to Him in the sight of all that live, because He hath shown His mercy to you." (Tob. xii. 6). For himself he asked nothing, not even the slightest token of gratitude or the least mark of respect. I can say no more in proof of the disinterested affection of our Angel Guardian than this: not all the offences we daily commit against him are enough to induce him to forsake us. Origen does indeed express a contrary opinion on this point, declaring it to be his belief that when we arrive at a certain point of wickedness our Angel Guardian abandons us; just as a physician leaves his patient when he finds the latter refuses to heed his prohibitions or to follow his prescriptions. But it is evident that Origen is in error here; hence an opposite view of the subject is unanimously taught by Saint Thomas, by Bonaventure, Egidius, Albert, Richard, in short, the great mass of theologians. Nor is it difficult to show the fallacy of his comparison, for a doctor only acts in accordance with the requirements of his profession, whereas the Angel Guardian may be more fitly likened to a benevolent person taking charge of some frenzied sick man, from whom he well knows that he will only meet with insults. What do you say to this, my brethren? Can you do otherwise than regard it as a very miracle of charity? "We daily offend in many ways against the Angels deputed to be our Guardians," exclaims Saint Peter Damian in astonishment, "and although they even suffer injuries from us frequently, they nevertheless bear them all, nor is their watchful care of us diminished thereby, but their solicitude is on the contrary continually increased." What earthly friend will you find who acts in this manner? The perfume of vines in flower is less efficacious in putting the serpent to flight, and the hiss of the snake the wild beast, than the slightest offence to drive away our friends, nay more, to convert them into our enemies?

And if our Angel Guardian ceases not to assist, to protect, to befriend us, in spite of all the affronts he experiences at our hands, we may rest assured that for no reason whatsoever will he ever leave us. Naturalists tell us of certain loving birds which, when the quails gather in flocks, preparing for their annual migration beyond seas, precede them as if they were their guides; but behold! hardly have they accomplished their first day's journey when they forsake them, remaining behind on the first island where they halt to take rest. Our Angel Guardian on the contrary helps, guides, and directs us from the moment when we enter upon our mortal pilgrimage, never leaving us until our death, that is until we reach the end of our journey. And in the hour of our death he displays greater anxiety than ever concerning our welfare; he offers our prayers to God, he soothes our anguish of mind, he strengthens us in our struggle with the enemy of mankind. Time would fail me to enumerate those who have received from this celestial friend distinct intelligence of their approaching end, in order that they might prepare for death with greater diligence and more pious assiduity. I might mention many holy Religious both men and women, many ascetic recluses and saintly solitaries to whom such an intimation was vouchsafed, amongst others Saint Maglorius, who having laid down the burden of the episcopate and retired into solitude, not only heard from his Angel Guardian the warning of which I spoke, but was further privileged to receive the Holy Viaticum at his hands; or another hermit, who was attended during his last illness by his Angel Guardian, who during a whole week fulfilled for him the office of

Infirmarian; or again, Bernard of Cluny, whose angelic friend defended him against the demons who fiercely assailed him in his last hour, casting in his teeth a sacrilegious confession made in times long past, and endeavouring to drive him to despair. And are not all these facts, my brethren, unquestionable proofs of true friendship ? I remember reading of Cyrus the younger, how, when he lay upon his deathbed, he declared that during his last sickness he had at length been able to distinguish his true from his false friends, and how deeply he deplored not having done this before it was too late for him to recompense them severally according to their deserts. God grant that in the hour of death a like experience may not be yours, my brethren! How many of those who now profess to be your friends, who offer you their services and beg of you to dispose of them at your pleasure, will, when you are lying prostrate upon your sick bed, show the most absolute indifference to your sufferings! Watch the self-interested bees, how in the garden they gather round a rose, freshly opened to the morning sun; they vie with one another which shall draw closest to its fragrant cup, they express their admiration by joyous humming and fond caresses; but return on the following day, when the faded rose droops languidly on its stem, and you will see it lonely and forsaken by all its flattering admirers. Thus it will be with more than one of you, my hearers. Where, O lady of fashion, will then be the crowd of adorers who now surround you? Where, O man of rank, will be the numerous friends of whose obsequious homage you now boast? Who will faithfully love us in that hour? None but our Guardian Angel. His affection alone will prove constant; anxiously solicitous for our welfare, he will be present with tender assiduity beside our sick-bed, and not content, as heretofore, with succouring us to the utmost of his own power alone, he will summon (as was the case with Lazarus whom the rich man despised) hosts of fellow-angels to his assistance, either to defend us more securely by their mighty aid against the attacks of hell, or to enhance the splendour of our triumph when we wing our flight to heaven. But I trust, my brethren, none of you will have to regret with Cyrus, that you only discovered the worth of so faithful a friend when it is already too late to offer him any suitable acknowledgment of his services. Alas! what grief, what remorse, what compunction will be ours, when, freed from the fetters of the flesh, we shall behold this faithful friend face to face, and know too late the true magnitude of the benefits he has conferred upon us, the dangers he has averted from us, the snares out of which he has delivered us; remembering at the same time in how small account we held him! How shall we be able to look him in the face and stand before his gaze? Shall we not be filled with confusion at the very sound of his voice? Pause for a moment, Christian brethren, and ask yourselves what single action of your whole life, done for the love of your Angel Guardian, shall you then be able to recall. Shall you be able to say that you have erected an altar in his honour, bestowed an alms for his sake on the indigent, observed a single fast, heard a Mass, made a Communion in his honour? God grant it may be possible to you to do so; but as far as my experience goes, it seems that to almost every other saint more affectionate homage is paid, more devoted veneration is shown, than to our Angel Guardian. What is the cause of this, my brethren? Since my subject has led us thus far, let me pray you, ere we proceed further, to answer me this question; is there perhaps amongst the saints one to whom we are under obligations of a more personal nature? It may be so, but I scarcely think it possible, for certainly no one makes us the object of his unwearying care in the way our Angel Guardian does.

I am fully conscious of the plausible excuse which will promptly rise to your lips, namely, that since the benefits you receive from your Angel Guardian are for the most part unknown to us, being performed in secret and hidden from our view, you know not how to be grateful for favours of whose existence you are unaware. But do you not perceive that in urging this plea, you are arguing against yourselves? Tell me, which benefactor do you esteem most highly, the one who ostentatiously tells you of all he does for you with noisy parade and pompous display, or the one who confers his favours so silently and secretly as to elude the notice of the recipient himself? It was not thus that Archesilaus judged on this point, for we are told how he, desirous of rendering pecuniary assistance to a sick friend in the most delicate manner possible, slipped a purse of gold under his pillow on taking leave of him, so that he might "discover it," to quote the words of Seneca, "rather than receive it." I will, for the sake of argument, grant that you are right in saying that we do not know the benefits our Angel Guardian confers on us, that they are performed secretly and hidden from our sight; but how wrong are you in the conclusion you appear to draw from this fact, namely, that you are thereby justified in showing him less gratitude on that account! It should on the contrary incite you to show him all the more, because this very secrecy is a fresh proof of his affection. But, you will ask, how am I to know that he confers on me all these benefits, the existence of which you assume as a matter of course? How are you to know this? Will you not believe Saint Augustine, who tells us the Angel appointed to be our guardian is in all times and in all places occupied in providing for our wants? Will you not believe Saint Cyril, who declares that our Angel acts continually towards us the part of a patient teacher, removing ignorance and error from our minds? Will you not believe Saint Bernard? He asserts that our Angel fulfils towards us the part of a loving monitor, exciting us to piety by his unwearied suggestions. Will you not believe Saint Ambrose? He says that our Angel encircles us as with a rampart, to protect us from the injuries and assaults of our enemies. Will you not believe Saint Lawrence Justinian? He affirms that we should not be able for a single moment to resist the dreadful snares of our infernal foes, were it not for the help of our Angel, who stands by us with a drawn sword in his hand. Who, I ask, unless supported by angelic aid, would be able to overcome the rage of such terrible foes, to escape their snares, resist their temptations, and detect their deceits? And should this testimony prove insufficient to convince you, will you not believe that of King David, who declares the same thing in the plainest language: "He hath given his Angels charge over thee, to keep thee in all thy ways" (Ps. xc. 11). Ponder the words well; he does not say in *one* of thy ways, but in *all* thy ways; whether on sea or on land, in peace or in war, when alone or in the company of others; whether we wake or sleep, whether in sickness or in health, in all things. And unless you persist in rejecting this mass of evidence, how can you continue to assert your ignorance of the benefits you receive from your Angel Guardian? You have not, I own, a distinct knowledge of each and all of them, for he never speaks of them, he never displays them, he never boasts of them. This silence however, as Seneca would tell you, forms part of the benefit. But what would you have him do? Would you have him present himself daily before you, speaking words such as these: "You were just now on the verge of a precipice, and would have fallen, had not I, unseen, held you by the hand; the lightning was about to strike you, but I, hidden from sight, extinguished it; your enemies were on the eve of attacking you, but I, under some pretext, led you to return at once to your home, and thus you escaped the dangerous onslaught." Your Angel leaves such vain boasting for human friends to make, such friends as are typified by that favourite of Cæsar's, who having by means of an urgent intercession availed to procure the pardon of a fellow-citizen, reminded him of the fact so frequently, and taxed him with it so incessantly, that at length the unfortunate individual lost all patience, and exclaimed: "Give me back to Cæsar!" for he judged it preferable to suffer death at the hands of the executioner than to owe the prolongation of his life to such an odious braggart. And what is a greater proof of weakness than not to be able to render the slightest service to any one without seeking to trumpet it abroad, without endeavouring to trade upon and exaggerate it, not perceiving that such conduct must infallibly tend to diminish instead of increasing its value, since the good we do is like the rain, which is all the more beneficial the more gently and quietly it falls. "Benefits should not be revealed without cogent necessity;" such is the rule laid down by Saint John Chrysostom, and thus it is that our Angel Guardian acts; and because he does so act, do you presume to consider yourself less bound to show him gratitude? Alas! what a strange mistake is this! what extraordinary perversity it exhibits!

Furthermore, would you know the reason why the benefits you receive from your Angel Guardian are less manifest and obvious than those which, from time to time, you receive from other saints, whom you consider as your special patrons? Listen, and I will tell you; the reason is this, because you do not take him for your patron; that is to say, you do not turn to him in time of need as you turn to the other saints. There is not the slightest doubt that were it your habit to have recourse to him, your supplications would soon win for you evident marks of his favouring protection, and your prayers would not long remain unanswered. Nor would you feel tempted to question whence these favours came, the very promptness with which they followed on your prayers would prove them to spring from no other source but from the hand of one who is always at your side. In illustration of my meaning, let me relate an occurrence, marvellous indeed, but for all that strictly true, with which some of you may, perhaps, not be familiar; and let those whom all my arguments have failed to convince, at least not refuse to yield to the irresistible force of reason. In bygone times, there lived in the imperial city of Constantinople a noble youth named Falco, who, for the love which from his earliest years he had borne to the Angel appointed as his guardian, made a vow never during his whole life to utter a falsehood, however unimportant it might appear; for he thought he could do nothing more calculated to give pleasure to a true friend than to pledge himself to adhere invariably to the truth. After the lapse of some years, the young man happened to fall out with one of his associates; from words they came to blows, and Falco, who was as complete a stranger to cowardice as he was to duplicity, and the warmth of whose passions equalled the piety of his mode of life, carried away by anger, threw his enemy to the ground and killed him on the spot. The place where this tragedy was enacted was so solitary that there was no witness of the deed; thus its perpetrator remained unknown; in fact, he continued to frequent his usual haunts and associate with his former companions, as persons often do in similar circumstances, hoping perhaps the more easily to avoid suspicion by assuming an air of innocence. But no delinquent has such difficulty in concealing his crime as the homicide, and in one way or other people began to talk about Falco, and some suspicious circumstances and vague reports having led to his arrest, he was imprisoned and brought before the judge. No proofs of his guilt were forthcoming, accusers and witnesses were alike wanting so that the judge could only appeal to the criminal himself, and ask him whether he had in reality committed the murder. What was the unhappy youth to reply? Was he bound to criminate himself? Surely the severest justice could not require an unconvicted culprit to pronounce judgment on himself. Will he, then, deny his guilt? This he cannot do, on account of the promise he made to his Angel Guardian always to speak the truth. He might, however, equivocate; and, by the use of ambiguous phrases, contrive to convey a false impression whilst employing words not untrue in themselves.

But the noble youth generously resolved to abide strictly by his promise, said within himself: "Let what may happen, at any rate I will not depart from the truth;" whereupon he boldly confessed himself the murderer, saying to the judge, "Yes, my lord, you see before you the criminal of whom you are in search; I am he." This extraordinary candour did not, however, have the effect of mitigating the sentence passed on him, much less of obtaining a free pardon for him; the party hostile to him being in a majority, he was condemned to be publicly beheaded. Alas! O unfortunate Falco! see to what straits imprudent devotion to your Angel Guardian has brought you. This it is that condemns thee to die in the flower of thy age, by the hand of the common hangman, in the sight of exultant enemies, who mock at what they are pleased to call thy simplicity! Do not distress yourselves, my hearers; in such a cause as this he can face death with courage, nay, more, he can even meet it with joy. With the same composure which characterised him when he confessed his secret crime, he now listened to the terrible sentence passed on him, and went forth to the place of execution, where, in the midst of a dense crowd of spectators, he mounts the scaffold, kneels down, prepares to receive the fatal stroke, stretches out his neck, and having briefly commended his soul to the mercy of God, calls on his Angel Guardian to succour him in that supreme moment. Wonderful to relate, at the very instant when the grim executioner, having drawn his sword, was about to strike the fatal blow, suddenly, to his astonishment, he beholds before him on the scaffold a youth of great beauty and imperious mien, who, in a vigorous grasp, arrests his uplifted arm, exclaiming: "Stop! for if you strike you are a dead man!" Terrified by the unlooked-for apparition, and startled by the unexpected words, the executioner was filled with dismay; but quickly recovering himself, four several times he endeavoured to shake off the hand which held him, and to repeat the blow, but all was in vain; at length he dropped his sword, and retreated pale and trembling, as if overcome by a sudden faintness. The spectators, ignorant of the real cause of this strange conduct, imagined the executioner to have been bribed by the criminal to feign sudden sickness; and a cousin of the murdered man, stepping out of the crowd, boldly ascended the scaffold, took up the fallen sword, and finding that threats had no effect on the executioner, advanced, maddened by rage, himself to perform the loathsome office. But he too, was soon fain to make a hasty retreat, for the same youth appeared to him, with a still more terrible aspect, and wrenched the sword from his grasp, vowing that if he did not desist from his intention, the sword should be plunged into his body. At the same time he explained the motive which had induced the criminal to make so generous a confession, though not convicted, nor even accused, showing him rather to deserve reward than punishment, glory than shame, for the great affection he had thus manifested to his celestial Guardian. All present recognised in this timely interposition the hand of the protecting Angel, to whom reverent submission must be yielded; it was unanimously decreed to absolve the delinquent, reverse the sentence passed on him, and set him free. This was forthwith done; Falco returned home, and shortly afterwards assumed the religious habit, changing his name of Falco to that of Angelus, out of gratitude to his kind deliverer; moreover, from that hour he made it his sole study to spread devotion to the Holy Angels, whom he closely resembled both in the manner of his life, and in his death.

And now, my hearers, can you any longer deny that the Angel Guardian is able to bestow upon those who invoke him benefits as tangible, favours as great, as those bestowed by other saints? And if, like the Nile, he conceals himself for the most part, because he loves to bestow on us splendid gifts, in a hidden way, and unknown to all, still from time to time he manifests himself to us in so plain a manner as to render it impossible for us any longer to plead ignorance of his power. Let us not, then, from henceforth seek an excuse for withholding from him the homage which is his due. You have heard how amply and how ably he fulfils all the duties of a true friend; let us, then, not be backward in doing our part, with equal love, by invoking him, by thanking him, by holding converse with him; endeavouring, by every means in our power, to show him to be second to none of the other saints in our devotion. But why need I mention the saints? It were well for us did we only esteem him as men esteem their human friends, false as these too often are; did we bear him the same affection, and pay him the same honour; for in that case we should soon see disappear from our midst one strange inconsistency at least, of which we must continue to be guilty so long as, whilst in regard to all other precious things we esteem the spurious to be of little worth in comparison with the real, we yet make friendship an exception to our rule, and persist in attaching greater value to the false than to the true.

THE END.

R. WASHBOURNE'S CATALOGUE.

18 *PATERNOSTER* ROW, LONDON.

Post Office Orders to be made payable at the General Post Office.

The Feasts of Camelot, with the Tales that were told there. By Eleanora Louisa Hervey. 3s. 6d.

"This is really a very charming collection of tales, told as is evident from the title, by the Knights of the Round Table, at the Court of King Arthur. It is good for children and for grown up people too, to read these stories of knightly courtesy and adventure and of pure and healthy romance, and they have never been written in a more attractive style than by Mrs. Hervey in this little volume."—*Tablet.* "Elegant and imaginative invention, well selected language, and picturesque epithet."—*Athenæum.* "Full of chivalry and knightly deeds, not unmixed with touches of quaint humour."—*Court Journal.* "The substance and spirit of Arthurian romance."—*Examiner.* "A graceful and pleasing collection of stories."—*Daily News.* "Quaint and graceful little stories."—*Notes and Queries.* "To those who wish to go back to the prehistoric days and indulge themselves in the old dream-land of romance, this is just the book."—*Guardian.* "There is a high purpose in this charming book, one which is steadily pursued—it is the setting forth of the true meaning of chivalry."—*Morning Post.*

My Godmother's Stories from many Lands. By Eleanora Louisa Hervey. 12mo, 3s. 6d.

"One hundred and twenty stories, enchanting to youth, and interesting to a degree to those of more mature age."——"Without doubt the most engaging tales that we have had placed before us for many years."——"Children, aye, mothers, and those interested in the early years of childhood, will hail with delight the rich treasure Mrs. Hervey has placed before us."

The Story of the Life of St. Paul. By M. F. S., author of "Legends of the Saints," &c., &c. Fcap. 8vo., 2s. 6d. In the press.

A Hundred Years Ago; or, a Narrative of Events leading to the Marriage and Conversion to the Catholic Faith of Mr. and Mrs. Sidney, of Cowper Hall, Northumberland, to which are added a few other Incidents in their Life. By their Granddaughter. In the press.

Cassilda; or, the Moorish Princess of Toledo. 2s.

⁎⁎ *Though this Catalogue does not contain many of the books of other Publishers, R. W. can supply all of them, no matter by whom they are published.*

Bertha; or, the Consequences of a Fault. 2s.
Captain Rougemont; the Miraculous Conversion. 2s.
The Little Hunchback. By the Countess de Ségur. With 8 full-page Illustrations. 3s.
The Irish Monthly. A Magazine containing several tales and interesting reading. Vol. 4, for 1876, 7s. 6d.; vols. 1 2 and 3, each, 7s. 6d.
The Franciscan Annals and Monthly Bulletin of the Third Order of S. Francis. Price 6d.
The Angelus. A Catholic Monthly Magazine, containing tales and other interesting reading. Price 2d.
Ritus Servandus in Expositione et Benedictione SS. 4to., red or purple cloth. 5s. 6d.
The Panegyrics of Fr. Segneri, S.J. Translated from the original Italian. With a preface by the Rev. Fr. W. Humphrey, S.J. In the press.
My Conversion and my Vocation. By Rev. Father Schouvaloff, Barnabite. In the press.
Spiritual Exercises according to the Method of S. Ignatius of Loyola. By Fr. Bellecius, S.J. 2s.
Albert the Great: his Life and Scholastic Labours. From original Documents. By Professor Sighart. Translated by Rev. Fr. T. A. Dixon, O.P. With a Photographic Portrait. 8vo., 10s. 6d.
Our Legends and Lives. A Gift for all Seasons. Poetry. By Eleanora Louisa Hervey. 6s.
Life of S. Patrick. By Miss Cusack. 6s.; gilt, 10s.
Mystical Flora of S. Francis de Sales, or the Christian Life under the Emblems of Plants. With coloured Illustrations. 8s.
Catholic Calendar for 1877, with Two Views of S. Etheldreda's Church, Ely Place, Holborn. 6d.
Legends of the Saints. By M. F. S., author of "Stories of the Saints." Square 16mo., 3s. 6d.
Stories of Martyr Priests. By M. F. S. 12mo., 3s. 6d.
The Three Wishes. A Tale. By M. F. S. 2s. 6d.
An Enquiry into the Nature and Results of Electricity and Magnetism. By Amyclanus. Illustrated. 6s. 6d.

Vespers and Benedictine Service. By Leopold de Prins.
A Devout Exposition of the Holy Mass; with an ample declaration of all the rites and ceremonies belonging to the same. By John Heigham, 1622. Edited by Austin Joseph Rowley, Priest. 12mo., 4s.
Life of Gregory Lopez, the Hermit. By Canon Doyle, O.S.B. With a Photograph. 12mo., 3s. 6d.
Road to Heaven. A game for family parties. 1s. With the Rules of the Game, bound, 2s.
Student's Handbook of British and American Literature. By Rev. O. L. Jenkins. 12mo., 8s.
The First Apostles of Europe; or the "Conversion of the Teutonic Race." By Mrs. Hope, author of "Early Martyrs," &c. 2 vols. 12mo., 10s.
Little Office of the Immaculate Conception. Translation approved by the Bishop of Clifton. 3d.
The Doctrine of Purgatory. By Rev. W. Marshall. 1s.

"This is unquestionably the best popular English treatise on this subject."—*Dublin Review*. "The evidence from passages of scripture amounts to proof the most incontestable."—*Tablet*. "This little treatise has astonished us by the amazing erudition which it compresses into so small a space, no less than by the irresistible cogency of the logic and the beauty of the style."—*Dolmun's Magazine*.

The Serving Boy's Manual and Book of Public Devotions, containing all those prayers and devotions for Sundays and Holidays, usually divided in their recitation between the Priest and the Congregation. Compiled from approved sources, and adapted to Churches, served either by the Secular or the Regular Clergy. 32mo., embossed, 1s.; French morocco, 2s.; calf, 4s.; with Epistles and Gospels, 6d. extra.
First Communion Picture. Tastefully printed in gold and colours. Price 1s., or 9s. a dozen, *net*.

"Just what has long been wanted, a really good picture, with Tablet for First Communion and Confirmation."—*Tablet*.

Düsseldorf Gallery. This volume contains 357 Engravings, handsomely bound in half morocco, full gilt. Cash £5 5s. A smaller volume containing 134 Engravings (8vo. and large 8vo.), handsomely bound in half morocco, full gilt, £2 2s.

R. Washbourne, 18 *Paternoster Row, London.*

GARDEN OF THE SOUL.
(Washbourne's Edition.)

Edited by the Rev. R. G. Davis. *With Imprimatur of the Cardinal-Archbishop.* Thirteenth Thousand. This Edition retains all the Devotions that have made the GARDEN OF THE SOUL, now for many generations, the well-known Prayer-book for English Catholics. During many years various Devotions have been introduced, and, in the form of appendices, have been added to other editions. These have now been incorporated into the body of the work, and, together with the Devotions to the Sacred Heart, to Saint Joseph, to the Guardian Angels, the Itinerarium, and other important additions, render this edition pre-eminently the Manual of Prayer, for both public and private use. The version of the Psalms has been carefully revised, and strictly conformed to the Douay translation of the Bible, published with the approbation of the LATE CARDINAL WISEMAN. The Forms of administering the Sacraments have been carefully translated, *as also the rubrical directions*, from the Ordo Administrandi Sacramenta. To enable all present, either at baptisms or other public administrations of the Sacraments, to pay due attention to the sacred rites, the Forms are inserted without any curtailment, both in Latin and English. The Devotions at Mass have been carefully revised, and enriched by copious adaptations from the prayers of the Missal. The preparation for the Sacraments of Penance and the Holy Eucharist have been the objects of especial care, to adapt them to the wants of those whose religious instruction may be deficient. Great attention has been paid to the quality of the paper and to the size of type used in the printing, to obviate that weariness so distressing to the eyes, caused by the use of books printed in small close type and on inferior paper.

"Garden of the Soul." Prices. 32mo. Embossed, 1s.; with rims and clasp, 1s. 6d.; with Epistles and Gospels, 1s. 6d.; with rims and clasps, 2s. French morocco, 2s.; with rims and clasp, 2s. 6d.; with E. and G., 2s. 6d.; with rims and clasp, 3s. French morocco extra gilt, 2s. 6d.; with rims and clasp, 3s.; with E. and G., 3s.; with rims and clasp, 3s. 6d. Calf, or morocco, 4s.; with rims and clasp, 5s. 6d.; with E. and G., 4s. 6d.; with rims and clasp, 6s. Calf or morocco extra gilt, 5s.; with rims and clasp, 6s. 6d.; with E. and G., 5s. 6d.; with rims and clasp, 7s. Velvet, with rims and clasp, 7s. 6d., 10s. 6d., and 13s.; with E. and G., 8s., 11s., and 13s. 6d. Russia, antique, with clasp, 10s., 12s. 6d.; with E. and G., 10s. 6d., 13s.; with corners and clasps, 20s.; with E. and G., 20s. 6d. Ivory, 14s., 16s., 20s., and 22s. 6d.; with E. and G., 14s. 6d., 16s. 6d., 20s. 6d., and 23s. Morocco antique, 10s.; with two patent clasps, 12s.; with E. and G., 10s. 6d. and 12s. 6d.; with corners and clasps, 18s.; with E. and G., 18s. 6d.

The Epistles and Gospels in cloth, 6d; roan, 1s. 6d.

"This is one of the best editions we have seen of one of the best of all our Prayer-books. It is well printed in clear large type, on good paper."—*Catholic Opinion.* "A very complete arrangement of this, which is emphatically the Prayer-book of every Catholic household. It is as cheap as it is good, and we heartily recommend it."—*Universe.* "Two striking features are the admirable order displayed throughout the book, and the insertion of the Indulgences, in small type, above Indulgenced Prayers."—*Weekly Register.*

The Little Garden of the Soul. 32mo. Cloth, 6d., with rims, 1s.; embossed, red edges, 9d., with rims 1s. 3d.; strong roan, 1s., with rims, 1s. 6d.; French morocco, 1s. 6d., with rims, 2s.; French morocco, extra gilt, 2s., with rims, 2s. 6d.; calf or morocco, 3s.; with rims, 4s.; calf or morocco, extra gilt, 4s.; with rims, 5s.; mor. antique, 7s. 6d., 10s. 6d. 12s. 16s.; velvet, with rims, 5s., 8s. 6d., 10s. 6d.; Russia, 5s.; with clasp, &c., 8s.; Russia antique, 17s. 6d.; ivory, with rims, 10s. 6d., 13s., 15s., 17s. 6d. Imitation ivory, with rims, 3s.; with oxydized silver or gilt mountings, in morocco case, 25s.

R. Washbourne, 18 Paternoster Row, London.

The Sacred Heart and St. Joseph.

Elevations to the Heart of Jesus. By Rev. Father Doyotte, S. J. Fcap. 8vo. 3s.

Paradise of God; or Virtues of the Sacred Heart. 4s.

Devotions to the Sacred Heart. By the Rev. S. Franco. 4s., paper covers, 2s.

Devotions to the Sacred Heart. By the Rev. J. Joy Dean. Fcap. 8vo. 3s.

Devotions to Sacred Heart of Jesus. By the Rt. Rev. Dr. Milner. *New Edition.* To which is added Devotions to the Immaculate Heart of Mary. 3d.; cloth, 6d.; gilt, 1s.

Sacred Heart of Jesus offered to the Piety of the Young engaged in Study. By Rev. A. Deham, S.J. 6d.

Pleadings of the Sacred Heart. By Rev. P. Comerford. 18mo. 1s.; gilt, 2s.; with the Handbook of the Confraternity, 1s. 6d.; Handbook, separately, 3d.

Treasury of the Sacred Heart. With Epistles and Gospels. 18mo. cloth, 3s. 6d.; roan, 4s. 6d. 32mo. 2s., roan 2s. 6d. calf 5s.; morocco, 6s.

Manual of Devotion to the Sacred Heart, from the Writings of Bl. Margaret Mary Alacoque. By Denys Casassayas. Translated. 3d.

Act of Consecration to the Sacred Heart. 1d.

Act of Reparation to the Sacred Heart. 1s. per 100.

The Power of St. Joseph. Meditations and Devotions. By Rev. Father Huguet. 18mo., 1s. 6d.

Novena of Meditations in Honour of S. Joseph, according to the method of S. Ignatius; preceded by a new exercise for hearing Mass according to the intentions of the souls in Purgatory. 18mo. 1s. 6d.

Novena to St. Joseph. Translated by M. A. Macdaniel. To which is added a Pastoral of the late Right Rev. Dr. Grant. 32mo. 4d.; cloth, 6d.

Devotions to St. Joseph. 1s. 2d. per 100, post free.

Litany of S. Joseph, &c. 1s. 2d. per 100, post free.

In Suffragiis Sanctorum. Commem S. Josephi. Commem S. Georgii. Set of five for 4d.

Religious Reading.

"Vitis Mystica;" or, the True Vine. A Treatise on the Passion of Our Lord. From the Latin. By the Rev. W. R. Bernard Brownlow. With Frontispiece. 18mo. 4s., red edges, 4s. 6d.

"It is a pity that such a beautiful treatise should for so many centuries have remained untranslated into our tongue."—*Tablet.*
"An excellent translation of a beautiful treatise."—*Dublin Review.*

The Sufferings of our Lord Jesus Christ. Preached in London by Father Claude de la Colombière, S. J., in the Chapel Royal, St. James's, in the year 1677. 18mo. 1s. and 1s. 6d.; red edges, 2s.

Lenten Thoughts. Drawn from the Gospel for each day in Lent. By the Bishop of Northampton. 2s.; red edges, 2s. 6d.

The Happiness of Heaven. By a Father of the Society of Jesus. Fcap. 8vo. 4s.

God our Father. By the same Author. Fcap. 8vo. 4s.

Holy Places; their Sanctity and Authenticity. By the Rev. Fr. Philpin. With Maps. Crown 8vo. 6s.

Fr. Philpin weighs the comparative value of extraordinary, ordinary, and natural evidence, and gives an admirable summary of the witness of the early centuries regarding the holy places of Jerusalem, with archæological and architectural proofs. It is a complete treatise of the subject."—*The Month.* "The author treats his subject with a thorough system, and a competent knowledge. It is a book of singular attractiveness and considerable merit."—*Church Herald.* "Dean Stanley and other sinners in controversy are treated with great gentleness. They are indeed thoroughly exposed and refuted."—*Register.* "Fr. Philpin has a particularly nervous and fresh style of handling his subject, with an occasional picturesqueness of epithet or simile."—*Tablet.*

The Consoler; or, Pious Readings addressed to the Sick and to all who are afflicted. By Lambilotte. Translated by the Right Rev. Abbot Burder. Fcp. 8vo. 4s. 6d., red edges, 5s.

"Written in plain and simple language, it is very specially adapted for one of the subjects which its writer had in view, namely, its introduction into hospitals."—*Tablet.* "A work replete with wise comfort for every affliction."—*Universe.* "A spiritual treatise of great beauty and value."—*Church Herald.*

Confidence in the Mercy of God. By Mgr. Languet. Translated by Abbot Burder. 3s.

Easy Way to God. By Cardinal Bona. Translated by Father Collins. Fcap. 8vo. 3s.

The Selva, or a Collection of Matter for Sermons. By St. Liguori. 5s.

The Souls in Purgatory. By Abbot Burder, 3d.
"It will be found most useful as an aid to the cultivation of this especial devotion."—*Register.*

Novena in favour of the Souls in Purgatory. By Abbé Serre. Translated by Abbot Burder, 3d.

Flowers of Christian Wisdom. By Lucien Henry. With a Preface by the Right Hon. Lady Herbert of Lea. 18mo. 2s.; red edges, 2s. 6d.
"A compilation of some of the most beautiful thoughts and passages in the works of the Fathers, the great schoolmen, and eminent modern Churchmen."—*Church Times.* "It is a compilation of gems of thought, carefully selected."—*Tablet.* "It is a small but exquisite bouquet, like that which S. Francis of Sales has prepared for *Philothea.*"—*Universe.*

Alzog's Universal Church History. Translated by Pabisch and Byrne. 8vo., 3 Vols., each 20s.

A General History of the Catholic Church: from the commencement of the Christian Era until the present time. By Abbé Darras. 4 vols., 48s.

The Book of Perpetual Adoration; or, the Love of Jesus in the most Holy Sacrament of the Altar. By Mgr. Boudon. Edited by the Rev. J. Redman, D.D. Fcap. 8vo. 3s.; red edges, 3s. 6d.
"One of Boudon's most beautiful works."—*Tablet.* "The devotions at the end will be very acceptable aids in visiting the Blessed Sacrament."—*The Month.* "It has been pronounced to be 'the most beautiful of all books written in honour of the Blessed Sacrament."—*The Nation.*

Before the Altar. Two short Meditations. 6d.

Ebba; or, the Supernatural Power of the Blessed Sacrament. In French. 12mo. 1s. 6d.; cloth gilt, 2s. 6d.

Apostleship of Prayer. By Rev. H. Ramière. 6s.

Spiritual Works of Louis of Blois, Abbot of Liesse. Edited by the Rev. John Edward Bowden, of the Oratory. Fcap. 8vo. 3s. 6d; red edges, 4s.
"No more important or welcome addition could have been made to our English ascetical literature than this little book. It is a model of good translation."—*Dublin Review.* "Elegant and flowing."—*Register.* "Most useful of meditations."—*Catholic Opinion.*

R. Washbourne, 18 Paternoster Row, London.

Heaven Opened by the Practice of Frequent Confession and Communion. By the Abbé Favre. Translated from the French, carefully revised by a Father of the Society of Jesus. Third Edition. Fcap. 8vo. 3s. 6d. ; red edges, 4s. Cheap edit. 2s.

"This beautiful little book of devotion. We may recommend it to the clergy as well as to the laity."—*Tablet*. "It is filled with quotations from the Holy Scriptures, the Fathers, and the Councils of the Church, and thus will be found of material assistance to the clergy, as a storehouse of doctrinal and ascetical authorities on the two great sacraments of Holy Eucharist and Penance."—*Register*.

The Spiritual Life.—Conferences delivered to the *Enfants de Marie* by Père Ravignan. Cr. 8vo. 5s.

"Ladies could not have a better book for their spiritual reading."—*Tablet*. "A depth of eloquence and power of exhortation which few living preachers can rival."—*Church Review*.

The Supernatural Life. Translated from the French of Mgr. Mermillod, with a Preface by Lady Herbert. Cr. 8vo. 5s.

Spiritual Conferences on the Mysteries of Faith and the Interior Life. By Father Collins. 4s.

The Eucharist and the Christian Life. By Mgr. de la Bouillerie. Translated. Fcap. 8vo. 3s. 6d.

Holy Communion: it is my Life. By H. Lebon. 4s.

The Blessed Sacrament of the Miracle. 10 Photographs. Price 2s. 6d.

On Contemporary Prophecies. By Mgr. Dupanloup. Translated by Rev. Dr. Redmond. 8vo. 1s.

Good Thoughts for Priests and People; or Short Meditations for Every Day in the Year. By Rev. T. Noethen. 12mo. 8s.

One Hundred Pious Reflections. Extracted from Alban Butler's "Lives of the Saints." 18mo. cloth, red edges, 2s. ; cheap edition, 1s.

"A happy idea. The author of 'The Lives of the Saints' had a way of breathing into his language the unction and force which carries the truth of the Gospel into the heart."—*Letter to the Editor from* THE RIGHT REV. DR. ULLATHORNE.

Some Documents concerning the Association of Prayers, in Honour of Mary Immaculate, for the Return of the Greek-Russian Church to Catholic Unity. By the Rev. C. Tondini. 3d.

R. Washbourne, 18 Paternoster Row, London.

Following of Christ. Small pocket edition, 1s. cloth; 1s. 6d. embossed; roan, 2s.; French morocco, 2s. 6d.; calf or morocco, 4s. 6d.; calf or morocco extra gilt, 5s. 6d.; ivory, 15s. and 16s.; morocco, antique, 17s. 6d.; russia antique, 20s.

The Imitation of Christ. With reflections. 32mo. 1s. Persian calf, 3s. 6d. Also an Edition with ornamental borders. Fcap. cloth, red edges, 3s. 6d.; morocco, 10s. 6d.; morocco antique, 25s.

The Apostles of Europe: or, the Conversion of the Teutonic Race. By Mrs. Hope, author of "Early Martyrs." Edited by the Rev. Father Dalgairns. 2 vols. crown 8vo. 10s.

"It is good in itself, possessing considerable literary merit; it forms one of the few Catholic books brought out in this country which are not translations or adaptations."—*Dublin Review.* "It is a great thing to find a writer of a book of this class so clearly grasping, and so boldly setting forth, truths which, familiar as they are to scholars, are still utterly unknown by most of the writers of our smaller literature."—*Saturday Review.* "A very valuable work . . . . Mrs. Hope has compiled an original history, which gives constant evidence of great erudition, and sound historical judgment."—*Month.* "This is a most taking book: it is solid history and romance in one."—*Catholic Opinion.* "It is carefully, and in many parts beautifully written."—*Universe.*

Contemplations on the Most Holy Sacrament of the Altar, drawn from the Sacred Scriptures. 18mo. cloth, 2s.; cloth extra, red edges, 2s. 6d.

"This is a welcome addition to our books of Scriptural devotion. It contains thirty-four excellent subjects of reflection before the Blessed Sacrament, or for making a spiritual visit to the Blessed Sacrament at home; for the use of the sick."—*Dublin Review.*

Cistercian Order: its Mission and Spirit. Comprising the Life of S. Robert of Newminster, and S. Robert of Knaresborough. By Fr. Collins. 3s. 6d.

Cistercian Legends of the 13th Century. Translated from the Latin by the Rev. Henry Collins. 3s.

"Interesting records of Cistercian sanctity and cloistral experience."—*Dublin Review.* "A casquet of jewels."—*Weekly Register.* "Most beautiful legends, full of deep spiritual reading."—*Tablet.* "Anecdotes, full of heavenly wisdom."—*Catholic Opinion.*

The Soul united to Jesus in the Adorable Sacrament. 1s. 6d.

The Dove of the Tabernacle. By Fr. Kinane. 1s. 6d.

Spalding's (Archbp.) Works. Miscellanea, 2 vols., 21s.; Protestant Reformation, 2 vols., 21s.; Evidences of Catholicity, 10s. 6d.

The Directorium Asceticum; or Guide to the Spiritual Life. By Scaramelli. Translated and edited at St. Beuno's College. 4 vols. crown 8vo. 24s.

Maxims of the Kingdom of Heaven. New and enlarged Edition. 5s.; red edges, 5s. 6d.; calf or morocco, 10s. 6d.

"Most suitable for meditation and reference."—*Dublin Review.*

Balmes' Letters to a Sceptic on Matters of Religion. 6s.

Thy Gods, O Israel. A Picture in Verse of the Religious Anomalies of our Time. Cr. 8vo. 2s.

BY ARTHUR AND T. W. M. MARSHALL.

Comedy of Convocation in the English Church. Edited by Archdeacon Chasuble, D.D. 2s. 6d.

The Oxford Undergraduate of Twenty Years Ago: his Religion, his Studies, his Antics. By a Bachelor of Arts. 2s. 6d.; cloth, 3s. 6d.

"The writing is full of brilliancy and point."—*Tablet.* "It will deservedly attract attention, not only by the briskness and liveliness of its style, but also by the accuracy of the picture which it probably gives of an individual experience."—*The Month.*

The Infallibility of the Pope. A Lecture. By the Author of "The Oxford Undergraduate." 8vo. 1s.

"A splendid lecture, by one who thoroughly understands his subject, and in addition is possessed of a rare power of language in which to put before others what he himself knows so well."—*Universe.* "There are few writers so well able to make things plain and intelligible as the author of 'The Comedy of Convocation.'... The lecture is a model of argument and style."—*Register.*

Reply to the Bishop of Ripon's Attack on the Catholic Church. By the same Author. 6d.

The English Religion. Letters addressed to an Irish Gentleman. By A. M. 1s.

The Harmony of Anglicanism. Report of a Conference on Church Defence. 8vo. 2s. 6d.

"'Church Defence' is characterized by the same caustic irony, the same good-natured satire, the same logical acuteness which distinguished its predecessor, the 'Comedy of Convocation.'... A more scathing bit of irony we have seldom met with."—*Tablet.* "Clever, humorous, witty, learned, written by a keen but sarcastic observer of the Establishment, it is calculated to make defenders wince as much as it is to make all others smile."—*Nonconformist.*

R. Washbourne, 18 *Paternoster Row, London.*

The Roman Question. By Dr. Husenbeth. 6d.
Consoling Thoughts of St. Francis de Sales. 2s.
Holy Readings. Short Selections from well-known Authors. By J. R. Digby Beste, Esq. 32mo. cloth, 2s.; cloth, red edges, 2s. 6d.; roan, 3s.; morocco, 6s. [See "Catholic Hours," p. 23.]
Anti-Janus. By Hergenröther. Translated by Professor Robertson. 6s.
St. Peter; his Name and his Office as set forth in Holy Scripture. By T. W. Allies. *Second Edition.* Revised. Crown 8vo. 5s.

"A standard work. There is no single book in English, on the Catholic side, which contains the Scriptural argument about St. Peter and the Papacy so clearly or conclusively put."—*Month.*

Sancti Alphonsi Doctoris Officium Parvum—Novena and Little Office in honour of St. Alphonsus. Fcap. 8vo. 1s.; cloth, 2s.; cloth extra, 3s.
The Life of Pleasure. Translated from the French of Mgr. Dechamps. Fcap. 8vo. 1s. 6d.
Sure Way to Heaven: a little Manual for Confession and Holy Communion. 32mo. cloth, 6d. Persian 2s. 6d. Calf or morocco, 3s. 6d.
Compendium of the History of the Catholic Church. By Rev. T. Noethen. 12mo. 8s.
History of the Catholic Church, for schools. By Rev. T. Noethen. 12mo. 5s. 6d.
The Rule of our most holy Father St. Benedict, Patriarch of Monks. From the old English edition of 1638. Edited by one of the Benedictine Fathers of St. Michael's, near Hereford. Fcap. 8vo. 4s. 6d.
Catholic Calendar and Church Guide. Price 6d.
Catholic Directory for Scotland. 1s.
Protestantism and Liberty. By Professor Ozanam. Translated by W. C. Robinson. 8vo. 1s.
Catholicism, Liberalism, and Socialism. Translated from the Spanish of Donoso Cortes, by Rev. W. M'Donald. 6s.
The Jesuits, and other Essays. By Willis Nevin. Fcap. 8vo., 1s. 6d.

Meditations on the Life of Our Lord. By Rev. J. Nouet, S.J. 2 vols., 7s. 6d.

The Tradition of the Syriac Church of Antioch, concerning the Primacy and Prerogatives of S. Peter, and of his successors, the Roman Pontiffs. By the Most Rev. C. B. Benni. 8vo., 7s. 6d.

Dr. Pusey's Eirenicon considered in Relation to Catholic Unity. By H. N. Oxenham. 2s. 6d.

Familiar Instructions on Christian Truths. By a Priest. No. 1, Detraction. 4d. No. 2, The Dignity of the Priesthood. 3d. No. 3, Necessity of hearing the Word of God. Why it produces no fruit, and how to be heard. On the necessity of Faith. 3d.

Sweetness of Holy Living; or Honey culled from the Flower Garden of S. Francis of Sales. 1s. French morocco, 3s.

"In it will be found some excellent aids to devotion and meditation."—*Weekly Register*.

Père Lacordaire's Conferences. God, 6s. Jesus Christ, 6s. God and Man, 6s. Life, 6s.

Commonitory of S. Vincent of Lerins. 12mo. 1s. 3d.

Men and Women of the English Reformation, from the days of Wolsey to the death of Cranmer. By S. H. Burke, M.A. Vol. ii., 6s. 6d.

The chief topics of importance in the second volume are: Archbishop Cranmer's opinions upon Confession; The Religious Houses of Olden England; Burnet as a Historian; What were Lord Cromwell's Religious Sentiments? Effects of the Confiscation on the People; The Church and the Holy Scriptures; Death-bed Horrors of Henry VIII.; Scenes upon the Scaffold—Lady Jane Grey's heroic Death; The Rack and the Stake; The Archbishop condemned to be Burnt Alive—Awful Scene; A General View of Cranmer's Life.

A Devout Paraphrase on the Seven Penitential Psalms; or, a Practical Guide to Repentance. By the Rev. Fr. Blyth. To which is added :—Necessity of Purifying the Soul, by St. Francis of Sales. 18mo., 1s. 6d.; red edges, 2s.; cheap edition, 1s.

"A new edition of a book well known to our grandfathers' The work is full of devotion and of the spirit of prayer."—*Universe*.

A New Miracle at Rome; through the Intercession of Blessed John Berchmans. 2d.

Cure of Blindness; through the Intercession of Our Lady and St. Ignatius. 2d.

Sanctuary Meditations for Priests and Frequent Communicants. Translated from the original Spanish of Father Baltasar Gracian, S.J., 1669. By Mariana Monteiro. Fcap. 8vo., 4s.
A Homely Discourse. Mary Magdalen. Cr. 8vo. 6d.
Extemporaneous Speaking. By Rev. T. J. Potter. 5s.
Pastor and People. By Rev. T. J. Potter. 5s.
Eight Short Sermon Essays. By Dr. Redmond. 1s.
One Hundred Short Sermons. By Canon Thomas. 12s.
Catholic Sermons. By Father Burke, and others. 2s.
The Light of the Holy Spirit in the World. Sermons by Bishop Hedley, O.S.B. 1s. ; cloth, 1s. 6d.
Sermon at the Month's Mind of the Most Rev. Dr. Spalding, Archbishop of Baltimore. 1s.
The Church of England and its Defenders. By the Rev. W. R. Bernard Brownlow. 8vo. 1s. 6d.
Lectures on the Life, Writings, and Times of Edmund Burke. By Professor Robertson. 3s. 6d.
Professor Robertson's Lectures on Modern History and Biography. Crown 8vo. cloth, 6s.
The Knight of the Faith. By the Rev. Dr. Laing.
1. A Favourite Fallacy about Private Judgment. 1d.
2. Catholic not Roman Catholic. 4d.
3. Rationale of the Mass. 1s.
4. Challenge to the Churches. 1d.
5. Absurd Protestant Opinions. 4d.
6. Whence the Monarch's right to rule. 2s. 6d.
7. Protestantism against the Natural Moral Law. 1d.
8. What is Christianity? 6d.
Explanation of the Medal or Cross of S. Benedict. 1d.
Diary of a Confessor of the Faith. 12mo. 1s.
Sursum, 1s. Homeward, 2s. Both by Rev. Fr. Rawes.
Commentary on the Psalms. By Bellarmin. 4to. 6s.

BY SISTER M. F. CLARE.

Woman's Work in Modern Society. 4s. 6d.
A Nun's Advice to her Girls. 2s. 6d.
Daily Steps to Heaven. Fcap. 8vo. 4s. 6d.
Book of the Blessed Ones. 4s. 6d.
Jesus and Jerusalem ; or, the Way Home. 4s. 6d.

Exposition of the Epistles of St. Paul. By the Right Rev. Dr. MacEvilly. 2 vols. 18s.

An Exposition of the Gospels. By the Right Rev. Dr. MacEvilly. Vol. i., 12s. 6d.

Monastic Legends. By E. G. K. Browne. 8vo. 6d.

A Few Words from Lady Mildred's Housekeeper. 2d.

"The good advice of an experienced upper servant on such subjects ought not to fall on unwilling ears."—*Register.*

BY HIS EMINENCE CARDINAL MANNING.

Confraternity of the Holy Family. 8vo. 3d.

Confidence in God. 1s.

The Convocation in Crown and Council. 6d.

Temporal Sovereignty of the Popes. 1s. ; cloth, 1s. 6d.

The Church, the Spirit, and the Word. 6d.

BY THE PASSIONIST FATHERS.

The Mirror of Faith: your Likeness in it. 3s.

The School of Jesus Crucified. 5s.

The Manual of the Cross and Passion. 32mo. 2s. 6d.

The Manual of the Seven Dolours. 32mo. 1s. 6d.

The Christian Armed. 32mo. 1s. 6d.

Guide to Sacred Eloquence. 2s.

Religious Instruction.

The Catechism of Christian Doctrine. Approved for the use of the Faithful in all the Dioceses of England and Wales. Price 1d. ; cloth, 2d.

The Catechism, Illustrated with Passages from the Holy Scriptures. Arranged by the Rev. J. B. Bagshawe, with Imprimatur. Crown 8vo. 2s. 6d.

"I believe the Catechism to be one of the best possible books of controversy, to those, at least, who are inquiring with a real desire to find the truth."—*Extract from the Preface.*

"An excellent idea. The very thing of all others that is needed by many under instruction."—*Tablet.* "It is a book which will do incalculable good. Our priests will hail with pleasure so valuable a help to their weekly instructions in the Catechism, while in schools its value will be equally recognized."—*Weekly Register.*

A First Sequel to the Catechism. By the Rev. J. Nary. 32mo. 1d.

Catechism made Easy. A Familiar Explanation of "The Catechism of Christian Doctrine." By Rev. H. Gibson. Vol. I., 4s. Vol. II., 4s.

R. Washbourne, 18 *Paternoster Row, London.*

The Threshold of the Catholic Church. A course of Plain Instructions for those entering her Communion. By Rev. J. B. Bagshawe. Cr. 8vo. 4s.

"A scholarly, well-written book, full of information."—*Church Herald.* "An admirable book, which will be of infinite service to thousands."—*Universe.* "Plain, practical, and unpretentious, it exhausts so entirely the various subjects of instruction necessary for our converts, that few missionary priests will care to dispense with its assistance."—*Register.* "It has very special merits of its own. . It is the work, not only of a thoughtful writer and good theologian, but of a wise and experienced priest."—*Dublin Review.* "Its characteristic is the singular simplicity and clearness with which everything is explained. . . It will save priests hours and days of time."—*Tablet.* "There was a great want of a manual of instruction for convents, and the want has now been supplied, and in the most satisfactory manner."—*The Month.*

A General Catechism of the Christian Doctrine. By the Right Rev. Dr. Poirier. 18mo. 9d.

Frassinetti's Dogmatic Catechism. Translated by the Oblate Fathers of St. Charles. 3s.

"We give a few extracts from Frassinetti's work, as samples of its excellent execution."—*Dublin Review.* "Needs no commendation."—*Month.* "It will be found useful, not only to catechists, but also for the instruction of converts."—*Tablet.*

Mgr. de Ségur's Books for Little Children. Translated. Confession; Holy Communion; Child Jesus; Piety; Prayer; Temptation. 3d. each.

The Seven Sacraments explained and defended. Edited by a Catholic Clergyman. 1s. 6d.

The Christian Instructed in the nature and use of Indulgences. By Rev. F. A. Maurel, S.J. 3s.

Protestant Principles Examined by the Written Word. Originally entitled, "The Protestant's Trial by the Written Word." *New edition.* 18mo. 1s.

"An excellent book."—*Church News.* "A good specimen of the concise controversial writing of English Catholics in the early part of the seventeenth century."—*Catholic Opinion.* "A little book which might be consulted profitably by any Catholic."—*Church Times.* "A clever little manual."—*Westminster Gazette.* "A useful little volume."—*The Month.* "An excellent little book."—*Weekly Register.* "A well-written and well-argued treatise."—*Tablet.*

Dr. Butler's *First* Catechism, ½d. ***Second* Catechism,** 1d.; ***Third* Catechism,** 1½d.

Dr. Doyle's Catechism, 1½d.

Lessons on the Christian Doctrine, 1½d.

Descriptive Guide to the Mass. By the Rev. Dr. Laing. 1s. ; extra cloth, 1s. 6d.
> "An attempt to exhibit the structure of the Mass. The logical relation of parts is ingeniously effected by an elaborate employment of differences of type, so that the classification, down to the minutest subdivision, may at once be caught by the eye."—*Tablet.*

The Necessity of Enquiry as to Religion. By Henry John Pye, M.A. 4d. ; cloth, 6d.
> "Mr. Pye is particularly plain and straightforward."—*Tablet.*
> "It is calculated to do much good. We recommend it to the clergy, and think it a most useful work to place in the hands of all who are under instruction."—*Westminster Gazette.*

The Grounds of Catholic Doctrine. By Dr. Challoner. Large type edition. 18mo. cloth, 4d.
Fleury's Historical Catechism. Large edition, 1½d.
Bible History for the use of Catholic Schools and Families. By the Rev. R. Gilmour. 2s.
Origin and Progress of Religious Orders, and Happiness of a Religious State. By Fr. J. Platus, S. J. 2s. 6d.
Children of Mary in the World. 32mo. 1d.
Christian Politeness. By the Ven. de la Salle. 1s.
Duties of a Christian. By the Ven. de la Salle. 2s.
The Young Catholic's Guide to Confession and Holy Communion. By Dr. Kenny. *Third edition.* Paper, 4d. ; cloth, 6d. ; cloth, red edges, 9d.
Instructions for the Sacrament of Confirmation. 6d.
Auricular Confession. By Rev. Dr. Melia. 1s. 6d.
Goffine's Explanation of the Epistles and Gospels. 7s.
Rules for a Christian Life. By S. Charles Borromeo. 2d.
Anglican Orders. By Canon Williams. 3s. 6d.
The Monks of Iona and the Duke of Argyll. By the Rev. J. Stewart M'Corry, D.D. 8vo. 3s. 6d.
The Child. By Mgr. Dupanloup. Translated, 3s. 6d.
The Penny Bank. By the Rev. Fr. Richardson. 1d.
The Crusade, or Catholic Association for the Suppression of Drunkenness. By the same. 1d.
The Catholic Total Abstinence League of the Cross. By the same. 1d. each ; or 6s. for 144, *net.*
Holy War, by the same, 1d. ; Cross, 2d.
Catholic Sick and Benefit Club ; or, the Guild of our Lady, and St. Joseph's Burial Society. By the Rev. Fr. Richardson. 32mo. 4d. Burial Society by itself, 2d.

Dramas, Comedies, Farces.

St. William of York. A Drama in Two Acts, for boys. 6d.
Major John André. An Historical Drama (Boys.) 2s.
He would be a Lord. Comedy in Three Acts. (Boys.) 2s.
St. Louis in Chains. Drama in Five Acts, for boys. 2s.
The Expiation. A Drama in Three Acts, for boys. 2s.
Shandy Maguire. A Farce for boys in Two Acts. 1s.
The Duchess Transformed. A Comedy in One Act, for girls. By W. H. A. 6d.
The Reverse of the Medal. A Drama in Four Acts, for young ladies. 6d.
Emscliff Hall: or, Two Days Spent with a Great-Aunt. A Drama in Three Acts, for young ladies. 6d.
Filiola. A Drama in Four Acts, for young ladies. 6d.
The Convent Martyr. By Dr. Husenbeth. 2s.
Road to Heaven. A game for family parties, 1s. & 2s.
Shakespeare. Expurgated edition, 6s. Comedies, 3s. 6d.

Lives of Saints, &c.

Lives of the Saints for every Day in the Year. Translated from M. Didot's edition. Beautifully printed on thick toned paper, with borders from ancient sources, scarlet cloth gilt, gilt edges, 4to. 16s.
Lives of the First Religious of the Visitation of Holy Mary. By Mother Frances Magdalen de Chaugy. With two Photographs. 2 vols., cr. 8vo. 12s.
S. Vincent Ferrer, of the Order of Friar Preachers: his Life, Spiritual Teaching, and practical Devotion. By Fr. Pradel. Translated by Fr. Dixon, O.P. With a Photograph. 5s.
Butler's Lives of the Saints. 2 vols., 8vo., cloth, 28s.; or in cloth gilt, 34s.; or in 4 vols., 8vo., cloth, 32s.; or in cloth gilt, 48s.; or in leather gilt, 64s.
Oratorian Lives of the Saints. Second Series. Post 8vo.
S. Bernardine of Siena. With a portrait, 5s.
S. Philip Benizi. With a portrait, 5s.
S. Veronica Giuliani, and Blessed Battista Varani. With a portrait, 5s.
S. John of God. With a portrait, 5s.

Life of Sister Mary Cherubina Clare of S. Francis, Translated from the Italian, with Preface by Lady Herbert. Cr. 8vo. with Photograph, 3s. 6d.

Stories of the Saints. By M. F S., author of " Tom's Crucifix, and other Tales," " Catherine Hamilton," &c. 2 vols., each 3s. 6d., gilt, 4s. 6d.

Stories of Holy Lives. By M. F. S. Fcp. 8vo., 3s. 6d.

Life of B. Giovanni Colombini. By Feo Belcari. Translated from the editions of 1541 and 1832. with a Photograph. Cr. 8vo. 3s. 6d.

Sketch of the Life and Letters of the Countess Adelstan. By E. A. M., author of " Rosalie, or the Memoirs of a French Child," " Life of Paul Seigneret, &c." 2s. 6d.

Life and Prophecies of S. Columbkille, 3s. 6d.

New Model for Youth; or, Life of Richard Aloysius Pennefather. 3s. 6d.

Recollections of Cardinal Wiseman, &c. By M. J. Arnold. 2s. 6d.

Life of St. Augustine of Canterbury. 12mo. 3s. 6d.

Life of St. German. 12mo. cloth, 3s. 6d.

Life of Stephen Langton. 12mo. cloth, 2s. 6d.

Prince and Saviour. A Life of Christ for the Young. By Rosa Mulholland. 6d. Illustrated, 2s. 6d.

The First Christmas for our dear little ones. By Miss Mulholland. 15 Illustrations, 4to. 5s.

S. Paul of the Cross. By the Passionist Fathers. 2s. 6d.

Nano Nagle. By Rev. W. Hutch, D.D. 7s. 6d.

Life of St. Boniface. By Mrs. Hope. 6s.

"Every one knows the story of S. Boniface's martyrdom, but every one has not heard it so stirringly set forth as in her 22nd chapter by Mrs. Hope."—*Dublin Review.*

Life of the Ven. Anna Maria Taigi. From the French of Calixte, by A. V. Smith Sligo. 5s.

Venerable Mary Christina of Savoy. 6d.

Memoirs of a Guardian Angel. Fcap. 8vo. 4s.

St. Patrick, the Apostle of Ireland. 1s.

Life of St. Patrick. 12mo. 1s.; 8vo., 6s.; gilt, 10s.

Life of St. Bridget, and of other Saints of Ireland. 1s.

Insula Sanctorum: the Island of Saints. 1s.; cloth, 2s.

R. Washbourne, 18 *Paternoster Row, London.*

Sufferings of Our Lord. With Introduction by Dr. Husenbeth. Illustrated. 5s.

Harmony of the Passion of Our Lord. In English and French. By Madame Paul Gayrard. 1s. 6d.

Life, Passion, Death, and Resurrection of Our Blessed Lord. Translated from Ribadeneira. 1s.

Life of Paul Seigneret, Seminarist of Saint-Sulpice. Fcap. 8vo., 1s.; cloth extra, 1s. 6d.; gilt, 2s.

"An affecting and well-told narrative... It will be a great favourite, especially with our pure-minded, high-spirited young people."—*Universe*. "We commend it to parents with sons under their care, and especially do we recommend it to those who are charged with the education and training of our Catholic youth."—*Register*.

A Daughter of St. Dominic. By Grace Ramsay. Fcap. 8vo. 1s. 6d.; cloth extra, 2s.

"A beautiful little work. The narrative is highly interesting."—*Dublin Review*. "It is full of courage and faith and Catholic heroism."—*Universe*. "A beautiful picture of the wonders effected by ubiquitous charity, and still more by fervent prayer."—*Tablet*.

Glory of St. Vincent de Paul. By Cardinal Manning. 1s.

Life of S. Edmund of Canterbury. From the French of the Rev. Father Massé, S. J. 1s. and 1s. 6d.

Life of St. Francis of Assisi. From the Italian of St. Bonaventure. By Miss Lockhart. 3s. 6d.; 4s. gilt.

Life of Fr. de Ravignan. Crown 8vo. 9s.

The Pilgrimage to Paray le Monial. 6d.

Patron Saints. By Eliza Allen Starr. Cr. 8vo. 10s.

His Eminence Cardinal Wiseman; with full account of his Obsequies. 1s.; cloth, 1s. 6d.

Count de Montalembert. By George White. 6d.

Life of Mgr. Weedall. By Dr. Husenbeth. 1s.

Life of Pope Pius IX. 6d. Cheap edition, 1d.

Challoner's Memoirs of Missionary Priests. 8vo. 6s.

BY SISTER MARY FRANCES CLARE.

O'Connell: his Life and Times. 2 vols., 18s.

The Liberator: his Speeches and Letters. 2 vols., 18s.

Life of Father Matthew. 2s. 6d.

Life of Mary O'Hagan, Abbess, Poor Clares. 6s.

Life of St. Aloysius. 6d.; St. Joseph, 6d., cloth, 1s.; St. Patrick, 6d., cloth, 1s.; 8vo., 6s.; gilt, 10s.

Life of St. Patrick. Illustrated by Doyle. 4to. 20s.

R. Washbourne, 18 Paternoster Row, London.

Our Lady.

Regina Sæculorum, or, Mary venerated in all Ages. Devotions to the Blessed Virgin from ancient sources. Fcap. 8vo. 3s.

Readings for the Feasts of Our Lady, and especially for the Month of May. By the Rev. A. P. Bethell. 18mo. 1s. 6d. ; cheap edition, 1s.

The History of the Blessed Virgin. By the Abbé Orsini. Translated by Dr. Husenbeth. With eight Illustrations. Crown 8vo. 3s. 6d.

The Path of Mary. By one of her loving children. 1s.

Manual of Devotions in Honour of Our Lady of Sorrows. Compiled by the Clergy at St. Patrick's Soho. 18mo. 1s. ; cloth, red edges, 1s. 6d.

Our Blessed Lady of Lourdes: a Faithful Narrative of the Apparitions of the Blessed Virgin. By F. C. Husenbeth, D.D. 18mo. 6d. ; cloth, 1s. ; with Novena, 1s. ; cloth, 1s. 6d. Novena, separately, 4d. ; Litany, 1d., or 6s. per 100.

Devotion to Our Lady in North America. By the Rev. Xavier Donald Macleod. 8vo. 7s. 6d.

"The work of an author than whom few more gifted writers have ever appeared among us. It is not merely a religious work, but it has all the charms of an entertaining book of travels. We can hardly find words to express our high admiration of it."—*Weekly Register.*

Letters to my God-Child. On the Veneration of the Blessed Virgin. By Mrs. Stuart Laidlaw. 4d.

Life of the Ever-Blessed Virgin. Proposed as a Model to Christian Women. 1s.

The Blessed Virgin's Root traced in the Tribe of Ephraim. By the Rev. Dr. Laing. 8vo. 10s. 6d.

Litany of the Seven Dolours. 1d. each, or 6s. per 100.

Month of Mary for all the Faithful. By Rev. P. Comerford. 1s.

Month of Mary for Interior Souls. By M. A. Macdaniel. 18mo. 2s.

Month of Mary, principally for the use of religious communities. 18mo. 1s. 6d.

Mariæ Lauretana ; or, Devotions and Exercises for the month of May. 2s.

A Devout Exercise in Honour ot the Blessed Virgin Mary. From the Psalter and Prayers of S. Bonaventure. In Latin and English, with Indulgences applicable to the Holy Souls. 32mo. 1s.
The Definition of the Immaculate Conception. 6d.
The Little Office of the Immaculate Conception. In Latin and English. By the Very Rev. Dr. Husenbeth. 32mo. 4d.; cloth, 6d.; roan, 1s.; calf or morocco, 2s. 6d.
The Little Office of the Immaculate Conception. In Latin and English. Translation approved of by the Bishop of Clifton. 3d.; or 100 for 16s. 8d.
Life of Our Lady in Verse. Edited by C. E. Tame. 2s.
Our Lady's Lament, and the Lamentation of St. Mary Magdalene. Edited by C. E. Tame. 2s.
Archconfraternity of Our Lady of Angels. 1s. per 100.
Litany of Our Lady of Angels. 1s. per 100.
Concise Portrait of the Blessed Virgin. 1s. per 100.
Origin of the Blue Scapular. 1d.
Miraculous Prayer—August Queen of Angels. 1s. 100.

Prayer-Books.

Washbourne's Edition of the "Garden of the Soul," in medium-sized type (small type as a rule being avoided). *For prices see page* 5.
The Little Garden. 6d., and upwards. *See page* 5.
Garden of the Soul. *Very large type*, 1s.; with E. & G., 1s. 6d.; French morocco, 2s. 6d.; with E. & G., 3s. 6d.; or superior edition, without E. & G., 3s. 6d.; morocco, turn over edges, 7s. 6d. Epistles and Gospels, in a separate volume, 2s.
Key of Heaven. *Very large type*, 1s. Leather 2s. 6d. gilt, 3s.
Catholic Piety; or, Key of Heaven. 32mo. 6d.; French morocco, 1s.; Velvet, 2s. 6d.; with E. & G., roan, 1s.; French morocco, 1s. 6d.; with rims, 2s.; French morocco, extra gilt, 2s.; Persian, 2s. 6d.; imitation ivory, with rims, 3s.; morocco, 3s. 6d.; velvet, with rims, 3s. 6d.
Manual of Catholic Piety. Edition with green border. French morocco, 2s. 6d.; morocco, 4s.

R. Washbourne, 18 *Paternoster Row, London.*

Holy Childhood. A book of simple Prayers and Instructions for very little children. 32mo., 1s.; gilt, 1s. 6d.

Catholic Piety, or Key of Heaven, with Epistles and Gospels. Large 32mo., roan, 1s. 6d. and 2s.; French morocco, with rims, 2s. 6d.; extra gilt, 3s.; with rims, 3s. 6d.; velvet, 3s. 6d. and 10s.

The Lily of St. Joseph; a little Manual of Prayers and Hymns for Mass. Price 2d.; cloth, 3d.; or with gilt lettering, 4d.; more strongly bound, 6d.; or with gilt edges, 8d.; roan, 1s.; French morocco, 1s. 6d.; calf, or morocco, 2s.; gilt, 2s. 6d.

" "A prayer-book for children, which is not a childish book, a handy book for boys and girls, and for men and women too, if they wish for a short, easy-to-read, and devotional prayer-book."—*Catholic Opinion*. It will be found very useful for children and for travellers."—*Weekly Register*. "A neat little compilation, which will be specially useful to our Catholic School-children. The hymns it contains are some of Fr. Faber's best."—*Universe*.

Devotions for Public and Private Use at the Way of the Cross. By Sister M. F. Clare. Illustrated, 1s.; red edges, 1s. 6d.

S. Patrick's Manual. By Sister M. F. Clare. 3s. 6d.

Path to Paradise. 3d. With 50 Illustrations, cloth, 4d.; superior paper, 6d.; with rims and clasp, 1s.

Manual of Catholic Devotion. 6d.; with Epistles and Gospels, 1s.; roan, with tuck, 1s. 6d.; calf or morocco, 2s. 6d.; imitation ivory, 2s. 6d.

S. Angela's Manual; a book of devout Prayers and Exercises for Female Youth. 16mo., cloth, red edges, 2s.; Persian, 3s. 6d.; calf, 4s. 6d.

Crown of Jesus. Persian calf, 6s.; calf or morocco, 7s. 6d. and 8s. 6d., with rims, 10s. 6d.; with turn-over edges, 10s. 6d.; morocco, extra gilt, 10s. 6d., with rims, 12s. 6d.; ivory, with rims, 21s., 25s., 27s. 6d. and 30s.

The Little Prayer-Book for Ordinary Catholic Devotions. Cloth, 3d.

Catholic Hours: a Manual of Prayer, including Mass and Vespers. By J. R. Digby Beste, Esq. 32mo. cloth, 2s; red edges, 2s. 6d.; roan, 3s.; morocco, 6s.

Ursuline Manual. Persian calf, 7s. 6d.; morocco, 10s.

Missal (complete). Persian, 8s. 6d.; calf or morocco, 10s. 6d., with rims, 13s. 6d.; calf or morocco, extra gilt, 12s. 6d., with rims, 15s. 6d.; morocco, with turn-over edges, 13s. 6d.; morocco antique, 15s.; morocco, with two patent clasps, 20s.; russia antique, 20s.; velvet, with rims, 20s.; ivory, with rims, 31s. 6d.; morocco, with gilt mounts, with engravings, and in morocco case, £5.

Missal and Vesper Book. In one volume, morocco, 6s.; with clasp, 8s.

A Prayer to be said for three days before Holy Communion, and another for three days after. 1d., or 6s. 100.

A New Year's Gift to our Heavenly Father. 4d.

Occasional Prayers for Festivals. By Rev. T. Barge. 32mo. 4d. and 6d.; gilt, 1s.

Illustrated Manual of Prayers. 32mo. 3d.; cloth, 4d.

The Mass: and a devout method of assisting at it. From the French of M. Tronson. 4d.

Devotions for Mass. Very large type, 2d.

Memorare Mass. By the Poor Clares of Kenmare, 2d.

Fourteen Stations of the Holy Way of the Cross. By St. Liguori. Large type edition, 1d.

Indulgences attached to Medals, Crosses, Statues, &c., by the Blessing of His Holiness and of those privileged to give his Blessing. 1s. 2d. per 100, post free.

A Union of our life with the Passion of our Lord by a daily offering. 1s. 2d. per 100, post free.

Prayer for one's Confessor. 1s. 2d. per 100, post free.

Prayer to S. Philip Neri. 1d. each, or 6d. a dozen.

Litany of Resignation. 1s. 2d. per 100, post free.

A Christmas Offering. 1s. a 100, or 7s. 6d. a 1000.

Intentions for Indulgences. 7d. per 100, post free.

Catholic Psalmist: or, Manual of Sacred Music, with the Gregorian Chants for High Mass, Holy Week, &c. Compiled by C. B. Lyons, 4s.

The Complete Hymn Book, 136 Hymns. Price 1d.

Douai Bible. 2s. 6d.; Persian calf, 5s.; calf or morocco, 7s.; gilt, 8s. 6d.

New Testament, Notes and References, Large 4to., 7s. 6d.; small 8vo., 2s. 6d.

Church Hymns. By J. R. Digby Beste, Esq. 6d.

Catholic Choir Manual : Vespers, Hymns and Litanies, &c. Compiled by C. B. Lyons. 1s.

Burial of the Dead (Adults and Infants) in Latin and English. Royal 32mo. cloth, 6d. ; roan, 1s. 6d.

"Being in a portable form, will be found useful by those who are called upon to assist at that solemn rite."—*Tablet.*

Prayers for the Dying. 1s. 2d. per 100, post free.

Indulgenced Prayer before a Crucifix. 1d. ea., or 6s. 100.

Indulgenced Prayers for Souls in Purgatory. 1s. per 100.

Indulgenced Prayers for the Rosary for the Holy Souls. 1d. each, 6d. a dozen, 3s. per 100.

The Rosary for the Souls in Purgatory, *with Indulgenced Prayer.* 6d., 8d. and 9d. each. Medals separately, 1d. each, 9s. gross.

Rome, &c.

The History of the Italian Revolution. The Revolution of the Barricades. (1796—1849.) By the Chevalier O'Clery, M.P., K.S.G. 8vo. 7s. 6d.

Two Years in the Pontifical Zouaves. By Joseph Powell, Z.P. With 4 Engravings. 8vo. 3s. 6d.

"It affords us much pleasure, and deserves the notice of the Catholic public."—*Tablet.* "Familiar names meet the eye on every page, and as few Catholic circles in either country have not had a friend or relative at one time or another serving in the Pontifical Zouaves, the history of the formation of the corps, of the gallant youths, their sufferings, and their troubles, will be valued as something more than a contribution to modern Roman history."—*Freeman's Journal.*

The Victories of Rome. By Rev. Fr. Beste. 1s.

Rome and her Captors. Letters collected and edited by Count Henri d'Ideville, and translated by F. R. Wegg-Prosser. Cr. 8vo. 4s.

The Pope of Rome and the Popes of the Oriental Orthodox Church. By the Rev. Cæsarius Tondini, Barnabite. Second edition. 3s. 6d.

Defence of the Roman Church against Fr. Gratry. By Dom Gueranger. 1s. 6d.

Personal Recollections of Rome. By W. J. Jacob, Esq., late of the Pontifical Zouaves. 8vo. 1s. 6d.

The Roman Question. By F. C. Husenbeth, D.D. 6d.
Supremacy of the Roman See. By C. E. Tame. 6d.
Rome: Present, Past, and Future. By Rev. Dr. M'Corry. 6d.
The Rule of the Pope-King. By Rev. Fr. Martin. 6d.
The Years of Peter. By an Ex-Papal Zouave. 1d.
The Catechism of the Council. By a D.C.L. 2d.
Civilization and the See of Rome. By Lord Robert Montagu, M.P. 6d.
Rome, semper eadem. By D. P. M.O'Mahony. 1s. 6d.
A Few Remarks on a pamphlet entitled the "Divine Decrees." 6d.

Tales, or Books for the Library.

Bessy; or the Fatal Consequence of Telling Lies. By the writer of "The Rat Pond, or the Effects of Disobedience." 1s.; stronger bound, 1s. 6d.; gilt, 2s.
Stories for my Children.—The Angels and the Sacraments. Square 16mo. 1s.
Canon Schmid's Tales, selected from his works. New translation, with Original Illustrations, 3s. 6d. Separately: Canary Bird, 6d.; Dove, 6d.; Inundation, 6d. Rose Tree, 6d.; Water Jug, 6d.; Wooden Cross, 6d.
Tom's Crucifix, and other Tales. By M. F. S. 3s.
"Eight simple stories for the use of teachers of Christian doctrine."—*Universe.* "This is a volume of short, plain, and simple stories, written with the view of illustrating the Catholic religion practically by putting Catholic practices in an interesting light before the mental eyes of children. The whole of the tales in the volume before us are exceedingly well written."—*Register.*
Catherine Hamilton. By the author of "Tom's Crucifix," &c. Fcap. 8vo. 2s. 6d.; gilt, 3s.
Catherine grown Older. Fcap. 8vo. 2s. 6d.; gilt 3s.
Simple Tales. Square 16mo. cloth antique, 2s. 6d.
"Contains five pretty stories of a true Catholic tone, interspersed with some short pieces of poetry. . . Are very affecting, and told in such a way as to engage the attention of any child."—*Register.* "This is a little book which we can recommend with great confidence. The tales are simple, beautiful, and pathetic."—*Catholic Opinion.* "It belongs to a class of books of which the want is generally much felt by Catholic parents."—*Dublin Review.* "Beautifully written. 'Little Terence' is a gem of a Tale."—*Tablet.*

R. Washbourne, 18 Paternoster Row, London.

Terry O'Flinn's Examination of Conscience. By the Very Rev. Dr. Tandy. Fcap. 8vo. 1s. 6d.; extra gilt, 2s.; cheap edition, 1s.

"The writer possesses considerable literary power."—*Register.*

The Adventures of a Protestant in Search of a Religion: being the Story of a late Student of Divinity at Bunyan Baptist College; a Nonconformist Minister, who seceded to the Catholic Church. By Iota. 5s.; cheap edition, 3s.

"Will well repay its perusal."—*Universe.* "This precious volume."—*Baptist.* "No one will deny 'Iota' the merit of entire originality."—*Civilian.* "A valuable addition to every Catholic library."—*Tablet.* "There is much cleverness in it."—*Nonconformist.* "Malicious and wicked."—*English Independent.*

The People's Martyr, a Legend of Canterbury. 4s.

Rupert Aubray. By the Rev. T. J. Potter. 3s.

Percy Grange. By the same author. 3s.

Farleyes of Farleye. By the same author. 2s. 6d.

Sir Humphrey's Trial. By the same author. 2s. 6d.

Fairy Tales for Little Children. By Madeleine Howley Meehan. Fcap. 1s.; cloth extra, 1s. 6d.; gilt, 2s.

"Full of imagination and dreams, and at the same time with excellent point and practical aim, within the reach of the intelligence of infants."—*Universe.* "Pleasing, simple stories, combining instruction with amusement."—*Register.*

Rosalie; or, the Memoirs of a French Child. Written by herself. Fcap. 8vo., 1s. and 1s. 6d.; extra gilt, 2s.

"It is prettily told, and in a natural manner. The account of Rosalie's illness and First Communion is very well related. We can recommend the book for the reading of children."—*Tablet.* "The tenth chapter is beautiful."—*Universe.*

The Story of Marie and other Tales. Fcap. 8vo., 2s.; gilt, 3s.; or separately:—The Story of Marie, 2d.; Nelly Blane, and A Contrast, 2d.; A Conversion and a Death-Bed, 2d.; Herbert Montagu, 2d.; Jane Murphy, The Dying Gipsy, and The Nameless Grave, 2d.; The Beggars, and True and False Riches, 2d.; Pat and his Friend, 2d.

"A very nice little collection of stories, thoroughly Catholic in their teaching."—*Tablet.* "A series of short pretty stories, told with much simplicity."—*Universe.* "A number of short pretty stories, replete with religious teaching, told in simple language."—*Weekly Register.*

Sir Ælfric and other Tales. By the Rev. G. Bampfield. 18mo. 6d.; cloth, 1s.; gilt, 1s. 6d.

The Last of the Catholic O'Malleys. A Tale. By M. Taunton. 18mo. cloth, 1s. 6d.; extra, 2s.

"A sad and stirring tale, simply written, and sure to secure for itself readers."—*Tablet.* "Deeply interesting. It is well adapted for parochial and school libraries."—*Weekly Register.* "A very pleasing tale."—*The Month.*

Eagle and Dove. From the French of Mademoiselle Zénaïde Fleuriot. By Emily Bowles. Cr. 8vo., 5s.

"We recommend our readers to peruse this well-written story."—*Register.* "One of the very best stories we have ever dipped into."—*Church Times.* "Admirable in tone and purpose."—*Church Herald.* "A real gain. It possesses merits far above the pretty fictions got up by English writers."—*Dublin Review.* "There is an air of truth and sobriety about this little volume, nor is there any attempt at sensation."—*Tablet.*

Cistercian Legends of the 13th Century. Translated from the Latin by the Rev. Henry Collins. 3s.

Cloister Legends: or, Convents and Monasteries in the Olden Time. *Second Edition.* Cr. 8vo. 4s.

Chats about the Rosary; or, Aunt Margaret's Little Neighbours. Fcap. 8vo. 3s.

"There is scarcely any devotion so calculated as the Rosary to keep up a taste for piety in little children, and we must be grateful for any help in applying its lessons to the daily life of those who already love it in their unconscious tribute to its value and beauty."—*Month.* "We do not know of a better book for reading aloud to children, it will teach them to understand and to love the Rosary."—*Tablet.* Illustrative of each of the mysteries, and connecting each with the practice of some particular virtue."—*Catholic Opinion.*

Margarethe Verflassen. Translated from the German by Mrs. Smith Sligo. Fcap. 8vo. 3s.; gilt, 3s. 6d.

"A portrait of a very holy and noble soul, whose life was passed in constant practical acts of the love of God."—*Weekly Register.* "It is the picture of a true woman's life, well fitted up with the practice of ascetic devotion and loving unwearied activity about all the works of mercy."—*Tablet.*

Keighley Hall and other Tales. By Elizabeth King. 18mo. 6d.; cloth, 1s.; 1s. 6d.; gilt, 2s.

Ned Rusheen. By the Poor Clares. Crown 8vo. 6s.

The Prussian Spy. A Novel. By V. Valmont. 4s.

Sir Thomas Maxwell and his Ward. By Miss Bridges. Fcap. 8vo. 2s.

Adolphus; or, the Good Son. 18mo. gilt, 6d.

Nicholas; or, the Reward of a Good Action. 6d.

The Lost Children of Mount St. Bernard. Gilt, 6d.

The Baker's Boy; or, the Results of Industry. 6d.
A Broken Chain. 18mo. gilt, 6d.
The Truce of God: a Tale of the Eleventh Century. By G. H. Miles. 4s.
Tales and Sketches. By Charles Fleet. 8vo. cloth, 2s. and 2s. 6d.; cloth, gilt, 3s. 6d.
The Artist of Collingwood. By Baron Na Carriag. 3s. 6d.; cheap edition, 2s.
The Convent Prize Book. By the author of "Geraldine." Fcap. 8vo. 2s. 6d.; gilt, 3s. 6d.
Munster Firesides; or, the Barrys of Beigh. By E. Hall. 3s. 6d.
The Village Lily. Fcap. 8vo. 1s.; gilt, 1s. 6d.
Forty Years of American Life. By Dr. Nichols. 5s.
The Journey of Sophia and Eulalie to the Palace of True Happiness. Translated by the Rev. Father Bradbury, Mount St. Bernard's. Fcap. 8vo. 3s. 6d.; cheap edition, 2s. 6d.
The Fisherman's Daughter. By Conscience. 4s.
The Amulet. By Hendrick Conscience. 4s.
Count Hugo of Graenhove. By Conscience. 4s.
The Village Innkeeper. By Conscience. 4s.
Happiness of being Rich. By Conscience. 4s.
Ludovic and Gertrude. By Conscience. 4s.
The Young Doctor. By Conscience. 4s.
Margaret Roper. By A. M. Stewart. 6s., gilt, 7s.
Florence O'Neill. By A. M. Stewart. 5s. and 6s.
Limerick Veteran. By the same. 5s. and 6s.
Life in the Cloister. By the same. 3s. 6d.
Alone in the World. By the same. 4s. 6d.
Festival Tales. By J. F. Waller. 5s.
My Dream; and Verses Miscellaneous. By Wallace Herbert. With a frontispiece. 12mo., 5s.
Poems. By H. N. Oxenham. *Third Edition.* 3s. 6d.
The Continental Fish Cook; or, a Few Hints on Maigre Dinners. By M. J. N. de Frederic. 18mo. 1s.
Certain Difficulties felt by Anglicans. Letters to Dr. Pusey and the Duke of Norfolk. By V. Rev. Dr. Newman. 5s. 6d.

Educational and Miscellaneous.

Horace. Literally translated by Smart. 2s.
Virgil. Literally translated by Davidson. 2s. 6d.
History of Modern Europe. With Preface by Bishop Weathers. cloth, 5s.; roan, 5s. 6d.; gilt, 6s.
Burton's Ecclesiastical History. 1s.
Biographical Readings. By A. M. Stewart. 4s. 6d.
General Questions in History, Chronology, Geography, the Arts, &c. By A. M. Stewart. 4s. 6d.
University Education; or, Monastic Studies. By a Monk of St. Augustine's, Ramsgate. 8vo. 2s. 6d.
Elements of Philosophy, comprising Logic, and General Principles of Metaphysics. By Rev. W. H. Hill, S.J. Second edition, 8vo. 6s.
Catechism of the History of England. Cloth, 1s.
History of Ireland. By T. Young. 18mo. cloth, 2s. 6d.
History of Ireland. By Miss Cusack. Illustrated. 11s.
The Patriots' History of Ireland. By Miss Cusack. 2s.; cloth gilt, 2s. 6d.
Ireland Ninety Years Ago. 12mo., 1s.
A Chronological Sketch of the Kings of England and France. With Anecdotes. By H. Murray Lane. 2s. 6d.; or England, 1s. 6d., France, 1s. 6d.

"Admirably adapted for teaching young children the elements of English and French history."—*Tablet.* "A very useful little publication."—*Weekly Register.* "An admirably arranged little work for the use of children."—*Universe.*

Extracts from the Fathers and other Writers of the Church. 12mo. cloth, 4s. 6d.
Brickley's Standard Table Book, ½d.
Washbourne's Multiplication Table on a sheet, 3s. per 100. Specimen sent for 1d. stamp.
Easy Lessons: or, Self-Instruction in Irish. By Rev. Ulick J. Bourke. 12mo., 3s. 6d.
The Catholic Alphabet of Scripture Subjects. Price, on a sheet, plain, 1s.; coloured, 2s.; mounted on linen, to fold in a case, 3s. 6d.; varnished, on linen, on rollers, 4s.
Book of Family Crests and Mottos. Upwards of four thousand engravings. 2 vols., cr. 8vo., 24s.

Culpepper. Brook's Family Herbal. Coloured Engravings. 5s. 6d.; plain, 3s. 6d.
Bell's Modern Reader and Speaker. Cloth, 3s. 6d.
Cogery's Third French Course, with Vocabulary. 2s.

Music (*Net*).

BY HERR WILHELM SCHULTHES.

Veni Domine. Motett for Four Voices. 2s.; vocal, 6d.
Cor Jesu, Salus in Te Sperantium. 2s.; with harp accompaniment, 2s. 6d.; abridged edition, 3d.
Mass of the Holy Child Jesus, and Ave Maria for unison and congregational singing, with organ accompaniment. 3s. Vocal Part, 4d.; cloth, 6d.
The Ave Maria of this Mass can be had for Four Voices, with the Ingressus Angelus. 1s. 3d.
Recordare. Oratio Jeremiæ Prophetæ. 1s.
Ne projicias me a facie Tua. Motett for Four Voices. (T.B.) 1s. 3d.
Benediction Service, with 36 Litanies. 6s.
Oratory Hymns. 2 vols., 8s.
Regina Cœli. Motett for Four Voices. 3s.; vocal, 1s.
Twelve Latin Hymns, for Vespers, &c. 2s.

Catholic Hymnal. English Words. For Children, Church, Convent, Confraternity and Catholic Family Use. For one, two, or four voices, with accompaniment. By Leopold de Prins. 4to., 2s., bound, 3s.

"Simple and effective. Once the Hymnal becomes known, it is sure to become popular."—*Freeman's Journal*.

Six Litany Chants. By F. Leslie. 6d.
Litanies. By Rev. J. McCarthy. 1s. 3d.
The Elements of Gregorian or Plain Chant and Modern Music. 2s. 6d.
Portfolio. With a patent metallic back. 3s.

A separate Catalogue of FOREIGN Books, Educational Books, Books for the Library or for Prizes; School and General Stationery, Second-hand Books, and Crucifixes and other Religious Articles.

R. Washbourne, 18 *Paternoster Row, London.*

INDEX TO AUTHORS.

Author	PAGE	Author	PAGE
Arnold, Miss M. J.	19	Husenbeth, Dr.	2, 18, 20, 21, 22
A'Kempis, Thomas	10	Kenny, Dr.	17
Allies, T. W., Esq.	12	King, Miss	28
Amherst, Bishop	7	Laing, Rev. Dr.	14, 17, 21
Bagshawe, Rev. J. B.	15, 16	Lane, H. Murray, Esq.	30
Bampfield, Rev. G.	27	M'Corry, Rev. Dr.	17, 26
Barge, Rev. T.	24	Macdaniel, Miss	6, 21
Beste, J. R. D., Esq.	12, 23, 25	Macleod, Rev. X. D.	21
Beste, Rev. K. D.	25	Manning, Most Rev. Dr.	15, 20
Bethell, Rev. A. P.	21	Marshall, T. W. M., Esq.	11
Blosius	8	Meehan, Madeleine Howley	27
Bona, Cardinal	8	Mermillod, Mgr.	9
Boudon, Mgr.	8	Milner, Bishop	6
Bowles, Emily	28	M. F. S.	2, 19, 26
Bradbury, Rev. Fr.	29	Nary, Rev. J.	15
Browne, E. G. K.	15	Newman, Dr.	2
Brownlow, Rev. W. R. B.	7, 14	O'Clery, Chevalier	25
Burder, Rt. Rev. Abbot	7, 8	O'Mahony, D. P. M.	26
Burke, S. H., M.A.	13	Oratorian Lives of the Saints	18
Butler, Alban	9, 18	Oxenham, H. N.	13, 29
Challoner, Bishop	17, 20	Ozanam, Professor	12
Collins, Rev. Fr.	9, 10	Philpin, Rev. Fr.	7
Compton, Herbert	3	Platus, Fr. Jerome	17
Dechamps, Mgr.	12	Poirier, Bishop	16
Deham, Rev. A.	6	Poor Clares	14, 20, 23
Dixon, Rev. Fr.	1, 18	Powell, J., Esq.	25
Doyle, Canon	2	Prins, Leopold de	31
Doyotte, Rev. Père	6	Pye, H. J., Esq.	17
Dupanloup, Mgr.	9, 17	Ravignan, Père	9
Francis of Sales, St.	12, 13	Redmond, Rev. Dr.	14
Frassinetti	16	Richardson, Rev. Fr.	17
Gibson, Rev. H.	15	Rowley, Fr. A. J.	2
Grace Ramsay	20	Schulthes, Herr	31
Gracian, Fr. Baltasar	3	Shakespeare	29
Grant, Bishop	6	Sligo, A. V. Smith, Esq.	19
Gueranger	25	Sligo, Mrs. Smith	28
Hedley, Bishop	14	Stewart, A. M.	23, 29, 30
Henry, Lucien	8	Tame, C. E., Esq.	22, 26
Herbert, Lady	8, 9, 19	Tandy, Very Rev. Dr.	27
Hervey, Mrs. T. K.	1	Taunton, Mrs.	28
Hill, Rev. Fr.	30	Tondini, Rev. C.	9, 25
Hope, Mrs.	10	Wegg-Prosser, F. R.	25
Humphrey, Rev. Fr., S.J.	1	Williams, Canon	17

CONTENTS.

	PAGE		PAGE
New Books	1	Our Lady, Works relating to	21
The Sacred Heart & St. Joseph	6	Prayer-Books	22
Religious Reading	7	Rome, &c.	25
Religious Instruction	15	Tales, or Books for Library	26
Dramas, Comedies, Farces	18	Educational Works	30
Lives of Saints, &c.	18	Music	31

R. WASHBOURNE, 18 PATERNOSTER ROW.

www.ingramcontent.com/pod-product-compliance
Lightning Source LLC
Chambersburg PA
CBHW020537300426
44111CB00008B/699